MUGHAL DYNASTY

Encyclopaedic History of India Series

MUGHAL DYNASTY

Dr. Mahesh Vikram Singh
Professor, Deptt. of History
Mahatma Gandhi Kashi Vidyapeeth
Varanasi (UP)

Dr. Brij Bhushan Shrivastava
Head of Deptt., Ancient History, Archeology & Culture
SMMTPG College, Ballia (UP)

CENTRUM PRESS
NEW DELHI-110002 (INDIA)

CENTRUM PRESS
H.O.: 4360/4, Ansari Road, Daryaganj,
New Delhi-110002 (India)
Tel: 23278000, 23261597, 23255577, 23286875
B.O.: No. 1015, Ist Main Road, BSK IIIrd Stage,
IIIrd Phase, IIIrd Block, Bangalore-560085 (INDIA)
Tel: 080-41723429
Email: centrumpress@gmail.com
Visit us at: www.centrumpress.com

Mughal Dynasty

First Edition, 2011

ISBN 978-93-80836-76-8

PRINTED IN INDIA

Printed at Mehra Offset Press, Delhi

प्रो. विपिन चंद्रा
अध्यक्ष
Prof. Bipan Chandra
Chairman

नेशनल बुक ट्रस्ट, इंडिया
नेहरू भवन
5 इंस्टीट्यूशनल एरिया, फेज़-II, वसंत कुंज, नई दिल्ली-110 070
फोन/ Phone: 011-26121880 फैक्स/ Fax: 011-26121883
NATIONAL BOOK TRUST, INDIA
Nehru Bhawan
5 Institutional Area, Phase II, Vasant Kunj, New Delhi-110 070
ई-मेल / E-mail: chairman@nbtindia.org.in
वेबसाइट / Website: www.nbtindia.org.in

FOREWORD

The term 'history' is derived from the Greek word 'historia' that means knowledge acquired through investigation. Obviously, this knowledge can be correct if the method of investigation is objective and not vitiated by any kind of bias. In other words, if the study of human past is comprehensive and obtained through scientific inquiry, it can provide perspective on the present day problems and help one plan for the future.

A true historian has to identify the sources that can be most useful in a given context. Documents, coins, archaeology, anthropology, geography, travel accounts, oral traditions, mythology and so on can be useful but they can be used only after their veracity is tested and they are critically examined. They should be checked and counter-checked.

Over the centuries, one finds the study and writing of history vitiated by biases. There are numerous instances in which historical data have been distorted to support or oppose certain preconceived ideas and purposes. Strictly speaking such history is just like fiction to accord with preconceived notions and serve some ulterior purposes.

The study of the past has never been static. Conclusions go on changing because of the discovery of new materials and tools of investigation. To give a concrete example, the carbon 14 or radiocarbon dating test has revolutionized the study of civilizations and settlements, especially of prehistoric times, for which written documents, coins, etc. are seldom available. This method has enabled historians to determine more accurately than before the time period of a particular civilization or settlement. This method was discovered only 70 years ago by American scientists.

In our country, excavations brought to light the Indus Valley Civilization and its various features, hitherto unknown. Similarly, no complete text of Kautilya's Arthashastra was available before it was discovered by Shamasastry, the chief of the Mysore Government Oriental Library in the first decade of the last century. Likewise, people's knowledge of the history of the Buddhist period got extended after excavations at Sarnath and the ruins of the Asokan period at Patna. In the future, if the Harappan inscriptions are deciphered, our knowledge of the Indus Valley Civilization will increase enormously. All these instances underline the fact that our knowledge of history is never static and its frontiers go on extending.

In the light of what has been said above the encyclopedic history is going to be of great help to students interested in Indian history. It is comprehensive and as far as possible free from biases. It includes the latest materials, and objective conclusions.

Prof . Bipan Chandra

Professor Emeritus, JNU

Chairman, National Book Trust, India

Contents

	Preface	*(viii)*
1.	Babur	1
2.	Humayun	33
3.	Akbar the Great	55
4.	Jahangir	141
5.	Shah Jahan	161
6.	Aurangzeb	185
7.	Later Mughals	237
	Bibliography	285
	Index	293

Preface

The people of India have had a continuous civilization since 2500 B.C., when the inhabitants of the Indus River valley developed an urban culture based on commerce and sustained by agricultural trade. This civilization declined around 1500 B.C., probably due to ecological changes. During the second millennium B.C., pastoral, Aryan-speaking tribes migrated from the northwest into the subcontinent. As they settled in the middle Ganges River valley, they adapted to antecedent cultures.

The political map of ancient and medieval India was made up of myriad kingdoms with fluctuating boundaries. In the 4th and 5th centuries A.D., northern India was unified under the Gupta Dynasty. During this period, known as India's Golden Age, Hindu culture and political administration reached new heights. Islam spread across the Indian subcontinent over a period of 500 years. In the 10th and 11th centuries, Turks and Afghans invaded India and established sultanates in Delhi. In the early 16th century, descendants of Genghis Khan swept across the Khyber Pass and established the Mughal (Mogul) Dynasty, which lasted for 200 years. From the 11th to the 15th centuries, southern India was dominated by Hindu Chola and Vijayanagar Dynasties. During this time, the two systems—the prevailing Hindu and Muslim—mingled, leaving lasting cultural influences on each other.

The first British outpost in South Asia was established in 1619 at Surat on the northwestern coast. Later in the century, the East India Company opened permanent trading stations at Madras, Bombay, and Calcutta, each under the protection of native rulers. The British expanded their influence from these footholds until, by the 1850s, they controlled most of present-day India, Pakistan, and Bangladesh. In 1857, a rebellion in north India led by mutinous Indian soldiers caused the British Parliament to transfer all political power from the East India Company to the Crown. Great Britain began administering most of India directly while controlling the rest through treaties with local rulers.

In the late 1800s, the first steps were taken toward self-government in British India with the appointment of Indian councillors to advise the British viceroy and the establishment of provincial councils with Indian members; the British subsequently widened participation in legislative councils. Beginning in 1920, Indian leader Mohandas K. Gandhi transformed the Indian National Congress political party into a mass movement to campaign against British colonial rule.

—*Authors*

1

Babur

Zahir ud-din Mohammad Babur (February 23 [O.S. February 14] 1483 – January 5 [O.S. December 26 1530] 1531) was a Turkic conqueror from Central Asia who, following a series of setbacks, finally succeeded in laying the basis for the Mughal dynasty of India. He was a direct descendant of Timur through his father, and a descendant also of Genghis Khan through his mother. Babur identified his lineage as Timurid and Chaghatay-Turkic, while his origin, milieu, training, and culture were steeped in Persian culture and so he was largely responsible for the fostering of this culture by his descendants, and for the expansion of Persian cultural influence in the Indian subcontinent, with brilliant literary, artistic, and historiographical results.

Overview

Babur's name: Zahir ud-Din Mohammad is more commonly known by his nickname, *Babur*.

According to Stephen Frederic Dale, the name *Babur* is derived from the Persian word *babr*, meaning "leopard" or "tiger", a word that repeatedly appears in Firdawsi's Shahnama and had also been borrowed by the Turkic languages of Central Asia. It is ultimately derived from the Indo-Iranian Sanskrit word *vyagr*. This thesis is supported by the Royal Asiatic Society of Great Britain and Ireland, explaining that the Turko-Mongol name *Timur* underwent a similar evolution, from the Sanskrit word *cimara* ("iron") via a modified version **eimr* to the final Turkicized version *timür*, with-*ur* replacing-*r* due to the Turkish vowel harmony (hence *babr* '! *Babur*).

"At that time the Chaghatai (descendants of Genghis Khan) were very rude and uncultured (*bazari*), and not refined (*buzurg*) as they are now; thus they found Zahir-ud-Din Mohammad difficult to pronounce, and for this reason gave him the name of Babar. In the public prayers (*khutba*) and in royal mandates he is always styled 'Zahir-ud-Din Babar Mohammad,' but he is best known by the name of Babar Padastha."

—Babur's cousin, Mirza Mohammed Haydar

Contradicting these views, W.M. Thackston argues that the name cannot be taken from *babr* and instead must be derived from a word that has evolved out of the Indo-European word for *beaver*, pointing to the fact that the name is pronounced *bahbor* in both Persian and Turkic, similar to the Russian word for beaver.

Sources for the Biography

The main source for Babur's biography is a written account of his life, written by Babur himself. His memoirs are known as the *Baburnama* and are considered the first true autobiography in Islamic literature.

He wrote the *Baburnama* in Chaghatai Turkic, his mother-tongue, though his prose was highly Persianized in its sentence structure, morphology, and vocabulary. The work gives a valuable impression of Babur's surrounding environment.

"I have not written all this to complain: I have simply written the truth. I do not intend by what I have written to compliment myself: I have simply set down exactly what happened. Since I have made it a point in this history to write the truth of every matter and to set down no more than the reality of every event, as a consequence I have reported every good and evil I have seen of father and brother and set down the actuality of every fault and virtue of relative and stranger. May the reader excuse me; may the listener take me not to task."

—*Baburnama*

History of the text and translations

The memoirs were originally much more extensive than they are now. The gaps in the text, particularly those between 1508 to 1519 and from 1520 to 1525, are likely the result of quires during a storm. A year before his death Babur was reworking parts of his memoirs in 1528-29. His son and successor Humayun knew Chaghatay well and read his father's memoirs. Babur corresponded with him in that language, correcting his spelling and commenting on his style. His grandson Akbar was enthroned at the age of fourteen when Humayun died in 1556.

The young emperor was raised by the regent, Bayram Khan, an Iranian statesman of whose father and grandfather had joined Babur's service. Bayram Khan himself wrote poetry in Chaghatay and Persian. His son, Abdul-Rahim, was fluent in Chaghatay, Urdu, and Persian and composed in all three languages. Using Babur's own text, he translated the *Baburnama* into Persian. The Chaghatay original was last seen in the imperial library sometime between 1628 and 1638 during Shah Jahangir's reign.

Biography

Babur was born on February 23 [O.S. February 14] 1483 in the town of Andijan, in the Fergana Valley which is in modern Uzbekistan. He was the eldest son of Omar Sheykh Mirza, ruler of the Fergana Valley, and his wife Qutluq Negar Khanum, daughter of Yonus Khan, the ruler of Moghulistan.

Although Babur hailed from the Barlas tribe which was of Mongol origin, his tribe had embraced Turkic and Persian culture, converted to Islam and resided in Turkestan and Khorasan. His mother tongue was the Chaghatai language (known to Babur as *Turki,* "Turkic") and he was equally at home in Persian, the *lingua franca* of the Timurid elite.

Hence Babur, though nominally a Mongol (or *Moghul* in Persian), drew much of his support from the Turkic and Iranian peoples of Central Asia, and his army was diverse in its ethnic makeup, including Persians (*Tajiks* or *Sarts,* as they were called by Babur), Pashtuns, and Arabs as well as Barlas and Chaghatayid Turco-Mongols from Central Asia. Babur's army also included Qizilbash fighters, a militant religious order of Shia *Sufis* from Safavid Persia who later became one of the most influential groups in the Mughal court.

Babur is said to have been extremely strong and physically fit. He could allegedly carry two men, one on each of his shoulders, and then climb slopes on the run, just for exercise. Legend holds that Babur swam across every major river he encountered, including twice across the Ganges River in North India.

His passions could be equally strong. In his first marriage he was "bashful" towards Ashah bultan Begum, later losing his affection for her. Babur was an orthodox Sunni Muslim and occasionally voiced distaste at the "deviations" of Shia Muslims. Though religion had a central place in his life, Babur and his fellow princes wore their Islam lightly. He approvingly quotes a line of poetry by one of his contemporaries: *"I am drunk, officer. Punish me when I am sober."* Babur related that one of his uncles *"was addicted to vice and debauchery. He kept a lot of catamites. In his realm, wherever there was a comely, beardless youth, he did everything he could to turn him into one. During his time this vice was so widespread, that to keep catamites was considered a virtue."*

He gave up drinking alcohol two years before his death, and demanded that his court do the same. But he did not stop chewing narcotic preparations, and did not lose his sense of irony. He wrote:

Everyone regrets drinking and swears an oath [of abstinence]; I swore the oath and regret that.

Military Career

In 1494, at only twelve years of age, Babur obtained his first power position, succeeding his father as ruler of Farghana, in present-day Uzbekistan. His uncles were relentless in their attempts to dislodge him from this position as well as many of his other territorial possessions to come. Thus, Babur spent a large portion of his life shelterless and in exile, aided only by friends and peasants. In 1497, Babur attacked the Uzbek city of Samarkand and after seven months succeeded in capturing the city. Meanwhile, a rebellion amongst nobles back home approximately 350 kilometers (200 miles) away robbed him of Farghana. As he was marching to recover it, Babur's troops deserted in Samarkand, leaving him with neither Samarkand nor Fergana.

By 1501, he was ready again to regain control of Samarkand, but was shortly thereafter defeated by his most formidable enemy, Mohammad Shaybani, khan of the Uzbeks. Samarkand, his lifelong obsession, was lost again. Escaping with a small band of followers from Fergana, for three years Babur concentrated on building up a strong army, recruiting widely amongst the Tajiks of Badakhshan in particular. In 1504, he was able to cross the snowy Hindu Kush mountains and capture Kabul from the Arghunids, who were forced to retreat to Kandahar. With this move, he gained a wealthy new kingdom and re-established his fortunes and assumed the title of *Badshah*. In the following year, Babur united with Husayn Bayqarah of Herat, a fellow Timurid and distant relative, against the usurper Mohammad Shaybani. However, the death of Husayn Bayqarah in 1506 delayed that venture. Babur instead occupied his allies' city of Herat, spending just two months there before being forced to leave due to diminishing resources.

Nevertheless, he marvelled at the intellectual abundance in Herat, which he stated was "filled with learned and matched men.", and became acquainted with the work of the Uzbek poet Mir Ali Shir Navai, who encouraged the use of Chagatai as a literary language. Navai's profiency with the language, which he is credited with founding, may have influenced Babur in his decision to use it for his memoirs, *Baburnama*.

A brewing rebellion finally induced him to return to Kabul from Herat. He prevailed on that occasion, but two years later a revolt among some of his leading generals drove him out of Kabul. Escaping with very few companions, Babur soon returned to the city, capturing Kabul again and regaining the allegiance of the rebels. Mohammad Shaybani was defeated and killed by Ismail I, Safavid ruler of Persia, in 1510, and Babur used this opportunity to attempt to reconquer his ancestral Timurid territories.

Over the following few years, Babur and Shah Ismail I would form a partnership in an attempt to take over parts of Central Asia. In return for Ismail's assistance, Babur permitted the Safavids to act as a suzerain over him and his followers. Conversely, Shah Ismail reunited Babur with his sister Khanzada, who had been imprisoned by and forced to marry the recently-deceased Shaybani. Ismail also provided Babur with a large wealth of luxury goods and military assistance, for which Babur reciprocated by adopting the dress and outward customs of the Shia Muslims.

The Shah's Persia had become the bastion of Shia Islam, and he claimed descent from Imam Musa al-kazim, the seventh Shia Imam. Coins were to be struck in Ismail's name, and the Khutba at the Mosque was also to be read in his name. In effect, Babur was supposed to be holding Samarkand as a vassal territory for the Persian Shah, though in Kabul, coins and the Khutba would remain in Babur's name.

With this assistance, Babur marched on Bukhara, where his army were apparently treated as liberators, Babur having greater legitimacy as a Timurid, unlike the Uzbegs. Towns and villages are said to have emptied in order to greet him, and aid and feed his army. At this point Babur dismissed his Persian aide, believing them no longer needed. In October 1511 Babur made a triumphant re-entry into Samarkand, ending a ten year absence.

Bazaars were draped in gold, and again villages and towns emptied to greet the liberator. Dressed as a Shia, Babur stood out starkly amongst the masses of Sunnis who had thronged to greet him. The original belief was that this show of Shivism was a ploy to garner Persian help which would soon be dropped. While it was indeed a ploy, Babur did not think it wise to drop the charade.

His cousin, Haidar, wrote that Babur was still too fearful of the Uzbegs to dismiss the Persian aid. Though Babur did not persecute the Sunni community, to please the Persian Shah, he did not drop the show of collaboration with the Shia either, resulting in popular disapproval and the re-conquering of the city by the Uzbegs eight months later.

Conquest of Northern India

Writing in retrospect, Babur suggested his failure in attaining Samarkand was the greatest gift Allah bestowed him. Babur had now resigned all hopes of recovering Fergana, and although he dreaded an invasion from the Uzbeks to his West, his attention increasingly turned towards India and its lands in the east, especially the rich lands of the Delhi Sultanate

Babur claimed to be the true and rightful Monarch of the lands of the Lodi dynasty. He believed himself the rightful heir to the throne of Timur, and it was Timur who had originally left Khizr Khan in charge of his vassal in the Punjab, who became the leader, or Sultan, of the Delhi Sultanate, founding the lodi dynasty. The lodi dynasty, however, had been ousted by Ibrahim Lodi, a Ghilzai Afghan, and Babur wanted it returned to the Timurids. Indeed, while actively building up the troop numbers for an invasion of the Punjab he sent a request to Ibrahim; "I sent him a goshawk and asked for the countries which from old had depended on the Turk," the 'countries' referred to were the lands of the Delhi Sultanate.

Following the un-surprising reluctance of Ibrahim to accept the terms of this "offer," and though in no hurry to launch an actual invasion, Babur made several preliminary incursions and also seized Kandahar — a strategic city if he was to fight off attacks on Kabul from the west while he was occupied in India-from the Arghunids. The siege of Kandahar, however, lasted far longer than anticipated, and it was only almost three years later that Kandahar and its Citadel (backed by enormous natural features) were taken, and that minor assaults in India recommenced. During this series of skirmishes and battles an opportunity for a more extended expedition presented itself.

Upon entering the Punjab plains, Babur's chief allies, namely *Langar Khan Niazi* advised Babur to engage the powerful Janjua Rajputs to join his conquest. The tribe's rebellious stance to the throne of Delhi was well known. Upon meeting their chiefs, *Malik Hast (Asad)* and *Raja Sanghar Khan,* Babur made mention of the Janjua's popularity as traditional rulers of their kingdom and their ancestral support for his patriarch Amir Timur during his conquest of Hind. Babur aided them in defeating their enemies, the Gakhars in 1521, thus cementing their alliance. Babur employed them as Generals in his campaign for Delhi, the conquer of *Rana Sanga* and the conquest of India.

The section of Babur's memoirs covering the period between 1508 and 1519 is missing. During these years Shah Ismail I suffered a large defeat when his large cavalry-based army was obliterated at the Battle of Chaldiran by the Ottoman Empire's new weapon, the matchlock musket. Both Shah Ismail and Babur, it appears, were swift in acquiring this new technology for themselves. Somewhere during these years Babur introduced matchlocks into his army, and allowed an Ottoman, Ustad Ali, to train his troops, who were then known as Matchlockmen, in their use. Babur's memoirs give accounts of battles where the opposition forces mocked his troops, never having seen a gun before, because of the noise they made and the way no arrows, spears, etc. appeared to come from the weapon when fired.

These guns allowed small armies to make large gains on enemy territory. Small parties of skirmishers who had been dispatched simply to test enemy positions and tactics, were making inroads into India. Babur, however, had survived two revolts, one in Kandahar and another in Kabul, and was careful to pacify the local population after victories, following local traditions and aiding widows and orphans.

The Battle with Ibrahim Lodi

However, while the Timurids were united, the Lodi armies were far from unified.

Ibrahim was widely detested, even amongst his nobles, and it was several of his Afghan nobles who were to invite Babur's intervention. Babur assembled a 12,000-man army, and advanced into India. This number actually increased as Babur advanced, as members of the local population joined the invading army. The first major clash between the two sides was fought in late February 1526. Babur's son, Humayun (then aged 17), led the Timurid army into battle against the first of Ibrahim's advance parties. Humayun's victory was harder fought than the previous skirmishes, but it was still a decisive victory.

Over one hundred prisoners of war were captured along with around eight war elephants. However, unlike after previous battles, these prisoners were not bonded or freed; by decree from Humayun, they were shot. In his memoirs, Babur recorded that "Ustad Ali-quli and the matchlockmen were ordered to shoot all the prisoners, by way of example; this had been Humayun's first affair, his first experience of battle; it was an excellent omen!" This is perhaps the earliest example of execution by firing squad.

Ibrahim Lodi advanced against him with 100,000 soldiers and 100 elephants; and though Babur's army had grown, it was still less than half the size of his opponents, possibly as few as 25,000 men. This was to be their main engagement, the First battle of Panipat, and was fought on April 21, 1526. Ibrahim Lodi was slain and his army was routed; Babur quickly took possession of both Delhi and Agra. That very day Babur ordered Humayun to ride to Agra (Ibrahim's former capital) and secure its national treasures and resources from looting. Humayun found the family of the Raja of Gwalior there — the Raja himself having died at Panipat — sheltering from the invaders, fearing the dreadful nature of the 'Mongols' from the stories that preceded their arrival.

After their safety was guaranteed they gave Humayun their family's most valuable jewel, a very large diamond, which some believe to be the diamond which came to be called the *Koh-i-Noor* or "Mountain of Light'. It is thought that they did this to retain their Kingdom. Whether it was because of the gift or not, the family remained the rulers of Gwalior, though now under their new rulers the Timurids. Babur, meanwhile, marched onward to Delhi reaching it three days after the battle. He celebrated his arrival with a festival on the river Jumna, and remained there at least until Friday (Jumah), when Muslim congregational prayers were said and he heard the Khutba, (sermon), read in his name in the *Jama Masjid*, a sign of the assumption of sovereignty. He then marched to Agra to join Humayun. Upon arrival Babur was presented with the fabulous diamond, and Babur reports that "I just gave it back to him", adding, "an expert in jewels said its value would provide two and a half days food for the whole world."

Battles with the Rajputs

Although master of Delhi and Agra, Babur records in his memoirs that he had sleepless nights because of continuing worries over Rana Sanga, the Rajput ruler of Mewar. The Rajput lords had, prior to Babur's intervention, succeeded in conquering some of the Sultanate's territory. They ruled an area directly to the southwest of Babur's new dominions, commonly known as Rajputana as well as fortified dominions in other parts of northern India. It was not a unified kingdom, but rather a confederacy of principalities, under the informal suzerainty of Rana Sanga, head of the senior Rajput dynasty.

The Rajputs had possibly heard word of the heavy casualties inflicted by Lodi on Babur's forces, and believed that they could capture Delhi, and possibly all Hindustan. They hoped to bring it back into Hindu Rajput hands for the first time in almost three hundred and fifty years since Sultan Shah-al Din Mohammad of Ghor defeated the Rajput Chauhan King Prithviraj III in 1192.

Furthermore, the Rajputs were well aware that there was dissent within the ranks of Babar's army. The hot Indian summer was upon them, and many troops wanted to return home to the cooler climes of Central Asia.

The Rajputs' reputation for valour preceded them, and their superior numbers no doubt further contributed to the desire of Babur's army to retreat. According to Babur's own calculations the potential strength of the Rajput army was much larger than that deployed by the Lodis at Panipat. Babur resolved to make this an extended battle, and decided to push further into India, into lands never previously claimed by the Timurids. He needed his troops to defeat the Rajputs.

Despite the unwillingness of his troops to engage in further warfare, Babur was convinced he could overcome the Rajputs and gain complete control over Hindustan. He made great propaganda of the fact that for the first time he was to battle non-Muslims, the *Kafir*, to the extent of taking a vow to abstain from drinking (a common fraction among his people) for the rest of his life to win divine favour, and declared the war against, Rana Sanga.

The two armies fought each other forty miles west of Agra at Khanwa. In a possibly apocryphal tale referred to in Tod's *Annals and Antiquities of Rajasthan*, Babar is supposed to have sent about 1,500 choice cavalry as an advance guard to attack Sanga. These were heavily defeated by Sanga's Rajputs. Babur then wanted to discuss peace terms. Sanga sent his general Silhadi (Shiladitya) to the parley. Babur is said to have won over this general by promising him an independent kingdom. Silhadi came back and reported that Babur did not want peace and preferred to fight.

Battle of Khanwa

The Battle of Khanwa also spelled as Khanua in some texts, was the second in a series of three major battles, victories in which gave Zahir ud-Din Babur overlordship over North India. The Battle of Panipat was the first of the series, the Battle of Ghaghra was the last. This battle was fought near the village of Khanwa, about 60 km west of Agra on March 17, 1527. Babur defeated a formidable army raised by Rana Sanga of Mewar in this ten hour battle and firmly established his rule over northern India. Babur's grandson Akbar the Great established the city and fort of Fatehpur Sikri in honour of his grandfather's victory in this battle.

Background

Maharana Sangram Singh better known as Rana Sanga was the ruler of Mewar, a region lying within the present-day Indian state of Rajasthan, between 1509 and 1527. He was a scion of the Sisodia clan of Suryavanshi Rajputs. He defended his kingdom bravely from repeated invasions from the Muslim rulers of Delhi, Gujarat and Malwa. He was the most powerful of the Hindu kings of that time. Above all, his continued expansion helped him unite the Rajputs under one confederacy.

This war was not the first event that introduced the two formidable commanders Rana Sanga and Babur. Before Emperor

Babur had set out from Kabul, his new dominion, on his last Indian expedition he had received from the Rana an embassy conveying expressions of regard and it seems to have been arranged that while Babur attacked Sultan Ibrahim Lodi by marching upon Delhi, Rana Sanga was to attack him on the side of Agra. Babur on his part complains that while he advanced and occupied these two capitals the Rana did not make a single movement. On the other hand the Rana complained of broken faith and in particular claimed Kalpi, Dholpur and Biana as his by agreement all of which had been occupied by Babur. And as Agra itself had till recent times been considered as only a dependency of Biana that city might also have been understood to accompany it. Successes of the mighty power of the Rana might seem to justify at once his hopes of seating himself on the vacant throne of the Lodi's and his more glorious ambition of expelling both the Afghan and the Turkic-Mongol invaders from India and restoring her own Hindu race of kings and her native institutions.

In the meanwhile however he acknowledged Sultan Mahmud Lodi the son of Sultan Sikandar Lodi who had been set up by the Western Afghan Confederates as the legal successor of Sultan Ibrahim Lodi. The preparations made by Rana Sanga evidently with the intention of marching towards Biana had induced Babur not only to collect a strong force near Agra for the purpose of repelling his attack but hastily to recall Humayun from Jaunpur. Soon after Rana Sanga was joined by Raja Hasan Khan Meo of Meo Rajputs who are Muslims of Indian descent, and ethnic cousins of the Jat and Gujjar castes. Raja Hasan Khan was ruler of Mewat a region lying south of Delhi, spread across south Haryana and North-East Rajasthan.

This news was particularly unwelcome to the Emperor Babur. The Khan was a chief of great power and influence. At the Battle of Panipat his son Naher Khan had been made prisoner and he had ever since kept up a friendly correspondence with the Emperor and a negotiation for his release. Babur hoping that if he set the son at liberty he would attach the father by the strongest ties of gratitude invested Naher Khan with a dress of honor and sent him back to his father. But though the son had made the fairest promises no sooner did the old man hear that he was out of Babur's hands and on his way to join him than without even waiting to see him he marched from Alwar his capital and joined the Rana Sanga.

Initial Skirmishes

On February 11, 1527, the Emperor Babur marched out of Agra to proceed against Rana Sanga but halted a few days near the city to collect and review his troops, and to get in order his train of artillery, the baggage and camp followers. As in this warfare he had little reliance on the Afghan chiefs or his Indian allies who had joined him, he sent several of them to strengthen his various garrisons.

He then marched westward to Medhakur where he had previously caused wells to be dug and thence next day to Fatehpur Sikri which from its having plenty of water he considered as a good situation for a camp but being apprehensive that the Rana who was now near at hand might attempt to occupy the ground before his arrival he marched out with his troops in order of battle ready to attack the enemy should they appear and took possession of the place which had been chosen for his encampment close by a tank.

He was now joined by Mahdi Khwaja and the troops from Bayana which he had called in. They had some sharp encounters with the Rajputs in which they had been severely handled and taught to respect their new enemy. A party from the garrison had some days before incautiously advanced too far from the fort when the Rajputs in great force fell upon them and drove them in.

All the troops that had been engaged in this affair united in bestowing unbounded praise on the gallantry and prowess of the enemy. Indeed the Chagatai Turkic-Mongols found that they had now to contend with a foe more formidable than either the Afghans of India or any of the natives of India to whom they had yet been opposed. The Rajputs energetic chivalrous fond of battle and bloodshed animated by a strong national spirit and led on by a hero were ready to meet face to face the boldest veterans of the camp and were at all times prepared to lay down their life for their honor. A small party being sent out to get notice of their motions discovered that they were encamped at Bisawer.

Emperor Babur was accustomed to commit to his principal Baigs in turn the charge of the advance and pickets. When it was Mir Abdal Aziz's, day that rash and impetuous youth pushed on seven or eight miles from Fatehpur Sikri. The Rajputs hearing of this incautious forward movement dispatched to meet him a body of 4000-5000 horsemen who without hesitation charged the instant they came up. His force did not exceed a 1000-1500.

Many of his men were killed others taken prisoners and carried off the field on the very first onset. The moment the news of what was going on reached the camp, Mohib Ali Khalifa Emperor Baburs' Grand Viziers' son and his followers were pushed forward to their assistance and there being no room for delay, numbers of separate horsemen, as fast as they were equipped, were sent off at the best of their speed while a regular detachment under Muhammed Ali moved forward to support them Mohib Ali who arrived first found every thing in disorder.

Mir Abdal Aziz's horse tail standard taken and many excellent officers slain. Not only was he unable to turn the tide of success but was himself unhorsed though finally brought off by a desperate charge of his followers. The Emperor's troops were then pursued for about two miles and it was only the arrival of the regular detachment under Mohammad Ali that checked the enemy. Meanwhile when the alarm reached the camp the whole troops were called out and marshaled in battle order to meet the hostile army which was thought to be approaching.

But after the imperial line had advanced a mile or two with all its artillery it was found that the enemy satisfied with their success had returned back to their camp. These repeated successes of the Rajputs, the unexpected valor and good conduct they displayed and their numbers for they are said to have amounted to a 120,000 horsemen along with their Mewat allies would have been considerably one of the largest armies Babur had to face, even in modern times such a huge army would have disheartened any battle hardened soldier.

Babur began to see the discouragement of his troops. Every precaution was now taken to strengthen his position and to give his troops time to recover their spirit. At this critical juncture he received a small yet welcome reinforcement of 500 men from Kabul. Babur decided to divert the attention of the enemy towards Mewat by sending some troops there, to ravage the territory. But the diversion did not answer his expectations.

Babur Rallies his Troops

Babur was now in some measure cooped up in his camp while

the enemy was in possession of the open country. The uneasiness which he in consequence experienced in this state of inaction appears very naturally to have excited feelings of religious compunction in his mind. When he reviewed his past life he keenly felt that he had long and openly violated one of the strictest injunctions of his faith by the use of wine. Like other habitual offenders he had all along firmly resolved to give up the evil custom at some future time but that time had been constantly deferred. He now resolved to perform his vows. Babur Said;

"Having sent for the gold and silver goblets and cups with all the other vessels used at drinking parties I directed them to be broken up and renounced the use of wine purifying my mind. The fragments of the goblets and other gold and silver drinking vessels I directed to be divided among derwishes and the poor. The first person who followed me in my repentance was Asas who also accompanied me in my resolution of ceasing to cut the beard and of allowing it to grow."

This was a visible sign commonly adopted by such as were under the influence of a vow. Many nobles and others to the number of 300 followed the example of their sovereign. Salt was thrown into the ample store of wine just arrived from Ghazni all the rest found in the camp was poured upon the ground and a well was ordered to be dug and an almshouse built on the spot to commemorate this great religious event of repentance. As a boon to his Muslim followers and subjects he gave up the Temgha or Stamp tax in all his dominions so far as concerned Muslims and published a firman (royal edict) to that effect on February 26.

The dejection and alarm of Babur's troops had at this time reached their extreme point. The contagion had infected even his highest officers. He excepts only Mir Ali Khalifa his Grand Vizier who he says all along behaved admirably. Babur whose bold and elastic mind never gave admittance to despair but even in the lowest depths of danger turned to any gleam of hope saw that matters were fast advancing to a crisis and that some stirring and energetic measures were indispensably required. He determined to make a bold exertion to infuse a portion of his own heroic ardor into the drooping spirits of his followers and for that purpose he addressed himself to the religious feelings so powerful with all Muslims but especially with such as are engaged in a Jihad against infidels. He thus made the most famous and most important speech of his life; "Noblemen and soldiers! Every man that comes into the world is subject to dissolution When we are passed away and gone, Allah survives One and Unchangeable. Whoever sits down to the feast of life must, before it is over, drink of the cup of death. He who arrives at the inn of mortality, the world must one day without fail take his departure from that mansion of sorrow. How much better then is it to die with honor than to live with infamy "

–He then quotes a couplet from Firdowsi's Shahnameh;

"Give me but fame and if I die I am contented
If fame be mine let Death claim my body "

He continues,

"Allah Almighty has been propitious to us. He has now placed us in such a crisis that if we fall in the field we die the death of martyrs, if we survive we rise victorious the avengers of his sacred cause. Let us therefore with one accord swear on Allah's Holy Word that none of us will for a moment think of turning his face from this warfare or shrink from the battle and slaughter that ensue till his soul is separated from his body."

Master and servant small and great all with emulation seizing the blessed Quran in their hands swore to fight to the finish. Babur's attempt at reinvigorating his men remains to this day one of the most excellent displays of military leadership.

Babur's Advance

With his troops now in high spirits Babur decided to advance from the entrenchments in which the army had so long been cooped up. It was on March 12, 1527 that Babur drew forward his guns and a kind of defensive cover that moved on wheels and which served as a breastwork supporting them by his matchlock men and all his army. He himself galloped along the line animating his troops and officers and giving them instructions how to conduct themselves in every emergency that could occur.

The army having advanced a mile or two halted to encamp. As soon as the Rajputs heard that they were in motion several bodies of them galloped close up to the guns. Babur not intending to engage in a general action that day quietly finished his entrenchments and ditches and then sent out a few horsemen to skirmish with them and try the temper of his men. They took several prisoners and returned with a number of heads elevated on their spears or dangling from their saddlebows which had a wonderful effect in restoring the confidence of the troops.

He now threw up other trenches in a position about a mile or two farther in advance near the spot which he had pitched upon as favourable for a general engagement and when they were finished advanced to occupy them dragging forward his guns. His people having reached their ground were still busy in pitching their tents when news was brought that the enemy was in sight. All were instantly ordered to their posts. Babur mounted and drew up his troops riding cheerfully along the ranks and confidently assuring them of victory.

Battle Positions of Babur

The center Babur took to himself assisted by Chin Taimur Sultan the right wing he committed to Humayun who had under him Kasim Hussein Sultan, Hindu Baig and Khusroe Kokultash the left wing he entrusted to Syed Mehdi Khwaja with Mohammad Sultan Mirza, Abdal Aziz and Mohammad Ali. He appointed strong reserves to carry out rescue efforts wherever required. On the right and left placed two flanking columns chiefly composed of Mughal troops who formed what is called the Tulughma and were on a signal given to wheel round on the enemy's flank and rear in the heat of battle. This arrangement he had learned to his cost in his early wars with the Uzbeks and he had practiced it in his later wars with brilliant success. His Indian allied troops appear to have been stationed chiefly in the left.

His artillery under Ustad Ali Kuli was placed in the center in front connected by chains and protected by the moveable defences or breastworks which he had constructed, behind which were placed matchlock men and in their rear a body of chosen troops ready either to repel any attack from behind or themselves to rush forward and charge the enemy whenever the chains that connected the guns were dropped to permit their passage. The army abounded with veteran commanders who had learned the art of war under the Emperor himself.

Battle Positions of Rana Sanga

In the Rajput army the commanders under Rana Sanga were

generally great chieftains who from their territorial possessions could bring a large force into the field. Thus Silhadi a Tomar Rajput chieftain of northeast Malwa the Chief of Bhilsa is rated at 30,000 *Purabiya Soldiers*; Hasan Khan of Mewat 12,000; Raul Uday Singh Nagari of Dongerpur 10,000; Medini Rao the Chief of Chanderi 10,000. The first and last of these had acted an important part in the history of Malwa. Sultan Mahmud Lodi a son of Sultan Sikander Lodi of Delhi who was acknowledged by the Afghans of the Delhi kingdom and by the Rana as the successor of his brother Ibrahim Lodi though he possessed no territory yet had with him a body of 10,000 adventurers who hoped to be liberally rewarded should fortune raise him to the throne. There were other chiefs who could command each from 4000-7000 men and all were animated by the most exalted hopes and by hatred of the common enemy. They also possessed 500 war elephants and included 7 Rajas, 9 Raos and 104 Rawals and Rawats (lesser chieftains). A more gallant army could not be put into the field.

The battle

Khanwa is about 60 km west of Agra. Here the epic battle between the Muslim Mughals and the Hindu Rajputs would play out and decide the fate of India. The battle began about 9:30 in the morning by a desperate charge made by the Rajputs on Babur's right. Bodies of the reserve were pushed on to its assistance and Mustafa Rumi who commanded one portion of the artillery on the right of the center opened a fire upon the assailants. Still new bodies of the enemy poured on undauntedly and new detachments from the reserve were sent to resist them.

The battle was no less desperate on the left to which also it was found necessary to dispatch repeated parties from the reserve. When the battle had lasted several hours and still continued to rage, Babur sent orders to the flanking columns to wheel round and charge and he soon after ordered the guns to advance and by a simultaneous movement the household troops and cavalry stationed behind the cannon were ordered to gallop out on right and left of the matchlockmen in the center who also moved forward and continued their fire hastening to fling themselves with all their fury on the enemy's center.

When this was observed in the wings they also advanced. These unexpected movements made at the same moment threw the enemy into confusion. Mughal cannon fire caused the elephants in the Rajput army to stampede. Mughal cavalry archers made repeated flanking charges from the left and right of their fortified position. These mounted archers inflicted maximum losses on Rajput ranks, as the latter were not accustomed to these tactics, their center was shaken, the men who were displaced by the attack made in flank on the wings and rear were forced upon the center and crowded together. Still the gallant Rajputs were not appalled. They made repeated desperate attacks on the Emperor's center in hopes of recovering the day but were bravely and steadily received by the Mughals and swept away in great numbers. Towards evening the Rajput defeat was complete and the slaughter was consequently dreadful. The fate of the battle was decided.

Nothing remained for the Rajputs to do but to force their way through the bodies of their kinsmen and enemy that were now in their rear and to affect a retreat.Emperor Babur pursued them as far as their camp which was about three or four miles from his own. On reaching it he halted but detached a strong body of horse with orders to pursue the broken troops of the Rajput Confederates without halting to cut up all they met and to prevent them from re assembling. But Rana Sanga escaped. Babur later mentions his regret in not going with the detachment in pursuing the broken Rajput troops because of Rana Sanga's escape.

Aftermath

No victory could be more complete. The enemy were quite broken and dispersed. The whole fields around were strewed with the dead as well as the roads to Bayana and Alwar. Among the slain were Hasan Khan who fell by a matchlock shot, Raul Uday Singh of Dongerpur, Rai Chanderbhan Chauhan, Manikchand Chauhan (later awarded Kotharia jagir posthumously) and many other chiefs of note. Clearly Babur's superior leadership and modern technology won the day. Babur henceforth assumed the proud title of Ghazi (Victorious Veteran of Jihad). Babur should be remembered more for this battle than for the Battle of Panipat. As for Sultan Mahmud Lodi, he also fled eastwards and would again pose a challenge to Babur two years later at the Battle of Ghaghra.

Since the time Babur had left Agra for this battle, insurrection and revolt appeared on every hand. The towns and forts of which with so much labour he had gained possession were fast changing masters. Raberi and Chandwar on the Yamuna River; Koel in the Doab and Sambhal beyond the Ganges all of them near Agra had been retaken by the Afghans. His troops had been obliged to abandon Kanauj. Gwalior was blockaded by the Rajputs of the vicinity Alim Khan Jilal Khan Jighat of Kalpi who was sent to relieve it instead of executing his orders had marched off to his own country. Many Hindu chiefs deserted the cause of Babur. Indeed the previous conquests and recent success of Rana Sanga a Hindu had inspired all his countrymen with hopes that a change of dynasty was about to take place and they hailed with joy the prospect of a native government. But after the battle of Khanwa, Babur sent forces to chastise the insurgents and quickly retook lost territories.

Being now disengaged of his most formidable enemies he was enabled to send a force to recover Chandwar and Raberi places not far distant from Agra of which the insurgents had made themselves masters during his operations against Rana Sanga. The consternation occasioned by his success was such that this object was affected with little difficulty and even Etawa lower down the Yamuna which had never yet submitted to his power, was surrendered by Kutb Khan. Rana Sanga died shortly after this battle in 1527 at Baswa on Mewar's northern border.

Rana Sanga

Maharana Sangram Singh (commonly known as Rana Sanga) (April 12, 1484 – March 17, 1527) was the ruler of Mewar state, a region lying within the present-day Indian state of Rajasthan, between 1509 and 1527. He was a scion of the Sisodia clan of Suryavanshi Rajputs.

Maharana Sangram Singh or Rana Sanga was the last ruler of medieval India who stood up against the invaders and was able to unite many Rajput states to fight against the foreigners. He was a Rajput in a true sense, a valiant fighter and a king who is legendary for his chivalry and generosity. He lost the battle to Babur but his gallantry inspired many others.

Rana Sanga succeeded his father Rana Raimal as the king of the Mewar in 1509. He defended his kingdom bravely from repeated invasions from the Muslim rulers of Delhi, Gujarat and Malwa. He was the most powerful of the Hindu kings of that time. During his rule, Mewar touched the pinnacle of prosperity and as an exemplary king he protected and developed his empire. He was a man with indomitable spirit and despite losing one arm, one eye and numerous other grave injuries he carried on with great valor. His chivalry was reflected when he treated Sultan Mahmud of Mandu with generosity and restored his kingdom even when he was defeated and taken as a prisoner by Rana.

Sanga had to face a new and powerful invader in the Moghul Babur, a descendant of Timur the Turk. In 1526 Babar invaded India and defeated Ibrahim Lodhi, Sultan of Delhi. In the face of this threat the Rajput clans united under Rana Sanga in a Rajput confederacy but the superior artillery of the Moghul prevailed against the cavalry charges of the Rajputs. At the battle of Khanwa, near Bharatpur in 1527, Babur defeated Sanga and the Rajput confederacy, and this victory established a new era in the history of India. Sanga sustained serious injuries in the battle and died shortly afterwards. He was succeeded by his son Ratan Singh. His tenacity and courage inspired many others including Rana Pratap.

Early Years

Mewar was a small kingdom in Rajasthan in North India. Chitor was its capital. Many famous Rajput kings and queens ruled over it. The Rajput kings were famous for their bravery, love of the country and attachment to dharma. Rana Sanga was the most noted Rajput king of his time.

Sanga was one of the three sons of Raimal, ruler of Mewar. He had two brothers Prithviraj and Jaimal. Legend had it that while they were all young, they used to go to a mountain cave near Mewar. In that cave lived a witch. The three brothers one day asked the woman, "Who will become the next king of Mewar?" The witch closed her eyes, uttered some mantra and said to them, " Rana Sanga! On hearing this, the other two brothers became jealous.

He and his brothers quarreled incessantly with each other, causing much grief to their father. The main villain of their fights was Surajmal (Sang's cousine brother). Sanga was younger brother of Prithviraj and Jaimal was their brother but his mother was different. Sanga had lost his one eye while fighting with Prithviraj. Sanga had to go into exile following a particularly bad *fracas* with his brothers. He spent this period *incognito,* working as a shepherd in a remote village in the Aravalli hills.

One day he slept under a banyan tree. A snake came out from a hole in the tree. It held its hood like a regal umbrella over his head. It remained in that position for a long time. Some shepherds were passing by. They saw the man and the hood over-head, and cried, "Look, he must be a prince!" So they took him to their chief The chief asked him, "'Who are you?" Rana Sanga told him the truth about himself. The chief gave him his daughter in marriage.

Meanwhile, both his brothers met their end violently. Following their deaths, Sanga returned to his father's court in order to succour his parents in their bereavement and to secure his patrimony. He succeeded his father as ruler of Mewar upon the death of the latter in 1509.

Rule

Sanga's reign was marked by a series of continual battles. He was engaged at least eighteen times in battle with Muslim forces, fighting the forces of the rulers of Delhi, Gujarat and Malwa on various occasions. In the course of these battles, he is said to have sustained eighty-four wounds on his body, losing one arm and being crippled in one leg. Despite all this, Sanga was magnanimous in victory: In 1519, after Sultan Mahmud of Mandu was trounced and taken prisoner, Rana Sanga extended traditional chivalry and benevolence to him. Sultan Mahmud was treated like a guest and his kingdom was restored to him by the Rana.

Sanga brought Mewar to the zenith of its prosperity and prominence, establishing it as the foremost Rajput state. Under Sanga, Mewar reached its zenith, controlling (directly and indirectly) a large part of Rajputana. More importantly, he succeeded in uniting several Rajput states and motivating them to make a united bid for control of northern India. This is Sanga's enduring claim to fame, and it is this that rendered the battle of Khanwa the seminal event it became in the history of north India.

Achievements and Ideals

The mantle of Rana Kumbha's greatness passed onto Maharana Sangram Singh. Rana Sanga, also known as Sangram Singh, was the rana (king) of Mewar, in present-day Rajasthan state of western India, from 1509 to 1527.

He brought Mewar to the peak of its prosperity and prominence, establishing it as the premier Rajput state.

With the collapse of power in Delhi, Rana Sanga emerged as the most powerful Hindu King in North India with a direct or indirect sway over the whole of Rajputana. His battles against the Lodhis and the Muslim rulers of Gujarat and Malwa are legendary.

He united the Rajput states and put up a strong unified defence against Babur's armies. It was a valiant struggle to protect the integrity of Hindu states. The Maharana lost the battle but not the principle of independence.

Like the illustrious Kshatriya Kings of ancient Bharat-varsha, the Maharanas exemplified the finest Hindu values and traditions in war and in peace: Honour and chivalry; selflessness and respect for humanity.

The pinnacle of prosperity, the heights of valour. Under the Mighty Sanga, Mewar reached its apex of prosperity and controlled, directly and indirectly, a large part of Rajputana.

Rana Sanga is the finest example of the Kshatriya King as the Protector, the Suryavanshi King whose focus was on consolidating and developing his state.

Though the power of Delhi was on the decline, Rana Sanga faced repeated invasions from the Muslim rulers of Delhi, Gujarat and Malwa. His powerful army engaged in battle over eighteen times with Muslim forces and the Maharana himself was battle-scarred : having lost an arm and eye, been crippled in one leg and suffered innumerable wounds. But his power and spirit remained indomitable.

In 1519 after Sultan Mahmud of Mandu was defeated and taken prisoner, Rana Sanga displayed the same chivalry and generosity which Rana Kumbha had demonstrated towards a defeated enemy. Mahmud was treated like a guest and his kingdom was restored by the Maharana who could have easily annexed it.

He too upon himself to unite the Rajput states into a confederacy. On February 1527 Rana Sanga led a combined Rajput force of over 200,000 men to drive Babur away. Rana Sanga's army engaged the Mughal force at the Battle of Khanwa.

In the Battle of Khanua in 1527, Rana Sanga's armies gained an initial advantage against Babur's forces. But the tides turned against the valiant Rajputs and Rana Sanga was himself wounded on the battlefield.

Babur's victory was his stepping stone to founding the Mughal Empire in India and in Rana Sanga's defeat the hopes of a Hindu revival were ruined. It is true lot of Rajputs clans fight for Babur against Sanga.

Rana Sanga's loyalty to the Rajput code of chivalry and generosity is legendary. He is regarded as the last Hindu emperor of medieval India who could stand up for the principle of independence and 'rashtra' against the march of the Mughals.

Consolidation

with the exception of Rajputana which would only be pacified in the reign of his grandson, Akbar, Babar was now the undisputed ruler of Hindustan (a term which at that time referred to northwestern India and the Gangetic Plain), and he began a period of further expansion. Each of the nobles or *Umarah* he appointed was granted leave to set up his own army. And, to facilitate Babur's expansionist aims, many were granted lands yet to be conquered as jaghirs, freeing Babur from many of the problems involved in raising troops. Meanwhile he granted his own sons the provinces furthest away from his new centre of operations: Kamran was given control over Kandahar, Askari was to control Bengal and Humayun was to govern Badakhshan, perhaps the most remote province of Babur's expanding empire.

Babar, with the aide of Ustad Ali continuously used new technology to improve his army. In addition to guns, Babur and Ali tested new types of Siege weaponry, such as cannons, which Babur recalls as being capable of firing a large rock almost a mile (although, he records, its initial test did leave eight innocent bystanders dead). Alongside this, they developed Shells which exploded on impact.

Lavish Lifestyle and Final Major Battle

Late in 1528 Babur celebrated a great festival, or *tamasha.* All nobles from the different regions of his empire were gathered, along with any noble who claimed descent from Timur or Genghis Khan. This was a celebration of his Khanal, Chingissid lineage, and when guests were sat in a semi-circle the farthest from Babur (who was, naturally, at the centre) was seated over 100 metres from him. The huge banquet involved giving presents and watching animal fights, wrestling, dancing and acrobatics. Guests presented

Babur with tribute of gold and silver, and were in turn presented with sword-belts and cloaks of honour (*khalats*). The guests even included Uzbegs (who under Shaybani Khan had ousted the Timurids from Central Asia and were now the occupiers of Samarkand) and a group of peasants from Transoxiana who were now being rewarded for befriending and aiding Babur before he was a leader.

After the festival, many of the other gifts given to Babur were sent to Kabul, "to adorn the ladies" of his family. Babur was far too generous concerning wealth, and by the time of his death the empire's coffers were almost empty; troops were even ordered to return a third of their income back to the treasury. He was known to cough up blood, had numerous boils on his person, suffered from Sciatica and also bled fluid from his ears. He was a heavy drinker and took hashish, perhaps as a means of alleviating the various illnesses he suffered from. These substances were strictly forbidden by the orthodox doctrines of Islam, although in the *Baburnama* Babur does write without censure of relatives in Ferghana who indulged in strong liquor. Nevertheless, Babur, who had fought as a warrior for Islam, was now indulging in the forbidden (*Haraam*). The evening before the battle of Khanwua, he smashed his drinking cups vowing never to drink again-a vow he kept.

On May 6, 1529, Babur defeated Mahmud Lodi, Ibrahim's brother, who led an army of those disaffected with his rule, at the Battle of Ghaghra, thus crushing the last remnant of Lodi resistance in North India.

Battle of Ghaghra

The Battle of Ghaghra, fought in 1529 and was the last major battle for the conquest of India by the Mughal Empire. It followed the first Battle of Panipat in 1526 and the Battle of Khanwa in 1527. The forces of now Emperor Zahir ud-Din Mohammad Babur of the emerging Mughal Empire were joined by Indian allies in battle against the Eastern Afghan Confederates under Sultan Mahmud Lodi and Kingdom of Bengal under King Nusrat Shah.

Background

Sultan Mahmud Lodi, who aspired to the throne of Delhi and who had been declared the rightful heir to the Delhi Sultanate by the Western Afghan Confederates and aided by the Rajput Confederates, was put to flight after the defeat at the Battle of Khanwa in 1527. He took refuge in Gujarat. After trying to get in touch with his kinsmen in the east he managed to join them. He at the head of the Eastern Afghan Confederates took Bihar.

On the death of Sultan Mohammad Shah Lohani the Pathan king of Bihar of the new dynasty, an event which occurred some time after Babur's expedition to Chanderi, he was succeeded by his son Sultan Jalal ud-Din Lohani a minor, that the chief management of affairs at least in Bihar then devolved on that prince's mother Dudu and on Farid Khan better known as Sher Shah Suri who had already risen into distinction; that the country was distracted by the rival claims of the Lohani nobles related to the young King, of Baban and Bayezid whose influence was very extensive, of Sher Shah Suri and of other chiefs, and that these factions added to the effects of the discomfiture which the Pathans received in the preceding campaigns from the armies of Babur at length induced the young prince to take refuge in the territories of the King of Bengal.

In this state of things the Afghans of Jaunpur and indeed of India in general, in order to avert the total ruin of their affairs and to unite all interests as far as was practicable resolved to call in Sultan Mahmud Lodi who had already with the support of Rana Sanga made an effort to mount the throne of Delhi. When defeated in that attempt he had retired to Gujarat whence he afterwards proceeded to Pana in Bundelkhand where he remained waiting for some favourable change of affairs and now accepted the invitation to ascend the throne of Bihar and Jaunpur.

He was speedily joined by his countrymen from every quarter and seems to have taken possession of nearly the whole of Bihar without opposition. What excites most surprise is the secrecy and success with which intrigues and movements so extensive appear to have been conducted a fact to be explained perhaps by the deep interest which every Pathan felt in the national success and the fidelity which tribesmen show to their chiefs and to each other.

The very day after receiving this news Babur returned to Agra where he intimated to his council his resolution immediately to assume the command of the eastern army and accordingly taking with him such troops as were at hand he set out on February 2,

1529 and crossing the Doab reached the right bank of the Ganges at Dakdaki on February 27, 1529. Here he was met by his son Humayun, General Askari and several generals who came from the other side. He arranged with them that while his army marched down the right bank of the river theirs should march down the left and should always encamp over against his.

The information which he here received was but little satisfactory. He found that the Pathans who were straining every nerve to recover their military and political ascendancy had gathered round Sultan Mahmud Lodi to the number of a 100,000 men that the Sultan had detached Baban and Sheikh Bayezid with a large force to Sirwar while he himself with Fateh Khan Shirwani the minister of Sultan Jalal ud-Din Lodi and of Sultan Ibrahim Lodi in succession by whom Mahmud had been joined and who had now deserted Babur as he had done his first master kept along the Bihar bank of the Ganges and was marching on Chunar that Sher Shah Suri, whom Babur had distinguished by marks of his favour having given him several perganas and entrusted him with a command, had joined the insurgents, had crossed the Ganges and occupied Benares from which the officers of Sultan Jalal ud-Din Sherki a descendant of the older dynasty of the country who held the city under Babur's authority had fled on his approach.

There were therefore at this time three competitors for the Eastern or Sherki kingdom

- Sultan Jalal ud-Din Sherki the representative of the older kings who ruled the country before it was conquered by Sultan Sikander Lodi. He had lately submitted to Babur and sought his protection. His claims had become rather obsolete but seemed to have been revived at this period, and acknowledged by Babur, evidently to serve an immediate purpose.
- Sultan Jalal ud-Din Khan Lohani whose father and grandfather had headed the revolt against Sultan Ibrahim Lodi. He was supported by many Afghan nobles in Bihar but had lately been forced to seek refuge with the King of Bengal his ally.
- Sultan Mahmud Lodi the brother of the late Sultan Ibrahim Lodi and the representative of the Lodi dynasty of Delhi whom the great body of the Pathans had now united to

support in his claims not on Bihar merely but on Delhi itself.

Babur informed of the real state of affairs continued his march down the banks of the Ganges. In passing Karra he was magnificently entertained by Sultan Jalal ud-Din Sherki the prince whose pretensions he favoured and on whom he bestowed the nominal command of a division of his army. When he had made a march or two below that city the effects of his activity became visible. He learned that Sultan Mahmud Lodi who had recently advanced to Chunar and even made an assault upon it had no sooner received certain information of the Emperor's approach than filled with consternation he raised the siege and retreated in confusion and that Sher Shah Suri had in like manner abandoned Benares and recrossed the river with such precipitation that two of his boats were lost in the passage.

The imperial army having reached Allahabad where the Ganges and Yamuna rivers unite, their streams began on March 10, 1529 to cross the latter river to Priag whence Babur proceeded by Chunar, Benares and Ghazipur hastening to attack Sultan Mahmud who had now taken a position behind the Son River. At Ghazipur, Mahmud Khan Lohani an Afghan of influence came and submitted to him and while yet near the same place Sultan Jalal ud-Din Khan Lohani the expelled prince and still one of the competitors for the throne of Bihar, Sher Shah Suri the future sovereign of Delhi and other Afghans of influence sent to tender their submission. This amounted to a breaking up of the Lohani dynasty of Bihar leaving only Sultan Mahmud Lodi and his adherents to be combated.

Babur now proceeded to cross the Kermnas and encamped beyond Chousa (that was to become celebrated by the calamity of his son) and Baksara or Buxar. Marching thence he found that Sultan Mahmud whose army had been daily suffering from defection and who had been lying not far off attended by only 2000 men had retired with precipitation on the approach of an advanced party of the imperial army had been pursued and several of his men slain.

He also now took refuge with the army of Bengal which had crossed the Ganges probably in the intention of co operating with him. Babur proceeded to the district of Ari in Bihar lying between the Ganges and the Son River at their confluence where he invested

Mohammad Zaman Mirza with the government of Bihar and fixed the revenue to be paid out of that province. The Emperor had now arrived opposite to where the Ghaghara River (also called Gogra in some texts) joins the Ganges from the north east and where apparently the kingdom of Bengal commenced on the left bank of that river.

Here he learned that Sultan Mahmud Lodi was in the Bengal camp at the junction of the two rivers with a body of Afghans and that when he and his followers wished to remove their families and baggage they were not permitted by the Bengalis probably wishing to retain them as hostages Sultan Jalal ud-Din Khan Lohani his rival who had lately sent his submission to Babur was in like manner hindered from departing in consequence of which he had come to blows with the Bengalis had effected a passage over the Ganges into Bihar with his followers and was on his march to join the imperial army.

The Emperor therefore who considered that the position of the army of Bengal and the conduct of its leaders had violated their neutrality prepared to call them to account. Nusrat Shah, the King of Bengal had recovered some of his lost territories from the Pathans after the collapse of the Delhi Sultanate.

Battle

Babur found the army of Kherid, as the Bengal army was called, lying between what is at present the territory of Saran . It was encamped near the junction of the Ganges and the Ghaghara River so as to be able to defend both the course of the Ghaghara River and the left bank of the Ganges after the union of the two rivers. He discovered too that the Bengal generals had collected about a 100-150 vessels on their side of the stream by means of which they were able at once to hinder the passage of an enemy and to facilitate their own.

Such an army he could not safely leave behind especially as the troops of Baban and Bayezid had also taken refuge upon and in strength occupied the upper course of the Ghaghra River. He was indeed at peace with Bengal but the shelter afforded to his flying enemy the position of the Kherid army and the equivocal conduct of its leaders made it indispensable that he should have a categorical declaration as to the disposition and intention of the Bengal government. He therefore dispatched an envoy to Nusrat

Shah the King of Bengal. Babur was now joined by Sultan Junaid Birlas from Jaunpur with about 20,000 men. The tardy arrival of these troops subjected their commander to a temporary disgrace. Not having received a satisfactory answer to his demands, the Emperor resolved to compel the army beyond the Ghaghra River to quit its strong position. He made the necessary arrangements for the intended attack. He formed his army into six divisions Four of these consisting of Askari's army which was already on the left bank of the Ganges and of Sultan Junaid's which had recently joined on the same side were ordered to be prepared to cross the Ghaghra River either in boats at Haldi or by fording still farther up that river.Askari was the youngest son of Babur. The other two divisions were still on the right bank of the Ganges. One of these under the Emperor's personal direction was to effect the passage of that river and then to cover the operations of Ustad Ali Kuli his chief engineer and commander of the Artillery who was directed to plant a battery on the banks of the Siru or Ghaghra River above its union with the Ganges directly opposite to the Bengal camp which it would be able to cannonade and afterwards to cover the passage of the Emperor's division when it crossed the Ghaghra River to attack the enemy. Mustafa Rumi another engineer who had a party of musketeers and artillery supported by Mohammad Zaman Mirza and the sixth division was to open a cannonade on the flank of the enemy's camp from the Bihar bank of the Ganges below the junction of the rivers. The main body of the army which was that under Askari after passing the Ghaghra River at Haldi was ordered to march down upon the enemy so as to draw them from their camp and induce them to march up that river and by this diversion to keep them occupied until the two divisions of Babur and Mohammad Zaman under cover of the fire of the artillery and matchlock men could be transported across.

The whole army was accordingly put in motion Askari's four divisions marched for Haldi . The batteries both on the Ghaghara River and Ganges were constructed and commenced their fire. The Bengal army behaved with great bravery and pushed parties across to attack the Emperor's troops both above and below the junction of the rivers. At length after various movements Babur received notice that Askari had effected a passage over the Ghaghra River at the Haldi Ghat and was now ready for action and that he had been strengthened by the defection of Shah Mohammad

Maaruf an Afghan nobleman of the highest rank and consequence who had deserted the confederacy with his followers and now joined his camp. The general attack was therefore fixed for next morning but in the mean while there was some fighting between the vessels in the river.

On the morning of May 6, 1529 as soon as Askari's army was known to be in motion the Bengal troops moved up to meet him whereupon Babur ordered both his division and that of Mohammad Zaman to cross over without delay. This was affected bravely though not without sharp resistance. The troops got across some in boats, some by swimming, some floating on reeds . They were met with equal gallantry on landing but kept together formed and made repeated vigorous charges. As Askari advanced downwards the enemy finding themselves surrounded and driven in on three sides finally quit the field in confusion.

Aftermath

This victory was decisive in its consequences. Numbers of the Afghan s who till now had been refractory having lost all hope of re establishing an Afghan government in the East submitted and Sultan Jalal ud-Din Khan Lohani the late King of Bihar whose escape from the Bengal camp has been mentioned arrived with many of his principal Amirs and acknowledged Babur. Other chiefs imitating their example petitioned to be received into the Emperor's service. 7000-8000 Lohani Afghans had already joined him and were now rewarded and employed. The feuds between the Lohani and Lodi factions in the Eastern provinces were fatal to the Pathan national interest. As for the King of Bengal Nusrat Shah, he hastily accepted peace proposals, previously communicated to him via the envoy Babur had sent before the battle.

This would be Baburs' last major engagement. He continued to consolidate his power and establish administrative infrastructure in his new Empire distributing *jagirs* (Estates) to loyal nobles and allies. He died at the age of 47 on December 26, 1530 of an unknown illness and was succeeded by his eldest son, Humayun.

Last Days

After Babar fell seriously ill, Humayun was told of a plot by the senior nobles of Babur's court to bypass the leader's sons and appoint Mahdi Khwaja, Babur's sister's husband, as his successor. He rushed to Agra and arrived there to see his father was well enough again, although Mahdi Khwaja had lost all hope of becoming ruler after arrogantly exceeding his authority during Babur's illness. Upon his arrival in Agra it was Humayun himself who fell ill, and was close to dying.

Babar is said to have circled the sick-bed, crying to God to take his life and not his son's. The traditions that follow this tell that Babur soon fell ill with a fever and Humayun began to get better again. This is not accurate, as there are months separating the recovery of Humayun and the death of Babur, and Babur's final illness was rather sudden. His last words apparently being to his son, Humayun, "Do nothing against your brothers, even though they may deserve it."

He died at the age of 47 on January 5 [O.S. 26 December 1530] 1531, and was succeeded by his eldest son, Humayun. Though he wished to be buried in his favourite garden in Kabul, a city he had always loved, he was first buried in a Mausoleum in the capital city of Agra. Roughly nine years later his wishes were fulfilled by Sher Shah Suri and Babur was buried in a beautiful garden Bagh-e Babur in Kabul, now in Afghanistan. The inscription on his tomb reads (in Persian):

If there is a paradise on earth, it is this, it is this, it is this!

Babar's legacy was a mixed one. He is considered a national hero in Uzbekistan and Kyrgyzstan, and is held in high esteem in Afghanistan where he is buried. However, the Sikh Guru, Nanak, wrote a series of complaints against Babur in the Guru Granth Sahib, claiming Babur "terrified Hindustan" and was a "messenger of death." He also claimed that women with braided hair "were shaved with scissors, and their throats were choked with dust" and that "the order was given to the soldiers, who dishonored them, and carried them away."

Impact on Architecture

Babar travelled the country, taking in much of the land and its scenery, and began building a series of structures which mixed the pre-existing Hindu intricacies of carved detail with the traditional Muslim designs used by Persians and Turks. He described with awe the buildings in Chanderi, a village carved from rock, and the palace of Raja Man Singh in Gwalior describing them as "wonderful buildings, entirely hewn from stone." He, was, however, disgusted by the Jain "idols" carved into the rock face below the fortress at Gwalior. "These idols are shown quite naked without even covering for the privities... I ordered them to be destroyed. " Fortunately, the statues were not destroyed entirely, rather the faces and genitalia of the offending pieces were removed. (Modern sculptors have restored the faces).

To remind himself of the lands he had left behind, Babur began a process of creating exquisite gardens in every palace and province, where he would often sit shaded from the fierce Indian sun. He tried to recreate the gardens of Kabul, which he believed were the most beautiful in the world, and in one of which he would eventually be buried. Almost thirty pages of Babur's memoirs are taken up describing the fauna and flora of his Hindustan.

Babri Masjid

Babur is believed to have built Babri Masjid in Ayodhya. The existence of a temple devoted to Lord Rama at the same location is the center of dispute between Hindus and Muslims.

2

Humayun

Humayun (March 17, 1508– March 4, 1556) was the second Mughal Emperor who ruled modern Afghanistan, Pakistan, and parts of northern India from 1530–1540 and again from 1555–1556. Like his father, Babur, he lost his kingdom early, but with Persian aid, he eventually regained an even larger one. On the eve of his death in 1556, the Mughal empire spanned almost one million square kilometers.

He succeeded his father in India in 1530, while his half-brother Kamran Mirza, who was to become a rather bitter rival, obtained the sovereignty of Kabul and Lahore, the more northern parts of their father's empire. He originally ascended the throne at the age of 22 and was somewhat inexperienced when he came to power.

Humayun lost his Indian territories to the Pashtun (Afghan) noble, Sher Shah Suri, and, with Persian aid, regained them fifteen years later. Humayun's return from Persia, accompanied by a large retinue of Persian noblemen, signaled an important change in Mughal court culture, as the Central Asian origins of the dynasty were largely overshadowed by the influences of Persian art, architecture, language and literature.

Subsequently, in a very short time, Humayun was able to expand the Empire further, leaving a substantial legacy for his son, Akbar.

Background

Babur's decision to divide the territories of his empire between two of his sons was unusual in India, but it had been a common Central Asian practice since the time of Genghis Khan. Unlike most European Monarchies which practised primogeniture, the

Timurids, following Genghis Khan's example, did not leave an entire kingdom to the eldest son. Although under that system only a Chingissid could claim sovereignty and khanal authority, any male Chinggisid within a given sub-branch (such as the Timurids) had an equal right to the throne.. While Genghis Khan's Empire had been peacefully divided between his sons upon his death, almost every Chinggisid succession since had resulted in fratricide.

Timur himself had divided his territories between Pir Mohammad, Miran Shah, Khalil Sultan and Shah Rukh, which resulted in inter-family warfare. Upon Babur's death, Humayun's territories were the least secure. Babur had ruled only four years, and not all *umarah* (nobles) viewed Humayun as the rightful ruler. Indeed earlier, when Babur had become ill, some of the nobles had tried to install Humayun's uncle, Mahdi Khwaja, as ruler. Although this attempt failed, it was a sign of problems to come.

Personal traits

Humayun was portrayed in the biography "Humayun-nama" written by his sister Gulbadan Begum, as being extraordinarily lenient, constantly forgiving acts which were deliberately aimed at angering him. In one instance the biography records that his youngest brother Hindal killed Humayun's most trusted advisor, an old Sheikh, and then marched an army out of Agra. Humayun, rather than seek retribution, went straight to his mother's home where Gulbadan Begum and other women were also present and swore on the Qur'an that he would bear no grudge against his younger brother, and insisted he return home. His many documented acts of mercy may have stemmed largely from weakness, but he does seem to have been a gentle and humane man by the standards of the day. He lacked his father's craftiness and athleticism. Though he could be a formidable warrior when he chose to be, he was more laid back and indolent.

He was also deeply superstitious, and fascinated by Astrology and the Occult. Upon his accession as *Padishah* (Emperor), he began to re-organise the administration upon mystically determined principles. The public offices were divided into four distinct groups, for the four elements. The department of Earth was to be in charge of Agriculture and the agricultural sciences, Fire was to be in charge of the Military, Water was the department of the Canals and waterways while Air seemed to have responsibility for everything else. His daily routine was planned in accordance with the movements of the planets, so too was his wardrobe. He refused to enter a house with his left foot going forward, and if anyone else did they would be told to leave and re-enter.

His servant, Jauhar, records in the Tadhkirat al-Waqiat that he was known to shoot arrows to the sky marked with either his own name, or that of the Shah of Persia and, depending on how they landed, interpreted this as an indication of which of them would grow more powerful. He was a heavy drinker, and also took pellets of Opium, after which he was known to recite poetry. He was, however, not enamoured of warfare, and after winning a battle would spend months at a time indulging himself within the walls of a captured city even as a larger war was taking place outside.

Early Reign

Upon his succession to the throne, Humayun had two major rivals interested in acquiring his lands — Sultan Bahadur of Gujarat to the south west and Sher Shah Suri (Sher Khan) currently settled along the river Ganges in Bihar to the east. Humayun's first campaign was to confront a Sher Khan Suri. Halfway through the counter offensive Humayun had to abandon it and concentrate on Gujarat, where a threat from Ahmed Shah had to be squelched. In this he succeeded and annexed Gujarat and Malwa. Champaner and the great fort of Mandu followed next.

During the first five years of Humayun's reign, these two rulers were quietly extending their rule, although Sultan Bahadur faced pressure in the east from sporadic conflicts with the Portuguese. While the Mughals had acquired firearms via the Ottoman Empire, Bahadur's Gujurat had acquired them through a series of contracts drawn up with the Portuguese, allowing the Portuguese to establish a strategic foothold in north western India.

Humayun was made aware that the Sultan of Gujarat was planning an assault on the Mughal territories with Portuguese aid. Showing an unusual resolve, Humayun gathered an army and marched on Bahadur. His assault was spectacular and within a month he had captured the forts of Mandu and Champaner. However, instead of pressing his attack and going after the enemy, Humayun ceased the campaign and began to enjoy life in his new forts. Bahadur, meanwhile, escaped and took up refuge with the Portuguese.

Shortly after Humayun had marched on Gujarat, Sher Shah saw an opportunity to wrest control of Agra from the Mughals. He began to gather his army together hoping for a rapid and decisive siege of the Mughal capital. Upon hearing this alarming news, Humayun quickly marched his troops back to Agra allowing Bahadur to easily regain control of the territories Humayun had recently taken. A few months later, however, Bahadur was dead, killed when a botched plan to kidnap the Portuguese viceroy ended in a fire-fight which the Sultan lost.

Whilst Humayun succeeded in protecting Agra from Sher Shah, the second city of the Empire, Gaur the capital of the *vilayat* of Bengal, was sacked. Humayun's troops had been delayed while trying to take Chunar, a fort occupied by Sher Shah's son, in order to protect his troops from an attack from the rear. The stores of grain at Gauri, the largest in the empire, were emptied and Humayun arrived to see corpses littering the roads. The vast wealth of Bengal was depleted and brought East giving Sher Shah a substantial war chest.

Sher Shah withdrew to the east, but Humayun did not follow: instead he "shut himself up for a considerable time in his Harem, and indulged himself in every kind of luxury." Hindal, Humayun's nineteen year old brother, had agreed to aid him in this battle and protect the rear from attack but abandoned his position and withdrew to Agra where he decreed himself acting emperor. When Humayun sent the grand *Mufti*, Sheikh Buhlul, to reason with him, the Sheikh was killed. Further provoking the rebellion, Hindal ordered that the *Khutba* or sermon in the main mosque at Agra be read in his name, a sign of assumption of sovereignty. When Hindal withdrew from protecting the rear of Humayun's troops, Sher Shah's troop quickly reclaimed these positions, leaving Humayun surrounded.

Humayun's other brother, Kamran, marched from his territories in the Punjab, ostensibly to aid Humayun. However, his return home had treacherous motives as he intended to stake a claim for Humayun's apparently collapsing empire. He brokered a deal with Hindal which provided that his brother would cease all acts of disloyalty in return for a share in the new empire which Kamran would create once Humayun was deposed.

Sher Shah met Humayun in battle on the banks of the Ganges, near Benares, in Chausa. This was to become an entrenched battle in which both sides spent a lot of time digging themselves into positions. The major part of the Mughal army, the artillery, was now immobile, and Humayun decided to engage in some diplomacy using Mohammad Aziz as ambassador. Humayun agreed to allow Sher Shah to rule over Bengal and Bihar, but only as provinces granted to him by his Emperor, Humayun, falling short of outright sovereignty. The two rulers also struck a bargain in order to save face: Humayun's troops would charge those of Sher Shah whose forces then retreat in feigned fear. Thus honour would, supposedly, be satisfied.

Once the Army of Humayun had made its charge and Sher Shah's troops made their agreed-upon retreat, the Mughal troops relaxed their defensive preparations and returned to their entrenchments without posting a proper guard. Observing the Mughals' vulnerability, Sher Shah reneged on his earlier agreement. That very night, his army approached the Mughal camp and finding the Mughal troops unprepared with a majority asleep, they advanced and killed most of them. The Emperor survived by swimming the Ganges using an air filled "water skin," and quietly returned to Agra.

In Agra

When Humayun returned to Agra, he found that all three of his brothers were present. Humayun once again not only pardoned his brothers for plotting against him, but even forgave Hindal for his outright betrayal. With his armies travelling at a leisurely pace, Sher Shah was gradually drawing closer and closer to Agra. This was a serious threat to the entire family, but Humayun and Kamran squabbled over how to proceed. Kamran withdrew after Humayun refused to make a quick attack on the approaching enemy, instead opting to build a larger army under his own name. When Kamran returned to Lahore, his troops followed him shortly afterwards, and Humayun, with his other brothers Askari and Hindal, marched to meet Sher Shah just 240 kilometres (150 miles) east of Agra at the Battle of Kanauj on May 17, 1540. The battle once again saw Humayun make some tactical errors, and his army was soundly defeated. He and his brothers quickly retreated back to Agra, humiliated and mocked along the way by peasants and villagers.

They chose not to stay in Agra, and retreated to Lahore, though Sher Shah followed them, founding the short-lived Sur Dynasty of northern India with its capital at Delhi.

In Lahore

The four brothers were united in Lahore, but every day they were informed that Sher Shah was getting closer and closer. When he reached Sirhind, Humayun sent an ambassador carrying the message "I have left you the whole of Hindustan (*i.e.* the lands to the East of Punjab, comprising most of the Ganges Valley). Leave Lahore alone, and let Sirhind be a boundary between you and me." Sher Shah, however, replied "I have left you Kabul. You should go there." Kabul was the capital of the empire of Humayun's brother Kamran Mirza, who was far from willing to hand over any of his territories to his brother. Instead, Kamran approached Sher Shah, and proposed that he actually revolt against his brother and side with Sher Shah in return for most of the Punjab. Sher Shah dismissed his help, believing it not to be required, though word soon spread to Lahore about the treacherous proposal and Humayun was urged to make an example of Kamran and kill him. Humayun refused, citing the last words of his father, Babur "Do nothing against your brothers, even though they may deserve it."

Withdrawing Further

Humayun decided that it would be wise to withdraw still further. He asked that his brothers join him as he fell back into Sindh. While the previously rebellious Hindal remained loyal, Kamran and Askari instead decided to head to the relative peace of Kabul. This was to be a definitive schism in the family.

Humayun expected aid from the Amir of Sindh, whom he had appointed and who owed him his allegiance. While the Amir, Hussein, tolerated Humayun's presence, he knew that raising an army against Sher Shah would ultimately end in disaster, and he therefore politely refused all of Humayun's requests for military assistance. Whilst in Sindh Humayun met and married Hamida — who was to become the mother of Akbar — on August 21, 1541. The date was selected after Humayun consulted his astrolabe to check the location of the planets.

In May 1542 the Raja of Jodhpur, Rao Maldeo Rathore, issued a request to Humayun to form an alliance against Sher Shah and so Humayun and his army rode out through the desert to meet with the Prince. As they made their way across the desert the prince became aware of how feeble Humayun's army had now become. Furthermore, Sher Shah had offered him more favourable terms and so he sent word that he no longer wanted to see Humayun, who was now less than 80 km (50 miles) from the city. Thus, Humayun and his troops, and his heavily pregnant wife, had to retrace their steps through the desert at the hottest time of year. All the wells had been filled with sand by the nearby inhabitants after Humayun's troops had killed several cows (a sacred animal to the Hindus), leaving them with nothing but berries to eat. When Hamida's horse died no one would lend the Queen (who was now eight months pregnant) a horse, so Humayun did so himself, resulting in him riding a camel for six kilometeres (four miles), although Khaled Beg then offered him his mount. Humayun was later to describe this incident as the lowest point in his life. He ordered Hindal to join his brothers in Kandahar.

However, while Humayun was on his travels, Hussein, the Amir of Sindh, had killed Maldeo's father, prompting the Raja to change his mind about Humayun. He decided to ride out to meet him in Umarkot, a small town by a desert oasis. Humayun was afforded full courtesies and was given new horses and weapons as the men formed an alliance against Sindh. Umarkot was to become the centre of operations for this battle, and it was here, on November 23, 1542 that the 15 year old Hamida, gave birth to her first child, a boy they called Akbar- (great), the heir-apparent to the 34 year old Humayun.

Retreat to Kabul?

The war against Sindh had led to a stalemate, and so Hussein decided to bribe Humayun to leave the area. Humayun accepted and in return for three hundred Camels (mostly wild) and two thousand loads of grain he set off to join his brothers in Kandahar, crossing the Indus on July 11, 1543.

In Kamran's territory, Hindal had been placed under house arrest in Kabul after refusing to have the *Khutba* recited in Kamran's name. His other brother Askari was now ordered to gather an army and march on Humayun. When Humayun received word of the approaching hostile army he decided against facing them, and instead sought refuge elsewhere. Akbar was left behind in camp close to Kandahar for, as it was December it would have been too cold and dangerous to include the 14 month old toddler in the forthcoming march through the dangerous and snowy mountains of the Hindu Kush. Askari found Akbar in the camp, and embraced him, and allowed his own wife to rear him. She apparently treated him as her own.

Refuge in Persia

Humayun fled to the refuge of the Safavid Empire in Iran, marching with forty men and his wife and her companion through mountains and valleys. Amongst other trials the Imperial party were forced to live on horse meat boiled in the soldiers' helmets. These indignities continued during the month it took them to reach Herat, however after their arrival they were reintroduced to the finer things in life. Upon entering the city his army was greeted with an armed escort, and they were treated to lavish food and clothing. They were given fine accommodations and the roads were cleared and cleaned before them. Shah Tahmasp, unlike Humayun's own family, actually welcomed the Mughal, and treated him as a royal visitor. Here Humayun went sightseeing and was amazed at the Persian artwork and architecture he saw: much of this was the work of the Timurid Sultan Husayn Bayqarah and his ancestor, princess Gauhar Shad, thus he was able to admire the work of his relatives and ancestors at first hand. He was introduced to the work of the Persian miniaturists, and Kamaleddin Behzad had two of his pupils join Humayun in his court. Humayun was amazed at their work and asked if they would work for him if he were to regain the sovereignty of Hindustan: they agreed. With so much going on Humayun did not even meet the Shah until July, some six months after his arrival in Persia. After a lengthy journey from Herat the two met in Qazvin where a large feast and parties were held for the event. The meeting of the two monarchs is depicted in a famous wall-painting in the Chehel Sotoun (Forty Columns) palace in Esfahan.

The Shah urged that Humayun convert from Sunni to Shia Islam, and Humayun eventually and reluctantly accepted, in order to keep himself and several hundred followers alive much to the disapproval of his biographer Jauhar. With this outward acceptance of Shivism the Shah was eventually prepared to offer Humayun more substantial support. When Humayun's brother, Kamran, offered to cede Kandahar to the Persians in exchange for Humayun, dead or alive, the Shah refused. Instead the Shah threw a party for Humayun, with three hundred tents, an imperial Persian carpet, 12 musical bands and "meat of all kinds". Here the Shah announced that all this, and 12,000 choice cavalry were his to lead an attack on his brother Kamran. All that Shah asked for was that, if Humayun's forces were victorious, Kandahar would be his.

Kandahar and Onwards

With this Persian aid Humayun took Kandahar from Askari after a two-week siege. He noted how the nobles who had served Askari quickly flocked to serve him, "in very truth the greater part of the inhabitants of the world are like a flock of sheep, wherever one goes the others immediately follow". Kandahar was, as agreed, given to the Shah who sent his infant son, Murad, as the Viceroy. However, the baby soon died and Humayun thought himself strong enough to assume power.

Humayun now prepared to take Kabul, ruled by his brother Kamran. In the end, there was no actual siege. Kamran was detested as a leader and as Humayun's Persian army approached the city hundreds of Kamran's troops changed sides, flocking to join Humayun and swelling his ranks. Kamran absconded and began building an army outside the city in November 1545 Hamida and Humayun were reunited with their son Akbar, and held a huge feast. They also held another, larger, feast in the childs' honour when he was circumcised.

However, while Humayun had a larger army than his brother and had the upper hand, on two occasions his poor military judgement allowed Kamran to retake Kabul and Kandahar, forcing Humayun to mount further campaigns for their recapture. He may have been aided in this by his reputation for leniency towards the troops who had defended the cities against him, as opposed to Kamran, whose brief periods of possession were marked by atrocities against the inhabitants who, he supposed, had helped his brother.

His youngest brother, Hindal, formerly the most disloyal of his siblings, died fighting on his behalf. His brother Askari was shackled in chains at the behest of his nobles and aides. He was allowed go on Hajj, and died en route in the desert outside Damascus.

Humayun's other brother, Kamran, had repeatedly sought to have Humayun killed, and when in 1552 he attempted to make a pact with Islam Shah, Sher Shah's successor, he was apprehended by a Gakhar.

The Gakhars were one of only a few groups of people who had remained loyal to their oath to the Mughals. Sultan Adam of the Gakhars handed Kamran over to Humayun. Humayun was tempted to forgive his brother, however he was warned that allowing Kamran's continuous acts to go unpunished could foment rebellion within his own ranks. So, instead of killing his brother Humayun had Kamran blinded which would end any claim to the throne. He sent him on Hajj, as he hoped to see his brother absolved of sin, but he died close to Mecca in the Arabian desert in 1557.

India Revisited

Sher Shah Suri had died in 1545, and, although he was a powerful ruler, his son Islam Shah died too in 1554. These two deaths left the dynasty reeling and disintegrating. Three rivals for the throne all marched on Delhi, while in many cities leaders tried to stake a claim for independence. This was a perfect opportunity for the Mughals to march back to India. Humayun placed the army under the able leadership of Bairam Khan. This was a wise move given Humayun's own record of military ineptitude, and turned out to be prescient, as Bairam was to prove himself a great tactician.

Bairam Khan led the army through the Punjab virtually unopposed. The fort of Rohtas, which was built in 1541-43 by Sher Shah Suri to crush the Gakhars who were loyal to Humayun, was surrendered without a shot by a treacherous commander. The walls of the Rohtas Fort measure up to 12,5 meters in thickness and up to 18,28 meters in height.

They extend for 4 km and feature 68 semi-circular bastions. Its sandstone gates, both massive and ornate, are thought to have exerted a profound influence on Mughal military architecture.

The only major battle faced by Humayun's armies was against Sikander Suri in Sirhind, where Bairam Khan employed a tactic whereby he engaged his enemy in open battle, but then retreated quickly in apparent fear. When the enemy followed after them they were surprised by entrenched defensive positions and were easily annihilated.

From here on most towns and villages chose to welcome the invading army as it made its way to the capital. On July 23, 1555 Humayun, once again, sat on Babur's throne in Delhi.

Ruling North India again

With all of Humayun's brothers now dead, there was no fear of another usurping his throne during military campaigns. He was also now an established leader, and could trust his generals. With this new-found strength Humayun embarked on a series of military campaigns aimed at extending his reign over areas to the East and West India.

His sojourn in exile seems to have reduced Humayun's reliance on astrology, and his military leadership instead imitated the methods he had observed in Persia, allowing him to win more effectively and quicker.

This also applied to the administration of the empire. Persian methods of governance were imported into North India in Humayun's reign. The system of revenue collection is held to have improved on both the Persian model and that of the Delhi Sultanate one. The Persian arts too were very influential, and Persian-style miniatures were produced at Mughal (and subsequently Rajput) courts. The Chaghatai language, in which Babur had written his memoirs, disappeared almost entirely from the culture of the courtly elite, and Akbar could not speak it. Later in life Humayun himself is said to have spoken in Persian verse more often than not.

Death and Legacy

On March 4, 1556, Humayun, his arms full of books, was descending the staircase from his library when the muezzin announced the Adhan (the call to prayer), reportedly after smoking a pipefull of opium. It was his habit, wherever he heard the summons, to bow his knee in holy reverence. Kneeling, he caught his foot in his robe, tumbled down several steps and hit his temple on a rugged stone edge. He died three days later, and was succeeded by the 13 year old Akbar.

Humayun loved astrology and astronomy and built observatories that lasted centuries. His life was chronicled in a slightly hagiographical work called the *Humayun-nama* written by his sister Gulbadan Begum at the request of his son, Akbar. His most lasting impact was the importing of Persian ideas into the Indian empire, something which was expanded on by later leaders. His support for the arts, following exposure to Safavid art, saw him recruit painters to his court who developed the celebrated Mughal style of painting.

Humayun's greatest architectural creation was the Din-Panah (Refuge of Religion) citadel, also known as *Purana Qila* at Delhi which was destroyed by Sher Shah Suri. He is best remembered today for his great Tomb, built by his widow after his death between 1562 and 1571. The ultimate model for Humayun's tomb is the Gur-e Amir in Samarkand, and it is best-known as a precursor to the Taj Mahal in style. However, in its striking composition of dome and *iwan*, and its imaginative use of local materials, it is one of the finest Mughal monuments in India in its own right.

Kamran Mirza

Kamran Mirza, sometimes known simply as Kamran, (born 1509, Kabul; died 5 (or 6) October 1557, Mecca) was the second son of Babur, the founder of the Mughal dynasty. He was half-brother to Babur's eldest son Humayun, who would go on and inherit the Mughal throne, but he was full brother to Babur's third son, Askari.

During the Reign of Babur

While his father, Babur, was conquering northern India from 1525 onwards, Kamran remained in Kandahar in order to secure his northern flank. He was still in charge of the northern part of the newly formed empire, when his father died in 1530. According to the Mughal historian Abul Fazl, Babur's last words to Humayun were "do nothing against your brothers, even though they may deserve it."

In India

In 1538 Kamran first crossed into India, bringing with him 12,000 soldiers, while Humayun was away fighting in Bengal. He appeared to have come in order to put down the rebellion of his brother Hindal against Humayun. However, despite Humayun's calls for help, Kamran offered him no aid whatsoever. After Humayun returned from his defeat at the Battle of Chausa, Kamran refused to place his troops under Humayun's command as he was more interested in taking power for himself. Seeing no chance of furthering his ambition, Kamran withdrew back to Lahore.

Rivalry with Humayun

Following his success in the Battle of Kaunaj in 1540, the new ruler of northern India, Sher Shah, ordered Humayun to leave India and settle in Kabul. Kamran was unwilling to hand the city over to his brother though. At this point Kamran went behind Humayun's back and offered to support Sher Shah, if the latter would give him the Punjab in return. His offer was refused. At this point Humayun was urged by his advisors to put his brother to death, but he refused. After a series of disastrous attempts to retake his throne, Humayun crossed the Indus in 1543. Rather than welcoming him, Kamran sent his younger brother Askari out to catch him and bring him to Kabul. Humayun managed to escape his brother's clutches though and sought refuge in the court of the ruler of Persia, Shah Tahmasp I. When Humayun was in Persia, Kamran offered the Shah, the city of Kandahar if he would hand his brother over to him. Shah Tahmasp favoured Humayun in this fraternal squabble however, and provided him with troops with which he defeated Kamran.

Exile and Death

Although Humayun resisted the pressure to put his rebellious brother to death, he was persuaded that something needed to be done about him so he reluctantly had him blinded. Humayun then sent him off to perform the Hajj to Makkah, where he died in 1557.

Personal Information

Kamran was the second or third son born to Babur, but the second surviving son. His mother was Gulrukh Begum, sister of Sultan Ali Mirza Taghai Begchik.

Wives and children:

- (Gulrukh?) Begum, his first cousin, daughter of his maternal uncle Sultan Ali Mirza Taghai Begchik; married at Kabul in November 1528; presumably mother of
  - Habiba Sultan Begum, born about 1530; married (A) in Hazara, 1544, Esan Daulat Aq Sultan Chaghatai, son of Aiman Kwaja Khan Chaghatai; divorced 1551/1552; married (B) 1551/1552 Mirza Abdu-r Rahman Khan Dughlat

  - o Gulrukh Begum, died after February 1615; married Ibrahim Husain Mirza Bayqra, died 1573, son of Sultan Mohammad Mirza.
- Hazara Begum, niece of Khizr Khan Hazara ; alive in October 1545
- Mah Begum Qibchaq Moghol, daughter of Sultan Wais Kulabi Qibchaq Moghol;alive in October 1545
- Mah Afroz Begum, alive in October 1545; mother of a daughter:
  - o Haji Begum, died 1583. Haji is evidently a surname. Mah Afroz Begum is said by Gulbadan Begum to be the mother of Haji Begum. When Gulbadan went on pilgrimage to Mekkah in 1575, she was accompanied by 2 daughters of her late brother Kamran: Haji Begum and Gulizar Begum. 4 daughters of Kamran are known by their names: Habiba, Gulrukh, Ayisha and Gulizar. None of them can be identified with Haji begum: Gulrukh was still alive in 1615; Ayisha's mother was Daulat Bakht Agacha; Gulizar went to Mekkah with Haji, and Habiba is mentioned by Gulbadan together with Mah Afroz, but the latter is identified at the same time as the mother of Haji Begum, and not of Habiba as well.
- Muhtarima Khanum, daughter of Shah Mohammed Sultan Chaghatai and Khadija Sultan Khanum Chaghatai; she married (B) in 1557/1558 Ibrahim Sultan Mirza Miranshah, died 1560, son of Suleiman Mirza Miranshah and Haram Begum. She had a daughter by Kamran:
  - o Gulizar Begum, born bef. 1550; went to Mekkah in 1575. Gulbadan Begum informs us that Muhtarima had a daughter by Kamran, but unfortunately does not name her. As Ayisha's mother was Daulat Bakht Agacha, and Habiba and Gulrukh were most presumably born of the first wife, Muhtarima's daughter must be Gulizar, or another unatested daughter of Kamran.
- Mah-i-Kuchuk Begum, married before 21 February 1547; died at Mekkah, May 1558), only child of Mir Shah Husain Arghun, Lord of Sind, Kandahar and Kabul, by his wife,

Mah-i-Kuchuk Begum, daughter of Mirza Mohammad Muqim Beg Aghun. She accompanied Kamran to Mekkah in 1553

- a daughter of 'Abdu'llah Khan Mughal.
- Daulat Bakht Agacha, a concubine, alive in 1550; mother of
  - o Ayisha Sultan Begum, born bef. 1550; presumably married to Fakhruddin Khan Mashhadi (died 1578)
  - by an unidentified concubine, Kamran had a son:
  - o Abul-Qasim Ibrahim Mirza, died 1567.

Gulbadan Begum

Gulbadan Begum (c. 1523 – 1603) was a daughter of Zâhir ud-Dîn Mohammad Babur, the first Mughal emperor of India, she is most known as the author of 'Humayun Nama', the account of the life of her brother, Humayun..

Her name means literally *princess with a body like roses* in Persian. She was a descendant of the lines of highest Central Asian aristocracy: Timur through his son Miran Shah, and Genghis Khan through his son Chagatai Khan. Her mother was Dildar Begum and she was sister to Humayun, the second Mughal emperor.

She also finds reference throughout, Akbarnama, the Book of Akbar, written by Abul Fazal, and much of her biographical details are accessible through the work.

Biography

When Princess Gulbadan was born her father had been lord in Kabul for nineteen years; he was master also in Kunduz and Badakhshan, had held Bajaur and Swat since 1519, and Qandahar for a year. During ten of those nineteen years he had been styled "padshah", in token of headship of the house of Timur and of his independent sovereignty. Two years later Babur set out on his last expedition across the Indus to conquer an empire in India. Gulbadan Begum was brought to India at the age of six. Gulbadan was married at 17, and had at least one son.

Humayun and his Sister

In 1540 Humayun lost the kingdom that his Kabul-born father Babur had established in India to Sher Shah Suri, an upstart from

Bihar. With only his pregnant wife, one female attendant and a few loyal supporters, Humayun first fled to Lahore, and then later to Kabul. He was in exile for the next fifteen years in Afghanistan and Persia. Gulbadan Begum went to live in Kabul again. Her life, like all the other Mughal women of the harem, was intricately intertwined with three Mughal kings – her father Babur, brother Humayun and nephew Akbar. Two years after Humayun re-established the Delhi Empire, she accompanied other Mughal women of the harem back to Agra at the behest of Akbar, who had begun his rule.

Writing of Humayun Nama

Akbar commissioned Gulbadan Begum to chronicle the story of her brother Humayun. He was fond of his aunt and knew of her storytelling skills. It was fashionable for the Mughals to engage writers to document their own reigns (Akbar's own history, Akbarnama, was written by the well-known Persian scholar Abul Fazl). Akbar asked his aunt to write whatever she remembered about her brother's life. Gulbadan Begum took the challenge and produced a document titled *Ahwal Humayun Padshah Jamah Kardom Gulbadan Begum bint Babur Padshah amma Akbar Padshah*. It came to be known as *Humayun-nama*.

Gulbadan wrote in simple Persian without the erudite language used by better known writers. Her father Babur had written Baburnama in the same style and she took his cue and wrote down from her memory. Unlike some of her contemporary writers, Gulbadan wrote a factual account of what she remembered, without embellishment. What she produced not only chronicles the trials and tribulations of Humayun's rule, but also gives us a glimpse of life in the Mughal harem. It is the only surviving writing penned by a woman of Mughal royalty in the sixteenth century.

The memoir had been lost for several centuries and what has been found is not well preserved, poorly bound with many pages missing. It also appears to be incomplete, with the last chapters missing. There must have been very few copies of the manuscript, and for this reason it did not receive the recognition it deserved.

Translation of Humayun Nama

A battered copy of the manuscript is kept in the British Museum. Originally found by an Englishman, Colonel G. W.

Hamilton. it was sold to the British Museum by his widow in 1868. Its existence was little known until 1901, when Annette S. Beveridge translated it into English (Beveridge affectionately called her Princess Rosebud).

Historian Dr. Rieu called it one of the most remarkable manuscripts in the collection of Colonel Hamilton (who had collected more than 1,000 manuscripts). A paperback edition of Beveridge's English translation was published in India in 2001.

Pradosh Chattopadhyay has translated Humayun Nama into Bengali in 2006. Chirayata Prokashan published the book.

Content of the Document

Upon being entrusted with the directive by Akbar to write the manuscript, Gulbadan Begum begins thus:

There had been an order issued, 'Write down whatever you know of the doings of Firdous-Makani (Babur) and Jannat-Ashyani (Humayun)'. At this time when his Majesty Firdaus-Makani passed from this perishable world to the everlasting home, I, this lowly one, was eight years old, so it may well be that I do not remember much. However in obedience to the royal command, I set down whatever there is that I have heard and remember.

From her account we know that Gulbadan was married by the age of seventeen to Khizr Khwaja Khan, a Chagtai Mughal by ancestry and her second cousin. She had at least one son. She had moved to Delhi/Agra in 1528 from Kabul with her foster mother. After the defeat of Humayun in 1540 she moved back to Kabul to live with one of her half brothers. She did not return to Agra immediately after Humayun won back his kingdom. Instead, she stayed behind in Kabul until she was brought back to Agra by Akbar, two years after Humayun died in a tragic accident in 1556. Gulbadan Begum lived in Agra and then Sikri for the rest of her life, except for a period of seven years when she undertook a pilgrimage to Mecca.

She appears to have been an educated, pious, and cultured woman of royalty. She was fond of reading and she had enjoyed the confidences of both her brother Humayun and nephew Akbar. From her account it is also apparent that she was an astute observer, well versed with the intricacies of warfare, and the intrigues of royal deal making. The first part of her story deals with Humayun's rule after her father's death and the travails of Humayun after his defeat. She had written little about her father Babur, as she was only aged eight when he died. However, there are anecdotes and stories she had heard about him from her companions in the Mahal (harem) that she included in her account. The latter part also deals with life in the Mughal harem.

She recorded one light-hearted incident about Babur. He had minted a large gold coin, as he was fond of doing, after he established his kingdom in India. This heavy gold coin was sent to Kabul, with special instructions to play a practical joke on the court jester Asas, who had stayed behind in Kabul. Asas was to be blindfolded and the coin was to be hung around his neck. Asas was intrigued and worried about the heavy weight around his neck, not knowing what it was. However, when he realized that it was a gold coin, Asas jumped with joy and pranced around the room, repeatedly saying that no one shall ever take it from him.

Gulbadan Begum describes her father's death when her brother had fallen ill at the age of twenty-two. She tells that Babur was depressed to see his son seriously ill and dying. For four days he circumambulated the bed of his son repeatedly, praying to Allah, begging to be taken to the eternal world in his son's place. As if by miracle, his prayers were answered. The son recovered and the forty-seven year old father died soon after.

Soon after his exile, Humayun had seen and fallen in love with a thirteen year old girl named Hamida Banu in the harem of Shah Husain Mirza. At first she refused to come to see the Emperor, who was much older than her. Finally she was advised by the other women of the harem to reconsider, and she consented to marry the Emperor. Two years later, in 1542, she bore Humayun a son named Akbar, the greatest of the Mughal rulers. Gulbadan Begum described the details of this incident and the marriage of Humayun and Hamida Banu with glee, and a hint of mischievousness in her manuscript.

Gulbadan also recorded the nomadic life style of Mughal women. Her younger days were spent in the typical style of the peripatetic Mughal family, wandering between Kabul and Delhi. During Humayun's exile the problem was further exaggerated. She had to live in Kabul with one of her step brothers, who later tried to recruit her husband to join him against Humayun. Gulbadan Begum persuaded her husband not to do so.

Pilgrimage to Mecca

Gulbadan Begum described in her memoir a pilgrimage she took to Mecca, a distance of three thousand miles, crossing treacherous mountains and hostile deserts. Though they were of royal birth, the women of the harem were hardy and prepared to face hardships, especially since their lives were so intimately intertwined with the men and their fortunes. Gulbadan Begum stayed in Mecca for nearly four years and during her return a shipwreck in Aden kept her from returning to Agra for several months. She finally returned in 1582, seven years after she had set forth on her journey.

Akbar had provided for safe passage of his aunt on her Hajj and sent a noble as escort with several ladies in attendance. Lavish gifts were packed with her entourage that could be used as alms. Her arrival in Mecca caused quite a stir and people from as far as Syria and Asia Minor swarmed to Mecca to get a share of the bounty.

If Gulbadan Begum had written about the death of Humayun, when he tumbled down the steps in Purana Qila in Delhi, it has been lost. The manuscript seems to end abruptly in the year 1552, four years before the death of Humayun. It ends in mid-sentence, describing the blinding of Prince Kamran. As we know that Gulbadan Begum had received the directive to write the story of Humayun's rule by Akbar, long after the death of Humayun, it is reasonable to believe that the only available manuscript is an incomplete version of her writing. It is also believed that Akbar asked his aunt to write down from her memory so that Abul Fazl could use the information in his own writings about the emperor Akbar.

Old Age and Death

When she was seventy, her name is mentioned with that of Mohammad-yar, a son of her daughter, who left the court in disgrace; again, she and Salima join in intercession to Akbar for Prince Salim; again, with Hamida, she receives royal gifts of money and jewels.

Her charities were large, and it is said of her that she added day unto day in the endeavour to please God, and this by succouring the poor and needy.

When she was eighty years old, in February, 1603, her departure was heralded by a few days of fever. Hamida was with her to the end, and it may be that Ruqaiya, Hindal's daughter, also watched her last hours. As she lay with closed eyes, Hamida-banu spoke to her by the long-used name of affection, "Jiu!" (elder sister). There was no response. Then, "Gul-badan!" The dying woman opened her eyes, quoted the verse, "I die—may you live!" and died. Akbar helped to carry her bier some distance, and for her soul's repose made lavish gifts and did good works. He will have joined in the silent prayer for her soul before committal of her body to the earth, and if no son were there, he, as a near kinsman, may have answered the Imam's injunction to resignation: "It is the will of God."

It is said that for the two years after her death, Akbar lamented constantly that he missed his favourite aunt, until his own death in 1605.

Gulbadan was also said to have been a poet, fluent in both Persian and Turkish. None of her poems have survived.

For much of history the manuscript of Gulbadan Begum remained in obscurity. There is little mention of it in contemporary literature of other Mughal writers, especially the authors who chronicled Akbar's rule. Yet, the little known account of Gulbadan Begum is an important document for historians, with its window into a woman's perspective from inside the Mughal harem.

Bibliography

Humayun-Nama ***: The History of Humayun*** by Gul-Badan Begam. Translated by Annette S. Beveridge. New Delhi, Goodword, 2001,ISBN 81-87570-99-7.

Hamida Banu Begum

Hamida Banu Begam, 'Maryam Makani' (1527-1604) was a wife of the second Mughal Emperor, Humayun, and the mother of Mughal Emperor, Akbar. Her important architectural legacy is the Humayun's Tomb, Delhi, which she commissioned in 1562 CE, and saw through its construction over the next eight years.

Biography

Hamida Banu Begum was born in 1527, to Shaikh Ali Akbar Jami, a Persian Shia, and a friend and preceptor to Mirza Hindal, the youngest son of first Mughal Emperor and Humayun's father, Babur. Ali Akbar Jami was also known as Mir Baba Dost, who belonged to the lineage of Ahmad Jami Zinda-fil. Hamida Banu's mother was Mah Afraz Begum, who married Ali Akbar Jami in Paat, Sindh.

Two years later, after a perilous journey through the desert, on 22 August 1542, she and Emperor Humayun reached at the Rajput Fortress of Umarkot in Sindh at a small desert town, where they were received its ruler, Rana Prasad Singh. Here two months later she gave birth future Emperor, Akbar on the early morning of 15 October 1542 (fourth day of Rajab, 949 AH), he was given the name Humayun had heard in his dream at Lahore-the Emperor Jalalu-d-din Mohammad Akbar

In coming years, she took on numerous tough journeys to follow her husband, who was still in flight. First the beginning of the following December she and her new born went into camp at Jun, after travelling for ten or twelve days. Then in 1543, she made the perilous journey from Sindh, which had Qandahar for its goal, but in course of which Humayun had to take hasty flight from Shal-mastan, 'through a desert and waterless waste.' Leaving her little son behind, she accompanied her husband to Persia, here they visited the shrines of her ancestor, Ahmad-e Jami and Shiites shrine, of Ardabil in Iran, the place of origin of Safavid dynasty which helped them immensely in the following years. In 1544, at a camp at Sabzawar, 93 miles south of Herat, she gave birth to a daughter, thereafter she returned from Persia with the army given to Humayun by Shah of Iran, Tahmasp I, and at Qandahar met Dildar Begum, and her son, Mirza Hindal. Thus, it was not until 15 November 1545 (Ramdan 10th, 952 AH) that she saw her son Akbar again, the scene of young Akbar recognizing his mother amongst a group of women has been keenly illustrated in Akbar's biography, *Akbarnama*. In 1548, she and Akbar accompanied Humayun to Kabul.

Meanwhile, Sher Shah Suri died in May 1545, and after that his son and successor, Islam Shah died too in 1554, disintegrating the Suri dynasty rule. In November 1554, when Humayun set out for India, she stayed back in Kabul. Though he took control of Delhi in 1555, he died within a year of his return, from a fall down the steps of his library at Purana Qila, Delhi, in 1556 at the age of 47, leaving behind a thirteen year old heir, Akbar, who was to become one of greatest emperors of the empire. Hamida Banu joined Akbar from Kabul, only during his second year of reign, 1557 CE, and stayed with him thereafter, she even intervened into politics on various occasions, most notable during the ouster of Mughal minister, Bairam Khan, when Akbar came of age in 1560.

Hamida now an Empress mother, commissioned the construction of Humayun's Tomb, Delhi, in around 1562 CE, six years after his death, and designed by Mirak Mirza Ghiyath, a Persian architect. Over the next eight years she personally supervised the construction of the tomb, where she too was buried after her death on 29 August, 1604 (19th Shahriyar, 1013 AH) in Agra, just a year before the death of her son Akbar and almost half a century after death of her husband, Humayun. Throughout her years, she was held in high regard by her son Akbar, as English traveller Thomas Coryat recorded, Akbar carrying her palanquin himself across the river, during one of her journeys from Lahore to Agra. Later when Prince Salim, future king Jahangir, revolted against his father Akbar, she took upon the case of her grandson, and a reconciliation ensued thereafter, even though has plotted and got Akbar's favourite minister Abul-Fazl killed. Akbar shaved his head and chin only on two occasions, one at the death of foster-mother Jiji Anga and another at the death of his mother.

She was given the title, *Maryam-makani*, dwelling with Mary, posthumously, as she was considered, 'epitome of innocence' by Akbar.. Details of her life are also found in *Humayun Nama*, written by Gulbadan Begum, sister of Humayun, as well as in *Akbarnama* and *Ain-i-Akbari*, both written during the reign of his son, Akbar.

3

Akbar the Great

Jalaluddin Mohammad Akbar (October 15, 1542 – October 27, 1605) was the third Mughal Emperor of India. He was of Timurid descent; the son of Humayun, and the grandson of Babur who founded the dynasty. At the end of his reign in 1605 the Mughal empire covered most of Northern India.

Akbar, widely considered the greatest of the Mughal emperors, was thirteen years old when he ascended the throne in Delhi, following the death of his father Humayun. During his reign, he eliminated military threats from the Pashtun descendants of Sher Shah Suri, and at the Second Battle of Panipat he defeated the Hindu king Hemu. It took him nearly two more decades to consolidate his power and bring parts of northern and central India into his realm. The emperor solidified his rule by pursuing diplomacy with the powerful Rajput caste, and by admitting Rajput princesses in his harem.

Akbar's reign significantly influenced art and culture in the region. Akbar took a great interest in painting, and had the walls of his palaces adorned with murals. Besides encouraging the development of the Mughal school, he also patronised the European style of painting.

He was fond of literature, and had several Sanskrit works translated into Persian, apart from getting many Persian works illustrated by painters from his court. He also commissioned many major buildings, and invented the first prefabricated homes. Akbar began a series of religious debates where Muslim scholars would debate religious matters with Sikhs, Hindus, Carvaka atheists and Portuguese Roman Catholic Jesuits. He founded a religious cult, the *Din-i-Ilahi* (Divine Faith), but it amounted only to a form of personality cult for Akbar, and quickly dissolved after his death.

Early Years

Akbar was born on October 15, 1542 (the fourth day of Rajab, 949 AH), at the Rajput Fortress of Umerkot in Sindh, where Humayun and his recently wedded wife, Hamida Banu Begum were taking refuge. Humayun gave the child the name he had heard in his dream at Lahore, Jalalu-d-din Mohammad Akbar Ghazi

Humayun had been driven into exile in Persia by the Pashtun leader Sher Shah Suri. Akbar did not go to Persia with his parents but grew up in the village of Mukundpur in Rewa (in present day Madhya Pradesh). Akbar and prince Ram Singh I, who later became the Maharaja of Rewa, grew up together and stayed close friends through life. Later, Akbar moved to the eastern parts of the Safavid Empire (now a part of Afghanistan) where he was raised by his uncle Askari. He spent his youth learning to hunt, run, and fight, but he never learned to read or write. Nonetheless, Akbar matured into a well-informed ruler, with refined tastes in the arts, architecture, music and a love for literature.

Following the chaos over the succession of Sher Shah Suri's son Islam Shah, Humayun reconquered Delhi in 1555, leading an army partly provided by his Persian ally Tahmasp I. A few months later, Humayun died. Akbar's guardian, Bairam Khan concealed the death in order to prepare for Akbar's succession. Akbar succeeded Humayun on February 14, 1556, while in the midst of a war against Sikandar Shah to reclaim the Mughal throne. In Kalanaur, Punjab, the 13 year old Akbar donned a golden robe and Dark Tiara was enthroned by Bairam Khan on a newly constructed platform, which still stands. He was proclaimed *Shahanshah* (Persian for "King of Kings"). Bairam Khan ruled on his behalf until he came of age.

Battle of Panipat (1556)

The Second Battle of Panipat was fought between the forces of Samrat Hem Chandra Vikramaditya, popularly called Hemu, and the army of Akbar, on November 5, 1556.It was a decisive victory for the Mughal Emperor Jalal ud-Din Mohammad Akbar's general Bairam Khan

Background

On January 24, 1556, Mughal ruler Humayun died and was succeeded by his son, Jalal ud-Din Mohammad Akbar who was only thirteen years old. On February 14, 1556, in a garden at Kalanaur in Punjab, Akbar was enthroned as the Emperor. At the time of his accession to the throne, the Mughal rule was confined to Kabul, Kandahar, parts of Delhi and Punjab. Akbar was then campaigning in Kabul with his guardian, Bairam Khan.

Samrat Hem Chandra Vikramaditya or Hemu was a Hindu leader who was an advisor to Sher Shah Suri's son Islam Shah earlier from 1545 to 1553 and had won 22 battles during 1553 to 1556 to quell the rebellion by Afghan rebels against Sur regime. At the time of Humayun's death in January 1556, Hemu had just quelled a rebellion in Bengal killing the Bengal ruler Mohammad Shah in the war. He made his intentions of winning Delhi for himself known to his commanders. He then started a campaign winning battles throughout northern India. When he attacked Agra, the commander of Akbar's forces in Agra ran away, leaving the state without a fight. A large area of Etawah, Kalpi and Agra states had come under Hemu's control.

Hemu then moved towards Delhi and stationed his forces outside the city at Tughlaqabad. On October 6, 1556, his army encountered Mughal resistance. After a fierce fight Akbar's forces were ousted, and Tardi Beg, the commander of the Mughal forces, escaped, allowing Hemu to capture Delhi without much difficulty. Around 3000 army personnel were killed. Hemu had himself crowned at Purana Quila on October 7, 1556, established Hindu Raj in North India, and was bestowed the title of Samrat Hem Chandra Vikramaditya.

Battle

Developments in Delhi and Agra disturbed the Mughals at Kalanaur. Many Mughal Generals advised Akbar and Bairam Khan to retreat to Kabul as Mughal forces may not face Hemu's might, but Bairam Khan decided in favour of war. Akbar's army marched towards Delhi. On November 5, both armies met at the historic battlefield of Panipat, where, thirty years earlier, Akbar's grandfather Babur had defeated Ibrahim Lodi in what is now known as the First Battle of Panipat. Hemu Vikramaditya showed most heroic courage during the battle. The Mughal forces were charged repeatedly by elephants to break their lines. Hemu was himself commanding his forces from atop an elephant like a Hindu Vikramaditya King. It seemed Hemu was on a winning track and Akbar's army will run away. Then suddenly an arrow struck Hemu in the eye and knocked him senseless in his Ohda on the elephant. Not seeing Hemu in his Ohda, Hemu's army was in disarray and defeated in the ensuing confusion. Almost dead Hemu was captured by Shah Quli Khan and brought to Akbar's tent. General Bairam Khan was desirous that Akbar should slay General Hemu himself and should establish his right to the title of "Ghazi" (Champion of Faith or war veteran). But Akbar, the spirited boy that he was, refused to strike a defeated and wounded enemy. Bairam Khan irritated by Akbar's scruples beheaded Hemu himself. His head was sent to Kabul, where it was hanged outside Delhi Darwaza, while his body was placed in a gibbet outside Purana Qila in Delhi.

Aftermath

Akbar, after the Battle of Panipat, let loose a reign of terror on Hindus and Afghan supporters of Hemu Vikramaditya, who was killed in the state of unconsciousness brutally. Thousands were killed by the army of Akbar. Heads were cut and minaretts were made of such heads, at public places, to terrorise people. At least one such picture is displayed at the Panipat Wars Museum at Panipat. Akbar took Agra and Delhi without much resistance. But soon after he took possession of his capital, he had to return to Punjab when intelligence informed him of Sikandar Shah Suri's (Adil Shah Suri's brother) advancing campaign in Punjab. He was however defeated and taken captive after the siege of Fort Mankot by Mughal forces and exiled to Bengal. The victory of Akbar at the Battle of Panipat in 1556 was the real restoration of the Mughal Dynasty to Power in India. It marked the fulfillment of the destiny of the House of Timur in India as rulers.

Samrat Hem Chandra Vikramaditya

Hem Chandra Vikramaditya, also known as Hem Chandra Bhargava, Hemu Vikramaditya or simply Hemu was a Hindu Emperor of India during the 1500s. He fought Afghan rebels across North India from the Punjab to Bengal and the Mughal forces of Akbar and Humayun in Agra and Delhi, winning 22 battles without a single setback. He assumed the title of

Vikramaditya after acceding to the throne of Delhi. This was one of the crucial periods in Indian history, when the Mughals and Afghans were desperately vying for power. The son of a food seller, and himself a vendor of saltpetre at Rewari, he rose to become Chief of Army and Prime Minister under the command of Adil Shah Suri of the Suri Dynasty. He acceded to the throne of Delhi on October 7, 1556. His *Rajyabhishek* or coronation was at Purana Quila in Delhi, where he was bestowed the title of Samrat. Hemu re-established the Hindu Kingdom (albeit for a short duration) after over 350 years. Hemu struck coins bearing his title.

Early Life

Hemu was born at Machheri village of Alwar District in Rajasthan in the year 1501. His father Rai Puran Das, a Brahmin, was engaged in *Purohiti,* the performing of Hindu religious ceremonies as a profession. However, due to persecution of Hindus, who performed religious ceremonies, by Mughals, Rai Puran Das could not make both ends meet as a *Purohit,* therefore he gave up *Purohiti* and moved to Qutabpur (now Hemu Nagar) in Rewari in Mewat, what is present day Haryana. Hemu's father started trading (breaking the caste barrier) in salt in Qutabpur, and Hemu was brought up and educated there.

Apart from learning Sanskrit and Hindi, he was educated in Persian, Arabic and Arithmetic. During his childhood, he was fond of exercise and *Kushti* (Wrestling) and while crushing salt in an *Imam Dasta* (an iron pot and hammer), he would monitor his strength. He trained in horse-riding at his friend Sehdev's village. His friend Sehdev was a Rajput and he participated in all the battles which Hemu fought later, except the Second Battle of Panipat. Hemu was brought up in religious environment; his father was a member of *Vallabh Sampradai* of *Vrindavan* and visited various *Teerth* (religious sites) as far as Sindh in present Pakistan.

Rise to Fame

At a very young age, Hemu, who was based at Rewari started supplying food/cereals to Sher Shah Suri's army. Slowly he started other supplies like Saltpetre or Potassium Nitrate (Gunpowder) to Sher Shah's army. Sher Shah had defeated Humayun in the year 1540 and had forced him to withdraw to Kabul. Hemu also laid the foundation of brass cannons casting and manufacturing industry in Rewari, which remains an important industrial Brass/ Copper sheets and utencils manufacturing centre even today.

After Sher Shah Suri's death in the year 1545, his son Islam Shah became ruler of North India. Islam Shah recognised the calibre, and administrative skills of Hemu and therefore made him his personal adviser. He consulted Hemu in matters relating not only to trade and commerce, but also pertaining to statesmanship, diplomacy and general politics. Islam Shah initially appointed Hemu as *Shahang-i-Bazar*, a Persian word meaning 'Market superintendent' who managed the mercantile system throughout the empire. This post gave Hemu an opportunity to interact with the king frequently in order to apprise him of the trade and commercial situation of the Kingdom. Abul Fazal says that Islam Shah held Hemu in great esteem. In 1550, Hemu accompanied Islam Shah to the Punjab where he was deputed along with other high officers to receive Mirza Kamran in the fort of Rohtas. Islam Shah consulted Hemu on a variety of matters. After serving as *Sahang-i-Bazar*, for some time, Hemu rose to become Chief of Intelligence or *Daroga-i-Chowki* (Superintendent of Post). Hemu held this position till October 30, 1553, when Islam Shah died.

Islam Shah was succeeded by his 12 year old son Firoz Khan who was soon killed by Adil Shah Suri. The new king Adil was an indolent, pleasure-seeker, drunkard and debauch as well as faced revolts all around. Adil Shah took Hemu as his Chief Advisor and entrusted all his work to him. Hemu now became the prime minister and chief of the Afghan army. After some time, Adil Shah became insane and Hemu became the virtual king.

Many Afghan governors rebelled against the weak King Adil Shah and refused to pay the taxes, Hemu went to various states in North India to crush rebellion. Ibrahim Khan, Sultan Muhhamad Khan, Taj Karrani, Rukh Khan Nurani and several other Afghan rebel officers were defeated and killed one by one by Hemu. At the battle of Chhapparghatta in December 1555, Hemu routed the Bengal forces under Mohammad Shah, who was killed in the battle.

At the time Afghans considered themselves to be natives (and were considered to be natives by the Hindus); on the other hand Akbar, writes Vincent Arthur Smith, was considered to be a foreigner. Writer K.K.Bhardwaj in his book "Hemu-Napoleon of medieval India" calimed that Hemu was a native ruler leading a native Afghan army to victory, battle after battle, thus Hemu was became popular among Hindus and Afghans. Another writer K.R.Qanungo claimed that Hemu's established commanding Afghan army was secular and nationalistic.

Victories against Mughals

After the victory of the Mughal ruler Humayun over Adil Shah's brother Sikander Suri, Mughals regained Punjab, Delhi and Agra after a gap of 15 years on July 23, 1555. Hemu was in Bengal when Humayun died on January 26, 1556. Humayun's death gave Hemu an ideal opportunity to defeat Mughals. He started a winning march from Bengal through present day Bihar, Eastern UP and Madhya Pradesh. The Mughal *fauzdars* evacuated their positions and fled in panic. In Agra, an important Mughal stronghold, the commander of Mughal forces Iskander Khan Uzbeg ran away from Agra hearing about Hemu's invasion without a fight. Etawah, Kalpi, Bayana, in the present day central and western UP, all came under Hemu's dominion.

In the words of K.K.Bhardwaj in HEMU-Napoleon of Medieval India, if Vincent A Smith describes Samudragupt as Indiạn Napolean we can certainly call Hemu "the Napolean of Medieval India" as the victor of 22 battles before dying fighting at Panipat due to sheer bad luck. His triumphant march from Bihar to Dilli (Delhi) can be equated to the Italian campaign of Napolean "He came, he saw, he conquered". Hemu never saw the defeat in a battle and romped from victory to victory throughout his life (he died in the only battle he lost). If Napoleon promised his soldiers a glorious future they fought bravely in his Italian campaign and instilled in them a new vigour and enthusiasm by an excellent address leading to glorious victories, Hemu practiced it by his lavish distribution of the spoils of war among his soldiers. After winning Agra, Hemu moved towards final assault on Delhi.

Ṭardi Beg Khan who was Governor of Delhi, representing Akbar, sent a despatch to Akbar and Bairam Khan that Hemu had captured Agra and was intending to attack the capital Delhi which could not be defended without adequate reinforcements. Bairam Khan who visualised the gravity of the situation, sent his ablest lieutenant Pir Mohammad Sharwani with other brave commanders to Tardi Beg to hearten him advising to do his utmost for the time being. Tardi Beg Khan summoned all the Mughal commanders of the neighbourhood to the rescue of Delhi and a war council was held. It was decided to fight Hemu and plans were made accordingly. Sir Jadunath Sarkar writes in detail about the battle of Tughlaqabad:

> *"The Mughal army was thus drawn up. Abdullah Uzbeg commanded the Van, Haider Mohammad the right wing, Iskander Beg the left and Tardi Beg himself the centre. The choice Turki Cavalry in the Van and left wing attacked and drove back the enemy forces before them and followed far in pursuit. In this assault the Victors captured 400 elephants and slew 3000 men of the Afghan army. Imagining victory already gained, many of Tardi Beg followers dispersed to plunder the enemy camp and he was left in the field thinly guarded. All this time Hemu had been holding 300 choice elephants and a force of select horsemen as a reserve in the centre. He promptly seized the opportunity and made a sudden charge upon Tardi Beg with this reserve."*

The result was confusion and defeat for the Mughals. Hemu was helped by reinforcements from Alwar with a contingent commanded by Hazi Khan and desertions of various Mughal Commanders along with Pir Mohammed Khan who fled away from the battle field to the utmost chagrin and surprise of Tardi Beg who followed suit.

Hemu won Delhi after a day's battle on October 6, 1556. Some 3000 army men died in this battle. However, Mughal forces lead by Tardi Beg Khan vacated Delhi after a day's fight and Hemu entered Delhi victorious under a royal canopy.

Hemu's Rajyabhishek (Coronation)

Sir Wolsey Haig writes, "Hemu was so elated by the capture of Delhi as to believe that he had already reached the goal of his ambition."

Vincent A. Smith who puts Hemu as the third claimant to the sovereignty of Hindustan at the time, the other two being the Suris and Akbar, affirms that Hemu after his occupation of Delhi came to the conclusion that he had better claim of the throne for himself rather than on behalf of Adil Shah and ventured to assume the royal state under the style of Raja Vikramaditya or Vikramaditya, a title borne by several renowned Hindu Kings in ancient times. Hemu assumed the royal robes and declared himself the Emperor of India under the glorious title of Vikramaditya.

His Afghan officers were reconciled to the ascendancy of an infidel by a liberal distribution of plunder. (and probably, also by the fact that Hemu had proved to be an invincible General)

Hemu had his formal *Rajyabhishek* or coronation following all Hindu religious ceremonies in Delhi and became the ruler under the title 'Raja Vikramaditya'. Hemu was crowned at Purana Qila, on 7 October 1556, in the presence of all Afghan Sardars and Hindu Senapatis (military commanders). The picture above shows a painting of the occasion of Hemu's coronation, where he is flanked by his Afghan and Hindu military commanders. K.K.Bhardwaj writes, thousands of guests would have been invited, along with various Rajput chiefs and Afghan governors along with various scholars and Pandits and the festivities continued for three or four days. "Essential parts of a Hindu King's coronation are" writes, Sir Jadunath Sarkar, "washing him (*abbhishake*) and holding the royal umbrella over his head (*Chhatra-Dharam*)" and Hemu must have followed these ancient traditions, accompanied by costly gifts and robes to priests. He made various appointments on the occasion, appointing his brother Jujharu Rai as governor of Ajmer and his nephew Rammayya as a general in his army. He also appointed his various supporters as *Chhaudhuris* and *Muqqudams* based on their merit so that they continued to maintain their respective positions in the reign of Akbar.

Thus Hemu was the last Hindu Emperor (albeit for a short duration) in North India, after over three centuries of rule by various Islamic invaders and rulers.

Administration under Hemu

Hemu revitalised the administrative set-up which had lagged after the demise of Sher Shah Suri. With his thorough knowledge of trade and commerce, which he achieved as Shangha-i-Bazar, injected fresh blood into the arteries of the mercantile system throughout the length and breadth of the country. He spared none indulging in black-marketing, hoarding, overcharging and less-weighing. After his victory over Agra and Delhi, he dismissed all the corrupt officers and replaced them. He also introduced coins bearing his pictures.

The Name Akbar

Akbar was originally named Badruddin Akbar, because he was born on the night of a *badr* (full moon). After the capture of Kabul by Humayun his date of birth and name were changed to throw off evil sorcerers. Contrary to some popular traditions, the name Akbar-meaning "Great"-was a not an honorific given to Akbar; rather he was named for his maternal grandfather, Shaikh Ali *Akbar* Jami.

Military Achievements

Early conquests: Akbar decided early in his reign that he should eliminate the threat of Sher Shah's dynasty, and decided to lead an army against the strongest of the three, Sikandar Shah Suri, in the Punjab. He left Delhi under the regency of Tardi Baig Khan. Sikandar Shah Suri presented no major concern for Akbar, and often withdrew from territory as Akbar approached.

The Hindu king Hemu, however, commanding the Afghan forces, defeated the Mughal army and captured Delhi on 6 October 1556. Tardi Beg Khan promptly fled the city. News of the capitulation of Delhi spread quickly to Akbar, and he was advised to withdraw to Kabul, which was relatively secure. But urged by Bairam Khan, Akbar marched on Delhi to reclaim it. Tardi Beg and his retreating troops joined the march, and also urged Akbar to retreat to Kabul, but he refused again. Later, Bairam Khan had the former regent executed for cowardice, though Abul Fazl and Jahangir both record that they believed that Bairam Khan was merely using the retreat from Delhi as an excuse to eliminate a rival.

Akbar's army, led by Bairam Khan, met the larger forces of Hemu on 5 November 1556 at the Second Battle of Panipat, 50 miles (80 km) north of Delhi. The battle was going in Hemu's favour when an arrow pierced Hemu's eye, rendering him unconscious. The leader less army soon capitulated and Hemu was captured and executed.

The victory also left Akbar with over 1,500 war elephants which he used to re-engage Sikandar Shah at the siege of Mankot. Sikandar, along with several local chieftains who were assisting him, surrendered and so was spared death. With this, the whole of Punjab was annexed to the Mughal empire. Before returning to Agra, Akbar sent a detachment of his army to Jammu, which defeated the ruler Raja Kapur Chand and captured the kingdom. Between 1558 and 1560, Akbar further expanded the empire by capturing and annexing the kingdoms of Gwalior, northern Rajputana and Jaunpur.

After a dispute at court, Akbar dismissed Bairam Khan in the spring of 1560 and ordered him to leave on Hajj to Mecca. Bairam left for Mecca, but on his way was goaded by his opponents to rebel. He was defeated by the Mughal army in the Punjab and forced to submit. Akbar, however forgave him and gave him the option of either continuing in his court or resuming his pilgrimage, of which Bairam chose the latter.

Bairam Khan

Bairam Khan also Bayram Khan (died 1561) was a powerful Turcoman noble and regent of eastern Anatolian and Azerbaijani origin at the court of the Mughal emperors Humayun and Akbar whose father and grandfather had joined Babur's service.

Bairam Khan was born in Badakhshan and belonged to the Baharlu clan of the Turkmen Kara Koyunlu tribe. The Qara Qoyunlu had ruled Western Persia for decades before being overthrown by their Ak Koyunlu rivals and, eventually, by the Safavid dynasty.

Bairam Khan contributed greatly to the reconquest of the Mughal empire under Humayun, while his most notable battle was at the Second Battle of Panipat. For four years he acted as the regent and raised the young emperor Akbar, who assumed the throne at the age of fourteen upon Humayun's death in 1556.

Bairam was dismissed upon Akbar's coming-of-age in 1560. He then left upon a hajj to Mecca.

While travelling through Gujarat, he was killed by a Lohani Pashtun assassin whose father had been killed five years ago in a battle led by Bairam. He died on January 31, 1561.

Legacy

Bairam Khan's accomplishments have been recognized both in Afghanistan and India. He was a perfect master of the sword and the pen. His liberal patronage attracted men of letters and masters of fine arts.

Bairam Khan has left a small divan of Chagatay, Persian and Turkish verses. The Persian section contains 618 verses, the Turkish

357 verses. However, an earlier copy of his divan preserved in the library of his son Mirza Abdul Rahim Khan-i-Khana consisted of about 2,000 couplets. Bairam Khan, a Shiite, praises the Imams Ali ibn Abu Talib and Ali al-Ridha in his Persian poetry. He also wrote panegyrics glorifying the emperors Humayun and Akbar.

His son Abdul Rahim Khan-I-Khana translated the *Baburnama* from Chagatay into Persian.

Maham Anga

Maham Anga (d.1562) was the wet nurse of the Mughal Emperor Akbar, and often referred as his foster mother as she took care of young Akbar, as his own mother, Hamida Banu Begum was mostly away, with his father, Humayun was i exile, thorough Akbar's growing years. She was the de facto regent of the Mughal state after the exclusion of Bairam Khan in 1560 to Akbar's assumption of full power in 1562, shortly before her death.

The period is referred to by some historians as the "The Petticoat Government", suggesting that the 'foster mother cohort' attempted to keep Akbar as a puppet ruler after Bairam Khan's death. An alternative perspective is that this regency was considerably less oppressive than that of Bairam Khan, and ended in considerably less destruction than the Uzbeg Revolt of 1564-7.

Maham Anga was the mother of Adham Khan, Akbar's foster brother, and his violent execution for the murder of Ataga Khan, Akbar's favourite general Shams-ud-Din, at the hands of the young Emperor himself no less in November, 1561, profoundly affected her. She famously commented 'You have done well' to Akbar when he broke the news to her; she died shortly afterwards.

Her tomb and that of her son, known as Adham Khan's Tomb, was built by Akbar, and popularly named *Bhul-bulaiyan*, owing to the labyrinth in its structure, lies north of the Qutub Minar in Mehrauli.

Khairul Manazil

She also built a mosque, 'Khairul Manazil' ca 1561 CE. It later served as a *madarsa*, and now stands opposite, Purana Qila, Delhi on Mathura Road, south eats to Sher Shah Gate.

It was here that A slave tried to kill Akbar, after his return from hunting and moving towards Nizamuddin Dargah, but the arrow hit a soldier in his entourage instead, who was hurt, albeit not gravely

Expansion

After dealing with the rebellion of Bairam Khan and establishing his authority, Akbar went on to expand the Mughal empire by subjugating local chiefs and annexing neighbouring kingdoms. The first major conquest was of Malwa in 1561, an expedition that was led by Adham Khan and carried out with such savage cruelty that it resulted in a backlash from the kingdom enabling its ruler Baz Bahadur to recover the territory while Akbar was dealing with the rebellion of Bairam Khan. Subsequently, Akbar sent another detachment which captured Malwa in 1562, and Baz Bahadur eventually surrendered to the Mughals and was made an administrator. Around the same time, the Mughal army also conquered the kingdom of the Gonds, after a fierce battle between the Asaf Khan, the Mughal governor of Allahabad, and Rani Durgavati, the queen of the Gonds. However, Asaf Khan misappropriated most of the wealth plundered from the kingdom, which Akbar subsequently forced him to restore, apart from installing Durgavati's son as the administrator of the region.

Over the course of the decade following his conquest of Malwa, Akbar brought most of present-day Rajasthan, Gujarat and Bengal under his control. A major victory in this campaign was the siege of Chittor. The fortress at Chittor, ruled by Maharana Udai Singh, was of great strategic importance as it lay on the shortest route from Agra to Gujarat and was also considered a key to central Rajasthan. On the advice of his nobles, Udai Singh retired to the hills, leaving two warriors Jaimal and Patta in charge of the fort. The Mughal army surrounded the fortress in October 1567 and it fell in February 1568 after a siege of six months. The fort was then stormed by the Mughal forces, and a fierce resistance was offered by members of the garrison stationed inside, as well as local peasants who came to their assistance. The women committed *jauhar* while over 30000 men were massacred by the Mughal army. It was for the first and last time that Akbar indulged in carnage of this magnitude. In commemoration of the gallantry of Jaimal and Patta, he ordered that stone statues of them seated on elephants be carved and erected at the chief gate of the Agra fort. The fortress was completely destroyed and its gates were carried off to Agra, while the brass candlesticks taken from the Kalika temple after its destruction were given to the shrine of Moinuddin Chishti in Ajmer.

After Akbar's conquest of Chittor, two major Rajput clans remained opposed to him-the Sisodiyas of Mewar and Hadas of Ranthambore. The latter, reputed to be the most powerful fortress in Rajasthan, was conquered by the Mughal army in 1569, making Akbar the master of almost the whole of Rajputana. As a result, most of the Rajput kings, including those of Bikaner, Bundelkhand and Jaisalmer submitted to Akbar. Only the clans of Mewar continued to resist Mughal conquest and Akbar had to fight with them from time to time for the greater part of his reign. Among the most prominent of them was Maharana Pratap who declined to accept Akbar's suzerainty and also opposed the marriage etiquette of Rajputs who had been giving their daughters to Mughals. He renounced all matrimonial alliances with Rajput rulers who had married into the Mughal dynasty, refusing such alliances even with the princes of Marwar and Amer until they agreed to sever ties with the Mughals.

Adham Khan

Adham Khan was a general of Akbar. He was the younger son of Maham Anga, he thus became the foster brother of Akbar. In his fourth regnal year, Akbar married him to the daughter of Baqi Khan Baqlani.

Conquest of Malwa

After the dismissal of Bairam Khan, Adham Khan was appointed as a general and was sent to Malwa to capture it.

In 1561, the Mughal army led by Adham Khan and Pir Mohammad Khan invaded Malwa. They defeated the army of Baz Bahadur, the Sultan of Malwa in the battle of Sarangpur on March 29, 1561. All his treasures, elephants and his harem was captured by the victors. Adham Khan tried to take possession of Baz Bahadur's Hindu mistress Rani Roopmati also, but she killed herself by consuming poison. According to the historian Badauni, both the commanders, Adham Khan and Pir Mohammad Khan perpetrated acts of barbaric cruelty, massacring the prisoners and killing even their wives and children. After the victory, Adham Khan sent to the emperor Akbar a report of victory along with only a few elephants, himself appropriating the rest of the spoils. Akbar resented this insolence and personally marched to Sarangpur. He took Adham Khan by surprise. Adham Khan surrendered to Akbar and his spoils were seized. Later he was recalled from Malwa and the command was made over to Pir Mohammad Khan.

Murder of Ataga Khan and its Aftermath

In November, 1561 Akbar's favourite general Shams-ud-Din Mohammad Ataga Khan, was appointed *wakil* (the prime minister), replacing Munim Khan. His appointment displeased Maham Anga.

On May 16, 1562, Adham Khan accompanied by a few ruffians burst in upon him as he sat in the hall of audience and murdered him. Adham Khan then rushed to the inner apartment where he was caught by Akbar, just roused from sleep by tumult. Akbar replied to the Adham Khan's explanation to palliate his crime by striking him down with a heavy blow of his fist. Adham was thrown down twice from the ramparts of the Agra Fort which was 40 ft (12 m) high from ground level by the royal order and put to death. Akbar himself broke this news to Maham Anga, who made a simple but dignified reply that he did well. This sudden demise of Adham Khan, made his mother mentally depressed and after forty days she also died.

After his death his body was sent with respect to Delhi. Akbar built the mausoleum of Adham Khan in Mehrauli, where both Adham Khan and his foster mother Maham Anga were buried. This mausoleum, popularly known as *Bhul-bhulaiyan,* due to a labyrinthine maze inside, and stands on the ramparts of the Lal Kot, located at the north of the Qutub Minar.

Ataga Khan

Shamsuddin Mohammad Atgah Khan (Ataga Khan), also known as Khan-e-Kalan Shamsud-Din Mohammad Khan Atgah Khan (d. 1562) held important positions in the court, including that of *wakil* (advisor or minister) to which he was appointed in November 1561, much to displeasure of Maham Anga, whose son Adham Khan, eventually murdered him in 1562. Ataga Khan was the husband of Ji Anga, one of Akbar's wet nurses.

Shamsuddin was the son of Mir Yar Mohammad of Ghazni, a simple farmer, and started life as a soldier in Kamran Mirza's army. He saved Humayun from drowning in the Ganges. As reward, Humayun took him into his personal service and his wife became one of Akbar's foster-mothers. She was called foster-mother (Anagah) and her husband Shamsuddin was designated foster-father (*Atgah*). He also received the title of Khan and his biological son, Aziz became Akbar's foster or milk-brother (*Kokah*).

Death

On May 16, 1562, Adham Khan accompanied by a few ruffians burst in upon him as he sat in the *Diwan-e-Aam*, the hall of audience, in Agra Fort, and murdered him, in the courtyard of *Diwan-e-Aam*.. Hearing of this murder, an enraged Akbar ordered Adham Khan to be thrown down the rampart of the fort, and when he survived the first fall, he was thrown a second time and killed instantly.

After the death of Ataga Khan, his tomb was built by the instructions of Mughal emperor Akbar and built by his son, Mirza Aziz Koka, in 1566-67. It is situated on the northern edge of Nizamuddin, most known for the dargah of 13th century Sufi saint Nizamuddin Auliya. Its architect was Ustab Khuda Quli and calligrapher Baqi Mohammad from Bukhara, who added Quranic verses on the white marble slabs, inlaid on the red sandstone exterior walls, which were suitably chosen reflecting his mode of death, considered a martyrdom by Mughal historian, Abul Fazal. An inscription on the southern door of the tomb mentions that it was finished in 974 AH (1566-67).

Rani Durgavati

Rani Durgavati (October 5, 1524- June 24, 1564) was born in the family of famous [Rajput] Chandel Emperor Keerat Rai. She was born at the fort of Kalanjar (Banda, Uttar Pradesh). *Chandel Dynasty* is famous in the Indian History for the defence of king *Vidyadhar* who repulsed the muslim attacks of Mahmud Ghaznavi. His love for sculptures is shown in the world famed temples of Khajuraho and Kalanjar fort. Rani Durgavati's achievements further enhanced the glory of her ancestral tradition of courage and patronage of arts.

In 1542, she was married to Dalpat Shah, the eldest son of king Sangram Shah of Gond Dynasty. Chandel and Gond dynasties got closer as a consequence of this marriage and that was the reason

Keerat Rai got the help of Gonds and his son-in-law Dalpat Shah at the time of muslim invasion of Sher Shah Suri in which Sher Shah died.

She gave birth to a son in 1545 CE. who was named Vir Narayan. Dalpat Shah died in about 1550 CE. As Vir Narayan was too young at that time, Durgavati took the reins of the Gond kingdom in her hands. Two ministers *Adhar Kayastha* and *Man Thakur* helped the Rani in looking after the administration successfully and effectively. Rani moved her capital to Chauragarh in place of Singaurgarh. It was a fort of strategic importance situated on the Satpura hill range.

After the death of Sher shah, Sujat Khan captured the Malwa zone and was succeeded by his son Baz Bahadur in 1556 CE. After ascending to the throne, he attacked Rani Durgavati but the attack was repulsed with heavy losses to his army. This defeat effectively silenced Baz Bahadurand the victory brought name and fame for Rani Durgavati.

In the year 1562 Akbar vanquished the Malwa ruler Baz Bahadur and annexed the Malwa under Mughal dominion. Consequently, the state boundary of Rani touched the Mughal Sultanate.

Rani's contemporary was a Mughal General, Khwaja Abdul Majid Asaf Khan, an ambitious man who vanquished Ramchandra, the ruler of Rewa. Prosperity of Rani Durgavati's state lured him and he invaded Rani's state after taking permission from Mughal emperor Akbar.

When Rani heard about the attack by Asaf Khan she decide to defend her kingdom with all her might although her minister Adhar pointed out the strength of Mughal forces. Rani maintained that it was better to die respectfully than to live a disgraceful life.

To fight a defensive battle, she went to Narrai situated between a hilly range on one side and two rivers Gaur and Narmada on the other side. It was an unequal battle with trained soldiers and modern weapons in multitude on one side and a few untrained soldiers with old weapons on the other side. Her *Faujdar* Arjun Das was killed in the battle and Rani decided to lead the defence herself. As the enemy entered the valley, soldiers of Rani attacked them. Both sides lost some men but Rani was victorious in this battle. She chased the Mughal army and came out of the valley.

At this stage Rani reviewed her strategy with her counselors. She wanted to attack the enemy in the night to enfeeble them but her lieutenants did not accept her suggestion. By next morning Asaf khan had summoned big guns. Rani rode on her elephant Sarman and came for the battle. Her son Vir Narayan also took part in this battle. He forced Mughal army to move back three times but at last he got wounded and had to retire to a safe place. In the course of battle Rani also got injured near her ear with an arrow. Another arrow pierced her neck and she lost her consciousness. On regaining consciousness she perceived that defeat was imminent. Her Mahout advised her to leave the battlefield but she refused and took out her dagger and killed herself on June 24, 1564.

Maharana Udai Singh

Maharana Udai Singh (August 4, 1522 – February 28, 1572) was a king of Mewar and the founder of the city of Udaipur in the present day Rajasthan state of India. He was the 53rd ruler of the Mewar dynasty. He was the fourth and posthumous son of Maharana Sangram Singh and Rani Karmavati, a princess of Bundi.

Early Life

Udai Singh was born in Chittor. In January, 1528 after the death of his father, Maharana Sangram Singh, he was succeeded by his eldest surviving son, Maharana Ratan Singh. Ratan Singh was assassinated in 1531. He was succeeded by his brother Maharana Vikramaditya Singh. During his reign, when the Sultan of Gujarat Bahadur Shah sacked Chittor in 1534, Udai Singh was sent to Bundi for safety. In 1537, Banbir killed Vikramaditya and usurped the throne. He tried to kill Udai Singh also, but Udai's nurse Panna Dhai sacrificed her own son to save him from his uncle Banbir and took him to Kumbhalgarh. He lived in secret in Kumbhalgarh for two years, disguised as a nephew of the governor Asha Shah. In 1540, he was crowned in Kumbhalgarh by the nobles of Mewar. His eldest son Maharana Pratap was born in the same year. He had twenty wives and twenty-five sons. Amongst his other sons, Sakta (Shakti), Jagmal and Viramdeo are well known.

The Reign

After defeating Banbir at Mavli, Udai Singh returned to Chittor. In 1559, his grandson Maharana Amar Singh was born. In the same year, he founded Udaipur. In 1562, he gave refuge to Baz Bahadur of Malwa. Using this as a pretext, Akbar attacked Mewar in October,1567. On October 23, 1567 Akbar formed his camp near Udaipur. According to Kaviraj Shyamaldas, Udai singh called a council of war. The nobles advised him to take refuge along with the princes in the hills, leaving a garrison at Chittor. Udai Singh retired to Gogunda (which later became his temporary capital) leaving Chittor in the hands of his loyal chieftains. Akbar captured Chittor after a long siege on February 25, 1568.. He later shifted his capital to Udaipur. He died in 1572 in Gogunda. Before his death, he nominated his favourite ninth son Jagmal as his successor. But after his death, the nobles of Mewar prevented Jagmal from succeeding and placed Maharana Pratap Singh on the throne on March 1, 1572.

Jaimal and Patta

Jaimal Rathore of Badnor and Patta of Kelwa (Jaimal Rathore: cousin of Meera Bai and Fateh Singh Sisodiya) were the warriors who faced attack of Akbar in 1567 and 1568 AD on the fort of Chittor. Both were aged 16 years. When Akbar attacked Chittor, Rana Udai Singh II left the fort together with his family. Jaimal Rathore of Merta was appointed *qiledar* (Commander in charge) of the fort. Akbar arrived at Chittor on 23 October 1567 AD and sieged the fort. The siege continued for at least four months. Ultimately Akbar ordered to dig mines and blast them to demolish walls of the fort so the Mughal army could enter into it. The people inside the fort were running short of food and water and other supplies. Finally one morning Akbar was able to damage a wall of the fort. Next morning on 23 February 1568 AD Jaimal Rathore started repairing of the damaged wall. Akbar noticed him walking on the walls. He guessed from his clothing that he was some important person and shot at him with his gun "Sangram". The bullet hit Jaimal in the leg and wounded him. When Rajputs in the fort felt that the war could not be carried out for long, they decided to die in the war. In the same night Jauhar was committed by Rajput ladies. When the flames were riding high atop the fort, Raja Bhagwandas of Amer immediately realised that the flames were of Jauhar. He cautioned the mughal forces to face the ferocious Rajput men anytime because Rajputs would now fight till their last breath. Next morning Rajput men under the command of lame but valiant Jaimal Rathore performed Saka (kesariya or Saffron) by wearing saffron clothes and fought their last fight with Mughal army. Since Jaimal was injured so he cannot ride a horse. His brother Kalla Rathore made him sit on his shoulders and they as a single entity fought with four hands which seemed as if god Charbhujanathji himself had incarnated. When Jaimal died in the war, Patta sisodia took the command, but he too died in the battle. These young men displayed true Rajput chivalry. Akbar was so impressed with the bravery of these two warriors that he commissioned a statue of Jaimal and Patta riding on elephants. The statue was fixed at the gates of Agra fort which were later destroyed by the pervert Aurangzeb.

Pratap Singh of Mewar

Maharana Pratap or Pratap Singh of Mewar (May 9, 1540-January 29, 1597) was a ruler of Mewar, a state in north-western India. He belonged to the Sisodia clan of Suryavanshi Rajputs. The epitome of fiery Rajput pride and self-respect, Pratap has for centuries exemplified the qualities to which Rajputs aspire.

Early Life and Background

Pratap, eldest of 25 brothers and 29 sisters, was born at Kumbhalgarh [now in Rajsamand District of Rajasthan] to Maharana Udai Singh II and Maharani Javanta Bai Songara.

Accession

In 1568, during the reign of Udai Singh II, Chittor was conquered by the Mughal emperor Akbar. The third *Jauhar* of Chittor transpired, with the ladies of the fort finding "safety from personal dishonour in the devouring element (fire)," while the remaining menfolk sallied forth to certain death in the battlefield.

Prior to this calamity, Udai Singh and his family had wisely moved to the safety of the nearby hills. He later moved base to another location in the foothills of the Aravalli Range. This new base gradually became the city of Udaipur, named after him. Udai Singh wanted Jagmal, his favourite son, to succeed him but his senior nobles wanted Pratap, the eldest son, to be their king. During the coronation ceremony Jagmal was physically moved out of the palace and Pratap was made the king. Pratap did not want to go against the wishes of his father but Rajput nobles convinced him that Jagmal was not fit to rule in the troubled times of the day. It was the beginning of a career of struggle and hardship.

Maharana Pratap never accepted Akbar as ruler of India, and fought Akbar all his life. Akbar first tried diplomacy to win over Maharana Pratap but nothing worked. Pratap maintained that he had no intention to fight with Akbar but he could not bow down to Akbar and accept him as the ruler. Some scholars argue that there was some possibility that Maharana could have become friends with Akbar, but in the siege of Chittor Akbar had killed 27,000 civilian, unarmed residents of Chittor, because they refused to convert to Islam. This left a lasting impression on Maharana's mind and he decided he could not bow to such an injustice and cruelty. (The Hindu warrior code was to refrain from attacking a non-combatant or a person who has laid down his weapons.)

Tod's *Annals and Antiquities of Rajasthan* relates that Pratap stopped the marriage etiquette of Rajputs who had been giving their daughters to Mughals and his supporting Rajputs instead:

With such examples as Marwar and Amber (of giving their daughters to Mughals), and with less power to resist the temptation, the minor chiefs of Rajasthan, with a brave and numerous vassalage, were transformed into satraps of Delhi.

But these were fearful odds against Pratap. The arms of his country turned upon him, derived additional force from their self-degradation, which kindled into jealousy and hatred against the magnanimous resolution they lacked the virtue to imitate. When Hindu prejudice was thus violated by every prince in Rajasthan, the Rana renounced all *matrimonial* alliance with those who were thus degraded. To the eternal honour of Pratap and his issue be it told that, to the very close of the monarchy of the Moguls, they refused such alliances not only with the throne, but even with their brother princes of Marwar and Ambar. It is a proud triumph of virtue to be able to record from the autograph letters of the most powerful of the Rajput princes, Bukhet Singh and Sawai Jai Singh, that whilst they had risen to greatness by the surrender of principle, as Mewar had decayed from her adherence to it, they should solicit, and that humbly, to be readmitted to the honour of matrimonial intercourse and "to be purified," " to be regenerated," " to be made Rajputs" and that this favour was granted only on condition of their abjuring the contaminating practice (of giving daughters to Mughals) which, for more than a century, had disunited them.

Conflict

Chittorgarh (Chittor fort), Pratap's ancestral home, was under Mughal occupation. Living a life on the run, the dream of reconquering Chittor (and thus reclaiming the glory of Mewar) was greatly cherished by Pratap, and his future efforts were bent towards this goal.

Nearly all of Pratap's fellow Rajput chiefs had meanwhile entered into the vassalage of the Mughals. Even Pratap's own brothers, Shakti Singh and Sagar Singh, were serving Akbar. Indeed, many Rajput chiefs, such as Raja Man Singh of Amber (later known as Jaipur) were serving as army commanders in Akbar's armies and members of his council. Akbar sent a total of six diplomatic missions to Pratap, seeking to negotiate the same sort of peaceful alliance that he had concluded with the other Rajput chiefs. Pratap roundly rebuffed every such attempt.

For the new capital-Udaipur, Maharana Udai Singh constructed a water reservoir–Udai Sagar in 1565. It was on its dam that in June 1573 Kunwar (Prince) Man Singh of Amber, as the emissary of Mughal Emperor Akbar, arrogantly demanded that Maharana Pratap should give up protocol and be present at the feast in his honour. Pratap and Man Singh were of the same generation, Kunwar Man Singh was born on Sunday the December 21, 1550, but Pratap was king while Man Singh was a prince.

Pratap, following the protocol, sent his son Kunwar Amar Singh to dine with Kunwar Man Singh, Akbar's special envoy. This incident precipitated the Mughal-Mewar conflict.

Since Man Singh was a Kunwar, his father Raja Bhagwan Das led another unsuccessful peace mission to Maharana Pratap in October 1573 at which Maharana Pratap was personally present.

Battle of Haldighati

The Battle of Haldighati was fought between the Mughal Empire and the forces of Mewar on June 21, 1576 at Haldighati in Rajasthan,In dia. It was a decisive victory for the Mughal Emperor Jalal ud-Din Mohammad Akbar's general Raja Man Singh against the Maharana Pratap Singh of Mewar.

Background

Pratap Singh became the Maharana of Mewar in 1572 after the death of his father Maharana Udai Singh. Pratap never accepted Emperor Jalal ud-Din Mohammad Akbar as ruler of India, and fought Emperor Akbar all his life. Emperor Jalal ud-Din Mohammad Akbar first tried diplomacy to win over Pratap Singh but nothing worked. Pratap Singh maintained that he had no intention to fight with Emperor Akbar but he could not bow down to Emperor Akbar and accept him as the ruler. Chittor fort, Pratap's ancestral home, was under Mughal occupation. Living a life on the run, the dream of reconquering Chittor was greatly cherished by Pratap, and his future efforts were bent towards this goal. Nearly all of Pratap's fellow Rajput chiefs had meanwhile entered into the vassalage of the Mughals. Even Pratap's own brothers, Shakti Singh and Sagar Singh, were serving Emperor Akbar. Indeed, many Rajput chiefs, such as Raja Man Singh of Amber (Jaipur) were serving as army commanders in Akbar's armies and members of his council. Akbar sent a total of six diplomatic missions to Pratap, seeking to negotiate the same sort of peaceful alliance that he had concluded with the other Rajput chiefs. Pratap roundly rebuffed every such attempt.

Battle

Raja Man Singh marched with his Mughal forces from Ajmer on April 3, 1576. On June 21, 1576 (June 18 in other texts), the two armies met at Haldighati, near the town of Gogunda in present-day Rajasthan. While accounts vary as to the exact strength of the two armies, all sources concur that the Mughal forces greatly outnumbered Pratap's men. The battle of Haldighati, lasted only four hours. Both sides fought bravely on the field. Folklore has it that Pratap personally attacked Man Singh: his horse Chetak placed its front feet on the trunk of Man Singh's elephant and Pratap threw his lance; Man Singh ducked, and the mahout or Elephant rider was killed.

However, the numerical superiority of the Mughal army and their artillery began to tell. Seeing that the battle was lost, Pratap's generals prevailed upon him to flee the field so as to be able to fight another day. To facilitate Pratap's escape, one of his lieutenants, a member of the Jhala clan, donned Pratap's distinctive garments and took his place in the battlefield. He was soon killed. Meanwhile, riding his trusty steed Chetak, Pratap made good his escape to the hills.

In terms of numbers the Mughal army suffered heavier losses. This was also because of the intensive arrow showers by the Bhil tribes of the surrounding mountains who had aided with Pratap. To honor their contribution, a Bhil warrior was placed next to Pratap in the Royal Coat of Arms of Mewar.

Aftermath

Pratap retreated into the hilly wilderness of the Aravalli hills and continued his struggle. His one attempt at open confrontation having thus failed, Pratap resumed the tactics of guerilla warfare. Using the hills as his base, Pratap harassed the large Mughal forces in their encampments. He ensured that the Mughal occupying force in Mewar never knew peace: Akbar dispatched three more expeditions to ferret Pratap out of his mountainous hideouts, but they all failed. During this era, Pratap received much financial assistance from Bhamashah, a well-wisher. The Bhil tribals of the Aravalli hills provided Pratap with their support during times of war and their expertise in living off the forests during times of peace. Thus the years passed. Pratap died of injuries sustained in a hunting accident. He died at Chavand, on January 29, 1597, aged 56. It is said that as he lay dying, Pratap made his son and successor, Amar Singh, swear to maintain eternal conflict against the Mughals.

Maharana Pratap's son, Amar Singh, fought 17 wars with the Mughals but he conditionally accepted them as rulers. At this time, a large chunk of Maharana Pratap's band of loyal Rajputs became disillusioned and left Rajasthan. This group included Rathores, Deora Chauhans, Pariharas, Tomaras, Kacchwaha and Jhalas. They are called "Rors" and settled mostly in Haryana, with some in Uttar Pradesh and Pakistan.

Generals

Hakim Khan Sur Pathan

Hakim Khan Sur Pathan was a descendant of the Afghan, Sher Shah Suri. To avenge the fall of his forefathers by the Mughals he joined Pratap. Numerous Hindu temples were systematically destroyed by the Mughals. Pratap and other Rajputs fought to save their religion. The presence of some Muslim mercenaries in

Rajput armies does not imply that the conflict with the Mughals was not to protect the Hindu religion.

Jhala Man Sinh

Jhala Man Sinh (also known as Jhala Sardar) set an example of extraordinary valour, bravery and sacrifice in the struggle for freedom. In the battle of Haldi Ghati in 1576, upon seeing Maharana Pratap wounded (three wounds were inflicted, sword, spear and shot by a musket) and unconscious on his horse, Chetak; Jhala immediately took the Crown and royal emblem of Pratap, thus confusing the enemy into thinking that he was Pratap and took the entire attack of the Mughal hordes upon himself. Ultimately he sacrificed his life to save the life of Pratap and freedom for his country. It is because of this sacrifice that Pratap continued to fight on against the Mughals and eventually reestablish and liberate all of Mewar except Chittor. In Present day Udaipur, the descendants of Jhala still carry the emblem of Mewar as their coat of arms as conferred upon them by Maharana Pratap. According to Shri Ashok Dattatraya Kulkarni the brave warrior was not Man Sinh Jhala but Beeda Jhala. Ref-Maharana Pratapaancha Rajvansh.

Tomars

Raja Ram Shah Tomar of Gwalior was married to a daughter of Rana Udai Singh, sought refuge in Mewar after he lost Gwalior to Mughals. He along with 300 of his men fought the battle of Haldighati. His only remaining son was sent to Bikaner so the line could survive, everyone else gave up their life for the cause of Mewar.

Bargujars

The Bargujars were the most trusted allies of Mewar and fought along with the Rana till the end. They were fierce fighters always in the frontline in any battle.

Bhim Singh Dodia

Bhim Singh Dodia, one of the Mewar nobles who took part in Maharana PRATAP SINGH's war council at Gogunda (1576) prior to the Battle of Haldighati.

Chetak

Chetak, the white horse of Marwari breed (an indigenous

Indian breed) had a short neck, a tail with bushy dense hair, narrow back, big eyes with sharp sight, sturdy shoulders, broad forehead and chest. Considered beautiful and poetically divine, this horse had balanced muscular body with an extremely attractive appearance, blessed with flying legs. He is described as possessing a rare, acute intelligence, restraint and courage coupled with unflinching faithfulness to his master.

Raja Poonja

The Bhil warriors in the battle of Haldi Ghati, participated under the leadership of Rana Poonja. The enthusiastic Bhils worked as secret informers and running messengers. In Mewar state the history of Guhil clan is full of daring deeds. The contribution of the Bhil community is unforgettable. At the time of Ghuhaditya's coronation the "Tilak ceremony was performed by the blood flowing from the thumb of Mandleek –a "Bhil" Sardar. "

For this, the royal emblem of Mewar State carries a Victory Tower, flanked by a Rajput warrior on one side and "a bow-and–arrow-bearing Bhil", on the other.

Bhama Shah (or Bhamashah)

Bhamashah made a mark in the history of Mewar. Son of Bharmal Kawadiya and born 450 years ago, he set an example of honesty, faith and duty. He was not only Pratap's treasurer, but also fought like a soldier when the need arose. Maharana Pratap was able to properly maintain his army of 25,000 soldiers for 12 years only because Bhamashah had gifted not only his property, but also a collection of 25Lakh rupees and 20,000 gold coins from Maalpura during a financial crisis. Bhamashah also served Maharana Amarsinh. Thereafter his son Jeev Shah was treasurer of the Maharana. At the time of his death Bhamashah asked his wife to handover the detailed record of royal treasury to Maharana Amarsinh then he left for heavenly abode. Ref. Maharana Pratapaancha Rajvansh-A marathi book by Shri Ashok Dattatraya Kulkarni published in 2008

Aftermath

Pratap retreated into the hilly wilderness of the Aravallis and continued his struggle. His one attempt at open confrontation having thus failed, Pratap resumed the tactics of guerilla warfare. Using the hills as his base, Pratap harassed the large and therefore awkward Mughal forces in their encampments. He ensured that the Mughal occupying force in Mewar never knew peace: Akbar dispatched three more expeditions to ferret Pratap out of his mountainous hideouts, but they all failed. During this era, Pratap received much financial assistance from Bhamashah, a well-wisher. The Bhil tribals of the Aravalli hills provided Pratap with their support during times of war and their expertise in living off the forests during times of peace. Thus the years passed. As James Tod writes: "There is not a pass in the alpine Aravalli that is not sanctified by some deed of the great freedom fighter, Maharana Pratap Singh; some brilliant victory or, more often, some glorious defeat." On one occasion, the Bhils saved the Rajput women and children in the nick of time by conveying them into the depths of the ancient zinc mines at Zawar, near Udaipur. Later, Pratap relocated to Chavand in the mountainous southeastern area of Mewar. Still harassed by the Mughals, the exiles survived in those ravines for many years by subsisted on wild berries and by hunting and fishing. Legends say that Pratap had to eat chapatees made of grass in troubled days.

Prithviraj Rathore's Letter

The letter from Prithviraj Rathore sent to Pratap in poetic language, ran like this.

Patal sun Patshah, bole mukh hunta bayan
Mihir picham dis mahn, uge kasap rao ut
Patakun munchyan pan, ke patakun nij tan karad
Dije likh Deewan, in do mahali bat ik.

(The mouth of Pratap has begun to say "Badshah". O Rao! has the sun started rising in the West, as well? Should I keep my hand over my mustache or should my body fall with my own hands? O Deewan! write an answer choosing between the two.)

Pratap replied to this letter like this.
Turak kahasi turakado, in mukh sun Ikling
Uge jya hi ugasi, prachi bich Patang
Khushi hunt Peethal Kamadh, patako munchyan pan
Jete hai pachatan Pato, kilama sir kewan.

(Lord Eklingji will always make my mouth call him "Turk". The sun will rise in the east always. O Prithviraj Rathore be happy and put your hand on your mustache. Till Pratap stands on his feet, his sword will keep hovering over the heads of the invaders.)

When the exiles were facing the prospect of actual starvation, Pratap wrote to Akbar indicating his readiness to negotiate a treaty. Pratap's first cousin (his mother's sister's son) Prithviraj Rathore, who was one of Akbar's courtiers, heard of this overture. He is said to have grown despondent and wrote thus to his cousin Pratap:

The hopes of the Hindu rest on the Hindu surya yet the Rana forsakes them. But for Pratap, all would be placed on the same level by Akbar; for our chiefs have lost their valour and our females their honour. Akbar is the broker in the market of our race; he has purchased all but the son of Udai (Singh II of Mewar); he is beyond his price. What true Rajput would part with honour for *nauroza* [the Persian new year's festival, where Akbar selected women for his pleasure]; yet how many have bartered it away? Will Chittor come to this market...? Though Patta (an affectionate name for Pratap Singh) has squandered away wealth (on warfare), yet he has preserved this treasure. Despair has driven man to this market, to witness their dishonour: from such infamy the descendant of Hammir (Maharana Hammir) alone has been preserved. The world asks, from where does the concealed aid of Pratap emanate? None but the soul of manliness and his sword.. The broker in the market of men (Akbar) will one day be surpassed; he cannot live forever. Then will our race come to Pratap, for the seed of the Rajput to sow in our desolate lands. To him all look for its preservation, that its purity may again become resplendent. It is as much impossible for me to believe that Pratap has called Akbar his emperor as to see the sun rising in the west. Tell me where do I stand? Shall I use my sword on my neck or shall I continue my proud bearing?

Pratap replied to him:

> *"By my God Eklinga, Pratap would call the emperor Turk alone (*the word 'Turk' carries a pejorative flavour in many Indian languages*) and the sun would rise in the east. You may continue your proud bearing as long as Pratap's sword dangles on the mughal head. Pratap would be guilty of Sanga's blood, if he was to tolerate Akbar. you would have the better of it, no doubt Prithviraj, in this wordy quarrel."*

Thus ended the incipient rapprochement between Pratap and Akbar. This Prithviraj Rathore was the husband of Kiranmayee, sister of Shakti Sinh (Stepbrother of Maharana Pratap). She once placed her dagger at the throat of Akbar and made him to promise that he would not held Meena Bazar thereafter. Ref. Maharana Pratapancha Rajvansh-A marathi book by Shri Ashok Dattatraya Kulkarni email-ashokakulkarni@yahoo.com

Akbar's Expeditions

Akbar kept sending expedition after expedition against Maharana Pratap, but never succeeded. He expended a lot of money and men in trying to defeat Maharana Pratap. For 30 years Pratap remained ahead of Akbar and in the last ten years of his life was able to free most of his kingdom.

Personal Life

Rana Pratap had 17 sons and five daughters. The male-line descendants of Udai Singh II bear the patronymic "Ranawat". The patronymic changes usually when rulers are forced to flee their country and establish new capital. Guhilot are descendants of Guha, Sisodia's are descendants of Hamir Guhilot of Sisoda village and Ranawats are descendants of Rana Udai Singh who had to flee Chittor and establish a new capital at Udaipur. The patronymic change is name is usually followed by a major migration of population or battle.

Final Days

Maharana Pratap died of injuries sustained in a hunting accident. He died at Chavand, on January 29, 1597, aged fifty-six. It is said that as he lay dying, Pratap made his son and successor, Amar Singh, swear to maintain eternal conflict against the Mughals. Thus, his strained circumstances did not overpower Pratap even in his declining years; he remained intrepid to the end. He also did not sleep on a bed because of a vow he took that until Chittor was freed he would sleep on the floor and live in a hut despite the fact that he had reconquered almost his entire kingdom from Akbar.

Maharana Pratap's son, Amar Singh, fought 17 wars with the Mughals but he conditionally accepted them as rulers. At this time, a large chunk of Maharana Pratap's band of loyal Rajputs became disillusioned by the surrender and left Rajasthan. This group included Rathores, Deora Chauhans, Pariharas, Tomaras, Kacchwaha and Jhalas. They are called "Rors" and settled mostly in Haryana, with some in Uttar Pradesh. Even today they do not intermarry with other Rajputs but "gotra permitting" within the Ror community only.

Maharana Pratap is a great hero in the eyes of Indians, much respected and loved by his people. During a dark chapter of Hindu history, Pratap alone stood firmly for his honour and dignity; he never compromised his honour for safety. He died a proud and free man.

Character

Before the Battle of Haldighati started, Man Singh Kacchwaha was out hunting with a few hundred retainers. Pratap's Bhil spies reported this to him at his camp a few kilometers away. Some of Pratap's nobles suggested that they seize the opportunity to attack and kill Man Singh. Pratap refused, demonstrating his sense of rectitude.

In another incident, the womenfolk of Abdur Rahim Khankhana, a Mughal officer, fell into the hands of Pratap's son, Amar Singh. At this point of time, Khankhana was actually on the march against Pratap, and was camping at Sherpur in order to make preparations for an assault against Pratap. Nonwithstanding all this, Pratap commanded his son Amar Singh (eldest of 17 sons and 5 daughters) to arrange for the safe conveyance of the Mughal ladies to their camp. Khankhana was so affected by this incident that he refused to campaign against such a chivalrous monarch. He petitioned Akbar to be relieved of his post and was subsequently (in 1581) appointed guardian of Akbar's own son, Salim. Also it is believed that the slogan " Jo dridh rakhe dharm, ne tahi rakhe kartar was spoken by Abdur Rahim Khankhana, who is also known as "Rahim das" in Hindi poetry.

Present-Day Status

Following India's independence in 1947, Maharana Bhupal Singh (reign 1930-1955) was made Maharaj Pramukh of Rajasthan State 1952-1955 – the only post in Republic of India specially created for Mewar! Maharana Bhupal Singh was the first ruler to merge his state with independent India (18 April 1948). India's first Union Home Minister (Loh Purush-the Iron Man) Sardar

Vallabh Bhai Patel reprimanded the reluctant Hyderabad and other states saying that "...if any ruler in India had any right to claim of independence it was Mewar, which has gladly and readily merged with the Indian Union saying that it was fulfillment of 13 centuries of their mission...but for Mewar no other rulers has that right..." Even in the post-independent period, the Indian public, Indian Presidents, Prime Ministers and politicians irrespective of their political affiliation, continued their appreciation and reverence to the values of Mewar.

The noted Indian freedom fighter, Union Minister and founder of Bharatiya Vidya Bhawan, and one of the great persons of literature of modern India, K. M. Munshi (1887-1971) has written,"...the Maharanas of Mewar represented the best and noblest in Hindu culture and polity...they translated into practice the Puranic concept of Ram Rajya...

Maharana Pratap has always been held in great esteem in India and was projected as a model of patriotism and freedom struggle against the Mughal rule in India. The names Pratap and Chetak, his stallion, are very famous and the Government of Republic of India has issued commemorative stamps (1967, 1998) and coins (2003) to honor this great Son of India. The grateful nation installed Pratap's Chetak-mounted statue along with those of his more renowned associates — Jhala Maan, Bhilu Raja (the tribal chief), Bhama Shah, Hakim Khan Soor and an attendant-foot-soldier in front of the Parliament House in New Delhi on August 21, 2007.

A feature film on Maharana Pratap is under post-production.

Moti Magri

An impressive bronze statue of Maharana Pratap and his favourite and loyal horse, who was fiercely protective of his master and stood by him till his last breath, stands at the top of Moti Magri (Pearl Mount) overlooking Fateh Sagar.

Local people climb the hill to pay homage to Maharana Pratap and his faithful charger 'Chetak', who was killed in the battle of Haldighati. There are the ruins of one of the first modest palaces of Udaipur and there is also a charming Japanese rock garden not far away. The memorial has the first Light & Sound program in Rajasthan, that presents the glorious 1400 years of Mewar's history.

Sword

The 25 kg weight sword was used by Rana Pratap Singh. Rana Pratap use to carry two swords with him always. Before any fight he uses to offer one sword to his opponent if he is not armed.

Consolidation

Having conquered Rajputana, Akbar turned to Gujarat, whose government was in a state of disarray after the death of its previous ruler, Bahadur Shah. The province was a tempting target as it was a center of world trade, it possessed fertile soil and had highly developed crafts. The province had been occupied by Humayun for a brief period, and prior to that was ruled by the Delhi Sultanate. In 1572, Akbar marched to Ahmedabad, which capitulated without offering resistance. He took Surat by siege, and then crossed the Mahi river and defeated his estranged cousins, the Mirzas, in a hard-fought battle at Sarnal. During the campaign, Akbar met a group of Portugese merchants for the first time at Cambay. Having established his authority over Gujarat, Akbar returned to Agra, but Mirza-led rebellions soon broke out. Akbar returned, crossing Rajasthan at great speed on camels and horses, and reached Ahmedabad in eleven days-a journey that normally took six weeks. Akbar's army of 3000 horsemen then defeated the enemy forces numbering 20000 in a decisive victory on September 2, 1573. The conquest of Gujarat marked a significant event of Akbar's reign as it gave the Mughal empire free access to the sea and control over the rich commerce that passed through its ports. The territory and income of the empire were vastly increased. The Mughal army also conquered Bengal (1574), Kabul (1581), Kashmir (1586), and Kandesh (1601), among others. Akbar installed a governor over each of the conquered provinces.

Administration

Taxation: Akbar set about reforming the administration of his empire's land revenue by adopting a system that had been used by Sher Shah Suri. A cultivated area was measured and taxed through fixed rates based on the area's crop and productivity. Because taxation rates were fixed on the basis of prices prevailing in the imperial court, however—which were often higher than those in the countryside — this placed hardship on the peasantry. Akbar changed to a decentralised system of annual assessment, but this resulted in corruption among local officials and was abandoned in 1580, to be replaced by a system called the *dahsala*. Under the new system, revenue was calculated as one-third of the average produce of the previous ten years, to be paid to the state in cash. This system was later refined, taking into account local prices, and grouping areas with similar productivity into assessment circles. Remission was given to peasants when the harvest failed during times of flood or drought. Akbar's *dahsala* system is credited to Raja Todar Mal, who also served as a revenue officer under Sher Shah Suri.

Other local methods of assessment continued in some areas. Land which was fallow or uncultivated was charged at concessional rates. Akbar also actively encouraged the improvement and extension of agriculture. *Zamindars* of every area were required to provide loans and agricultural implements in times of need, to encourage farmers to plow as much land as possible and to sow seeds of superior quality. In turn, the Zamindars were given a hereditary right to collect a share of the produce. Peasants had a hereditary right to cultivate the land as long as they paid the land revenue.

Mansabdar

Mansabdar was the generic term for the military-type grading of all imperial officials of the Mughal Empire. The mansabdars governed the empire and commanded its armies in the emperor's name. Though they were usually aristocrats, they did not form a feudal aristocracy, for neither the offices nor the estates that supported them were hereditary.

The term is derived from *Mansab*, meaning 'rank'. Hence, Mansabdar literally means rank-holder.

History

The Moghals ruled India from 1526 AD, when Babur defeated Ibrahim Lodi at the Battle of Panipat, till 1707 AD when the Emperor Aurangzeb died and thereafter nominally till the Indian Mutiny in 1857 AD.

When Babur invaded India to establish his kingdom his army consisted of tribes and clans that followed him from Kabul, some joined him later, after the Battle of Panipat, he awarded the leaders of these tribes and clans in accordance to their performance in the battle and many of them who had joined Babur for the booty, chose to return to their homes.

Babur and Humayun ruled over territory that was not too far flung, after the tribes and the clans that had joined Babur for booty returned after the Battle of Panipat, their place was taken by foreign adventurers, Uzbeks, Persians, Arabs, Turks etc. who thronged to the court with contingents of troops. Since the Moghals were foreigners there were no hereditary nobles related to the rulers or ancient families to depend upon, the court consisted of adventurers from different nations, the ruler raised them to dignity or degraded them; up to the early rule of Akbar the Moghal armies consisted of contingents commanded by these adventurers.

Akbar, Babur's grandson, who ruled from 1556 to 1605, organized the 'mansabdari' system in the 19th year of his rule. The system classified the functionaries of the kingdom as fighters, 'ashab-u's-saif', (masters of the sword); clerks 'ashab-u'l-qalam' (masters of the pen); theologians, 'ashab-u'l-amamah'. The 'mansab' denoted a rank of office, it had its obligations, precedence and grade of pay; it was for life but it was not hereditary, heirs could not demand continuity of office.

The status of the 'ashab-u's-saif (military) and ashab-u'l-qalam' (clerical and administrative), was denoted by military rank, originally 66 grades but later only 33 grades existed. Every official of the empire above the rank of a sepoy or a servant held an army rank, the lowest was the commander of twenty; the highest the commander of seven thousand.

Mansabs were ranked as of 7,000, 6,000, 5,000, intervals of 500 between 5,000 and 1,000, intervals of 100 between 1,000 and 200, intervals of 50 between 200 and 100, finally intervals of 20 between 100 and 20. Mansabs were of three classes, 7,000 to 3,000- 'Amir-i-Azam' the greater nobles; 2,500 to 500-'Amir', noble; 400 to 20-'Mansabdar' office holder. Commanders of higher ranks were of three classes according to the proportion of horsemen, first class if the whole command was of 'horse', second class if the 'horse' element was more than half and third class if less than half.

Compensation per annum started at rupees 350,000 with intervals of 50,000 between mansabs of 7,000 and 5,000; rupees 250,000 with intervals of 25,000 between mansabs of 5,000 and 1,000; the mansab of 20 received 1,000.

Compensation was either 'naqdi' meaning cash compensation or by the revenue of a 'jagir', an area of land which was not given to the 'mansabdar' but he could use the revenue from the land for his expenses and compensation. The 'mansab' could be increased or decreased on the wishes of the ruler and reports of performance and two lists were maintained, 'Hazir-i-rikah' present at court and 'Ta-inat' on duty elsewhere.

For a military mansab an application could be made for a mansab with troops or without troops. Those applying for a mansab with troops brought their retainers, mounted and equipped at their expense, these were known as 'silladars' and their men were known as 'bagirs'. (The system continued under the British till 1914.) When a silladar brought his men, they were paraded for inspection, their descriptive rolls were prepared and the horses were branded; these mansabdars were paid for the maintenance of horses and the salaries of the men. Men considered fit to command but lacking resources were given money to purchase horses and received the salaries of the men only. Men who could not be mansabdars but too good to be employed as soldiers were given the higher rank of a 'ahadi'.

Military mansabdars were required to maintain troops according to the mansab including beasts of burden, elephants, camels, mules, carts etc., they maintained horses for their troopers and a prescribed number in their own stables.

Military command was at the will of the emperor, Akbar held that anyone could be a military commander and often appointed commanders who had no military knowledge or experience.

Mansabdars were given control over an area of land, a 'jagir' whose revenue was to be used for maintaining troops; if not given a 'jagir' they were paid in cash through a complicated accounting system, with deductions for various things including 'the rising of the moon'; it was a normal practice to pay for only eight or ten months in the year. The mansabdars were allowed to keep five percent of the income of the 'jagir' or five per cent of the salaries received. The accounting system was complex, mansabdars usually borrowed money for expenses and when they died their private property was seized against any outstanding balances.

With a corrupt system of accounting and inspection very few mansabdars kept their units up to strength. When a mansabdar was ordered to take part in an expedition, he was required to parade his unit outside the palace and the emperor inspected it from a window in the palace.

Cavalry made up the bulk of the Moghal army; they enjoyed the prestige of warriors. Individual troopers took great care to keep themselves fit, they exercised, engaged each other in mock fights, practiced horsemanship, they were personally brave and trained themselves for person to person combat, but were unwilling to endanger their mounts because their salary depended on these; there was no training for units to act collectively.

Infantry was despised as drudges, they were considered little more than watchmen to guard the baggage, labourers, porters etc. The infantry consisted of matchlock men and archers, in the ratio of one matchlock man to four archers because of the greater rate of fire of the archers since both weapons had about the same effective range; there was no infantry training, no discipline and very little reliance was placed on them.

The 'Mir Atish', the 'master gunner', was responsible for the manufacture, supply of ordnance and was the artillery commander. Gunners were called 'golandaz' (the bringer of round shot, a term also used by the British till 1857), they were paid directly from the treasury and were the most reliable part of the army. The efficiency of the Moghal artillery was poor, the rate of fire was very low and the pieces were difficult to move. Europeans as artillerymen were prized and were paid as much as ten times the amount paid to locals.

The recruitment of men was by 'classes'; it was specified that an officer from Iran could not recruit more than one third Moghals, the rest had to be Syeds or Sheikhs, Afghans could not be more than one sixth or Rajputs more than one seventh of a force. The British adopted this system of recruitment by 'classes'.

The Moghal army consisted of bands of horsemen, each band linked by some personal loyalty to its leader but without any loyalty to the emperor or any national or religious loyalty. These soldiers of fortune depended on their commanders; their pay was always kept in arrears to prevent desertion.

There was a theoretical pattern to which the army conformed in battle; this consisted of three divisions, the center, right and left wing, each of these had an advance guard, a screen of skirmishers and there was a rear guard to the whole force. Once a formation was adopted there was very little capability for maneuver and there was no system of communicating between the parts.

Open country was necessary for successful action by a Moghal army because it was mostly cavalry. The opposing armies deployed guns on a line protected by earthwork and tied together with chains or ropes to prevent cavalry riding through as Babur had done at Panipat. Battle started with artillery fire, the heavy guns fired one round every three hours while the others about four rounds per hour. When it was considered that the artillery had sufficiently demoralized the enemy, successive charges were delivered from one wing then the other; the cavalry first fired their matchlocks and arrows then closed with the sword, spear and the mace, fighting was series of skirmishes ending in individual combat. The cavalry was not trained to act collectively on command, once dispersed it could not be formed again but since cavalry was the bulk of the army, the object of the Moghal commander was to engage the enemy on an open plain where he could deliver a massed charge of mail clad warriors. Up to the time of Aurangzeb, the Moghals fielded much larger armies than their opponents and usually managed to defeat their enemy, either on the battlefield or after a siege.

During battle the overall commander or the king had to prominently show his presence on the battlefield, usually riding an elephant, the battle objective was usually the elephant of the opposing commander and around it raged the fiercest battle; the decisive event of a battle was the death or disappearance of the leader, if he was known to have been killed or could not be seen the troops dispersed and sought their own safety. Aurangzeb when fighting his brothers for succession, in two battles, the rival to the throne was induced by treacherous advice to dismount and their armies automatically dispersed; this was because the remuneration of the army was from individual princes. The British used this custom to their advantage by knocking off the commanders with a four-pounder artillery piece and causing the dispersion of the opponents, eventually the princes and commanders learnt to ride horses instead of elephants and not to prominently show themselves.

The Emperor usually did not personally command the army unless it was a very large force in an important campaign; when the army moved out to war with the emperor in command, the whole apparatus of government moved with it. Aurangzeb's army on the move included camels bearing treasure, one hundred loaded with gold, two hundred with silver; the emperor's hunting establishment, with hawks and cheetahs; official records, on eighty camels, thirty elephants and twenty carts, these could never be parted from the emperor; a hundred camels carried water and kitchen utensils; fifty milch-cows, a hundred cooks, each a specialist in a dish; fifty camels and a hundred carts carried the emperor's and his ladies wardrobe; thirty elephants carried the women's jewellery and presents for successful commanders.

The mass of the cavalry, the main strength of the army, led, then the way was leveled for the emperor and his women; a rear guard largely of infantry brought up the tail. When the army halted the emperor's camp was about a mile long, a square enclosure was roped off and surrounded by a ditch, heavy artillery defended the approaches, the emperor's tent was in the center, divided into four courts with the entrance facing the direction of the next day's march.

The army transport consisted of elephants, camels, packhorses, bullocks, bullock carts and porters. Every man provided for himself by buying for his needs, on a daily basis from 'banyas' who erected their shops in the camps. Supplies of grain were brought to the camp by 'banjarahs' on bullocks, which moved at two miles an hour, they formed a square in the evening with bags of grain. Either side did not attack the 'banjarahs' and the grain taken was paid for. Fodder was taken from the countryside and foragers looted the villages in the path of the army.

The armies of the Moghal times consisted of bands without military training and discipline; there was no loyalty owed to the ruler or the state; band leaders could be bought; half hearted support during battle, treachery and desertion were therefore negotiable. The two opposing armies would camp on the battlefield and for several days negotiations would be conducted to entice commanders to change sides before the battle, to refuse to act at a critical moment or to desert with their commands during a battle. The British successfully exploited this mercenary soldiering, in its worst form, when they fought the princes who had seized bits and pieces of the Moghal Empire. Insulated by the mountains and the seas, the Moghals developed a military system which, though locally successful, did not improve on the weapons, organization and tactics, failed miserably when it clashed with the European military system of the period. Instituted by the Mughal emperor Akbar, *mansabdari* was a system common to both the military and the Civil department. Basically the Mansabdari system was borrowed from Persia. It was prevalent during the reign of Babur and Humayun. Akbar made some important changes to the system and made it more efficient. Mansabdar was referred to as the official, rank, or the dignity.

Two grades delineated the mansabdars. Those mansabdars whose rank was one thousand (hazari) or below were called the Amir. Those mansabdars whose rank was above 1000, were called the Amiral Kabir (Great Amir). Some Great Amirs whose rank were above 5000 were also given the title of Amir-al Umara (Amir of Amirs)

Political Government

Akbar's system of central government was based on the system that had evolved since the Delhi Sultanate, but the functions of various departments were carefully reorganised by laying down detailed regulations for their functioning.

- The revenue department was headed by a *wazir*, responsible for all finances and management of *jagir* and *inam* lands.
- The head of the military was called the *Mir bakshi*, appointed from among the leading nobles of the court. The *Mir bakshi* was in charge of intelligence gathering, and also made recommendations to the emperor for military appointments and promotions.
- The *Mir saman* was in charge of the imperial household, including the harems, and supervised the functioning of the court and royal bodyguard.
- The judiciary was a separate organization headed by a chief *qazi*, who was also responsible for religious endowments.

Akbar departed from the policy of his predecessors in his treatment of the territories he conquered. Previous Mughals extracted a large tribute from these rulers and then leave them to administer their dominions autonomously; Akbar integrated them into his administration, providing them the opportunity to serve as military rulers. He thus simultaneously controlled their power while increasing their prestige as a part of the imperial ruling class. Some of these rulers went on to become the navaratnas in Akbar's court.

Capital of the Empire

Akbar was a follower of Salim Chishti, a holy man who lived in the region of Sikri near Agra, who later blessed him with three sons. Believing the neighbourhood to be a lucky one for himself, he had a mosque constructed there for the use of the saint. Subsequently, he celebrated the victories over Chittor and Ranthambore by laying the foundation of a new walled capital, 23 miles (37 km) west of Agra in 1569, which was named Fatehpur ("*town of victory*") after the conquest of Gujarat in 1573 and subsequently came to be known as Fatehpur Sikri in order to distinguish it from other similarly named towns. Palaces for each of Akbar's senior queens, a huge artificial lake, and sumptuous water-filled courtyards were built there. However, the city was soon abandoned and the capital was moved to Lahore in 1585. The reason may have been that the water supply in Fatehpur Sikri was insufficient or of poor quality. Or, as some historians believe, Akbar had to attend to the northwest areas of his empire and therefore moved his capital northwest. Other sources indicate Akbar simply lost interest in the city or realized it was not militarily defensible. In 1599, Akbar shifted his capital back to Agra from where he reigned until his death.

Matrimonial Alliances

Akbar persuaded the Kacchwaha Rajput, Raja Bharmal, of Amber (modern day Jaipur) into accepting a matrimonial alliance for his daughter Harka Bai. This was the first instance of royal matrimony between Hindu and Muslim dynasties in India. Harka Bai was rechristened Mariam-uz-Zamani. After her marriage she was treated as an outcaste by her family and for the rest of her life never visited Amber. She was not assigned any significant place either in Agra or Delhi, but rather a small village in the Bharatpur district. She died in 1623. As a custom Hindus were cremated and never buried; her burial near Agra signifies that she converted to Islam. A mosque was built in her honor by her son Jahangir in Lahore.

Other Rajput kingdoms also established matrimonial alliances with Akbar. The law of Hindu succession has always been patrimonial, so the Hindu lineage was not threatened in marrying their princesses for political gain. Rajputs who married daughters to Mughals still did not treat Mughals as equals, however, they would not dine with Mughals or take Muslim wives.

Two major Rajput clans remained against him, the Sisodiyas of Mewar and Hadas (Chauhans) of Ranthambore. In another turning point of Akbar's reign, Raja Man Singh I of Amber went with Akbar to meet the Hada leader, Surjan Hada, to effect an alliance. Surjan grudgingly accepted an alliance on the condition that Akbar did not marry any of his daughters. Surjan later moved his residence to Varanasi.

Other Rajput nobles did not like the idea of their kings marrying their daughters to Mughals. Rathore Kalyandas threatened to kill both Mota Raja Udai Singh (of Jodhpur) and Jahangir because Udai Singh had decided to marry his daughter Jodha Bai to Jahangir. Akbar on hearing this ordered imperial forces to attack Kalyandas at Siwana. Kalyandas died fighting along with his men and the women of Siwana committed Jauhar.

Entering into alliance with Rajput kingdoms enabled Akbar to extend the border of his Empire to far off regions, and the Rajputs became the strongest allies of the Mughals. Rajput soldiers fought for the Mughal empire for the next 130 years till its collapse following the death of Aurangzeb. To foster their compliance, Akbar kept the eldest sons of his Rajput allies as hostages.

Personality

Akbar's reign was chronicled extensively by his court historian Abul Fazal in the books *Akbarnama* and *Ain-i-akbari*. Other contemporary sources of Akbar's reign include the works of Badayuni, Shaikhzada Rashidi and Shaikh Ahmed Sirhindi.

Akbar was an artisan, warrior, artist, armourer, blacksmith, carpenter, emperor, general, inventor, animal trainer (reputedly keeping thousands of hunting cheetahs during his reign and training many himself), lacemaker, technologist and theologian.

Akbar is said to have been a wise ruler and a sound judge of character. His son and heir, Jahangir, in his memoirs, wrote effusive praise of Akbar's character, and dozens of anecdotes to illustrate his virtues. According to Jahangir, Akbar's complexion was like the yellow of wheat. Antoni de Montserrat, the Catalan Jesuit who visited his court described him as plainly white. Akbar was not tall but powerfully built and very agile. He was also noted for various acts of courage. One such incident occurred on his way back from Malwa to Agra when Akbar was 19 years of age.

Akbar rode alone in advance of his escort and was confronted by a tigress who, along with her cubs, came out from the shrubbery across his path. When the tigress charged the emperor, he was alleged to have dispatched the animal with his sword in a solitary blow. His approaching attendants found the emperor standing quietly by the side of the dead animal.

Abul Fazal, and even the hostile critic Badayuni, described him as having a commanding personality. He was notable for his command in battle, and, "like Alexander of Macedon, was always ready to risk his life, regardless of political consequences". He often plunged on his horse into the flooded river during the rainy seasons and safely crossed it. He rarely indulged in cruelty and is said to have been affectionate towards his relatives. He pardoned his brother Hakim, who was a repented rebel. But on rare occasions, he dealt cruelly with offenders, such as his maternal uncle Muazzam and his foster-brother Adham Khan.

He is said to have been extremely moderate in his diet. *Ain-e-Akbari* mentions that during his travels and also while at home, Akbar drank water from the Ganga river, which he called 'the water of immortality'. Special people were stationed at Sorun and later Haridwar to dispatch water, in sealed jars, to wherever he was stationed. According to Jahangir's memoirs, he was fond of fruits and had little liking for meat, which he stopped eating in his later years. He was more religiously tolerant than many of the Muslim rulers before and after him. Jahangir wrote:

"As in the wide expanse of the Divine compassion there is room for all classes and the followers of all creeds, so... in his dominions, ... there was room for the professors of opposite religions, and for beliefs good and bad, and the road to altercation was closed. Sunnis and Shias met in one mosque, and Franks and Jews in one church, and observed their own forms of worship."

To defend his stance that speech arose from hearing, he carried out a language deprivation experiment, and had children raised in isolation, not allowed to be spoken to, and pointed out that as they grew older, they remained mute.

During Akbar's reign, the ongoing process of inter-religious discourse and syncretism resulted in a series of religious attributions to him in terms of positions of assimilation, doubt or uncertainty, which he either assisted himself or left unchallenged. Such hagiographical accounts of Akbar traversed a wide range of denominational and sectarian spaces, including several accounts by Parsis, Jains and Jesuit missionaries, apart from contemporary accounts by Brahminical and Muslim orthodoxy. Existing sects and denominations, as well as various religious figures who represented popular worship felt they had a claim to him. The diversity of these accounts is attributed to the fact that his reign resulted in the formation of a flexible centralised state accompanied by personal authority and cultural heterogeneity.

Religion at Akbar's Court

Of all the aspects of Akbar's life and reign, few have excited more interest than his attitude toward religion. There is every indication that he began his rule as a devout, orthodox Muslim. He said all the five prayers in the congregation, often recited the call for prayers, and occasionally swept out the palace mosque himself. He showed great respect for the two leading religious leaders at the court, Makhdum-ul-Mulk and Shaikh Abdul Nabi. Makhdum-ul-Mulk, who had been an important figure during the reign of the Surs, became even more powerful in the early days of Akbar. Shaikh Abdul Nabi, who was appointed *sadr-ul-sadur* in 1565, was given authority which no other holder of the office (the highest religious position in the realm) had ever enjoyed. Akbar would go to his house to hear him expound the sayings of the Prophet, and he placed his heir, Prince Salim, under his tutorship. "For some time the Emperor had so great faith in him as a religious leader that he would bring him his shoes and place them before his feet."

Further indication of Akbar's orthodoxy and of his religious zeal was shown in his devotion to Khwaja Muin-ud-din, the great Chishti saint whose tomb at Ajmer was an object of veneration. He made his first pilgrimage to the tomb in 1565, and thereafter he went almost every year. If there was a perplexing problem or a particularly difficult expedition to undertake, he would make a special journey to pray at the tomb for guidance. He always entered Ajmer on foot, and in 1568 and 1570, in fulfillment of vows, walked the entire way from Agra to Ajmer.

It was probably devotion to Khwaja Muin-ud-din that was responsible for Akbar's interest in Shaikh Salim Chishti, a contemporary saint who lived at the site of what was to become Akbar's capital at Fathpur Sikri. It was there that he built the Ibadat Khana, the of Worship, which he set apart for religious discussions. Every Friday after the congregational prayers, scholars, dervishes, theologians, and courtiers interested in religious affairs would assemble in the Ibadat Khana and discuss religious subjects in the royal presence.

The assemblies in the Ibadat Khana had been arranged by Akbar out of sincere religious zeal, but ultimately they were to drive him away from orthodoxy. This was partly the fault of those who attended the gatherings. At the very first session there were disputes on the question of precedence, and when these were resolved, a battle of wits started among the participants. Each tried to display his own scholarship and reveal the ignorance of the others. Questions were asked to belittle rivals, and soon the gatherings degenerated into religious squabbles. The two great theologians of the court, Makhdum-ul-Mulk and Shaikh Abdul Nabi, arrayed on opposite sides, attacked each other so mercilessly that Akbar lost confidence in both of them. His disillusionment extended to the orthodoxy they represented.

Of the two, Makhdum-ul-Mulk was a powerful jurist and had received the title of Shaikh-ul-Islam from Sher Shah Suri. He used his position for two main purposes: to persecute the unorthodox and to accumulate fabulous wealth. Badauni says that when he died, thirty million rupees in cash were found in his house, and several boxes containing gold blocks were buried in a false tomb.

Shaikh Abdul Nabi, although not personally accused of graft, is said to have had corrupt subordinates. He was a strict puritan, and his hostility toward music was one of the grounds on which his rival attacked him in the discussions in the House of Worship. The petty recriminations of the ulama disgusted the emperor, but probably a deeper cause for his break with them was an issue that is comparable in some ways to the conflict between the church and the state in medieval Europe. The interpretation and application of Islamic law, which was the law of the state, was the responsibility of the ulama. Over against this, and certain to come in conflict with it, was Akbar's concentration of all ultimate authority in himself. Furthermore, with Akbar's organization of the empire on new lines, problems were arising which the old theologians were unable to comprehend, much less settle in a way acceptable to the emperor.

One such problem brought matters to a climax in 1577. A complaint was lodged before the emperor by the qazi of Mathura that a rich Brahman in his vicinity had forcibly taken possession of building material collected for the construction of a mosque and had used it for building a temple. "When the qazi had attempted to prevent him, he had, in presence of witnesses, opened his foul mouth to curse the Prophet, ... and had shown his contempt for Muslims in various other ways." The question of suitable punishment for the Brahman was discussed before the emperor, but, perplexed by conflicting considerations, he gave no decision. The Brahman languished in prison for a long time. Ultimately Akbar left the matter to Shaikh Abdul Nabi, who had the offender executed. This led to an outcry, with many courtiers like Abul Fazl expressing the view that although an offence had been committed, the extreme penalty of execution was not necessary. They based their opinion on a decree of the founder of the Hanafi school of Islamic law. Abdul Nabi's action was also severely criticized by the Hindu courtiers and by Akbar's Rajput wives.

Akbar was troubled not only by this incident but by the general legal position which gave so much power to the ulama that he was at their mercy on such vital issues. He explained his difficulties to Shaikh Mubarik, the father of Faizi and Abul Fazl, who had come to the court on business. The shaikh, who was liberal minded and independent in his views, had suffered at the hands of Makhdum-ul-Mulk. He stated that according to Islamic law, if there was a difference of opinion between the jurists, the Muslim ruler had the authority and the right to choose any one view, his choice being decisive. He drew up a brief but important document, the arguments of which were supported by quotations from the Holy Quran and traditions of the Prophet. It read as follows:

Whereas Hindustan has now become the center of security and peace, and the land of justice and beneficence, a large number of people, especially learned men and lawyers, have immigrated and chosen this country for their home. Now we, the principal ulama, who are not only well versed in the several departments of the law and in the principles of jurisprudence, and well acquainted with the edicts which rest on reason or testimony, but are also known for our piety and honest intentions, have duly considered the deep meaning, first, of the verse of the Quran: "Obey God and obey the Prophet, and those who have authority among you"; and secondly, of the genuine tradition: "Surely, the man who is dearest to God on the day of judgment is the *imam-i-adil*; whosoever obeys the Amir obeys Thee; and whoever rebels against him rebels against Thee"; and thirdly, of several other proofs based on reasoning or testimony; and we have agreed that the rank of a *sultan-i-adil* is higher in the eyes of God than the rank of a *mujtahid*. Further, we declare that the King of Islam, Amir of the Faithful, Shadow of God in the world, Abul Fath Jalal-ud-din Mohammad Akbar Padshah Ghazi (whose kingdom God perpetuate), is a most just, most wise, and a most God-fearing king. Should, therefore, in the future, a religious question come up, regarding which the opinions of the *mujtahids* are at variance, and His Majesty, in his penetrating understanding and clear wisdom, be inclined to adopt, for the benefit of the nation, and as a political expedient, any of the conflicting opinions, which exist on that point, and issue a decree to that effect, we do hereby agree that such a decree shall be binding on us and on the whole nation.

Further, we declare that should His Majesty think it fit to issue a new order, we and the nation shall likewise be bound by it, provided always that such order be not only in accordance with some verse of the Quran, but also of real benefit to the nation; and further, that any opposition on the part of his subjects to such an order passed by His Majesty shall involve damnation in the world to come, and loss of property and religious privileges in this life.

This document has been written with honest intentions, for the glory of God and the propagation of Islam, and is signed by us, the principal ulama and lawyers, in the month of Rajab of the year nine hundred and eight-seven.

The document has been referred to as the "Infallibility Decree of 1579," with the implication that it gave to Akbar unlimited powers in both the spiritual and temporal spheres. This is an erroneous reading, for the king's authority was confined to measures which were "in accordance with some verse of the Quran" and were of "real benefit for the nation." The modern Islamic scholar Abul Kalam Azad has argued that the central thesis of the document was in line with traditional Islamic political theory. "The khalifa of the day and those in charge of affairs, and their advisers have the right of *ijtihad* (independent judgment) at all times and in all ages, and its denial has been responsible for all the misfortunes of Islam."

But the limitations laid down in the declaration of 1579 were not observed by Akbar, and in practice it became an excuse for the exercise of unrestrained autocracy. Soon the gatherings of the Ibadat Khana were exposed to new and more hostile influences. Before long, in addition to the Muslim scholars, Hindu pandits, Parsi mobeds and Jain sadhus began to attend the gatherings. They expressed their own points of view, and the emperor, ever open to new ideas, was attracted by some of their practices. A more serious complication arose when the emperor invited Jesuits from Goa to the discussions. They did not confine themselves to the exposition of their own beliefs, but reviled Islam and the Prophet in unrestrained language.

When the news of these discussions and the new decrees promulgated by the emperor became known, there was serious disaffection among the Muslims. The first to criticize the new developments was Mullah Mohammad Yazdi, the Shia qazi of Jaunpur, who declared in 1580 that the emperor had ceased to be a Muslim and the people should rise against him. Even some courtiers like Qutb-ud-din Khan Koka and Shahbaz Khan Kamboh criticized the emperor in the court. Akbar sent for Mullah Mohammad Yazdi and Muiz-ul-Mulk, the chief qazi of Bengal, and had them put to death by drowning. His punitive action against others did not prevent open rebellion from breaking out in 1581. Akbar's enemies did not confine themselves to sporadic outbursts and regional risings, but made a serious attempt to dethrone him and place his brother Mirza Mohammad Hakim, ruler of Kabul, on the throne. Akbar's brilliant Diwan, Khawaja Shah Mansur, was executed for alleged conspiracy with Mirza Hakim, who got as far as Lahore, but being no match for Akbar, was driven back to Kabul.

The historian Vincent Smith, in his biographical study of Akbar, declares that the emperor, after he had returned from his successful expedition against the rebels, called a formal council to promulgate his new religion the Din-i-Ilahi. This reading of the evidence is, however, almost certainly erroneous. The Jesuits apparently had not heard of any such proclamation. In fact, Father Monserrate, who accompanied Akbar to Kabul and back, thought that the emperor had grown more cautious in the expression of his views. On the return journey Akbar performed prayers in the customary Muslim manner in a mosque near Khyber, was reluctant to have religious discussions with the Jesuits, and during one debate in which Muslim spokesmen appeared likely to lose, Akbar took their side and brought his own knowledge into play. Not only Smith, but most European historians, have assumed that Akbar abandoned Islam. Hindu writers, on the other hand, have generally held that although he followed a tolerant policy, he lived and died a Muslim. Muslim historians are about equally divided on the question. These conflicting judgments partly reflect the inevitable differences that result from assessing a complex personality, but they are due also to conflicting contemporary accounts and, in no small degree, to erroneous translations of the relevant Persian texts.

The foundation for the misunderstanding of Akbar's religious history was laid by Blochmann in the introduction to his translation of Abul Fazl's *Ain-i-Akbari*; here he set the pattern for relying on Badauni, Akbar's enemy, rather than Abul Fazl, his friend, for studying Akbar's religious history. The crucial question about Akbar's religious activity is whether he established a new religion or a new spiritual order. Badauni's account is clearly intended to give the impression that Akbar no longer respected Islam and, indeed, actively persecuted it. The expressions used by both Abul Fazl and Badauni in this connection, however, are *iradat* or *muridi* (discipleship) but Blochmann habitually translates these expressions as "divine faith," thus converting a religious order (or even a bond of loyalty) into a new religion. He translated the expression *ain-i-iradat gazinan*, which correctly means "rules for the (royal) disciples," as the "principles of divine faith," and gives the subsection the heading, "ordinances of the divine faith," although there is no such heading in the original text.

The sharp difference between the viewpoints of Abul Fazl and Badauni is obvious, but our study of the subject has revealed a surprisingly large area of common ground between them, and if the present divergence of opinion about Akbar's religion is to be resolved, more attention will have to be given to what is common ground between these two principal sources of our information. It appears that modern historians, fascinated by the wit and sarcasm of Badauni, have paid scant attention to Abul Fazl's informative sections on Akbar's religion contained in his *Akbar-Nama* and *Ain-i-Akbari*. Akbar's regulations which were not of an ephemeral or tentative character have been preserved in the voluminous *Ain-i-Akbari*, and it would be illogical to suppose that important royal orders, which were to be given general currency in the empire, would have been omitted. Since the *Ain*'s accounts of Akbar's religious innovations and of the practices of the royal disciples contain much that would shock an orthodox Muslim, there is no reason to suppose that regulations for the Din-i-Ilahi would not have been included. Judging by its contents and the public nature of the information which is sought, the *Ain* appears to be the most dependable source of information regarding Akbar's religious regulations and spiritual practices.

According to *Ain-i-Akbari* the emperor discouraged people from becoming his disciples, but the person whom he accepted for initiation approached him with his turban in his hand and put his head on the emperor's feet. This was to express that the novice had "cast aside conceit, selfishness—the root of so many evils." The emperor then stretched out his hand, raised up the disciple and replaced the turban on his head. ... The novice was given a token containing the ruler's symbolic motto Allah-u-Akbar (God is Great). When the disciples met each other, one would say, "Allah-u-Akbar" and the other responded, "Jall-u-Jallaluhu." "The motives of His Majesty in allowing this mode of salutation," Abul Fazl wrote, "is to remind men to think of the origin of their existence and to keep the Deity in their fresh, lively and grateful remembrance." The disciples were to endeavor to abstain from flesh and not to make use of the same vessels as butchers, fishermen, and bird catchers. Each disciple was to give a party on the anniversary of his birthday and to bestow alms. The dinners customarily given after a man's death were to be given by a disciple during his lifetime.

For students of history, general orders intended for compliance by all are more important than the regulations framed for the royal disciples. According to Abul Fazl, the kotwals were asked to ensure that no ox or bufalo or horse or camel was slaughtered, and the killing of all animals was prohibited on many days of the year—including the whole month of Aban—except for feeding the animals used in hunting and for the sick.

Akbar interested himself in the reform of marriage customs. He abhorred marriages before the age of puberty, and also considered marriages between near relations highly improper. He disapproved of large dowries, but admitted that they acted as a preventative to rash divorces. "Nor does His Majesty approve of everyone marrying more than one wife; for this ruins the man's health, and disturbs the peace of the home." Circumcision before the age of twelve was forbidden. The kotwals were to "forbid the restriction of personal liberty and the selling of slaves," and a woman was not to be burned on her husband's funeral pyre without giving her consent. Government officers were not to consider homage paid to the sun as worshiping fire. A governor was expected to accustom himself to night vigils and to partake of sleep and food in moderation. He was to pass the dawn and evening in meditation and pray at noon and midnight. Nauroz, the Parsi New Year, was to be celebrated officially, with the kotwal keeping a vigil on that night.

It was true that Akbar adopted and prescribed for his disciples and even others many practices which were borrowed from alien creeds, but precedents for this may be found in the lives of many Sufi saints who continue to be considered Muslims in spite of wide departures from traditional Islam. For all of his innovations, Islamic texts or precedents, genuine or spurious, were cited by his courtiers. But while Akbar did not claim to be a prophet or to establish a new religion, Islam lost its privileged position and many of his practices and regulations differed widely from the normal Muslim practices. It is not surprising that by many Muslims he was—and is—regarded as having gone outside the pale of Islam. Writing of the proclamation of 1579, Abul Fazl very ably summed up the popular misconceptions concerning Akbar, noting that he was accused by the "ill-informed and the unfair" of claiming divinity, or at least prophethood, of being anti-Muslim, a Shia, and partial to Hinduism. While Abul Fazl answered these criticisms, he admitted that Akbar's policy and some of his regulations facilitated the task of his enemies. Possibly Akbar sincerely believed that the powers conferred on him by the ulama in 1579 authorized him to initiate his regulations, and the court flatterers pandered to this belief by citing precedents in Islamic history. That they caused serious misgivings and resentment among orthodox Sunni Muslims was to be expected.

In any assessment of Akbar's religious policy, it is important to see that it had two quite distinct aspects. On the one hand were the political and administrative measures which he took to broaden the basis of his government and secure the goodwill of all his subjects. For this policy of religious tolerance and of giving an adequate share in the administration to all classes there can be nothing but praise, and it became a part of the Mughal political code. In themselves, these measures involved nothing more than what Mohammad ibn Qasim, the Arab conqueror of Sind, had adopted eight centuries before with full concurrence of the ulama of Damascus. Zain-ul-Abidin introduced similar measures in Kashmir without a murmur on the part of Muslims. They were adopted by Akbar in the very beginning of his reign—mainly between 1662 and 1665—at a time when the ulama were dominant at the court, without offending Muslim opinion.

An aspect of Akbar's religious policy that began several years after the acrimonious debates of the House of Worship was on a different footing. His attempt to set himself up as a *jagat guru*, the spiritual leader of the people, was a political mistake. Akbar's Hindu well-wishers like Raja Bhagwan Das and Raja Man Singh left him in no doubt about their dislike of his religious innovations. The only prominent Hindu who became his disciple was Birbal, regarded by succeeding generations as the court jester. Muslims were greatly offended and a reaction began against Akbar's policy which was to destroy much that he had created.

Akbar's failure was also due to forces operating outside the court. At this time a great Hindu religious revival was sweeping the country. It commenced in Bengal, but under Chaitanya's successors, Mathura in northern India became the great center of resurgent Hinduism. It was there that the great crisis had arisen over the wealthy Brahman who had taken building material collected for the construction of a mosque, and used it for building a Hindu temple. It is possible that this particular incident occurred in connection with the large-scale Vaishnava temple-building operations which were going on at Mathura at this time. Among the temple-builders was Raja Man Singh, Akbar's great Hindu general. The defiant spirit which had been inculcated by the new movement can be seen in the Brahman's action. With such developments in the country, possibly with the support of his Hindu officers, Akbar's efforts at religious syncretion were doomed to failure. In fact, as we shall see, the new aggressive attitude of the Hindu revivalists and the offence which the emperor's religious innovations gave to the Muslims led to a reaction which was to destroy even the existing basis of harmony.

Relation with Hindus

However, historian Dasharatha Sharma states that court histories like the Akbarnama idealize Akbar's religious tolerance, and give Akbar more credit than he is due.

Akbar in his early years was not only a practising Muslim but is also reported to have had an intolerant attitude towards Hindus. It was during this period that he boasted of being a great conqueror of Islam to the ruler of Turan, Abdullah Khan, in a letter in 1579, and was also looked upon by orthodox Muslim elements as a devout believer committed to defending the religion against infidels. However, his attitude towards the Hindu religion and its practices no longer remained hostile after he began his marriage alliances with Rajput princes. He was also perceived as not being averse to performing Hindu rituals despite his Islamic beliefs.

Hindus boycotted the Vishwanath temple built by Akbar's general Man Singh (which he built after taking Akbar's permission) because Man Singh's family had marital relations with Akbar. Akbar's Hindu generals could not construct temples without the emperor's permission. In Bengal, after Man Singh started the construction of a temple in 1595, Akbar ordered him to convert it into a mosque.

Akbar allowed the conversion of a mosque into Hindu temple at Kurukshetra. He gave two villages for the upkeep of a mosque and a Madras which was setup by destroying a Hindu temple. Akbar's army was responsible for the demolition of rich Hindu temples which had gold idols in the Doab region. He changed the name of some Hindu holy places to Islamic ones; for example changing Prayag to Allahabad in 1583.

Relations with other Muslims

During the early part of his reign, Akbar adopted an attitude of suppression towards Muslim sects that were condemned by the orthodoxy as heretical. In 1567, on the advice of Shaikh Abdun Nabi, he ordered the exhumation of Mir Murtaza Sharifi Shirazi-a Shia buried in Delhi-because of the grave's proximity to that of Amir Khusrau, arguing that a "heretic" could not be buried so close to the grave of a Sunni saint, reflecting a restrictive attitude towards Shivism which continued to persist till the early 1570s. He suppressed Mahdavism in 1573 during his campaign in Gujarat, in the course of which the Mahdavi leader Miyan Mustafa Bandagi was arrested and brought in chains to the court. However, as Akbar increasingly came under the influence of pantheistic Sufi mysticism from the early 1570s, it caused a great shift in his outlook and culminated in his ultimate rejection of Islam as traditionally professed, in favour of a new concept of Islam transcending the limits of religion.

In 1580, a rebellion broke out in the eastern part of Akbar's empire, and a number of *fatwas,* declaring Akbar to be a heretic, were issued by qazis. Akbar suppressed the rebellion and handed out severe punishments to the qazis. In order to further strengthen his position in dealing with the qazis, Akbar issued a *mazhar* or declaration. The *Mahzar* asserted that Akbar was the *Khalifa* of the age, the rank of the *Khalifa* was higher than that of a *Mujtahid,* in case of a difference of opinion among the mujtahids, Akbar could select any one opinion and could also issue decrees which did not go against the *nass*. Given the prevailing Islamic sectarian conflicts in various parts of the country at that time, it is believed that the *mazhar* helped in stabilising the religious situation in the empire.

Akbar's relations with the Ottoman Empire are believed to have strained. He sent a Hajj caravan, including members of his harem, from Surat, which reached Mecca and Medina in 1577. Four more caravans were sent from 1577 to 1580, with gifts and *sadaqah* for the authorities of Mecca and Medina. The pilgrims in these caravans were poor, however, and their stay strained the resources of these cities. Ottoman authorities requested that the pilgrims return home, but the ladies of the harem did not want to leave Hejaz. At length they were forced to return. The Governor of Aden insulted the ladies of the harem on their way back to India. These events persuaded Akbar to stop sending Hajj caravans and *sadaqat* to Mecca and Medina. From 1584 onwards, Akbar seriously considered attacking the Ottoman port of Yemen with the help of the Portuguese. To forge an alliance, a Mughal envoy was stationed in Goa permanently as of October 1584. In 1587 a Portuguese fleet sent to attack Yemen was defeated. The Mughal-Portuguese alliance fell through.

Relation with Christians

Akbar met Portugese Jesuit priests and sent an ambassador to Goa, requesting them to send two missionaries to his court so that he could understand Christian doctrines better. In response, the Portugese sent Monserrate and Aquiviva who remained at Akbar's court for three years and left accounts of their visit. In 1603 a written *firman* was granted at the request of the Christian priests allowing them to make willing converts. Even armed with the firman, the missionaries however found it extremely difficult to carry out their work as the Viceroy of Lahore, [Qulij Khan, who was a staunch Muslim official, was so harassing in his tactics that many Christians fled from Lahore and Father Pinheiro went in fear of death.

The Orthodox Reaction

The Old spiritual orders of Islam in India adopted the practice of keeping out of affairs of state, but toward the end of Akbar's reign a new religious group, following quite different traditions, entered the subcontinent. This was the Naqshbandi movement, which was introduced into India under the leadership of Khwaja Baqi Billah. The order's intention of seeking to influence temporal rulers is indicated in the statement of one of its leaders: "If I were after spiritual prominence, no disciple would be left with the other saints. But I have another mission—to bring comfort to the Muslims. To achieve this, I have to associate with the worldly rulers, gain influence over them, and thereby fulfill the objects of the Muslims."

Khwaja Baqi Billah was born at Kabul in 1563, and after completing his scholastic education there and at Samarqand he visited several saints for spiritual training. Ultimately he was initiated in the Naqshbandi order by a leading saint of Bukhara, who asked him to make India the center of his work. Khwaja Baqi Billah came first to Lahore, where he spent more than a year before moving to Delhi. Partly owing to his great spiritual powers, and partly because he represented the order belonging to the native land of the ruling family, he acquired a prominent position in the religious life of the capital. He was particularly active as a link between the various nobles who were displeased with Akbar's religious innovations. One of these was Shaikh Farid, who, according to Jesuit accounts, extracted a promise from Jahangir, Akbar's heir, to uphold Islam in the kingdom. Other nobles who had great regard for the khwaja included Qulich Khan, the devout viceroy of Lahore, Abdul Rahim Khan-i-Khanan, the commander-in-chief of the Deccan, and Khan-i-Azam, the deputy of the realm. In some of the khwaja's letters there are references to Sadr Jahan (the head of the religious endowments under Akbar) coming to him for spiritual training. The khwaja died in 1603, but before his death the Naqshbandi order had been firmly established in India.

Khwaja Baqi Billah's most prominent disciple was Shaikh Ahmad, popularly known as Mujaddid Alif Sani (reviver of Islam during the second millennium). He was born at Sirhind on June 26, 1564, and was educated there and at Sialkot. He established himself at Sirhind, but he was soon attracted to Akbar's capital, Fathpur Sikri. Here he moved in the most distinguished intellectual circles, and seems to have favourably impressed Abul Fazl and his versatile brother, Faizi. Shaikh Ahmad's views and temperament had little in common with those of the two brothers (though he himself passed through a period of youthful free-thinking and at one time wrote verses with the poetic surname of Kufri, the "heretic"), but they had enough respect for each other's learning to be able to carry on this intellectual comradeship in spite of the difference in views. The shaikh is even stated to have helped Faizi in the completion of his commentary on the Quran.

He visited Delhi in 1599 and went to see Khwaja Baqi Billah, who asked him to spend a few days in his hospice. Within two days Ahmad requested the khwaja to take him into discipleship. After having initiated Shaikh Ahmad into various stages of spiritual development under the Naqshbandi order, the khwaja wrote: "Shaikh Ahmad is ... rich in knowledge and vigorous in action. I associated with him for a few days, and noticed truly marvellous things in his spiritual life. He will turn into a light which will illuminate the world."

Shaikh Ahmad returned to Sirhind, convinced that he had a major role to play in the religious life of the times. He twice visited Delhi during the lifetime of the khwaja, who deputed him to work at Lahore. After the khwaja's death, he retired to Sirhind, which remained the main seat of his activities. He carried on his work partly through personal guidance and oral instructions, but he had discovered his literary gifts, and believed that he could also fulfill his mission by writing letters on religious and public subjects to important personages of the day. Khwaja Baqi Billah had, by his warm praise and encouragement, made Shaikh Ahmad aware of his potentialities. He had also facilitated the achievement of his task by providing him useful contacts with persons in key positions in the state. Shaikh Ahmad was able to make full use of these opportunities. A profound scholar, a master of polemics, and possessing a polished and forceful literary style, he began sending letters to important nobles bemoaning the sad state into which Islam had fallen in India and reminding them of their duty. The rhetoric and appeal of these letters kindled a religious fervour which, although it took some time to bear fruit, profoundly affected the history of Islam in India by strengthening the position of the orthodox in places of power.

But Shaikh Ahmad's letters touched on more than just religious revival, and it was this that placed him in serious difficulties. Some of his letters stated that in his trances he saw that at one time he had gone ahead of all the Companions of the Prophet. The theologians criticized these claims, and asked Emperor Jahangir to take action. The wazir, Asaf Khan, who was a Shia, could not have been fond of the anti-Shia views of Shaikh Ahmad, and he is said to have pointed out the political dangers inherent in the growing influence and organization of Shaikh Ahmad. In 1619, through the governor of Sirhind, he was summoned to the emperor's court and asked to explain his statements. The shaikh behaved at the court with great dignity and courage. He made it clear that there could be no question of his considering himself superior to the Companions of the Prophet, and gave an explanation of the relevant entry in his letters. The emperor seemed to be satisfied with this, but he took offence when somebody pointed out that the shaikh had not performed the *sijdah* (deep obeisance), which Akbar had prescribed for everybody coming in the royal presence. The shaikh's reply that he was not prepared to perform the sijdah before any human being seemed to be open defiance, and he was imprisoned in Gwalior fort.

After about a year the shaikh was released from the fort, presented with a dress of honor and a thousand rupees for expenses and given an option of accompanying the royal camp or returning to Sirhind. The shaikh preferred to remain in the royal camp, and this enabled him to visit the whole of the empire, and even establish friendly contacts with the emperor. It appears that Jahangir came to hold the shaikh in great respect; in his autobiography he twice refers to having made large offerings to the saint, and among the shaikh's letters there is one addressed to the emperor. In another letter the shaikh gave a detailed account of a lengthy conversation he had with the emperor on religious subjects, with the emperor apparently taking a great interest.

Shaikh Ahmad was in the royal camp for nearly three years. His letters written during this period contain few biographical details, but the entries in Jahangir's autobiography suggest that during this period the easy-going Jahangir was unusually religious. It would not be surprising if the emperor's orthodox mood were due to the shaikh's presence in the camp. For example, in describing the conquest of Kangra and his visit there in early 1622, Jahangir says: "I went to see the fort of Kangra, and gave an order that the qazi, the Chief Justice, and other learned men of Islam should accompany me and carry out in the fort whatever was customary, according to the religion of Mohammad. Briefly ... by the grace of God, the call to prayer and the reading of the khutba and the slaughter of a bullock, which had not taken place from the commencement of the building of the fort till now, were carried out in my presence. I ... ordered a lofty mosque to be built inside the fort." It is more than probable that Shaikh Ahmad was one of "the learned men of Islam" who accompanied Jahangir to Kangra. Soon after, the saint's health began to fail, and with the emperor's permission he returned to Sirhind. Here he lived in seclusion, devoting himself to charity and prayers, until his death on December 10, 1624. Shaikh Ahmad was the most forceful and original thinker produced by Muslim India before the days of Shah Waliullah and Iqbal. Indeed he occupies a high place in the religious history of the entire Muslim world, for his exposition of *tawhid-i-shahudi* was a distinct contribution to Islamic thought. Perhaps even more important was the attitude of vigorous self-confidence and self-assertion which he contributed to Muslim thinking, the like of which had been seen rarely since the days of Ibn Taimiya in the eighth century.

The white heat of revivalist fervour which one finds in his writings is not visible among early members of his order, the

Naqshbandi. In spite of Shah Waliullah's emphasis on moderation, the Mujaddidiya revival, associated with the shaikh, ultimately superseded other branches of the Naqshbandi order, not only in the subcontinent but in the Ottoman empire as well. This is remarkable considering that the main order was of Central Asian and Turkish origin. The influence of the Mujaddidiya seems to have been a factor in creating those forces which ultimately led to the rise and widespread acceptance of Wahhabism.

In discussing Akbar's religious policy, reference was made to the circumstances which made its failure inevitable. The inability of the Hindus and Muslims to evolve a common spiritual brotherhood was the result of the basic fact that to the Hindus the Muslims were (and are) untouchables. This attitude of the Hindus, nourished by the revivalistic fervour of the Vaishnava Gosains of Mathura, became more marked during Akbar's era of toleration. The writings of the shaikh, which reveal the anguish he felt at the low position of Islam under Akbar and even later, also militated against the success of Akbar's policy. In fact, it would not be wrong to say that the swing of religious policy from Akbar to Aurangzeb was in some measure due to the influence and teachings of Shaikh Ahmad.

His forceful and eloquent letters addressed to the leading nobles at Jahangir's court, calling on them to rise in defence of Islam and uphold the dignity of their religion, have great power and effectiveness. These letters were meant not only for the individuals to whom they were addressed; they were really "open letters" and were no less forceful than the poems with which Byron tried to engender enthusiasm for the cause of Greek independence, or with which Hali tried to reawaken Indian Muslims. Copies of them were supplied to the shaikh's disciples and admirers, and given wide circulation.

Some Naqshbandi writers state that Aurangzeb became a disciple of Khwaja Mohammad Masum, son and successor of Shaikh Ahmad, but even though Aurangzeb's contemporary, the satirist Nimat Khan Ali, refers to it in his *Wiqaya,* the connection is not certain, since it is not mentioned in the historical accounts of the reign. The official history of the period, however, does refer to his visits to the emperor's court, where he received high honours and rich gifts. After his death, his son, Shaikh Saif-ud-din, came to stay at the royal capital and apparently was in close contact with

Aurangzeb. The court history speaks of his being a formal witness at the wedding of Prince Azam Shah. Next year, on June 3, 1669, the emperor visited the saint at his residence for one hour late at night, and then returned to the palace.

Even more remarkable than these historic links between Aurangzeb and Shaikh Ahmad's family is the fact that almost all the steps which are associated with Aurangzeb's religious policy had been advocated so forcefully by the shaikh in his letters. Shaikh Ahmad had seen those days when, according to him, "non-Muslims carried out aggressively the ordinances of their own religion in a Muslim state and the Muslims were powerless to carry out the ordinances of Islam; if they carried them out, they were executed." He had described with great anguish those tragic days those who believed in the Holy Prophet were "humiliated and powerless, while those who denied his prophethood enjoyed high position, and used to sprinkle salt on the wounds of the Muslims with ridicule and taunts."

These developments had filled Shaikh Ahmad with anger and hatred against Akbar and the non-Muslims. What had troubled him even more was that with Akbar's withdrawal of patronage from Islam, and an aggressive religious revival among the Hindus, non-Muslims had started persecuting Islam. "The non-Muslims in India," he wrote, "are without any hesitation demolishing mosques and setting up temples in their place. For example, in Kurukshetra there was a mosque and the tomb of a saint. They have been demolished and in their place a very big temple has been erected." Hindus were even interfering with Muslim observances. "Moreover, non-Muslims openly carry out their observances, but Muslims are powerless to carry out openly many of the Islamic injunctions. During Ekadashi, Hindus fast and strive hard to see that in Muslim towns no Muslim cooks or sells food on these days. On the other hand, during the sacred month of Ramadan, they openly prepare and sell food, but owing to the weakness of Islam, nobody can interfere. Alas, the ruler of the country is one of us, but we are so badly off!"

Shaikh Ahmad was convinced that the considerations shown to Hindus in Akbar's reign had emboldened them, and that this policy must be reversed. In a number of his letters he expressed regret at the abolition of jizya and urged its revival. In another letter he demanded the abolition of the ban on cow slaughter. He called upon the Muslim nobles not to associate with non-Muslims and unorthodox Muslims, including Shias. In a letter to Shaikh Farid, one of the chief nobles, he went so far as to say that the company of Muslim nonconformists was worse than that of non-Muslims. Once the preacher at the principal mosque of Samana did not follow the Sunni practice of mentioning all the four caliphs in his Id sermon; Shaikh Ahmad immediately wrote an open letter to the religious leaders of the city, rebuking them for the neglect of their duties, and for their failure to deal "aggressively and offensively" with that "unjust preacher."

Shaikh Farid and other leaders did not accept the extremist point of view, and in some of his letters Shaikh Ahmad has expressed his disappointment with Farid's failures and omissions. But his warnings and his denunciations had their effect, and there is no doubt that he had a wide following in the highest places. Is it a mere coincidence that the attitude which Aurangzeb had toward Shias—at least during his early days—was identical with that of Shaikh Ahmad?

Elsewhere in India other saints and prophets were upholding orthodoxy with scarcely less vigor and success than Khwaja Baqi Billah and Shaikh Ahmad. On the northwest frontier Sayyid Ali Shah Tirmiz, known as Pir Baba, and his disciple Akhund Darweza took as their special task the uprooting of the heretical Raushaniya sect which flourished in the mountains. Pir Baba's descendants wielded great influence among the Pathan tribesmen, and three centuries later provided a rallying point against the Sikhs and the British.

Signs of religious activity of a somewhat different nature, but conducive to the strengthening of the forces of orthodox Islam, were visible at about the same time in Bengal. The religious history of Muslim Bengal is as yet unwritten, but there are indications that after the vigor and energy displayed by Chaitanya and his prominent disciples, and particularly the vigorous expression which their devotions and religious yearnings found in the new Bengali literature, Islamic influences in the area gradually weakened, especially outside the principal cities. This happened partly because the waves of the immigrant Sufis and preachers had subsided, but the lack of knowledge of Persian and Arabic among the general populace also prevented the propagation of Islam. At the same time, a vigorous new Bengali literature was coming into existence, often under the patronage of the Muslim rulers. This was concerned largely with the stories of the Ramayana and the Mahabharata, and the Muslim masses, not well-versed in any language other than Bengali, heard the Bengali poems and stories connected with these themes or saw them acted at Hindu festivals under the patronage of the Hindu landlords. Their mental background thus became more Hindu than Islamic.

As a counter-measure to the popular Bengali Hindu literature, marked literary activity among Bengali Muslims took place at the end of the sixteenth and the beginning of the seventeenth century, with a special emphasis on the writing of lives of the prophets and other saints in the language of the people. Sayyid Sultan, a leader of this movement, gave the reasons for the literary activity in his *Wafat-i-Rasul*:

All the Bengalis do not understand Arabic;

None understands the words of your religion.

Everyone remains satisfied with [Hindu] tales.

I, the despised and sinful, am in the midst of these people.

I do not know what Ilahi [God] will ask me in the afterlife.

If He asks, " Having been in their midst, why did you not tell them about the religion?" and blames me for this fault, I will have no power to give a proper reply. Considering this, I have composed *Nabi-vamsa* [a history of the Prophet's family] for the benefit of the ignorant people. For this reason many people blame me for having polluted this religious book.

When the learned read from the books, which are in Arabic, and do not translate them into Hindustani [i.e., Bengali], how can our people follow? In whatever language God has given one birth, that alone is his highest treasure.

Thus, as men like Shaikh Ahmad appealed to the upper classes to maintain the Faith through their political power, men like Sayyid Sultan took the Prophet's message to the common people. Both appeals explain the resurgent power of Islam in the century following Akbar's experiments.

Ibadat Khana

The Ibadat Khana (*House of Worship*) was a meeting house built in 1575CE by the Mughal Emperor Akbar (r. 1556-1605) at his palace in Fatehpur Sikri to gather religious leaders of many faiths in discussion.

Akbar built the Ibadat Khana originally as a debating house open only to Sunni Muslims, but following a series of petty squabbles which turned ugly, Akbar encouraged Hindus, Roman Catholics and even atheists to participate. Religious leaders and philosophers from around this diverse empire, as well as those passing through, were invited to Akbar's Thursday evening discussions.

By the late 1580s CE, Akbar began to reconcile the differences of all religions by creating a new faith called the Din-i-Ilahi ("Faith of the Divine"), which incorporated both 'pantheistic' versions of Islamic Sufism (most notably the Ibn Arabi's doctrine of 'Wahdat al Wajood' or Unity of existence) and 'bhakti' or devotional cults of Hinduism. Even some elements of Christianity (like crosses), Zoroastrianism (fire ceremonies) and Jainism were amalgamated in the new religion. Akbar was greatly influenced by the teachings of Jain Acharyas Hir Vijay Suri and Jin Chandra Suri and gave up non-vegetarian food by their influence. He declared "Amari" or non-killing of animals on the holy days of Jains like Paryushan and Mahavir Jayanti. He rolled back Jizya Tax from Jain Pilgrim places like Palitana.

This faith, however, was not for the masses. In fact, the only "converts" to this new religion were the upper nobility of Akbar's court. Historians have so far been able to identify only 18 members of this new religion.

The exact site of the Ibadat Khana within the palace complex is unknown, and has likely been long demolished. There is conjecture that the ornate single storey *Diwan-I-Khas* was the Ibadat Khana's original site.

Alfred Tennyson's poem *Akbar's Dream* lauds the Ibadat Khana, ascribing tolerance and humanity to his "Divine Faith", while implicitly criticising the intolerance of 19th century British Christianity.

Din-i-Ilahi

The Dîn-i Ilahi, was a syncretic religious doctrine propounded by the Mughal emperor Jalalu d-Din Mohammed Akbar ("Akbar the Great"), who ruled the Indian subcontinent from 1556 to 1605, intending to merge the best elements of the religions of his empire, and thereby reconcile the differences that divided his subjects. The elements were primarily drawn from Hinduism and Islam, but some others were also taken from Christianity, Jainism and Zoroastrianism

Akbar was tolerant of religions other than Islam. In fact, not only did he tolerate them, he encouraged debate on philosophical and religious issues. This led to the creation of the *Ibadat Khana* ("House of Worship") at Fatehpur Sikri.

From the discussions he led there in 1575, Akbar concluded that no single religion could claim the monopoly of truth. This inspired him to create the *Dîn-i Ilahi* in 1581. Various Muslim clerics, among them the Qadi of Bengal and the seminal Sufi personality Shaykh Ahmad Sirhindi, responded by declaring this to be blasphemy.

Dîn-i Ilahi as propounded by Akbar combined mysticism, philosophy and nature worship. It also recognized no gods or prophets.

Dîn-i Ilahi appears to have survived Akbar according to the Dabestan-e Mazaheb of Mubad Shah (Mohsin Fani). However, the movement never numbered more than 19 adherents.

Din-i-Ilahi was more of an ethical system. It prohibits lust, sensuality, slander and pride, considering them sins. Piety, prudence, abstinence and kindness are the core virtues. The soul is encouraged to purify itself through yearning of God. Celibacy is respected and the slaughter of animals is forbidden. There are neither sacred scriptures nor a priestly hierarchy in this religion.

Disciples of Din-i-Ilahi

The initiated disciples of Din-i-Ilahi during emperor Akbar the Great's time included:

- Birbal.
- Prince Salim.
- Abul-Fazl ibn Mubarak.
- Qasim Khan.
- Azam Khan.
- Shaikh Mubarak.
- Abdus Samad.

- Mulla Shah Mohammad Shahadad.
- Sufi Ahmad.
- Mir Sharif Amal.
- Sultan Khwaja.
- Mirza Jani Thatta.
- Taki Shustar.
- Shaikhzada Gosala Benarasi.
- Sadar Jahan.
- Sadar Jahan's first son.
- Sadar Jahan's second son.
- Shaikh Faizi.
- Jafar Beg.

The Nine Gems of Akbar

The Mughal Emperor Akbar (1543-1605), though illiterate and unable to read or write, demonstrated a remarkable appreciation of other religious thoughts. He was also a connoisseur of music and fine arts. The Mughal architecture, that later culminated in the glorious Taj Mahal, found its beginnings in Akbar's rule. Music and miniature paintings reached their zenith. His tolerance to other religions perhaps came from his many queens including his principle wife who was a Hindu. He had also married a Christian, and several Indian and Persian Muslim women. Akbar reigned as the Mughal monarch for several decades and established himself as the most benevolent, tolerant Emperor; and history knows him as Akbar the Great.

The court of Akbar held some of the best India had to offer at that time. The Emperor had an enormously curious intellect. He would routinely assemble religious leaders of other religions in his court and patiently listen to them. Thus it was not only Hinduism he was curious about but had Christian missionaries who were more and more common after Vasco da Gama visited India. Buddhism, Sikhism and Jainism also were his fascinations. He eventually formed his own religion, Din Ilahi, gathering the best from his understanding of the various religions. Akbar married thirty three times and had brides from all faiths. With his alliances with the daughters of nobles, he was able to bring peace in his empire. Several Rajput kings were his relatives by marriage and were loyal to him. *Diplomacy through matrimony!* The great administrator who was also an aficionado of the arts attracted the best contemporary minds to his court. Nine such extraordinary talents, who shone brightly in their respective fields, were known as Akbar's nine gems. The nomenclature as nine gems is chosen because there are nine well-known gems (*nava-rathna*). There were endless lists of worthy people in his court that shone like the brightest gems, and to choose only nine amongst them is a difficult task indeed.

Abul Fazl (1551-1602)

Shaikh Abu al-Fazl ibn Mubarak also known as Abul-Fazl, Abul Fadl and Abul-Fadl 'Allami (January 14, 1551-August 12, 1602) was the vizier of the great Mughal emperor Akbar, and author of the *Akbarnama,* the official history of Akbar's reign in three volumes, the third volume is known as the *Ain-i-Akbari* and a Persian translation of the Bible. He was also the brother of Faizi, the poet laureate of emperor Akbar.

Biography

Abul Fazl was the fifth descendant of Shaikh Musa who lived in Rel Sindh. His grandfather, Shaikh Khizr settled at Nagaur, where his father Shaikh Mubarak was born. Initially Shaikh Mubarak studied in Nagaur under Khwaja Ahrar. Later he went to Ahmedabad and studied under Shaikh Abul Fazl, Shaikh Umar and Shaikh Yusuf.

Finally, he settled in Agra, where his eldest son, poet Abul Faizi and his second son Abul Fazl were born He came to Akbar's court in 1575 and was influential in Akbar's religious views becoming more liberal into the 1580s and 1590s. He also led the Mughal imperial army in its wars in the Deccan.

He was assassinated by Vir Singh Bundela (who later became the ruler of Orchha) between Sarai Vir and Antri (near Narwar) in a plot contrived by the Mughal Prince Salim, who later became the Emperor Jahangir in 1602, because Abul Fazl was known to oppose the accession of Prince Salim to the throne. His severed head was sent to Salim at Allahabad. Abul Fazl was buried at Antri. Abul Fazl's son Shaikh Abdur Rahman Afzal Khan (December 29, 1571-1613) was later appointed governor of Bihar in 1608 by Jahangir.

His Own Account of the First Twenty Years

As I have now recounted somewhat of my ancestors, I proceed to say a few words regarding myself and thus unburden my mind, in order to refresh this narrative and loosen the bonds of my tongue. In the year 473 of the Jalali era, corresponding to the night of Sunday, the 6th of Muharram 958 of the lunar reckoning (14 January 1551), my pure spirit joined to this elemental body came forth from the womb into this fair expanse of the world. At a little over one year I had the miraculous gift of fluent speech and at five years of age I had acquired an unusual stock of information and could both read and write. At the age of seven I became the treasurer of my father's stores of knowledge and a trusty keeper of the jewels of hidden meaning and as a serpent, guarded the treasure. And it was strange that by a freak of fortune my heart was disinclined, my will ever averse, and my disposition repugnant to conventional learning and the ordinary courses of instruction. Generally I could not understand them. My father in his way conjured with the spell of knowledge and taught me a little of every branch of science, and although my intelligence grew, I gained no deep impressions from the school of learning. Sometimes I understood nothing at all, at others doubts suggested themselves which my tongue was incapable of explaining. Either shame made me hesitate or I had not the power of expression. I used to weep in public and put all the blame upon myself. In this state of things I came into fellowship of mind with a congenial helper and my spirit recovered from that ignorance and incomprehension. Not many days had elapsed before his conversation and society induced me to go to college and there they restored to rest my bewildered and dissipated mind and by the wondrous working of destiny they took me away and brought another back.

The temple as I entered, drew they nigh

And brought their gift, a wine-cup brimming high.

Its strength snatched all my senses, self from self,

Wherein some other entered and not I.

The truths of philosophy and the subtleties of the schools now appeared plain, and a book which I had never before seen gave me a clearer insight than any thing I could read. Although I had a special gift which came down upon me from the throne of holiness, yet the inspirations of my venerable father and his making me commit to memory the essential elements of every branch of science, together with the unbroken continuity of this chain, were of immense help, and became one of the most important causes of my enlightenment.

For ten years longer I made no distinction between night and day, teaching and learning, and recognized no difference between satiety and hunger, nor discriminated between privacy and society, nor had I the power to dissever pain from pleasure. I acknowledged nothing else but the bond of demonstration and the tie of knowledge. Those who had a regard for my constitution, from seeing that two and sometimes three days passed without my taking food, and that my studious spirit had no inclination therefore, were amazed, and stood out strongly against it.

I answered that my withdrawal, was now a matter of habit and custom, and how was it that no one was astonished when the natural inclination of a sick man on an attack of illness was averse from food. If therefore my love of study induced forgetfulness, where was the wonder? Most of the current arguments of the schools, frequently misquoted and misunderstood when heard, and abstruse questions from ancient works, had been presented to the fresh tablet of my mind.

Before these points had been elucidated and the attribution to me of extreme ignorance had passed to that of transcendent knowledge, I had taken objection to ancient writers, and men learning my youth, dissented, and my mind was troubled and my inexperienced heart was in agitation. Once in the early part of my career they brought the gloss of Khwajah Abul Qasim, on the Mutawwal. All that I had stated before learned doctors and divines of which some of my friends had taken notes, was there found, and those present were astounded and withdrew their dissent, and began to regard me with other eyes and to raise the wicket of misunderstanding and to open the gate of comprehension. In my early days of study, the gloss of Isfahani more than half of which had been eaten by white ants, came under my observation.

The public being in despair at profiting by it, I removed the parts that had been eaten and joined blank paper to the rest. In the serene hours of morning, with a little reflection, I discovered the beginnings and endings of each fragment and conjecturally penned a draft text which I transcribed on the paper. In the meanwhile the entire work was discovered, and when both were compared, in two or three places only were there found differences of words, though synonymous in meaning; and in three or four others, (differing) citations but approximate in sense. All were astounded.

The more my will was engaged, the more my mind was illumined. At the age of twenty the good tidings of my independence reached me. My mind cast off its former bonds and my early bewilderment recurred. With a parade of much learning, the intoxication of youth effervescing, the skirts of pretension spread wide, and the world-displaying cup of wisdom in my hand, the ringings of delirium began to sound in my ears, and suggested a total withdrawal from the world. Meanwhile the wise prince-regnant called me to mind and drew me from my obscurity, somewhat of which I have in its entirety and somewhat but approximately suggested and acknowledged. Here my coin has been tested and its full weight passed into currency. Men now view me with a different regard, and many effusive speeches have been made amid felicitous congratulations evoked.

On this day which is the last of the 42nd year of His Majesty's reign (A.D. 1598), my spirit again breaks away from its yoke and a new solicitude arises within me.

My songster heart knows not King David's strains:

Let it go free—'tis no bird for a cage.

I know not how it will all end nor in what resting-place my last journey will have to be made, but from the beginning of my existence until now the grace of God has continuousiy kept me under its protection. It is my firm hope that my last moments may be spent in doing His will and that I may pass unburdened to eternal rest.

Works

The Akbarnama: The Akbarnma, which literally means *Book of Akbar*, is a official biographical account of Akbar, the third Mughal Emperor (r. 1556–1605), written in Persian. It includes vivid and detailed descriptions of his life and times.

The work was commissioned by Akbar, and written by Abul Fazl, one of the *Nine Jewels* (Hindi: Navaratnas) of Akbar's royal court. It is stated that the book took seven years to be completed and the original manuscripts contained a number of paintings supporting the texts, and all the paintings represented the Mughal school of painting, and work of masters of the imperial workshop, including Basawan, whose use of portraiture in its illustrations was an innovation in Indian art.

Contents of the Volumes I and II

The Akbarnama consists of three volumes or parts. The first volume deals with the genealogy of the descendants of Timur, and detailed information from the birth of Akbar, his accession to the throne, and the first seventeen years of his reign. The second volume narrates the reign of Akbar from the eighteenth year of his reign to the forty sixth year of his reign. It stops there because Abul Fazl was assassinated at the order of Jahangir, Akbar's son and heir on August 12, 1602. The account of Akbar's reign from the 46th regnal year, where Abul Fazl's work stops till his death in October, 1605 was later added to the second volume by Inayat Ullah or Mohammad Salih. This work is known as *Takmil-i-Akbarnama*. This work omits many happenings between 1602 and 1605.

Besides recording Akbar's life and reign, the Akbarnâma also includes many descriptions of the social order of India. Both Abul Fazl and Akbar had very tolerant religious ideas, and Fazl used his writing to show Hinduism in a good light to the Muslims of the Mughal ruling class.

Volume III: The Ain-i-Akbari

The Ain-i-Akbari or the "Institutes of Akbar", is a 16th century, detailed document recording the administration of emperor Akbar's empire, written by his vizier, Abul-Fazl ibn Mubarak. It makes the Volume III and the final part of the much larger document, the Akbarnama, the Book of Akbar, also by Abul Fazl, and it itself is in three volumes.

Contents

The Ain-i-Akbari is the third volume of the Akbarnama contains information regarding Akbar's reign in the form of, what would be called in modern times, administration reports, statistical compilations, or gazetteers. It contains the ain (i.e., mode of governing) of Akbar, and is, in fact, the administration report and statistical Return of his government. The first volume of the

Akbarnama contains the history of Timur's family and the reigns of Babar, the Sur kings, and Humayun. The second volume is devoted to the detailed history of the nearly forty-six years of the Akbar's reign. Since it was written around 1590, it also contains details of Hindu beliefs and practices as well as a history of India.

The Ain-i-Akbari is itself divided into five books. The first book deals with the imperial household, and the second with the servants of the emperor, the military and civil services. The third book deals with the imperial administration, containing the regulations for the judicial and executive departments. The fourth book contains information about Hindu philosophy, science, social customs and literature. The fifth book contains sayings of Akbar, along with an account of the ancestry and biography of the author.

Translations

The original Persian text was translated into English in three volumes. The first volume, translated by H. Blochmann (1873) consisted of Books I and II. The second volume, translated by Colonel H.S. Jarrett (1891), consisted of Book III. The third volume, also translated by Colonel H.S. Jarrett (1896), consisted of Books IV and V. These three volumes were published by the Asiatic Society of Bengal, Calcutta as a part of their *Bibliotheca Indica* series.

The Akbarnama of Faizi Sirhindi

The *Akbarnama* of Shaikh Illahdad Faizi Sirhindi is another contemporary biography of the Mughal emperor Akbar. This work is mostly not original and basically a compilation from the *Tabaqat-i-Akbari* of Khwaja Nizam-ul-Mulk-ud-Din Ahmad and the more famous *Akbarnama* of Abul Fazl. The only original elements in this work are a few verses and some interesting stories. Very little is known about the writer of this *Akbarnama*. His father Mulla Ali Sher Sirhindi was a scholar and Khwaja Nizam-ul-Mulk-ud-Din Ahmad, the writer of the *Tabaqat-i-Akbari* was his student. He lived in Sirhind sarkar of Delhi Subah and held a *madad-i-ma'ash* (a land granted by the state for maintenance) village there. He accompanied his employer and patron Shaikh Farid Bokhari (who held the post of the *Bakhshi-ul-Mulk*) on his various services. His most important work is a dictionary, the *Madar-ul-Afazil,* completed in 1592. He started writing this *Akbarnama* at the age of 36 years. His work also ends in 1602 like the one of Abu'l Fazl. This work provides us some additional information regarding the services rendered by Shaikh Farid Bokhari. It also provides valuable information regarding the siege and capture of Asirgarh.

Ruqaat

The Ruqaat or the Ruqaat-i-Abul Fazl is a collection of private letters from Abu al-Fayl to Murad, Daniyal, Akbar, Mariam Makani, Salim (Jahangir), Akbar's queens and daughters, his father, mother and brothers and several other notable contemporaries compiled by his nephew Nur al-Din Mohammed.

Insha-i-Abul Fazl

The Insha-i-Abul Fazl or the Maqtubat-i-Allami contains the official despatches written by Abul Fazl. It is divided into two parts. The first part contains Akbar's letters to Abdullah Khan Uzbeg of Turan, Shah Abbas of Persia, Raja Ali Khan of Khandesh, Burhan-ul-Mulk of Ahmadnagar and his own nobles such as Abdur Rahim Khan Khanan. The second part consists Abul Fazl's letters to Akbar, Daniyal, Mirza Shah Rukh and Khan Khanan. This collection was compiled by Abd-us-samad, son of Afzal Mohammad, who claims that he was Abul Fazl's sister's son as well as his son-in-law.

Faizi (1547-1595)

Faizi (1547-1595) was the poet laureate of Akbar's Court. He was the brother of Akbar's historian Abul Fazl. He composed beautiful poetry in Persian and is estimated by his contemporaries to have composed nearly 100 poetic works. He wanted to produce a Panj Ganj (lit. five treasures) in imitation of the Persian poet Nezami, but died after writing only three out of the five works. Towards this end he wrote *Nal u Daman*, *Makhzan ul-advar*, and *Bilqis va Salman*. These were in imitation of Nezami's *Layla va Majnun*, *Makhzan ul-Asrar*, and *Shirin va Khusrau*, respectively. Akbar highly recognized the genius in him and appointed him teacher for his son and gave place to him among his decorative 'Nav Ratnas'. He also wrote a commentary on the Quran and translated *Lilavati*, a Sanskrit work on mathematics, into Persian. His father was Mubarak Nagori, a scholar in the philosophy and literature of Greece as well as in Islamic theology.

His brother Abul-Fazl about him

Of my eldest brother what shall I say? who notwithstanding his spiritual and worldly perfections, took no step without my concurrence, indiscreet as I am, and devoting himself to my interests, advanced my promotion and was an aid to good intentions.

In his poems he speaks of me in a manner which I cannot sufficiently acknowledge, as he says in his eulogium :

- My verse may share both great and little worth,
- Its theme sublime—I lowlier than the earth.
- A father's virtues shall it far proclaim
- And vaunt the glory of a brother's fame:
- He, touchstone of all wisdom, who inspires
- My strain with sweetness that a world admires;
- If through a riper age, I pass him by,
- In merit, centuries between us lie.
- What though the branching savin taller grows,
- What gardener mates its beauty with the rose?

He was born in the Jalali year 469, corresponding to A.H. 954 (A.D. 1547). In what tongue shall I indict his praise? In this work I have already written of him and poured forth the anguish of my heart, and quenched its furnace with the water of narration and broken the dam of its torrents and alleviated my want of resignation. His works which are the scales of eloquence and penetration and the lawns of the birds of song, praise him and speak his perfections and recall his virtues.

Mian Tansen

Miyan Tansen or Ramtanu Pandey (1493 or 1506 – 1586 or 1589) is considered among the greatest composer-musicians in Hindustani classical music. He was an extraordinarily gifted vocalist, known for a large number of compositions, and also an instrumentalist who popularized and improved the rabab (of Central Asian origin).

He was among the Navaratnas (nine jewels) at the court of the Mughal Emperor Akbar. Akbar gave him the title *Miyan* (an honorific, meaning learned man).

Early Life and Background

Tansen as a historical personality is difficult to extract from the extensive legend that surrounds him. It is reasonably certain that he was born into a Hindu Brahmin family, possibly in 1506, though some legends give it as 1493; possibly in the village Behat near Gwalior. His father Mukund Mishra was a poet and accomplished musician, who for some time was a temple priest in Varanasi. Tansen's name as a child was Ramtanu (he may have had other nicknames/names like Tanna and Mukul).

He was born at a time when a number of Persian and Central Asian motifs were fusing with Indian classical music, his influence was central to creating the Hindustani classical ethos as we know today. A number of descendants and disciples have also considerably enriched the tradition. Almost all gharanas of Hindustani classical music claim some connection with the Tansen lineage. Tansen later converted to Islam from Hinduism.

According to legend, he was noted for his imitations of animal calls and birdsong.

Career

At some point, he was discipled for some time to Swami Haridas, the legendary composer from Vrindavan and part of the stellar Gwalior court of Raja Mansingh Tomar (1486-1516 AD), specializing in the dhrupad style of singing. One legend has that Haridas was passing through the forests when the five-year old Ramtanu's imitation of a tiger impressed the musician saint. Another version is that his father sent him to Haridas. From Haridas, Tansen acquired not only his love for dhrupad but also his interest in compositions in the local language. This was the time when the Bhakti tradition was fomenting a shift from Sanskrit to the local idiom (Brajbhasa and Hindi), and Tansen's compositions also highlight this trend. At some point during his apprenticeship, Tansen's father died, and he returned home, where it is said he used to sing at a local Shiva temple.

In any event, Tansen went to Mohammad Ghaus who eventually became his spiritual mentor. He also married Husseini (lit. *beautiful one*),

> *"However, beyond a reference of Tansen's name in a list of his disciples Miyan Tansen's name is found among the names of*

the Mureeds (Fans) of the Shuttari Tariqat-a Sufi spiritual lineage founded by Shaykh Mohammad Ghaus of Gwalior."

The burial of Tansen in his shaykh's mausoleum is thought to indicate proof of his conversion to the faith of his spiritual guide. Usually, the most prominent disciples of a saint are buried near the master's mausoleum, not much historical detail is known about their actual encounter.

The interaction with Ghaus in the Sufi tradition and the earlier training with Swami Haridas in the Bhakti tradition led to a fusion of these streams in the work of Tansen. As it is, the mystic streams of Sufism and Bhakti had considerable philosophical and stylistic overlap; Ghaus in his text *Bahr-ul-Hayat* (Ocean of Life) devotes several chapters to Yoga practices. In Tansen's music, we find he continues to compose in Brajbhasha invoking traditional motifs such as Krishna or Shiva.

Tansen was also influenced by other singers in the Gwalior court and also the musically proficient queen, Mriganayani (lit. *doe-eyed*), whose romance with the king had been forged on her singing; she remained a friend even after the death of the king. Other musicians at Gwalior may have included Baiju Bawra.

Eventually, he joined the court of King Ramachandra Baghela of Rewa, India, where he remained from 1555-1562. It appears that the Mughal emperor Akbar heard of his prowess and sent his emissary Jalaluddin Qurchi to Ramachandra, who had little choice but to acquiesce, and Tansen went to Akbar's court in 1562.

Another legend is that Akbar's daughter Meherunnissa was enamoured by Tansen and had a role in his coming to Akbar's court.

Tansen joined Akbar's court eventually becoming one of the treasured Navaratnas (lit. *nava*=nine, *ratna*=jewel) of his court. It was Akbar who gave him the honorific title *Miyan*, and he is usually referred to today as Miyan Tansen. Legend has it that in his first performance, he was gifted one lakh (100,000) gold coins.

The presence of musicians like Tansen in Akbar's court has been related by historians to the theoretical position of making the empire's audible presence felt among the population, a mechanism related to *Naubat* or ritual performance.

The fort at Fatehpur Sikri is strongly associated with Tansen's tenure at Akbar's court. Near the emperor's chambers, a pond was built with a small island in the middle, where musical performances were given. Today, this tank, called *Anup Talao*, can be seen near the public audience hall *Diwan-i-Aam*-a central platform reachable via four footbridges. It is said that Tansen would perform different ragas at different times of day, and the emperor and his select audience would honour him with coins.

Family

Tanras Khan, Bilas Khan, Hamirsen, Suratsen and Saraswati Devi, all musicians. Bilas Khan is said to have created raga Bilaskhani Todi after Tansen's death; an interesting legend of this improvisation (it differs only in detail from Tansen's Todi), has it that Bilas composed it while grief-stricken at the wake itself, and that Tansen's corpse moved one hand in approval of the new melody.

Tansen's blood descendants – the Senia gharana-held considerable prestige in musical circles for several centuries. The royal courts of Rewa, India, Rampur and Jaipur among others, retained many noted members of Tansen lineage, including Nayak Wazir Khan (guru of Allauddin Khan) and Mohammed Ali Khan. Wazir Khan, who is of Saraswati Devi lineage, was also a musicologist who wrote the *Risala Mousibi*. One of the last of the line, Dr Dabir Khan, (1905-1972, Saraswati Devi lineage) was a dhrupadiya and a beenkar, at Radio Calcutta.

Musical Legacy

The legendary musical prowess of Tansen surpasses all other legends in Indian music. In terms of influence, he can be compared only to the prolific sufi composer Amir Khusro (1253-1325), or to bhakti tradition composers such as Kabir or Haridas. The Indian sitar is said to have been invented by Amir Khusro (1253-1325), a devotee of the Chistiyya order, after the Persian 'Setar', from the saz group of musical instruments

Several of his raga compositions have become mainstays of the Hindustani tradition, and these are often prefaced with *Miyan ki* ("of the Miyan"), e.g. Miyan ki Todi, Miyan ki Malhar, Miyan ki Mand, Miyan ka Sarang; in addition he is the creator of major ragas like Darbari Kanada, Darbari Todi, and Rageshwari.

Tansen also authored *Sangeeta Sara* and *Rajmala* which constitute important documents on music.

Almost every gharana (school) tries to trace its origin to him, though some try to go further back to Amir Khusro. As for the Dhrupad style of singing, this was formalized essentially through the practice by composers like Tansen and Haridas, as well as others like Baiju Bawra who may have been a contemporary.

After Tansen, some of the ideas from the rabab were fused with the traditional Indian stringed instrument, veena; one of the results of this fusion is the instrument sarod, which does not have frets and is popular today because of its perceived closeness to the vocal style.

The famous qawwals, the Sabri Brothers claim lineage from Miyan Tansen

Legends

The bulk of Tansen's biography as it is handed down in the musical literature consists of legends.

Among the legends about Tansen are stories of his bringing down the rains with Raga Megh Malhar and starting fires with the legendary raga Deepak. Other legends tell of his ability to bring wild animals to listen with attention (or to talk their language). Once, a wild white elephant was captured, but it was fierce and could not be tamed. Finally, Tansen sang to the elephant who calmed down and the emperor was able to ride him.

Many aficionados are convinced that his death was caused by a conflagration while he was singing the raga Deepak.

Death

According to one version of the story, Tansen died on 26 April 1586, and that Akbar and much of his court attended the funeral procession. Other versions give 1589 as the year of his death. Tansen was buried in the mausoleum complex of his Sufi guru Shaikh Mohammad Ghaus in Gwalior. According to legend, Tansen's son Bilas Khan, in his grief, composed Bilaskhani Todi.

Every year in December, an annual festival, the *Tansen Samaroh*, is held in Gwalior to celebrate Tansen.

Birbal (1528-1583)

Raja Birbal (1528-1586) (real name: Maheshdas Bhat) was the Grand Vizier (Wazir-e Azam) of the Mughal court in the administration of the Mughal emperor Akbar and one of his most trusted members along with being a part of Akbar's inner council of nine advisors, known as the *navaratna*, a Sanskrit word meaning nine jewels. He was the only person other than Akbar who was a Din-i-Ilahi believer.

Birbal's duties in Akbar's court were mostly military and administrative but he was also a very close friend of the emperor, who liked Birbal most for his wit and wisdom, as a result of which they frequently had witty and humorous exchanges between them. These exchanges and stories have become part of a rich tradition of folklore and legend.

Early Years

Born Mahesh Das in 1528 in the village Ghoghara of Sihawal tehsil in Sindhi district of Madhya Pradesh, abrahmin by birth. Birbal grew up in a Brahmana household, educated but impoverished. He was a poet and author whose wit and wisdom led the Emperor Akbar to invite him to be a part of the royal court and to bestow upon him a new name-Birbal (Bir means Brain, Bal means Strong). Akbar also conferred on him the title of *Raja*.

Meeting with Sikh Guru

According to Giani Gian Singh, The author of the Book Twarikh Guru Khalsa in 1626, Raja Birbal met Guru Amar Das, the third guru of Sikhism. He and his army had their meals in the Langar, when some unscrupulous individual told him that Guru Amar Das had a precious rasayana (a rejuvenating ointment that promised eternal youth according to Ayurveda's Bhoota Vidya). He demanded this rasayana from Guru Amar Das. But Guru Amar Das replied *God's name is the true rasayana and this rasayana is only gifted to the previous Gurus.*

Birbal did not believe him and instead got angry. He said that he would take the rasayana the next day but at night. However, he had orders to reach Malandri (Muhim) the next day. Abandoning his plans for the rasayana, he journeyed onward.

Death

Raja Birbal died in the battle of Malandari Pass, attempting to quell unrest amongst Afghan or Pashtun tribes in Northwest India. Akbar was said to have mourned for a long time on hearing the news. The death was said to be caused by treachery, not military defeat. Sanchit Fazal killed Birbal because of his close relationship with Akbar. A quote from Birbal's last wish was that upon his (Birbal) death, his ashes be immersed in the River Ganges at Haridwar, but Akbar did not grant this wish and instead he had a well dug, near the river and buried his ashes there. (Location: Thanda kua near Harki Pauri, Haridwar)

Raja Todar Mal

Raja Todar Mal was born at Lahore. He rose to become the Finance Minister in Akbar's Darbar. Todar Mal overhauled the revenue system of Akbar's Mughal empire. Perhaps he was from the Khatri (or Khattri/Khattree) community of Punjab but some consider him to be belonging to Kayastha community. That he was a Khatri and not a Kayastha is also supported by the fact (as found in his many paintings) that he wore a sacred thread (Yagnopavit), which is traditionally worn only by Brahmins, Kshatriya and Kharis but not Kayasthas. It is also well known that Kayastha community is a sub sector of Brahmins and most of them wore sacred thread (Yagnopavit) also so it is very difficult to identify his caste. Todar Mal had developed his expertise in Sher Shah's employ.

Todar Mal as a soldier

Todar Mal is recognized as an able warrior, and lead in various battles.

> *"In 971, he was employed under Muzaffar (9Bad.1165) and in 972, he served under Akbar against Khan Zaman (vide no 61). "*

> *"In the 19th year, after the conquest of Patna, he got an Salam and naqqara (Ain 19) and was ordered to accompany Munsim Khan to Bengal. He was the soul of the expedition. In the battle with Daud Khan-i-Kharani, when Khan Alam (vide No.58) had been killed, and Munsim Khan 's horse had run away, the Raja held his ground bravely, and 'not only was there no defeat but an actual vbictory " What harm* said Todar Mal, *if Khan Alam is dead ;what fear if the Khan Khanan's horse has run away, the empire is ours ! "*

Todar Mal as a Finance Minister of Akbar

Todar Mal succeeded Khwaja Malik Itimad Khan in 1560. Raja Todar Mal introduced standard weights and measures, a land survey and settlement system, revenue districts and officers. He can be thought of one of first statisticians in India and perhaps in the world. Many of the fundamental data collection schemes as practiced over the centuries in the Indian subcontinent and neighboring countries can be attributed to him.

In 1582, Akbar bestowed on Raja Todar Mal the title, *Diwan-I-Ashraf*. His systematic land reforms of 1582, popularly known as the Bandobast System, provided the framework of subsequent land taxation systems, including that introduced by Thomas Munro. India travelogue Impressions of India: Kashi Viswanath

Todar Mal died in Lahore on 8th November, 1589.

Todar Mal is also featured in the video game Sid Meier's Civilization 4: Beyond the Sword as a "great merchant" available in the game.

Raja Man Singh

Raja Shri Man Singh Ji Saheb (Man Singh I) (May 9, 1540-July 6, 1614) was the Kacchwaha Rajah Saheb of Amber, a state later known as Jaipur. He was a trusted general of the Mughal emperor Akbar, who included him among the Navaratnas, or the nine gems of the royal court. However, he was a devotee of Shri Krishna, and not an adherent of Akbar's religion, Din-i-Ilahi.

Early Life

He was the son of Rani Sa Bhagawati Ji Sahiba at Amber; his father was Raja Bhagwant Das of Amber. He was born on Sunday, December 21, 1550. He was about eight years younger than Mughal Emperor Akbar who was born on November 23, 1542 and about ten years younger than Rana Pratap who was born on May 9, 1540, These three great personalities, of the same generation, had a great impact on sixteenth century India's polity, society, and history. They are remembered with reverence in India, although Rana Pratap fought unrelenting wars with both of them. Raja Bharmal, the first Rajput ruler to marry his daughter to a Mughal, was Man Singh I's grandfather.

Initially known as *Kunwar* (prince), Man Singh received the title of *Mirza Raja* and the *mansab* (rank) of 5000 after the death of his father on December 10, 1589 from Akbar. On August 26, 1605, Man Singh became a mansabdar of 7,000, i.e., a commander of 7,000 cavalry in the Mughal forces, which was the maximum command for anyone other than a son of the Mughal emperor and the guardian of Khusrau, the eldest son of Jahangir. Akbar called him "Farzand" (son). He fought many important campaigns for Akbar. Kunwar Man Singh led the Mughal army in the well-known battle of Haldighati fought in 1576 between the Mughal Empire and Maharana Pratap.

Conflict with Rana Pratap

Man Singh was sent by Akbar to persuade Rana Pratap to make a treaty with Akbar and accept Mughal sovereignty. But Rana Pratap, as a grandson of Rana Sanga, considered the Mughals invaders and intruders on Indian territory; he declined to accept Akbar's sovereignty. The great grandfather of Man Singh, Raja Prithviraj, was married to Rana Sanga's niece (Raṇa Raimal's daughter). Thus Rana Pratap was his relative.

On the day of their meeting Rana Pratap invited Man Singh for dinner. Rana Pratap deliberately avoided attending the dinner in person and sent his son "Kunwar" Amar Singh to dine with "Kunwar" Man Singh (as a custom Rajput men are called "Kunwar" in the life time of their father). The attitude of other Rajput nobles was also discouraging. They were secretly making mockery of Man Singh as his aunt Hira kunwar or Jodhabai was married to Akbar. Man Singh took this as an insult to Akbar and himself. He knew Rana Pratap was making an excuse to avoid him. He refused to dine with Amar Singh. He remarked, "I will come again and then will have a dinner". Understanding the hidden meaning a noble of Pratap remarked "well, don't forget to bring your uncle Akbar". This laid the foundation of war between the Mughals and Rana Pratap, who already had many decades of rivalry and enmity.

Appointed by Akbar to lead the Mughal Army against Rana Pratap, Kunwar Man Singh started from Ajmer on 3 April 1576. A gruesome battle was fought on June 18, 1576 at Haldi Ghati. Rana Pratap personally attacked Man Singh, who defended himself by ducking. Man Singh's "Mahout" (the driver of his elephant) was killed. Rana Pratap's famous warhorse "Chetak" was mortally wounded. Rana Pratap, himself, amazingly survived this battle. A nobleman, Jhala Man Singh, who pretended to be Rana Pratap, was killed by the Mughal forces. Jhala Man Singh put the helmet of Rana Pratap on his head, though he knew he would be killed soon by doing this. Ultimately, the Mughal army won the battle. The next day Man Singh advanced and captured Gogunda, the seat of Pratap's coronation. But the geographical situation of Mewar was such that Rana Pratap could hide between hills. He exploited this and began guerrilla warfare. Ultimately Pratap was able to liberate all of Mewar except the fort of Chittor. Despite his success Akbar was not happy with Man Singh, and stopped conversing with him for some time. Perhaps he thought Man Singh was responsible for Pratap's escape from the battlefield. Conspirators also fed this to his ears, but Akbar's doubts cleared when he visited Ajmer's shrine of Khwaja Moinuddin Chishti the following year.

In the Battle of Haldighati, despite exaggerated figures, it is estimated that Rana Pratap had 3,000 horsemen, some elephants and the same number of Bhil warriors under Rao Poonja or Rana Poonja. A small artillery unit was also with him under Hakim Khan Sur. The force was divided into five wings. Advance wing was under Hakim Khan Sur, Bhim Singh Dodiya, and Ramdas Rathore. The right wing was under Bhamashah and Ramshah Tanwar. The left wing was under Jhala Man Singh. Rana Pratap was in the centre. Behind him was Rao Poonja with his Bhil warriors.

The Mughal army had 10,000 horsemen, some elephants and infantry. Among the horsemen 4,000 were Kachwaha Rajput warriors. One thousand other Hindu warriors and rest were Uzbeks, Turks, Kazzakhs, Saiyads and other Muslims. This force divided into five wings. There were two advance wings. The first was under Sayyad Hashim Barah Jagganath Kachwaha and Asaf Ali Khan. The second advance troop was under Madho Singh Kachwaha. Behind this was Man Singh. To his right was Mulla Kazikhan Badkhsi and to left were Sayyads of Barah. At first Rana Pratap attacked and scattered the advance and left wings of the Mughal army. Jagnnath Kachwaha killed Ramshah Tanwar. Rajput warriors of both sides engaged in fierce battle. The Mughal army could not distinguish between friend and foe and killed Rajputs of both sides. The Mughal army surrounded Rana Pratap; so to save his life Jhala Man put the Rana's helmet on his head and died in his place. This provided Rana Pratap a chance to escape. After this, Rana's army dispersed. The Mughal Army, expecting another attack, remained vigilant all night. Only in the morning they were able to judge their success. Almost half of Rana's army was finished. The battle was won but the Rana had survived.

Expedition to Kabul

In 1580 CE some prominent Muslim officers of Akbar, displeased with his liberal religious policies, started to conspire against him. One Qazi Mohammad Yazdi declared it the duty of every Muslim to rebel against Akbar. In Bihar and Bengal they declared Mirza Hakim, Akbar's stepbrother and Governor of Kabul, to be the emperor. Akbar sent armies to Bihar and Bengal to crush this rebellion, while he himself started towards Kabul; Man Singh was with him. On March 8, 1581 Akbar reached Macchiwara and soon arrived on the banks of river Indus. Here he sent an advance force led by Man Singh to Kabul.

Although Akbar's army was hesitating to cross the swelling Indus River, Man Singh was able to cross it first followed by troops. Hearing the news Mirza Hakim fled to Gurband. Following the army, Akbar himself arrived at Kabul on August 10, 1581. Hakim was pardoned by Akbar but his sister "Bakhtunissa Begum" was appointed Governor of Kabul. Akbar returned to Fatehpur Sikri. After the return of Akbar, Bakhtunissa remained as the nominal head of state while Hakim acted as the Governor in fact. Hakim died in July, 1582. Kabul was annexed by the Mughal Empire and Man Singh was appointed Governor. He remained there for some years and built a fortress there, used by succeeding Mughal Governors. Man Singh brought many talented men with him when he returned from Kabul. Some of their descendants still live in Jaipur.

Again in 1585 CE some Afghan tribes rose against the Mughal empire. The "Yusufzai" and "Mandar" tribes were the main ones among them. Akbar sent an army under Zain Khan, Hakim Abul Fateh and Raja Birbal to control these revolting tribes. However they failed to control the revolting Afghans and Raja Birbal, friend of Akbar and one of his Navratnas was also killed in the battle with Afghans. Akbar then sent Raja Todar Mal to crush the revolt and called Raja Man Singh to help Todar Mal. Todarmal had some success in controlling the rebellious Afghan tribes. But the real source of the revolt was behind the Khyber Pass. It was hard to cross this pass which was dominated by Afghan "Kabailies". Man Singh was accompanied by "Rao Gopaldas" of Nindar in this expedition, who bravely made way for Mughal army in the pass. After crossing the pass Man Singh decisively defeated five Major tribes of Afghans including "Yusufzai" and "Mandar" tribes. The flag of Amber was changed from "Katchanar" (green climber in white base) to "Pachranga" (five coloured) to commemorate this victory. This flag continued in use until accession of Jaipur state in India. This permanently crushed the revolt and the area remained peaceful thereafter.

In 1586 CE Akbar sent another army under Raja Bhagwant Das, father of Kunwar Man Singh to win Kashmir. Kashmir was included in the Mughal Empire and made a Sarkar (district) of Kabul province. Man Singh and his father Raja Bhagwant Das are reputed to have brought the technology of cannon production from Kabul and Lahore to Amber.

Conquest of Orissa

In 1588 Man Singh was appointed Governor of Bihar. In 1590, "Qatlu Khan Lohani" of Orissa declared himself independent and assumed the name of "Qatlu Shah". Raja Man Singh started an expedition against him. Before facing Man Singh, Qatlu Shah was killed by Rao Gopaldas of Nindar. Qatlu Khan's son Nasir Khan, after little resistance, accepted Mughal sovereignty. Nasir Khan was then appointed Governor of Orissa. Nasir Khan remained faithful to the Mughal empire for two years but after that he violated the conditions of his treaty and seized the Jagannath temple of Puri, which was Mughal territory. Man Singh again attacked Orissa and decisively defeated Nasir Khan on April 9, 1592 in a battle near the present day Medinipur town and ousted him from Orissa. Orissa then was annexed to the Mughal Empire and included in Bengal "Subah" (Province).

Governor of Bengal, Bihar, and Orissa

On March 17, 1594 Raja Man Singh was appointed Subahdar (Governor) of Bengal, Bihar, and Orissa. He made his headquarters in Rohtas, in Bihar. He built a Haveli (Palatial House) in Rohtas Fort. During his tenure as Governor Man Singh further expanded the Mughal Empire by defeating and subduing the old kingdoms of Bengal, Bihar and Orissa. He defeated the Raja of Jessore, now part of Bangladesh, and brought the famous idol of "Shila Devi" to Amber. The temple of this goddess is still present in Amber fort. During Navratris lakhs of people gather here. Raja Man Singh served three successive terms as Governor of this area, in 1594-98, 1601-1605, 1605-1606.

Jahangir and Twilight of Man Singh I

Prince Salim was born after many prayers. But he soon became addicted to alcohol and opium. He disobeyed royal orders and became infamous for torture. He had Abul Fazal murdered. Akbar tried hard to reform him. Salim had a son, Khusrau. Two of Akbar's sons, Murad and Danial, died in his lifetime. The royal court was divided into two factions, one favouring Khusrau and the other Salim to be the next emperor. Raja Man Singh and Mirza Ajij Koka were in Khusrau's favour. In 1605, when Akbar fell ill, he appointed Salim to be his heir. Though Man Singh opposed Salim's accession to the throne during Akbar's lifetime, he never opposed Jahangir after his coronation. After Akbar's death, Jahangir (Salim) became emperor. Man Singh was initially sent as Subahdar of Bengal on November 10, 1605 for a short period, but soon he was replaced by Qutb-ud-Din Khan Koka on September 2, 1606. Jahangir also ordered removal of some of the modifications which had been made by Raja Man Singh to his palace at Amber. But in 1611 CE the southern provinces of Ahmad Nagar, Berar and Khandesh defied Mughal sovereignty under Malik Ambar. Jahangir sent Raja Man Singh and others to crush the revolt.

Man Singh died a natural death on July 6, 1614 at Ellichpur. Following his death, he was succeeded by his son Mirza Raja Bhau Singh. His direct descendants became known (to this date) as the Rajawats who had the privilege to the Gaddi (throne) of Amber and subsequently Jaipur.

Cultural Achievements

Raja Man Singh was a devotee of Shri Krishna. He had a seven-storey temple of Krishna constructed at for Srila Rupa Goswami, disciple of Sri Caitanya Mahaprabhu, in Vrindavan. The cost of construction was one crore rupees at that time. Akbar is also believed to have donated the red sandstone for this temple. Aurangzeb later demolished three storeys of this temple. The four-storey temple is still present at Vrindavan. He also constructed a temple of Krishna at his capital, Amber. The place is now known as "Kanak Vrindavan" near Amber Ghati of Jaipur. He constructed the temple of Shila Devi at Amber Fort. He also constructed and repaired many temples at Benaras, Allahabad and various other places. He added much beautification to his palace at Amber. When Akbar called a meeting of his nobles at Fatehpur Sikri in

1582, to discuss Din-i-Ilahi, Raja Bhagwant Das was the only man to oppose this religion. Later Man Singh also refused to convert to Din-i-Ilahi. It is believed his son Jagat Singh I received education from Goswami Tulsidas and Man Singh himself used to attend his religious lectures. Tulsidas was a contemporary of Akbar and author of Ramcharit Manas, known as Tulsi Ramayana, and much other famous poetry devoted to Rama and Hanuman. He used to be accompanied by Charan poets.

Abdul Rahim Khan-i-Khan

Abdul Rahim Khan-e-Khana also known as Rahim was a composer in the times of Mughal emperor Akbar, and one of his main nine ministers (Diwan) in his court, also known as the Navaratnas; he is most known for his Hindi couplets and his books on Astrology.

The village of Khankhana, named after him, is located in the Nawanshahr district of the state of Punjab in northwest India.

Biography

Mirza Abdul Rahim Khan-i-Khana was the son of Akbar's trusted caretaker, Bairam Khan who had Turk ancestry. When Humayun returned to India, from his exile, he is asked the nobles in court to forge matrimonial alliances with various zamindars, feudal lords, across the nation. While Humayun himself married the elder daughter of Jamal Khan of Mewat (present Mewat district of Haryana), he asked Bairam to marry the younger daughter.

Abdul Rahim was born in Lahore (now in Pakistan) on 14th Cafar 964.

After Bairam Khan was murdered in Patan, Gujarat, his wife and young Rahim were brought safely to Ahmedabad, from they brought to Delhi and presented to the royal courts of Akbar, who gave him the title of 'Mirza Khan', and subsequently married him to Mah Banu, sister of Mirza Aziz Kokah, son of Ataga Khan, a noted Mughal noble. Later, Bairam Khan's wife became the second wife of Akbar, which made Abdul Rahim Khan-e-Khan his stepson, and later he became one of his nine prominent ministers, the Navaratnas, or nine gems.

Although a Muslim by birth, Rahim was a devotee of Lord Krishna and wrote poetry dedicated to him. He was also an avid

Astrolger, and the writer if two important works in Astrology Khet Kautukam and Dwawishd Yogavali are still popular.

He is well known for his strange manner of giving alms to the poor. He never looked at the person he was giving alms to, keeping his gaze downwards in all humility. When Tulsidas heard about Rahim's strange method of giving alms, he promptly wrote a couplet and sent it to Rahim:-

> *"Sir, Why give alms like this? Where'd you learn that?, Your hands are as high as your eyes are low"*

Realizing that Tulsidas was well aware of the truth behind creation, and was merely giving him an opportunity to say a few lines in reply, he wrote to Tulsidas in all humility:-

> *"The Giver is someone else, giving day and night. So they won't give me the credit, I lower my eyes."*

His two sons were killed by Akbar's son Jehangir and their bodies left to rot at the Khooni Darwaza because Rahim was not in favour of Jehangir's accession to the throne at Akbar's death.

His tomb is situated in Nizamuddin on the Mathura Road ahead of Humayun's Tomb in New Delhi, it was built by him for his wife in 1598, and later he was himself buried in it in 1627. Later, in 1753-4, marble and sandstone from this tomb was used for the making of Safdarjung's Tomb, also in New Delhi.

Major Works

Apart from writing various *dohas*, Rahim translated Babar's memoirs, *Baburnama* from Chagatai language to Persian language, which was completed in AH 998 (1589-90). His command over Sanskrit was very good. He wrote two books on Astrology, *Kheta Kautukama* and *Dwawishd Yogavali.*

4

Jahangir

Nur-ud-din Salim Jahangir (full title: *Al-Sultan al-Azam wal Khaqan al-Mukarram, Khushru-i-Giti Panah, Abul-Fath Nur-ud-din Mohammad Jahangir Padshah Ghazi [Jannat-Makaani]*) (September 20, 1569 – November 8, 1627) (OS August 31, 1569 – NS November 8, 1627) was the ruler of the Mughal Empire from 1605 until his death. The name Jahangir is from Persian Acoin, meaning "Conqueror of the World". Nur-ud-din or Nur al-Din is an Arabic name which means " Light of the Faith."

Born as Prince Mohammad Salim, he was the third and eldest surviving son of Mughal Emperor Akbar. Akbar's twin sons, Hasan and Hussain, died in infancy. His mother was the Rajput Princess of Amber, Jodhabai (born Rajkumari Hira Kunwari, eldest daughter of Raja Bihar Mal or Bharmal, Raja of Amber, India).

Jahangir was a child of many prayers. It is said to be by the blessing of Shaikh Salim Chishti (one of the revered sages of his times) that Akbar's first surviving child, the future Jahangir, was born. He was born at the dargah of the Shaikh Salim Chishti, within the fortress at Fatehpur Sikri near Agra. The child was named Salim after the darvesh and was affectionately addressed by Akbar as Sheikhu Baba.

Akbar developed an emotional attachment with the village Sikri (abode of Chishti). Therefore, he developed the town of Sikri and shifted his imperial court and residence from Agra to Sikri, later renamed as Fatehpur Sikri. Shaikh Salim Chishti's daughter was appointed Jahangir's foster mother as a mark of respect to the Shaikh. Jahangir's foster brother Nawab Kutb-ud-din Khan was private secretary to the emperor Jahangir and afterwards governor of Bengal. Nawab Kutb-ud-din Khan's son Nawab Mohtashim. Khan was granted by Jahangir 4,000 bigas of land in Badaun District (United Provinces) where he built a small fort named Sheikhupur, Badaun after Jahangir, who was caned Sheikhu-baba in his childhood.

Revolt

In 1600, when Akbar was away from the capital on an expedition, Salim broke into an open rebellion, and declared himself Emperor. Akbar had to hastily return to Agra and restore order. There was a time when Akbar thought of putting Khusraw on the throne instead of Salim. Prince Salim forcefully succeeded to the throne on November 3, 1605, eight days after his father's death. Salim ascended to the throne with the title of Nur-ud-din Mohammad Jahangir Badshah Ghazi, and thus began his 22-year reign at the age of 36. Jahangir soon after had to fend off his son, Prince Khusraw, when he attempted to claim the throne based on Akbar's will to become his next heir. Khusraw was defeated in 1606 and confined in the fort of Agra. As punishment Khusraw was blinded, and the Sikh Guru Arjun (the religious spiritual head of the sect at the time) was put to death, for giving the then fugitive Khusraw money when he visited Guru Arjun. Jahangir's rule was characterized by the same religious tolerance as his father Akbar, with the exception of his hostility with the Sikhs, which was forged so early on in his rule.

In 1622, Khurram (Shah Jahan), younger brother of Khusraw, had Khusraw murdered in a conspiracy to eliminate all possible contenders to the throne. Taking advantage of this internal conflict, the Persians seized the city of Qandahar and as a result of this loss, the Mughals lost control over the trade routes to Afghanistan, Persian and Central Asia and also exposed India to invasions from the north-west.

Reign

An aesthete, Jahangir decided to start his reign with a grand display of "Justice", as he saw it. To this end, he enacted Twelve Decrees that are remarkable for their liberalism and foresight. During his reign, there was a significant increase in the size of the Mughal Empire, half a dozen rebellions were crushed, prisoners of war were released, and the work of his father, Akbar, continued to flourish. Much like his father, Jahangir was dedicated to the expansion of Mughal held territory through conquest. During this regime he would target the peoples of Assam near the eastern frontier and bring a series of territories controlled by independent rajas in the Himalayan foothills from Kashmir to Bengal. Jahangir would challenge the hegemonic claim over Persia by the Safavid rulers with an eye on Kabul, Peshawar and Qandahar which were important centers of the central Asian trade system that northern India operated within. In 1622 Jahangir would send his son Prince Khurram against the combined forces of Ahmednagar, Bijapur and Golconda. After his victory Khurram would turn against his father and make a bid for power. As with the insurrection of his eldest son Khusraw, Jahangir was able to defeat the challenge from within his family and retain power.

Jahangir promised to protect Islam and granted general amnesty to his opponents. He was also notable for his patronage of the arts, especially of painting. During his reign the distinctive style of Mughal painting expanded and blossomed. Jahangir supported a flourishing culture of court painters.

Jahangir is most famous for his golden "chain of justice." The chain was setup as a link between his people and Jahangir himself. Standing outside the castle of Agra with sixty bells, anyone was capable of pulling the chain and having a personal hearing from Jahangir himself.

Furthermore, Jahangir preserved the Mughal tradition of having a highly centralized form of government. The son of a Hindu Rajput mother who converted to Islam, Jahangir made the precepts of Sunni Islam the cornerstone of his state policies. A faithful Muslim, as evidenced by his memoirs, he expressed his gratitude to Allah for his many victories. Jahangir, as a devout Muslim, did not let his personal beliefs dictate his state policies. Sovereignty, according to Jahangir, was a "gift of God" not necessarily given to enforce God's law but rather to "ensure the contentment of the world." In civil cases, Islamic law applied to Muslims, Hindu law applied to Hindus, while criminal law was the same for both Muslims and Hindus. In matters like marriage and inheritance, both communities had their own laws that Jahangir respected. Thus Jahangir was able to deliver justice to people in accordance of their beliefs, and also keep his hold on empire by unified criminal law. In the Mughal state, therefore, defiance of imperial authority, whether coming from a prince or anyone else aspiring to political power, or a Muslim or a Hindu, was crushed in the name of law and order.

Jahangir's relationship with other rulers of the time is one that was well documented by Sir Thomas Roe, especially his relationship with the Persian King, Shah Abbas. Though conquest was one of Jahangir's many goals, he was a naturalist and lover of the arts and did not have quite the same warrior ambition of the Persian king. This led to a mutual enmity that, while diplomatically hidden, was very clear to observers within Jahangir's court. Furthermore, Abbas had, for many years, been trying to recover the city of Kandahar, which Jahangir was not keen to part with, especially to this king whom he did not particularly care for, despite seeing him as an equal.

In this state, Jahangir was also open to the influence of his wives, a weakness exploited by many. Because of this constant inebriated state, Nur Jahan, the favourite wife of Jahangir, became the actual power behind the throne.

Marriage

Salim was made a Mansabdar of ten thousand (Das-Hazari), the highest military rank of the empire, after the emperor. He independently commanded a regiment in the Kabul campaign of 1581, when he was barely twelve. His Mansab was raised to Twelve Thousand, in 1585, at the time of his betrothal to his cousin Manbhawati Bai, daughter of Bhagwan Das of Amber. Raja Bhagwant Das, was the son of Raja Bharmal and the brother of Akbar's wife Rajkumari Hira Kunwari, also known as Mariam Zamani.

The marriage with Manbhawati Bai took place on February 13, 1585. Manbhawati gave birth to Khusrau Mirza. Thereafter, Salim was allowed to marry, in quick succession, a number of accomplished girls from the aristocratic Mughal and Rajput families. One of his favourite wives was a Rajput Princess, known as Jagat Gosain and Princess Manmati, who gave birth to Prince Khurram, the future Shah Jahan, Jahangir's successor to the throne. The total number of wives in his harem was more than eight hundred.

Jahangir married the extremely beautiful and intelligent Mehr-ul-Nisa (better known by her subsequent title of Nur Jahan), in May 1611. She was the widow of Sher Afghan. She was witty, intelligent and beautiful, which was what attracted Jahangir to her. Before being awarded the title of Nur Jahan ('Light of the World'), she was called Nur Mahal ('Light of the Palace'). Her abilities are said to range from fashion designing to hunting. There is also a myth that she had once killed four tigers with six bullets.

Nur Jahan

Begum Nur Jahan (alternative spelling Noor Jahan, Nur Jehan, Nor Jahan, etc.) (1577– 1645) also known as Mehr-un-Nisaa was an Indian Empress of the Mughal Dynasty, of Persian origin whose tomb lies in Lahore, Pakistan. Begum Nur Jahan was the twentieth and favourite wife of Mughal Emperor Jahangir, who was her second husband-and the most famous Empress of the Mughal Empire. The story of the couple's infatuation for each other and the relationship that abided between them is the stuff of many (often apocryphal) legends. She remains historically significant for the sheer amount of imperial authority she wielded-the true "power behind the throne," as Jehangir was battling serious addictions to alcohol and opium throughout his reign-and is known as one of the most powerful women who ruled India with an iron fist.

Birth

Begum Nur Jahan was born in 1577 in Kandahar (now in Afghanistan) to travelling Persians from Tehran (now in Iran). Her Persian-born grandfather, who was in the service of Shah Tahmasp I, died in Yazd, laden with honours. His heirs, however, soon fell upon hard times. His son Mirza Ghias Beg (known as *Itmad-ud-Daulah,* "Pillar of the State", a title conferred on him by Akbar) travelled to India with his family where he rose to become an administrative official in the Mughal court. For their journey, Ghias Beg and his wife, Asmat Begum, joined a caravan travelling southward under the leadership of a merchant noble named Malik Masud. While still in Persian territory, less than half the way to their destination, Ghias Beg's party was attacked by robbers and the family lost almost everything it owned. Left with only two mules, Ghias Beg, his expectant wife, their children, Mohammad Sharif, Abdul Hasan Asaf Khan, and one daughter, took turns riding on the backs of the animals. When the group reached Kandahar, Asmat Begum gave birth to her fourth child and second daughter, Mehr-un-Nisaa.

Marriage with Jahangir

The emperor Akbar died in 1605 and was succeeded by prince Salim, who took the regal name *Jahangir.* After her husband Sher Afghan (who was appointed as jagirdar of Bardhaman, a city in Bengal) was killed in 1607, Mehr-un-Nisaa became a lady-in-waiting to one of the Jahangir's stepmothers, Ruqayya Sultana Begum. Ruqayya was the most senior woman in the harem and had been Akbar's first and principal wife and was also the daughter of Mirza Hindal. The father of Mehr-un-Nisaa was, at that time, a Diwan to an amir-ul-umra, decidedly not a very high post.

The year 1607 had not been particularly good for Mehr-un-Nisaa. Her family had fallen into disgrace. Her father, who had been holding important posts under Akbar and Jahangir, had succumbed to his only weakness, money, and had been charged with embezzlement. Moreover, due to possible involvement in the pro-Khusrau assassination attempt on Jahangir in 1607, two of Mehr-un-Nisaa's family members (one brother named Mohammad Sharif and her mother's cousin) were executed on the orders of the Emperor.

In march 1611, her fortune took a turn for the better. She met the emperor Jehangir at the palace *meena bazaar* during the spring festival Nowruz new year. Jahangir grew so infatuated by her beauty that he proposed immediately and they were married on May 25 of the same year becoming his twentieth wife.

Mehr-un-Nisaa received the name Nur Mahal (Light of the Palace), upon her marriage in 1611 and was conferred the title *Nur Jahan* (Light of the world) in 1616. Jahangir's actual name was Nur-ud-din Mohammad, and thus the name that he gave to his wife was his own first name combined with the first part of his regal name.

Mughal empress: For Mehr-un-Nisaa's own immediate family, marriage to Jahangir became a great boon with several members receiving sizeable endowments and promotions as a result. This affection led to Nur Jahan wielding a great deal of actual power in affairs of state. The Mughal state gave absolute power to the emperor, and those who exercised influence over the emperor gained immense influence and prestige. Jahangir's addiction to opium and alcohol made it easier for Nur Jahan to exert her influence. For many years, she effectively wielded imperial power and was recognized as the real force behind the Mughal throne. She even gave audiences at her palace and the ministers consulted with her on most matters. Indeed, Jahangir even permitted coinage to be struck in her name, something that traditionally defined sovereignty.

Through Nur Jahan's influence, her family, including her brother Asaf Khan, consolidated their position at court. Asaf Khan was appointed grand Wazir (minister) to Jahangir, and his daughter Arjumand Banu Begum (later known as Mumtaz Mahal) was wed to Prince Khurram (the future Shah Jahan), the third son of Jahangir, born by a Rajput princess, Jagat Gosaini. Jahangir's eldest son Khusrau had rebelled against the Emperor and was blinded as a result. The second son, Parviz, was weak and addicted to alcohol. The fourth son was Prince Shahryar, born by a royal concubine. Khurram rebelled against his father and a war of succession broke out. Due to Khurram's intransigence, Nur Jahan shifted her support to his younger brother, Shahryar. She arranged the marriage of her own daughter Ladli Begum, born of her first marriage, to her stepson Shahryar. The two weddings ensured that one way or another, the influence of Nur Jahan's family would extend over the Mughal Empire for at least another generation.

Jahangir was captured by rebels in 1626 while he was on his way to Kashmir. Nur Jahan intervened to get her husband released. Jahangir was rescued but died on October 28, 1627. After Jahangir's death, Nur Jahan devoted some of her life to the making of perfume, an art form her mother had passed down.

Death

When Jahangir died in 1628, Nur Jahan's brother Asaf Khan took the side of his son-in-law Khurrum against his sister. It was Khurram who became the new Mughal emperor under the regal name Shah Jahan. Nur Jahan was confined to a comfortable mansion for the rest of her life.

During this period, she paid for and oversaw the construction of her father's mausoleum in Agra, known now as Itmad-Ud-Daulah's Tomb, and occasionally composed Persian poems under the assumed name of *Makhfi*.

Nur Jahan died in 1645 at age 68, and is buried at Shahdara Bagh in Lahore Pakistan in a tomb she had built herself, near the tomb of Jahangir. Her brother Asaf Khan's tomb is also located nearby. The tomb attracts many visitors, both Pakistani and foreign, who come to enjoy pleasant walks in its beautiful gardens. All had been personally laid out and designed by Nur Jahan herself.

Sher Afghan Quli Khan

Ali Quli Istajlu, 'Sher Afghan Khan', also mentioned as Ali Quli Khan Istaju 'Sher Afghan Khan' was a Mughal courtier, earlier serving in Persia, who became the *jagirdar* of Burdwan in West Bengal (1605-1607). He was also the first husband of Nur Jahan (*Mehrunissa*), who later married Jahangir and became Empress of India.

He was given the title Sher Afghan Khan, by Prince Salim, Jahangir, after his meritorious actions, during a war with the Rana of Mewar. Ali Kuli Istaju, was educated under the instructions of Shah Ismail II of Safavid dynasty in Iran Like his wife, Sher Afghan was also an immigrant from Persia, who fled from Iran, to Kandahar, then in India.

He was the father of Mehrunissa's only child, a daughter, also called *Mehurinissa*, like her mother, though later called Ladli Begum, after she married Prince Shahryar, the fifth and youngest son of Jahangir and rival to Shah Jahan.

Biography

Ali Quli Khan Istaju was the *safarchi*, or table-attendant, of Ismail II, the third Safavid Shah of Persia (1576-78), after whose death, he came to Kandahar, and at Multan met, Abdul Rahim Khan-I-Khana, who placed him amongst royal employees, while in the field. Later, on his recommendation, Ali Quli received a mansab, Thatta (in present day Pakistan), in the coming years during a war he rendered distinguished services to Akbar, and moved to the royal courts at Lahore. Soon after his arrival at the royal courts in 1594, Ain-e-Akbari suggests, Akbar married him to Mehrunissa (the future Nur Jahan), daughter of Mirza Ghias Beg, who was seventeen Ghias's wife had access to the royal harem, and was on her visits often accompanied by her daughter, Mehrunissa, it here that Prince Salim (Jahangir) reportedly saw her, and fell in love with her, and Akbar, to avoid scandal, married her quickly to 'Ali Quli'. Though some historians suggest that at the time, her marriage was already fixed with a rising Persian soldier, Ali Quli Istajlu, and thus Jahangir couldn't marry her on that account. When he revolted against Akbar, Ali Quli sides Akbar, this led to a fall out between the two, though when Jahangir finally ascended to the Mughal throne in 1605, he excused him along with all those who favoured Akbar instead of him, and Ali Quli was made a 'jagirdaar' and received the region of Bardhaman in east Bengal as a tuyul.

Death

Shaikh Khubu, Qutbuddin Khan Koka, (Khan-i-Chishti), was the foster-brother of Jahangir, as his mother was a daughter of Shaikh Salim. When Jahangir ascended the throne of Mughal Empire in 1605, Qutbuddin was made the 'subedar' (Governor) of Bengal, by replacing Raja Man Singh. Meanwhile Sher Afkan 'Ali Quli Istajlu was tuyuldar of Bardhaman, also in the province of Bengal, and as his wife Mehrunissa (Nur Jahan) was coveted by the emperor. Subsequently in 1607, Qutb was instructed to send Sher Afghan Khan to the court as he was accused of negligence and siding with Afghan rebels and transferred, which he refused to obey. Seeing this, Qutbuddin started off for Bardhaman, while he sent Ghiasa, the son of his sister, in advance to pacify Sher Afghan and bring him to the court. So upon his arrival on May 30, 1607, Sher Afghan duly went to meet him, accompanied by two men, in that moment Qutb signaled his men to arrest Sher Afghan, this alarmed Sher Afghan, and he stepped forward questioning his motive, and attacked Qutbuddin sensing treachery. Qutbuddin was fatally wounded, and seeing this, his men, surrounded Sher Afghan a killed him instantly.

Qutbuddin, who was fatally wounded, died later in the night, causing much grief to Jahangir as he mentions in his memoirs, Tuzk-e-Jahangiri, where he also mentions his elation at the death of Ali Quli and hopes that "the black faced wretch will for ever remain in hell.".

That he was killed because of the supposed love triangle, between Nur Jahan, Jahangir and Sher Afghan has been view as an assumption by many later historians, who cite the fact that if Jahangir had any such intentions, he wouldn't have had ever bestowed upon Sher Afghan the aforesaid title, or pardoned him after he ascended the throne, or given him Bardhaman.

Another historical writer, Khafi Khan mentions another extraordinary circumstance surrounding the circumstances of his death, which is said to have been related by Nur Jahan's mother. According to her, Sher Afkan was not killed by Qutbuddin's men, but, wounded as he was, managed to get to the door of his house, with the intention of killing his wife, Mehrunissa, whom he did not wish to fall into the emperor's hands. But her mother would not let him enter, and told him to mind his wounds, especially as Mehrunissa had committed suicide by throwing herself into a well. "Having heard the sad news, Sher Afkan went to the heavenly mansions." Though this story, seems far too improbable to be true.

His tomb is today, situated, within the shrine complex of the poet 'Bahram Saqqa', in present day city of Bardhaman in West Bengal, along with tomb, Qutbuddin

Nur Jahan's Remarriage

After Ali Quli's death, his wife, Mehrunissa, and their young daughter, were send to the royal harem, where she spent next four years as *lady-in-waiting* to one of the Jahangir's stepmothers, *Sultana Begum,* the mother of Khusrau Mirza at Agra. As the story progress, in March 1611, during the New Year day's (Nauroz) celebrations, Prince Salim happened to see Mehrunissa, at Meena Bazar, Agra, and immediately fell in love with her. Mehrunissa and Prince Salim were married two months later, on May 25, 1611,, which made her Jahangir's twentieth wife as Nur Mahal, 'Light of the harem', and in 1616, she was given the title Nur Mahal or Nur Jahan, 'the Light of the World'. Ali Quli's daughter, who, like her mother, was named Mehrunissa, later named Ladli Begum, was married to Prince Shahryar, Jahangir's fifth son in 1620,, Shahryar went on to briefly occupy the Mughal throne at Lahore, under the manoeuvring of Nur Jahan, after the death of Jahangir on October 27, 1627. He was later captured by Mughal forces led by Asaf Khan, and first blinded by the orders of Prince Dawar, was later executed by Asaf Khan, at the order of Shah Jahan, who finally ascend to the Mughal throne after executing all this remainder brothers. After Qutbuddin's death, the next subedar of Bengal was Quli Khan (1607–1608) and when he died, Islam Khan (June 1608–died August 1613).

Ladli Begum

Ladli Begum (born 1594) was the daughter of Nur Jahan (Mehrunnisa) and her first husband Sher Afghan, and was married to Mughal prince, Shahryar. Ladli's father (Sher Afghan) was killed in 1607. Her mother later wed the Mughal Emperor Jehangir and took the name Nur Jahan. As the favourite wife of Jehangir, Nur Jahan used her great influence to arrange the marriage of Ladli with Shahryar, son of Jehangir by a different wife. Thus, Ladli came to wed her mother's stepson.

She had a daughter from Shahryar, *Arzani Begum.*

Mirza Ghiyas Beg

Mirza Ghiyas Beg was an important official in the Mughal empire, whose children served as wives, mothers, and generals of the Mughal emperors.

Biography

Ghiyas Beg immigrated to India from Persia after the death of his father and his family's fall from grace. He was received by the Emperor Akbar, and quickly climbed his way through the intricate Mughal court, serving as a court official under Akbar and his son, Jahangir. He was an important official the rule of the Mughal Emperor Jahangir, and served as the *Diwan* of the Empire, the chief treasurer, and he was given the title 'Itimad-ud-Daulah', which means 'Pillar of the State'. His daughter, Mehrunnisa' (Nur Jahan) married Jahangir in 1611, and his son Abdul Hasan Asaf Khan served as a general to Jahangir.

He was also the grandfather of Mumtaz Mahal (originally named Arjumand Bano, daughter of Abdul Hasan Asaf Khan), the wife of the emperor Shah Jahan, responsible for the building of the Taj Mahal. Jahangir was succeeded by his son Shah Jahan, and Abdul Hasan served as one of Shah Jahan's closest advisors. Shah Jahan married Abdul Hasan's daughter Arjumand Banu Begum, Mumtaz Mahal, who was the mother of his four sons, including his successor Aurangzeb. Shah Jahan built the Taj Mahal to serve as Mumtaz Mahal's tomb.

Ghiyas Beg died shortly before Jahangir's death in 1627. Nur Jahan commissioned the construction of Itimad-ud-Daulah's Tomb in Agra, which is as an architectural predecessor of the Taj Mahal.

Abdul Hasan Asaf Khan

Abdul Hasan Asaf Khan was the father of Arjumand Banu Begum, also known as Mumtaz Mahal, who was the wife of the

Mughal Emperor Shah Jahan. Asaf Khan was also the elder brother of Mehrunissa, (better known as Nur Jehan), the empress of Shah Jahan's father, Jahangir. Many scholars have been researching on the origins of Asaf Khan's clan. Some researches claim they are descending from Armenia.

Asaf Khan was appointed Governor of Lahore by Emperor Jahangir in 1625. After the demise of Jahangir in 1627, he was instrumental in securing the accession of his son-in-law Shah Jahan by colluding with Dawar Bakht (Jahangir's other son) and defeating the rival claimant Prince Shahryar (Nur Jahan's son-in-law, married to her daughter by her previous marriage to Sher Afghan) in a battle near Lahore. Asaf Khan enjoyed a position even more elevated than in the preceding reign and retained it until 1632, when he failed in the siege of Bijapur, from which time he seems to have lost favour.

Asaf Khan died on 12 June 1641 and his tomb was commissioned to be built in Shahdara tomb complex in Lahore by Shah Jahan. It is built to the west of Jahangir's mausoleum, facing it. The tomb is built entirely of brick. It is of octagonal plan, with a large central double-layered bulbous dome. Each side has a deeply recessed *iwan*, or alcove, with a door and arched window looking into the tomb. Marble, and blue *kashi* tiles typical of Lahore once covered the mausoleum; they have since been stripped off. The interior was renowned for its lavish use of white marble and precious stone inlay, which had been removed and reused in temples during the rapacious Sikh rule (1799-1849). The inner dome ceiling is decorated in a high plaster relief of interlacing patterns, but much of it has fallen off. The tomb contains the marble sarcophagus, carved with Koranic inscriptions, similar to that in Emperor Jahangir's adjacent tomb.

The historian Hargreaves says about the tomb, "Despite its simplicity, there is a sense of restful quietude at this site (Asaf Khan's Tomb) which renders it one of the most fascinating monuments in the neighbourhood of Lahore."

Conquests

Jahangir was responsible for ending a century long struggle with the state of Mewar. The campaign against the Rajputs was pushed so extensively that the latter were made to submit and that too with a great loss of life and property.

Jahangir also thought of capturing Kangra Fort, which Akbar had failed to do. Consequently a siege was laid, which lasted for fourteen months, and the fort was taken in 1620.

The district of Kistwar, in the state of Kashmir, was also conquered.

Death

The health of Jahangir was completely shattered by too much drinking of alcohol. He was trying to restore it by visiting Kashmir and Kabul. He went from Kabul to Kashmir but returned to Lahore on account of a severe cold.

Jahangir died on the way from Kashmir in 1627 and was buried in Shahdara Bagh, a suburb of Lahore, Punjab, Pakistan. He was succeeded by his third son, Prince Khurram who took the title of Shah Jahan. Jahangir's elegant mausoleum is located in the Shahdara locale of Lahore and is a popular tourist attraction in Lahore. On his death in 1627 he uttered 'Kashmir only Kashmir'.

Autobiography

Tuzk-e-Jahangiri or *Tuzk-i-Jahangiri* is the autobiography of Mughal Emperor Nor-u-Din Mohammad Jahangir (1569-1609). Also referred to as *Jahangirnama,* Tuzk-e-Jahangiri is written in Persian, and follows the tradition of his great-grandfather, Babur (1487-1530), who had written the Baburnama; though Jahangir went a step further and besides the history of his reign, he includes details like his reflections on art, politics, and also information about his family.

The Writer

Jahangir was a good writer and loved nature. Jahangir recorded detailed description about wildlife in his autobiography. Jahangir admired paintings and collected them in his palace. Many of them survived and are found in museums around the world.

Overview

The text details the first nineteen years of his reign, but gave up the writing of his Memoirs in the seventeenth year of his reign. He then entrusted the task to Mu'tamad Khan, the author of the Iqbal-nama, who continued the Memoirs to the beginning of the nineteenth year. From where, it was taken up by Mohammad Hadi, who continued it to Jahangir's death. It forms an important reference point for the era along with his father, Akbar's, Akbarnama. First important printed version of 'Jahangirnama', was by, Sayyid Ahmad printed at Ghazipur in 1863 and at Aligarh in 1864

Jahangir's autobiography also reflects the royal ideology of Jahangir's views on various political, religious and social issues. Within the memoir, he noted many of his local level legislative policies in his large empire consisting of all of modern day India. Among them were his decrees to manage and regulate the jagirdars. Jagirdars were holders of the jagir, the emperor's land grant title. The jagirdars were to take the income of the land and use it mainly to finance the maintenance of the troops and to address the town needs. Jahangir made various attempts to halt corruption within the jagirdars. He prohibited each of them from using the money for personal profit by ordering that part of the land income to go to hospitals and infirmaries and for each town to be equipped with religious buildings according to the religion of that area. Jahangir also kept the jagirdars from gaining interest in family or land riches by ordering for jagirdars to seek his approval before marrying someone from the town they ruled in.

Jahangir and Religion

While Sunni Islam was the state religion, there was no widespread pressure to convert; indeed, Jahangir specifically warned his nobles that they "should not force Islam on anyone." In the first century of Islamic expansion this attitude was taken partially because of concerns that an absence of non-Muslims would deprive the state of a valuable source of revenue. However, as the jizya was not imposed by Jahangir, there might have been more behind this policy of toleration than mere economic reasoning. Jahangir was certainly willing to engage with other religions, and Edward Terry, an English chaplain in India at the time, saw a ruler under which "all Religions are tolerated and their Priests [held] in good esteeme." Brahmins on the banks of the Ganges received gifts from the emperor, while following a meeting with Jadrup, a Hindu ascetic, Jahangir felt compelled to comment that "association with him is a great privilege." He enjoyed debating theological subtleties with Brahmins, especially about the possible existence of avatars. Both Sunnis and Shias were welcome at court, and members of both sects gained high office. When drunk, Jahangir swore to Sir Thomas Roe, England's first ambassador to the Mughal court, that he would protect all the peoples of the book. Many contemporary chroniclers were not even sure quite how to describe his personal belief structure.

Roe labelled him an atheist, and although most others shied away from that term, they did not feel as though they could call him an orthodox Sunni. He relied greatly on astrologers, though that was not seen as unusual for a ruler at the time, even to the extent that he required that they work out the most auspicious time for the imperial camp to enter a city. Roe believed Jahangir's religion to be of his own making, "for he envyes Mahomett, and wisely sees no reason why he should not bee as great a prophet as he, and therefore proffeseth him selfe soe ... he hath found many disciples that flatter or follow him." At this time, one of those disciples happened to be the current English ambassador, though his initiation into Jahangir's inner circle of disciples was devoid of religious significance for Roe, as he did not understand the full extent of what he was doing: Jahangir hung "a picture of him selfe sett in gold hanging at a wire gold chaine, with one pendent soule pearle" round Roe's neck. Roe thought it "an specially favour, for that all the great men that were the Kings image (which none may doe but to whom it is given) receive no other then a meddall of gold as bigg as six pence."

Had Roe intentionally converted, it would have caused quite a scandal in London. But since there was no intent, there was no resultant problem. Such disciples were an elite group of imperial servants, with one of them being promoted to Chief Justice. However, it is not clear that any of those who became disciples renounced their previous religion, so it is probable to see this as a way in which the emperor strengthened the bond between himself and his nobles. Despite Roe's somewhat casual use of the term 'atheist', he could not quite put his finger on Jahangir's real beliefs. Roe lamented that the emperor was either "the most impossible man in the world to be converted, or the most easy; for he loves to heare, and hath so little religion yet, that he can well abide to have any derided." Broad toleration for other religions made little sense to Europeans forged in the heat of religious conflict, while the lifestyle and pretensions Jahangir afforded himself meant that it was difficult to see him as a devout Muslim. Sri Ram Sharma argues though that contemporaries and some historians have been too disparaging about Jahangir's beliefs, simply because he did not persecute non-believers and enforce his views on others.

This should not imply that the multi-confessional state appealed to all, or that all Muslims were happy with the situation in India. In a book written on statecraft for Jahangir, the author advised him to direct "all his energies to understanding the counsel of the sages and to comprehending the intimations of the 'ulama." At the start of his regime many staunch Sunnis were hopeful, because he seemed less tolerant to other faiths than his father had been. At the time of his accession and the elimination of Abul Fazl, his father's chief minister and architect of his eclectic religious stance, a strong orthodox nucleus of noblemen had gained power in administration." Jahangir did not always benevolently regard some Hindu customs and rituals. On visiting a Hindu temple, he found a statue of a man with a pig's head, which was supposed to represent God, so he "ordered them to break that hideous form and throw it in the tank." If the Tuzuk is reliable on this subject (and there is no reason to suspect that it is not), then this was an isolated case.

J. F. Richards argues that "Jahangir seems to have been persistently hostile to popularly venerated religious figures." This is perhaps misleading. Hindu ascetics like Jadrup were treated with respect, and it was only those who upset the order of the state that were seen as a threat to the state, with their popularity making them even more dangerous. A Muslim, who had gained some followers by claiming that he had surpassed the understanding of the companions of Mohammad, was imprisoned in Gwalior Fort. If he had been allowed to spread his message there was potential for serious disturbance, so he had to be stopped.

Most notorious was the execution of the Sikh Guru Arjun. It is unclear that Jahangir even understood what a Sikh was, referring to Guru Arjun as a Hindu, who had "captured many of the simple-hearted of the Hindus, and even of the ignorant and foolish followers of Islam, by his ways and manners ... for three or four generations (of spiritual successors) they had kept this shop warm." The trigger for Guru Arjun's execution was his support for Jahangir's rebel son Khusrau, yet it is clear from Jahangir's own memoirs that he disliked Guru Arjun before then: "many times it occurred to me to put a stop to this vain affair or bring him into the assembly of the people of Islam."

Guru Arjun was handed over to the Mughal governor of Lahore, and was tortured to death for refusing to convert to Islam. Jahangir ordered his execution, but it is unlikely that he also ordered Guru Arjun to be tortured and converted, for two reasons; one, because we have no other examples from Jahangir's generally tolerant reign to support the idea that he forced people to convert to Islam, and two, because Jahangir makes no note of Guru Arjun's torture, yet cheerfully describes the torture of two other rebels, as well as Guru Arjun's execution. Jahangir maintained his hostility towards the Sikhs, imprisoning Guru Hargobind, the successor of Guru Arjun, for several years.

A rana was described as an infidel, but only because he was fighting against the Mughals, and infidel was used as an everyday phrase to describe all non-Muslims anyway. Admittedly Muslims were discouraged from performing most Hindu rites, with Jahangir lamenting that many Muslims prayed at a temple dedicated to Durga, and worshipped at a black stone. With Jahangir himself occasionally taking part in Hindu ceremonies, the aforementioned example was probably one way of showing support for the idea that Muslim and Hindus should not mix their rituals. His attitude to religion in his domain was relaxed yet diligent. He saw himself as doing Allah's bidding, yet he was inquisitive enough to explore new ideas about religion, intelligent enough to understand that Hindus were in the majority and grand enough in his pretensions not to need to obey every line of the Qur'an.

Such a religious situation allowed the more recently arrived form of Christianity to have opportunity to grow. Jahangir did not seem to have anything against Christianity. He wrote fondly of Akbar's reign, when "Sunnis and Shias met in one mosque, and Franks and Jews in one church, and observed their own forms of worship." Roe noted that "of Christ he never utters any word unreverently."

His prayer room in Agra contained pictures of "our Lady and Christ." In the imperial palace in Lahore, over one of the doors, according to William Finch, a merchant, was "the Picture of our Sauiour," with an image of the Virgin Mary facing it. Elsewhere, the emperor had pictures of angels and demons, with the demons having a "most ugly shape, with long hornes, staring eyes ... with such horrible difformity and deformity, that I wonder the poore women are not frightened therewith."

It is possible that Jahangir might have seen these images in their Islamic persona, as the Qur'an features such creatures, yet depiction of living things was harem (forbidden), so the images could well have been created by a Christian artist. However, as Mughal art was still heavily Persian-influenced, images of living beings were allowed, and widespread, so perhaps the other worldly images had nothing to do with Christianity at all; they nonetheless caught Finch's eye. Muqarrab Khan sent to Jahangir "a European curtain (tapestry) the like of which in beauty no other work of the Frank painters has ever been seen." One of his audience halls was "adorned with European screens." Christian themes attracted Jahangir, and even merited a mention in the Tuzuk. One of his slaves gave him a piece of ivory into which had been carved four scenes. In the last scene "there is a tree, below which the figure of the revered (hazrat) Jesus is shown. One person has placed his head at Jesus' feet, and an old man is conversing with Jesus and four others are standing by." Though Jahangir believed it to be the work of the slave who presented it to him, Sayyid Ahmad and Henry Beveridge suggest that it was of European origin, and possibly showed the Transfiguration. Wherever it came from, and whatever it represented, it was clear that a European style had come to influence Mughal art, otherwise the slave would not have claimed it as his own design, nor would he have been believed by Jahangir.

There was even some baseless suggestion that Jahangir had converted to Christianity. Thrown by the religious tolerance of Akbar and Jahangir's rule, the Jesuits had long thought that they were always on the verge of conversion. Finch recounted how there "was much stirre with the King about Chrytianitie, he affirming before his Nobles, that it was the soundest faith, and that of Mahomet lies and fables." This is an extremely implausible story, yet the fact that Finch told it at all shows the extent to which Christianity was evident in the Mughal court. Jahangir apparently allowed a Jesuit to teach some Indian boys Portuguese and elements of Christian doctrine, and the Jesuits were also allowed to open churches in Ahmadabad and Hooghly. Christians were allowed to openly celebrate Christmas, Easter and other such festivals, and the Jesuits were even given an allowance and gifts in order to carry on with their work, with a few Indians converting to Christianity. Given the toleration of Hinduism, such imperial leeway was not shocking. Christianity occupied a special place in Islamic canon, as did Isa (Jesus), who was considered to be amongst the greatest prophets. What did surprise some observers was the forcible conversion of three sons of Jahangir's brother, Prince Daniyal, to Christianity, followed by a parade to celebrate their conversions. This was seen by the Jesuits as a gigantic step forward, but the English and the locals knew better. Hawkins dryly commented that Jahangir made his nephews Christian "not for any zeale he had to Christianitie, as the [Jesuit] Fathers, and all Christians thought; but upon the prophecie of certain learned Gentiles [Hindus], who told him that the sonnes of his should be disinherited, and the children of his brother should raigne. And therefore he did it, to make these children hatefull to all Moores." This highlighted the likely limits of Christianity in India. Its inhabitants already had mono-and poly-theistic religions from which to choose, and the European Christians had done little to demonstrate the attractiveness of conversion. A few did convert, though Terry believed that this was only for Jesuit money, as they did not appear to know anything about their new religion, and Roe agreed on this matter. Even Jahangir's nephews were allowed to return to the Islamic fold, because "the King of Portugall sent them no presents nor wives." Christianity was tolerated because it posed no real threat. It certainly had an effect on the arts, but it is difficult to discern any other lasting impact on Mughal India.

Jahangir and Art

Jahangir was fascinated with art and architecture. Jahangir himself is far from modest in his autobiography when he states his prowess at being able to determine the artist of any portrait by simply looking at a painting. As he said:

> *"...my liking for painting and my practice in judging it have arrived at such point when any work is brought before me, either of deceased artists or of those of the present day, without the names being told me, I say on the spur of the moment that is the work of such and such a man. And if there be a picture containing many portraits, and each face is the work of a different master, I can discover which face is the work of each of them. If any other person has put in the eye and eyebrow of a face, I can perceive whose work the original face is, and who has painted the eye and eyebrow."*

Jahangir took his connoisseurship of art very seriously. Paintings created under his reign were closely catalogued, dated and even signed, providing scholars with fairly accurate ideas as to when and in what context many of the pieces were created, in addition to their aesthetic qualities.

He was not only an admirer of Christian artwork but also a purveyor of it. This was largely due to earlier Jesuit missions during his father's reign. Jesuits had brought with them various books, engravings, and paintings and, when they saw the delight Akbar held for them, sent for more and more of the same to be given to the Mughals, as they felt they were on the "verge of conversion," a notion which proved to be very false. Instead, both Akbar and Jahangir studied this artwork very closely and replicated and adapted it, adopting much of the early iconographic features and later the pictorial realism for which Renaissance art was known. Jahangir was notable for his pride in the ability of his court painters. A classic example of this is described in Sir Thomas Roe's diaries, in which the Emperor had his painters copy a European miniature several times creating a total of five miniatures. Jahangir then challenged Roe to pick out the original from the copies, a feat Sir Thomas Roe could not do, to the delight of Jahangir.

Jahangir was also revolutionary in his adaptation of European styles. A collection at the British Museum in London contains seventy-four drawings of Indian portraits dating from the time of Jahangir, including a portrait of the emperor himself. These portraits are a unique example of art during Jahangir's reign because before, and for sometime after, faces were not drawn full, head-on and including the shoulders as well as the head as these drawings are.

During his time, Jahangir also pioneered several ornate genealogies illustrated with portraits of each family member in the style of Italian Renaissance painters. Jahangir's love for hunting met his love for art as he commissioned artists on multiple occasions to paint him while hunting and would even paint scenes himself, from time to time. Jahangir was also known for his vast collection of illuminated Persian albums that contained writings as well as paintings.

5

Shah Jahan

Shahab-ud-din Mohammad Shah Jahan I (full title: *Al-Sultan al-Azam wal Khaqan al-Mukarram, Abul-Muzaffar Shihab ud-din Mohammad, Sahib-i-Qiran-i-Sani, Shah Jahan I Padshah Ghazi Zillu'llah [Firdaus-Ashiyani]*) (also spelled Shah Jehan, Shahjehan, January 5, 1592 – January 22, 1666) was the ruler of the Mughal Empire in the Indian subcontinent from 1628 until 1658. The name Shah Jahan comes from Persian meaning "King of the World." He was the fifth Mughal ruler after Babur, Humayun, Akbar, and Jahangir. While young, he was a favourite of Akbar.

Even while very young, he could be pointed out to be the successor to the Mughal throne after the death of Jahangir. He succeeded to the throne upon his father's death in 1627. He is considered to be one of the greatest Mughals and his reign has been called the Golden Age of Mughals. Like Akbar, he was eager to expand his empire. The chief events of his reign were the destruction of the kingdom of Ahmadnagar (1636), the loss of Kandahar to the Persians (1653), and a second war against the Deccan princes (1655). In 1658 he fell ill, and was confined by his son Aurangzeb in the citadel of Agra until his death in 1666. On the eve of his death in 1666, the Mughal Empire spanned almost 750,000,000 acres (3,000,000 km^2), about 9/10 the size of modern India.

The period of his reign was the golden age of Mughal architecture. Shah Jahan erected many splendid monuments, the most famous of which is the Taj Mahal at Agra built as a tomb for his wife Mumtaz Mahal (birth name Arjumand Banu Begum). The Pearl Mosque at Agra, the palace and great mosque at Delhi also commemorate him. The celebrated Peacock Throne, said to be worth millions of dollars by modern estimates, also dates from his reign. He was the founder of Shahjahanabad, now known as 'Old Delhi'. The important buildings of Shah Jahan were the Diwan-i-Am and Diwan-i-Khas in the fort of Delhi, the Jama Masjid, the Moti Masjid and the Taj. It is pointed out that the Palace of Delhi is the most magnificent in the East.

Biography

Birth And Early Years: Shah Jahan was born as Prince Khurram Shihab-ud-din Mohammad, in 1592 in Lahore as the third and favourite son of the emperor Jahangir, his mother being a Rathore Rajput Princess, known as Princess Jagat Gosain who was Jahangir's second wife. The name Khurram-Persian for 'joyful'- was given by his grandfather Akbar. His early years saw him receive a cultured, broad education and he distinguished himself in the martial arts and as a military commander while leading his father's armies in numerous campaigns-Mewar (1615 CE, 1024 AH), the Deccan (1617 and 1621 CE, 1026 and 1030 AH), Kangra (1618 CE, 1027AH). He was responsible for most of the territorial gains during his father's reign. He also demonstrated a precocious talent for building, impressing his father at the age of 16 when he built his quarters within Babur's Kabul fort and redesigned buildings within Agra fort.

Marriage: In 1607 CE (1025 AH), at the age of fifteen, Khurram was to marry Arjumand Banu Begum, the grand daughter of a Persian noble, who was 14 years old at the time. She would become the unquestioned love of his life. They would, however, have to wait five years before they were married in 1612 CE (1021 AH). After their wedding celebrations, Khurram "finding her in appearance and character elect among all the women of the time," gave her the title Mumtaz Mahal (Jewel of the Palace).

She had 18 children. Despite her frequent pregnancies, Mumtaz Mahal travelled with Shah Jahan's entourage throughout his earlier military campaigns and the subsequent rebellion against his father. Mumtaz Mahal was utterly devoted — she was his constant companion and trusted confidante and their relationship was intense.

She is portrayed by Shah Jahan's chroniclers as the perfect wife with no aspirations to political power. This is in direct opposition to how Nur Jahan had been perceived.

Mumtaz Mahal

Mumtaz Mahal (April, 1593-17 June 1631) is the common nickname of Arjumand Banu Begum, an Indian Empress of the Mughal Dynasty. She was born in Agra, India. Her father was the Persian noble Abdul Hasan Asaf Khan, the brother of Empress Nur Jehan (who subsequently became the wife of the emperor Jahangir). She was religiously a Shia Muslim. She was married at the age of 19, on 10 May 1612, to Prince Khurram, who would later ascend the Peacock Throne as Mughal Emperor Shah Jahan I. She was his third wife, and became his favourite. She died in Burhanpur in the Deccan (now in Madhya Pradesh) during the birth of their fourteenth child, a daughter named Gauhara Begum. Her body remained at Burhanpur for 23 years until the Taj was completed. Only then was her coffin shifted to Agra. Her body was then buried in the Taj Mahal in Agra.

Biography

In 1607 AD (1016 AH), Prince Khurram was betrothed to Arjumand Banu Begum, who was just 14 years old at the time. She would become the unquestioned love of his life. They would however, have to wait five years before they were married in 1612 AD (1021 AH), on a date selected by the court astrologers as most conducive to ensuring a happy marriage. After their wedding celebrations, Khurram "finding her in appearance and character elect among all the women of the time", gave her the title 'Mumtaz Mahal' Begum (Chosen One of the Palace). 18 AH). The intervening years had seen Khurrum take two other wives. By all accounts however, Khurram was so taken with Mumtaz, that he showed little interest in exercising his polygamous rights with the two earlier wives, other than dutifully siring a child with each. According to the official court chronicler, Qazwini, the relationship with his other wives "had nothing more than the status of marriage. The intimacy, deep affection, attention and favour which His Majesty had for the Cradle of Excellence (Mumtaz) exceeded by a thousand times what he felt for any other."

Mumtaz Mahal had a very deep and loving marriage with Shah Jahan. Even during her lifetime, poets would extol her beauty, gracefulness and compassion. Mumtaz Mahal was Shah Jahan's trusted companion, travelling with him all over the Mughal Empire. His trust in her was so great that he even gave her his imperial seal, the Muhr Uzah. Mumtaz was portrayed as the perfect wife with no aspirations to political power in contrast to Nur Jehan, the wife of Jahangir who had wielded considerable influence in the previous reign. She was a great influence on him, apparently often intervening on behalf of the poor and destitute. But she also enjoyed watching elephant and combat fights performed for the court. It was quite common for women of noble birth to commission architecture in the Mughal Empire. Mumtaz devoted some time to a riverside garden in Agra.

Despite her frequent pregnancies, Mumtaz travelled with Shah Jahan's entourage throughout his earlier military campaigns and the subsequent rebellion against his father. She was his constant companion and trusted confidant and their relationship was intense. Indeed, the court historians go to unheard lengths to document the intimate and erotic relationship the couple enjoyed. In their nineteen years of marriage, they had fourteen children together, eight of whom died at birth or at a very young age.

Mumtaz died in Burhanpur in 1631 AD (1040 AH), while giving birth to their fourteenth child. She had been accompanying her husband whilst he was fighting a campaign in the Deccan Plateau. Her body was temporarily buried at Burhanpur in a walled pleasure garden known as Zainabad originally constructed by Shah Jahan's uncle Daniyal on the bank of the Tapti River. The contemporary court chroniclers paid an unusual amount of attention to Mumtaz Mahal's death and Shah Jahan's grief at her demise. In the immediate aftermath of his bereavement, the emperor was reportedly inconsolable. Apparently after her death, Shah Jahan went into secluded mourning for a year. When he appeared again, his hair had turned white, his back was bent, and his face worn. Jahan's eldest daughter, the devoted Jahanara Begum, gradually brought him out of grief and took the place of Mumtaz at court.

Her personal fortune valued at 10,000,000 rupees was divided by Shah Jahan between Jahanara Begum, who received half and the rest of her surviving children. Burhanpur was never intended by her husband as his wife's final resting spot. As a result her body was disinterred in December 1631 and transported in a golden casket escorted by her son Shah Shuja and the head lady in waiting of the deceased Empress back to Agra. There it was interred in a small building on the banks of the Yamuna River. Shah Jahan stayed behind in Burhanpur to conclude the military campaign that had originally bought him to the region. While there he began planning the design and construction of a suitable mausoleum and funerary garden in Agra for his wife, a task that would take more than 22 years to complete, the Taj Mahal.

Today, the Taj Mahal stands as the ultimate monument to love, and a homage to her beauty and life.

The intervening years had seen Khurrum take two other wives known as Akbarabadi Mahal (d.1677 CE, 1088 AH), and Kandahari Mahal (b. c1594 CE, c1002 AH), (m.1609 CE, 1018 AH).

According to the official court chronicler Qazwini, the relationship with his other wives "had nothing more than the status of marriage. The intimacy, deep affection, attention and favour which His Majesty had for the Cradle of Excellence [Mumtaz] exceeded by a thousand times what he felt for any other." Several European chroniclers suggested that Shah Jahan had an incestuous relationship with his daughter Jahanara Begum. The European traveller Francois Bernier wrote, "Begum Sahib, the elder daughter of Shah Jahan was very handsome... Lal pointed out that Aurangzeb may have been involved in "magnifying a rumour into a full-fledged scandal", and wrote: "Aurangzeb had disobeyed Shahjahan, he had incarcerated him for years, but if he really helped give a twist to Shahjahan's paternal love for Jahan Ara by turning it into a scandal, it was the unkindest cut of all his unfilial acts."

Accession

Inheritance of power and wealth in the Mughal empire was not determined through primogeniture, but by princely sons competing to achieve military successes and consolidating their power at court. This often led to rebellions and wars of succession. As a result, a complex political climate surrounded the Mughal court in Khurram's formative years. In 1611 his father married Nur Jahan, the widowed daughter of a Persian immigrant. She rapidly became an important member of Jahangir's court and, together with her brother Asaf Khan, wielded considerable influence. Arjumand was Asaf Khan's daughter and her marriage to Khurrum consolidated Nur Jahan and Asaf Khan's positions at court.

Khurram's intense military successes of 1617 CE (1026 AH) against the Lodi in the Deccan effectively secured the southern border of the empire and his grateful father rewarded him with the prestigious title 'Shah Jahan Bahadur' (Brave King of the World) which implicitly sealed his inheritance. Court intrigues, however, including Nur Jahan's decision to have her daughter from her first marriage wed Shah Jahan's youngest brother and her support for his claim to the throne led Khurram, supported by Mahabat Khan, into open revolt against his father in 1622.

The rebellion was quelled by Jahangir's forces in 1626 and Khurram was forced to submit unconditionally. Upon the death of Jahangir in 1627, Khurram succeeded to the Mughal throne as Shah Jahan, King of the World, the latter title alluding to his pride in his Timurid roots. Shah Jahan's first act as ruler was to execute his chief rivals and imprison his step mother Nur Jahan. This allowed Shan Jahan to rule without contention.

Rule

Although his father's rule was generally peaceful, the empire was experiencing challenges by the end of his reign. Shah Jahan reversed this trend by putting down a Islamic rebellion in Ahmednagar, repulsing the Portuguese in Bengal, capturing the Rajput kingdoms of Baglana and Bundelkhand to the west and the northwest beyond the Khyber Pass. Shah Jahan's military campaigns drained the imperial treasury. Under his rule, the state became a huge military machine and the nobles and their contingents multiplied almost fourfold, as did the demands for more revenue from the peasantry. It was however a period of general stability — the administration was centralised and court affairs systematised. Historiography and the arts increasingly became instruments of propaganda, where beautiful artworks or poetry expressed specific state ideologies which held that central power and hierarchical order would create balance and harmony. The empire continued to expand moderately during his reign but the first signs of an imperial decline were seen in the later years.

Under Shah Jahan the Mughal Empire attained its highest union of strength with magnificence. The land revenue of the Mughal Empire under Shah Jahan was 20¾ millions. The magnificence of Shah Jahan's court was the wonder of European travellers. His Peacock Throne, with its trail blazing in the shifting natural colours of rubies, sapphires, and emeralds, was valued by the jeweler Tavernier at 6½ millions sterling.

His political efforts encouraged the emergence of large centres of commerce and crafts – such as Lahore, Delhi, Agra, and Ahmedabad – linked by roads and waterways to distant places and ports. He moved the capital from Agra to Delhi.

Under Shah Jahan's rule, Mughal artistic and architectural achievements reached their zenith. Shah Jahan was a prolific builder with a highly refined aesthetic. He built the legendary Taj Mahal in Agra as a tomb for his beloved wife, Mumtaz Mahal. Among his other surviving buildings are the Red Fort and Jama Masjid in Delhi, the Shalimar Gardens of Lahore, sections of the Lahore Fort (such as Sheesh Mahal, and Naulakha pavilion), and his father's mausoleum.

Legend has it that Shah Jahan wanted to build a black Taj Mahal for himself. There is no reputable scholarship to support this hypothesis, however, nor other horrific legends that Shah Jahan maimed, blinded, or killed those responsible for designing and building his tomb.

Fate

His son Aurangzeb led a rebellion when Shah Jahan became ill in 1657 CE (1067 AH) and publicly executed his brother and the heir apparent Dara Shikoh. Dara was the eldest of the sons and the Emperor's favourite. With this Dara assumed the role of Regent in his father's stead which brought animosity towards him swiftly by his brothers. Upon receiving this information, his younger brothers, Shuja, Viceroy of Bengal, and Marad, Viceroy of Gujarat, declared their independence, and marched upon Agra in order to claim their riches. Aurangzeb, the third son, the ablest and most virile of the brothers join them and being placed in chief command, attacked Dara's army close to Agra and completely defeated him. Although Shah Jahan fully recovered from his illness, Aurangzeb declared him incompetent to rule and put him under house arrest in Agra Fort.

Jahanara Begum Sahib voluntarily shared his 8-year confinement and nursed him in his dotage. In January of 1666 CE (1076 AH), Shah Jahan fell ill with strangury and dysentery. Confined to bed, he became progressively weaker until, on January 22, he commanded the ladies of the imperial court, particularly his consort of later years Akbarabadi Mahal, to the care of Jahanara. After reciting the Kalima and verses from the Quran, he died.

Jahanara planned a state funeral which was to include a procession with Shah Jahan's body carried by eminent nobles followed by the notable citizens of Agra and officials scattering coins for the poor and needy. Aurangzeb refused to accommodate such ostentation and the body was washed in accordance with Islamic rites, taken by river in a sandalwood coffin to the Taj Mahal and was interred there next to the body of his beloved wife Mumtaz Mahal.

Jahanara Begum Sahib

Shahzadi (Imperial Princess) Jahanara Begum Sahib was the eldest daughter of Shah Jahan and Mumtaz Mahal.

Influence at Court

Upon the death of Mumtaz Mahal in 1631, Jahanara, who was just 17, took the place of her mother as first lady in the country, despite her father having one other wife. As well as caring for her younger brothers and sisters, she is also credited with bringing her father out of mourning and restoring normality to a court darkened by her mother's death and her father's grief. One of her tasks after the death of her mother was to oversee the betrothal and wedding of her brother, Dara Shikoh, to a begum, Nadira Banu which had been originally planned by Mumtaz Mahal but postponed by her death. Jahanara's mother Arjumand Banu Begum, Empress Mumtaz Muhal died while giving birth.

Mumtaz Mahal's personal fortune valued at 10,000,000 rupees was divided by Shah Jahan between Jahanara Begum, who received half and the rest of her surviving children.

Her father frequently took her advice and entrusted her with charge of the imperial seal. Shah Jahan's fondness for his daughter was reflected in the multiple titles he bestowed upon her, which include Sahibat al-Zamani (Lady of the Age) and Padishah Begum (Lady Emperor) or Begum Sahib (*Princess of Princesses*).

Her power was such that, unlike the other royal princesses, she was allowed to live in her own palace, outside the confines of the Agra Fort.

Accident

On the night of the 4 April 1644, while she was heading towards her sleeping quarters her dress brushed against a lamp left burning on the floor. Her garment caught fire and she was enveloped in flames. Two of the attendants who had tried to help Jahanara died of their burns. Her injuries were such that it was not until late in 1644 that she was deemed to be out of danger and an 8 day festival of thanks celebrated. With the assistance of numerous physicians Shah Jahan himself nursed her back to health.

After her recovery Shah Jahan gifted her rare gems and jewellery and bestowed upon her the revenues of the port of Surat. She made a pilgrimage to Ajmer, following the example set by her great-grandfather Akbar.

Relations with Family

Historians report a deep love and genuine liking between Jahanara and her brother Dara Shikoh, unlike the cool politeness that existed between Aurangzeb and herself. Jahanara had referred to Aurangzeb as the "white serpent" in a kind of diary she had written also calling him a tiger and panther. Legend says that once when Aurangzeb was severely sick, Jahanara took care of him. Later when he asked her whether or not she would support him for the throne and she said that he would not be emperor, Aurangzeb became very angry at her. When Aurangzeb fell out of favour with his father during the time of Jahanara's convalescence she is credited with using the celebrations of her recovery to encourage her father to restore Aurangzeb to his former positions.

There is record of tensions with her sister Roshanara Begum, three years her junior who resented her elder sister's position as first lady of the empire.

Struggle for Power

Jahanara took the side of Dara Shikoh in the struggle for the throne. Dara had promised her to lift the ban on marriage for Moghul princesses, which Akbar had introduced. Had he triumphed, her power would likely have continued.

Care of her Father

On Aurangzeb's usurpation of the throne, Jahanara joined her father in imprisonment at the Agra Fort where she devoted herself to his care until his death.

Relations with Aurangzeb

After the death of their father Jahanara and Aurangzeb were reconciled. He gave her the title, 'Empress of Princesses' and she replaced Roshanara as first lady. Jahanara's sister Roshanara Begum was reportedly very jealous of her sister's return to power. Jahanara was soon secure enough in her position to occasionally argue with Aurangzeb-something which generally resulted in the death of anyone doing so-and have certain rights other women did not have.

She argued against Aurangzeb's strict regulation of public life in accordance with his conservative religious beliefs and his decision in 1679 to restore the poll tax on non-Muslims, which she said would alienate his Hindu subjects.

Burial

Upon her death Aurangzeb gave her the posthumous title 'Sahibat-uz-Zamani' ('Mistress of the Age'). Jahanara is buried in a tomb in the Nizamuddin Dargah complex in New Delhi which is remarkable for its simplicity. The inscription on the tomb reads as follows:

He is the Living, the Sustaining.

Let no one cover my grave except with greenery, for this very grass suffices as a tomb cover for the poor.

The annihilated fakir Lady Jahanara, Disciple of the lords of Chisht, Daughter of Shah Jahan the Warrior (may God illuminate his proof).

Personal Attributes

No formally attributed likeness of her is known to exist. She was highly educated and well versed in Persian and Arabic, as well as a poet of some repute.

Sufism

Together with her brother Dara Shikoh she was a disciple of Mullah Shah Badakhshi, who initiated her into the Qadiriyya Sufi order in 1641. Jahanara Begum made such progress on the Sufi path that Mullah Shah would have named her his successor in the Qadiriyya, but the rules of the order did not allow this.

She wrote a biography of Moinuddin Chishti, the founder of the Chishtiyah order, titled *Munis al-Arwah*, as well as a biography of Mullah Shah, titled *Risalah-i bahibiyah*, in which she also described her initiation by him. Her biography of Moinuddin Chishti is highly regarded for its judgment and literary quality. In it she regarded him as having initiated her spiritually four centuries after his death, described her pilgrimage to Ajmer, and spoke of herself as a *faqirah* to signify her vocation as a Sufi woman.

Jahanara Begum stated that she and her brother Dara were the only descendants of Timur to embrace Sufism. As a patron of Sufi literature, she commissioned translations of and commentaries on many works of classical literature.

Charitable Works

Jahanara was known for her active part in looking after the poor and financing the building of mosques and gardens. In Agra she is best known for sponsoring the building of the Jami Masjid in 1648 in the heart of the old city.

She also made a significant impact on the landscape of the capital city of Shahjahanabad. Of the eighteen buildings in the city of Shahjahanabad commissioned by women, Jahanara commissioned five of them. All of Jahanara's building projects were completed around the year 1650 inside the city walls of Shahjahanabad. The best known of her projects is Chandni Chowk, the central bazaar.

Roshanara Begum

Roshanara Begum was the second daughter of the Mughal ruler, Shah Jahan and Mumtaz Mahal. Born on September 3, 1617, Roshanara was a brilliant woman, a talented poetess, the mastermind behind Aurangazeb's accession to the Mughal throne, and by the time of her death in 1671, one of the most notorious women in the Mughal kingdom. Today, however, Roshanara is best known for the Roshanara Bagh, a pleasure garden located in north Delhi, next to Kamala Nagar Road and Grand Trunk Road. The present-day Roshanara Club which was constructed in the late 1800s by the British is a famous country club that was actually originally a part of the Roshanara Bagh.

Of his four sons, his oldest, Dara Shikoh, was Shah Jahan's favourite son, and heir apparent to the Peacock Throne. Shah Shuja, the second son, was the rebellious Governor of Bengal, with open designs on his father's throne. Aurangzeb, the third son, was the nominal Governor of Deccan. Murad, the youngest son, was granted Governorship of Gujarat, at which position he proved so weak and so ineffectual that Shah Jahan had him stripped of his titles, offering them to Dara Shikoh, instead. This precipitated a family struggle between Shah Jahan and his embittered younger sons, who resolved to depose the aging emperor and seize the throne for themselves. During this power struggle, Dara Shikoh received the support of his oldest sister, Jahanara Begum while Roshanara Begum sided with Aurangzeb, instead.

Roshanara's rise to power began when she successfully foiled a plot by her father and Dara Shikoh to kill Aurangazeb. According to history, Shah Jahan sent a letter of invitation to Aurangazeb to visit Delhi, in order to peacefully resolve the family crisis. In truth, however, Shah Jahan planned to capture, imprison and kill Aurangazeb in prison as he viewed his third son as a serious threat to the throne. When Roshanara got wind of her father's plots, she sent a messenger to Aurangazeb, outlining their father's true intentions, and warning Aurangazeb to stay away from Delhi.

Aurangazeb was extremely grateful to Roshanara for her timely warning. When the war of succession was resolved in favour of Aurangazeb, she quickly became a powerful figure at court. Fearing that Dara Shikoh would kill her for her role in the war of succession if he ever returned to power, Roshanara insisted that Aurangazeb order Dara's execution. Legend has it that Dara was bound in chains, paraded around Chandni Chowk and beheaded. Roshanara then had his bloody head wrapped in a golden turban, packaged neatly and sent to her father as a gift from Aurangazeb and her. Shah Jahan, who opened the package just as he was sitting down to dinner, was so distressed by the sight of his favourite son's head that he fell unconscious to the floor. He remained in a stupor for many days after the incident.

Roshanara's relationship with her older sister, Jahanara, was troubled and tinged by jealousy as the latter was undisputedly their father's favourite daughter. Roshanara scored a major victory against her sister when Aurangazeb, who had been displeased with Jahanara for supporting their father and brother during the war of succession, removed her (Jahanara) from her position as head of the Imperial harem, installing Roshanara in her stead.

Eventually, however, Roshanara and Aurangazeb fell out with each other. Roshanara, who was obliged to remain single, as was the tradition with Mughal princesses, instead took many lovers, some openly, some secretly. In addition, she ruled Aurangazeb's harem with an iron hand and earned the hatred of her brother's many wives. She also had a love of gold and land, and accumulated wealth on a large scale, often by corrupt methods. This resulted in numerous complaints against her, none of which were brought to justice due to her position at Court. In addition, she blatantly misused the sweeping powers Aurangazeb had granted her just before leaving for his long military campaign in the Deccan, to further her own financial ends.

Her enemies soon brought these acts of financial and moral turpitude to Aurangazeb's notice. Himself a very strict Muslim, Aurangazeb frowned on Roshanara's libertine lifestyle and her greed. On his return to Delhi, he stripped Roshanara of her powers, banished her from his court, and ordered her to remain in seclusion and live a pious life in her garden palace outside of Delhi. Finally realizing that Roshanara was fast becoming a dangerous liability and afraid that the scandal following his sister would attach itself to his own name, he actively sought an opportunity to eliminate her from the picture.

That opportunity presented itself in late 1671, when Roshanara was discovered with yet another secret lover in her garden. The incident enraged Aurangazeb and sealed Roshanara's end. At the counsel of his ministers, he had her condemned as a "Kafir" for violating Muslim law and ordered her to be poisoned with her lover. Roshanara died a slow and agonizing death three days later at the age of 54. Aurangazeb had her interred in the Roshanara Bagh, a garden that she had designed and commissioned herself.

Legacy

Shah Jahan's legacy was one of the most profound of all the Mughals. A patron of the fine arts, he continued the Mughal patronage of painting, although his passion was architecture, with the highlight being undoubtedly the Taj Mahal. Painting during his reign reflected the serene prosperity that the Mughals enjoyed with many scenes reflecting Shah Jahan's interest in romance.

One of the greatest legacy that Shah Jahan was a part of during the Mughal rule of India was that of the ferocity of his successor to gain control of the empire. Shah Jahan exemplified one of the highest points in the Mughal Empire but also foreshadowed its downfall through the succession of emperors in the Mughal line. With his accession and downfall at the hands of his sons aside, Shah Jahan can clearly be seen as a leader who changed the landscape of India dramatically in the course of his reign; when you take into consideration that the legacy that brought him down as well as his great accomplishment, Shah Jahan gives us a great wealth of knowledge into the internal workings of an empire that was built from conquering, violence, and tolerance while alluding to the unstable hierarchy and the right to power in the Mughal Empire. He came to power through violence and betrayal and was ultimately brought down by the same means, exacerbating the legacy of the Mughals.

Notable Structures Associated with Shah Jahan

Shah Jahan has left behind a grand legacy of structures constructed during his reign. The most famous of these is the Taj Mahal in Agra built to hold the tomb for his favourite wife, Mumtaz Mahal. Upon his death, his son Aurangazeb had him interred in it next to Mumtaz Mahal. Among his other constructions are Delhi Fort also called the *Red Fort* or *Lal Qila* (Urdu) in Delhi, large sections of Agra Fort, the Jama Masjid (Grand Mosque), Delhi, the Wazir Khan Mosque, Lahore, Pakistan, the Moti Masjid (Pearl Mosque), Lahore, the Shalimar Gardens in Lahore, sections of the Lahore Fort, Lahore, the Jahangir mausoleum -- his father's tomb, the construction of which was overseen by his stepmother Nur Jahan and the Shahjahan Mosque, Thatta, Pakistan. He also had the Peacock Throne, Takht e Taus, made to celebrate his rule.

There is a crater named after Shah Jahan on the asteroid 433 Eros. Craters on Eros are named after famous fictional and real-life lovers.

European Accounts of Shah Jahan's Personal Life

Numerous accounts of Shah Jahan's personal life were recounted by contemporary European writers.

Shah Jahan's Family

Like all his ancestors, Shah Jahan's court included many wives, concubines, and dancing girls. Several European chroniclers have noted this. Niccolao Manucci wrote that "it would seem as if the only thing Shah Jahan cared for was the search for women to serve his pleasure" and "for this end he established a fair at his court. No one was allowed to enter except women of all ranks that is to say, great and small, rich and poor, but all beautiful." When he was detained in the Red Fort at Agra, Aurangzeb permitted him to retain "the whole of his female establishment, including the singing and dancing women." Manucci notes that Shah Jahan didn't lose his "weakness for the flesh" even when he had grown very old. However, most of the European travellers in India had access to such information primarily through bazaar gossip and not first hand.

Dara Shikoh

Dara Shikoh (March 20, 1615-August 30, 1659) was the eldest son and the heir apparent of the Mughal Emperor Shah Jahan and his wife Mumtaz Mahal. He was favoured as a successor by his father and his sister Jahanara Begum, but was defeated by his younger brother Aurangzeb in a bitter struggle for the Mughal throne. The trajectory of the historical evolution of the Indian subcontinent, had Dara prevailed over Aurangzeb, has been a matter of some conjecture among historians..

The Struggle for Succession and Death

On September 6, 1657, the illness of emperor Shah Jahan triggered a desperate struggle for power among the four Mughal princes, though realistically only Dara and Aurangzeb had a chance of emerging victorious. Shah Shuja was the first to make his move, declaring himself emperor in Bengal and marching towards Agra while Murad Baksh allied himself with Aurangzeb.

Despite strong support from Shah Jahan, who had recovered enough from his illness to remain a strong factor in the struggle for supremacy, and the victory of his army led by his eldest son Sulaiman Shikoh over Shah Shuja in the battle of Bahadurpur on February 14, 1658, Dara was defeated by Aurangzeb and Murad at the battlefield of Samugarh, 13 km from Agra on May 30, 1658. Subsequently Aurangzeb took over Agra fort and deposed emperor Shah Jahan on June 8, 1658.

After the defeat Dara retreated from Agra to Delhi and thence to Lahore. His next destination was Multan and then to Thatta (Sindh). From Sindh, he crossed the Rann of Kachchh and reached Kathiawar, where he met Shah Nawaz Khan, the governor of the province of Gujarat who opened the treasury to Dara and helped him to recruit a new army. He occupied Surat and advanced towards Ajmer. Foiled in his hopes of persuading the fickle but powerful Rajput feudatory, Maharaja Jaswant Singh of Marwar, to support his cause, the luckless Dara decided to make a stand and fight Aurangzeb's relentless pursuers but was once again comprehensively routed in the battle of Deorai (near Ajmer) on March 11, 1659. After this defeat he fled to Sindh and sought refuge under Malik Jiwan, a Baluch chieftain whose life had on more than one occasion been saved by the Mughal prince from the wrath of Shah Jahan. However, Malik betrayed Dara and turned him (and his second son Sipihr Shikoh) over to Aurangzeb's army on June 10, 1659.

Dara was brought to Delhi, placed on a filthy elephant and paraded through the streets of the capital in chains. Dara's fate was decided by the political threat he posed as a prince popular with the common people-a convocation of nobles and clergy, called by Aurangzeb in response to the perceived danger of insurrection in Delhi, declared him a threat to the public peace and an apostate from Islam. He was murdered by assassins on the night of August 30, 1659.

Intellectual Pursuits

Dara Shikoh is widely renowned as an enlightened paragon of the harmonious coexistence of heterodox traditions on the Indian subcontinent. He was an erudite champion of mystical religious speculation and a poetic diviner of syncretic cultural interaction among people of all faiths. This made him a heretic in the eyes of his orthodox brother and a suspect eccentric in the view of many of the worldly power brokers swarming around the Mughal throne. Dara was a follower of Lahore's famous Qadiri Sufi saint Hazrat Mian Mir, whom he was introduced to by Mullah Shah Badakhshi (Miaņ Mir's spiritual disciple and successor) and who was so widely respected among all communities that he was invited to lay the foundation stone of the Golden Temple in Amritsar by the Sikhs. Dara subsequently developed a friendship with the seventh Sikh Guru, Guru Har Rai. Dara devoted much effort towards finding a common mystical language between Islam and Hinduism. Towards this goal he completed the translation of 50 Upanishads from its original Sanskrit into Persian in 1657 so it could be read by Muslim scholars. His translation is often called *Sirr-e-Akbar* (The Greatest Mystery), where he states boldly, in the Introduction, his speculative hypothesis that the work referred to in the Qur'an as the "*Kitab al-maknun*" or the *hidden book* is none other than the Upanishads. His most famous work, Majma ul-Bahrain ("The Mingling of the Two Seas"), was also devoted to a revelation of the mystical and pluralistic affinities between Sufic and Vedantic speculation.

Patron of Art

He was also a patron of fine arts, music and dancing, a trait frowned upon by his sibling Aurangzeb. In fact many of his paintings are quite detailed and compare well to a professional artist of his time. The 'Dara Shikoh album' is a collection of paintings and calligraphy assembled from the 1630s until his death. It was presented to his wife Nadira Banu in 1641-42 and remained with her until her death after which the album was taken into the royal library and the inscriptions connecting it with Dara Shikoh were deliberately erased; however not everything was vandalised and many calligraphy scripts and paintings still bear his mark.

Dara Shikoh is also credited with the commissioning of several exquisite, still extant, examples of Mughal architecture-among them the tomb of his wife Nadira Banu in Lahore, the tomb of Hazrat Mian Mir also in Lahore, the *Dara Shikoh Library* in Delhi, the *Akhun Mullah Shah Mosque* in Srinagar in Kashmir and the *Pari Mahal* garden palace (also in Srinagar in Kashmir).

Mian Mir

Baba Sain Mir Mohammed Sahib, (c. 1550 – 11 August 1635) popularly known as Mian Mir is a famous Sufi saint who resided in Lahore, specifically in the town of *Begampura* (in present-day Pakistan). He belonged to the Qadiri order of Sufism. He is famous for being a spiritual instructor of Dara Shikoh, the eldest son of Mughal emperor Shah Jahan. He is identified as the founder of the Mian Khail branch of the Qadiri order.

Mian Mir and Emperor Jahangir

Mian Mir was a friend of God-loving people and he would shun worldly, selfish men, covetous Emirs and ambitious Nawabs who ran after faqirs to get their blessings. To stop such people from coming to see him, Mian Mir posted his *mureeds* (disciples) at the gate of his house.

Once, Jahangir, the Mughal emperor, with all his retinue came to pay homage to the great faqir. He came with all the pomp and show that befitted an emperor. Mian Mir's sentinels however, stopped the emperor at the gate and requested him to wait until their master had given permission to enter. Jahangir felt slighted. No one had ever dared delay or question his entry to any place in his kingdom. Yet he controlled his temper and composed himself. He waited for permission. After a while, he was ushered into Mian Mir's presence. Unable to hide his wounded vanity, Jahangir, as soon as he entered, told Mian Mir in Persian: *Ba dar-e-darvis darbane naa-bayd* ("On the doorstep of a faqir, there should be no sentry").

Pir Mian Mir, whose mind and soul were one with the Lord, caring little for the emperor's angst, replied in Persian: *Babayd keh sag-e-dunia na ayad* ("They are there so that the dogs of the world/ selfish men may not enter").

The emperor was ashamed and asked for forgiveness. Then, with folded hands, Jahangir requested Mian Mir to pray for the success of the campaign which he intended to launch for the conquest of the Deccan. Meanwhile, a poor man entered and, bowing his head to Mian Mir, made an offering of a rupee before him. The Pir asked the devotee to pick up the rupee and give it to the poorest, neediest person in the audience. The devotee went from one dervish to another but none accepted the rupee. The devotee returned to Mian Mir with the rupee saying: "Master, none of the dervishes will accept the rupee. None is in need, it seems."

"Go and give this rupee to him," said the faqir, pointing to Jahangir. "He is the poorest and most needy of the lot. Not content with a big kingdom, he covets the kingdom of the Deccan. For that, he has come all the way from Delhi to beg. His hunger is like a fire that burns all the more furiously with more wood. It has made him needy, greedy and grim. Go and give the rupee to him."

Mian Mir, the Sikh Gurus and his Place in Sikhism

Mian Mir, holds a pivotal legendary place in Sikhism and in Sikh history. Sikh Children and Sikh people around the world learn about him, his spiritual contribution and his place in Sikh history.

Mian Mir and Guru Arjan Meet

Guru Arjan Dev, the fifth Sikh Guru, often visited Lahore, the birth-place of his father (the fourth Guru, Guru Ram Das) to meet his relatives. On the occasion of one of such visit, he called on *Mian Mir*. The two men of God met and became very close lifelong friends. *Mian Mir* was thirteen years older than Guru Arjan.

The Foundation-Stone of the Harimandir Sahib

Guru Arjan was responsible for the construction of many tanks and buildings. In 1588, he planned to build a temple in the centre of the holy tank called *Amritsar* or the *pool of nectar.* As the temple was to be thrown open to people of all castes, creeds and climes, he invited Mian Mir to lay the foundation stone of the Harmandir Sahib. He came to the city of Amritsar wearing a religious mendicant's long cloak made up of patches of coarse wool and a cone-shaped cap, with a rose flower on top.

Mian Mir was given one of the warmest welcomes for which Guru Arjan was famous. The two holy men embraced each other in sincere love and regard. The purpose of the temple was disclosed to the Sufi saint. Mian Mir was delighted at the fine objectives the Guru had in mind. The foundation-stone was laid. Hymns were sung in praise of God and sweets were distributed among the audience.

Guru Arjan's Death

In 1606, Guru Arjan was implicated in the affair of Prince Khusraw, who had rebelled against his father, Jahangir. He was imprisoned in the Lahore fort and tortured. When Mian Mir heard about it, he came to see the Guru. He found Guru Arjan calm and serene, having completely resigned himself to the will of God. Mian Mir suggested to the Guru whether he should intercede with Emperor Jahangir on his behalf. The Guru forbade him saying that God's will must have its course unchecked, as it was not proper to interfere with its working. He only asked for the saint's blessings for his son, Har Gobind.

Guru Har Gobind

A couple of years after the death of Guru Arjan, his son and successor Guru Har Gobind, a lad of thirteen, called on Mian Mir at Lahore.

Guru Tegh Bahadur

Guru Tegh Bahadur, the son of Guru Har Gobind and the ninth Guru, as a child met Mian Mir who blessed him.

Death

After having lived a long life of piety and virtuosity, Mian Mir died on 11 August 1635 (7 Rabi' al-awwal, 1045 according to the Islamic Calendar), after having suffered from severe dysentery for some time. He was eighty-eight years old.

His funeral was read by Mughal prince Dara Shikoh, who was a highly devoted disciple of the Saint.

He was buried at a place which was about a mile from Lahore near Alamganj, that is at the south-east of the city. Mian Mir's spiritual successor was Mullah Shah Badakhshi.

Mian Mir's *Mazar* (Mausoleum) still attracts hundreds of devotees each day and he is revered by many Sikhs as well as Muslims.

Mullah Shah Badakhshi

Mullah Shah Badakhshi, popularly known as "Mullah Shah" was a Muslim Sufi, spiritual successor of the famous Mian Mir. He belonged to the Qadiri order of Sufism. He was the spiritual mentor of the mughal prince Dara Shikoh Qadri. Dara Shikoh desired to be initiated into the Qadri order at the hands of Hazrat Mian Mir. After Hazrat Mian Mir's *wisal*, Dara Shikoh's search for a murshid took him to Kashmir where he met Hazrat Mulla Shah Badakhsi. In Sakinatul Awliya Dara Shikoh writes in the chapter titled "Mulla Shah Badakhsi":

> *"This faqir is his (Mulla Shah's) servant and disciple. His blessed name is Shah Mohammad. Hazrat Mian Mir used to call him Mohammad Shah and Mian Mir's disciples and devotees would refer to him as Hazrat Akhund."*

Sai Hazrat Abu Saeed Fateh Ullah Masoom Al-Gillani Al-Qadri (Mullah Shah) was the caliph and deputy of Sai Hazrat Mian Mir Sahib Ji.Hazrat Abu Saeed was powerful cleric of Mohammadan law and the pronounced professor of his times. His actual name was "Syed Fateh Ullah Gillani" and family name (patronymic identify) was Abu Saeed, his title was Khwaja Masoom, and Mulla Masoom, which was bestowed from threshold of Sai Hazrat Mian Mir Sahib Ji and Mulla Abu Saeed Khan also used in history references. He perceived the given title a component of the faith and overlooked all other names. That's why Crown Prince of India "Shahzada Darashikoh" in his manuscript on Sai Hazrat

Mian Mir Sahib Ji "Sakeena Tul Awliya" at various places calls him "Abu Saeed", "Mulla Saeed", "Khwaja Masoom", "Mulla Masoom", "Khan e Jahan", "Abu Saeed Khan", and "Khan e Khanan (chief of the chief)" are also available. Other authors also used titles like Makhdom ul Asr, and Makhdom ul Mashaikh etc.

In his institution, pupils from far boarded to fulfill the thirst of knowledge. Abu Saeed had two sons, Syed Saeed Ud Din Gillani, titled by "Surkh Poosh" was the elder one. He was lunatic and acceptable close to Allah by birth. He was out of worldly dependency therefore never married. He was buried next to Hazrat Abu Saeed in "Rattar Chattar", near Dera Baba Nanak, Tehsil/ Distt Gordaspur, Punjab, India. The Shrine of Sai Hazrat Makhdom Syed Abu Saeed Fateh Ullah Masoom is as high as 150fts, 12 ft (3.7 m) wide Nanak Shahi brink's walls. Inside the shrine, beside the grave of Khawaja Abu Saeed, are the graves of his Wife, Syed Saeed Udin Surkh Posh and Syed Zain Udin Sher Sawar.

Younger son was Syed Zain Ud Din Gillani Qadri renowned as Zain Ul Awliya, the one by whom, the genealogy of Abu Saeed is trickled down up till now. Hazrat Abu Saeed had one daughter, Makhdoma Syeda Fatima Gillani who's married with Abu Saeed's nephew in Uchh Shreef.

Mian Mir remained practicing spirituality for three years at Abu Saeed's residence. Abu Saeed served Mian Mir day and night with great purity. He thanked Abu Saeed, as he was set to depart from Uchh Shreef, and said, whatever demanded should be granted ask Abu Saeed what do you need? Abu Saeed replied Hazrat! Seems tough to stay away from you, just want to be a plaintiff. Hazrat Mian Mir accepted him in fealty and ordered him to first accomplish all responsibilities and tasks from Uchh Shreef and come to my permanent threshold Lahore.

Sai Makhdom Abu Saeed Syed Fateh Ullah Masoom left every thing and came to Lahore where Sai Hazrat Mian Mir Sahib Ji granted him the first ever deputyship (a caliph).

Nadira Banu

Nadira Banu was the wife of Dara Shikoh, the heir to Shah Jahan's throne and the crown prince of his Indian empire. After his brother's rise to power, Prince Dara's immediate family and all of his supporters were in grave danger. She died in 1659, several months before his execution, and was survived by two daughters.

Personality and Lineage

Nadira Banu was considered to be rather beautiful, and considerably intelligent. Her husband-to-be was reportedly eager for the marriage and they had a good relationship throughout his turbulent life. Nadira was the daughter of Shah Jahan's half-brother, Pawaz, and therefore his cousin, but there were no real objections to this from either party. This sort of thing was probably commonplace in seventeenth century India.

Relationship with Jahanara

Nadira and Jahanara Begum, her sister-in-law, were said to have gotten on well; a fact which probably sprung from Jahanara's involvement in her wedding and her closeness to her brother. Jahanara had consciously decided to support Dara, the most beloved to her of all of her siblings, over Aurengzeb, and she made outward demonstrations of this decision.

According to legend, Aurengzeb had fallen sick sometime during his teen years. It was at this time he called Jahanara in. He then asked her outright if she would support him in his bid for the crown. She refused. Despite how unpopular this must have made her in his sight, and her undying loyalty to her brother Dara, she went on to become the head of the harem in Aurengzeb's court.

Jahanara's outward declarations of love for her eldest brother no doubt strengthened the relationship between herself and his wife, and when she died, she left the cream of her fortune to one of the daughters Nadira had borne him.

Wedding and Married Life

The marriage was originally arranged when the couple were both teenagers, by Dara's mother, Mumtaz Mahal. When the Empress died with the birth of her last child, a girl, the wedding arrangements halted as India plunged into mourning and Shah Jahan was consumed in his grief. After much coaxing by many, including his favourite daughter Jahanara, he resumed life as normal and let her oversee the remaining aspects of the wedding. Before Shah Jahan died, he and Jahanara had been shunned from their lovely palace by Aurangzeb, the third son in line for the throne. Driven by his ambition and his fanatical Islamic views, he seized the throne and eventually defeated his brother (who was considerably more well-liked than he, a fact which was highlighted later on in his strict, extremist rule). While Shah Jahan's eldest son was said to be tolerant, wise and beloved, he was nonetheless overrun and eventually executed, leaving the crown to his brother, who ruled his empire harshly and assured that he was one of the remembered, if not fondly.

For these reasons, Nadira and her children were caught in a dangerous feud. She remained faithful to her husband until her death in the late sixteen-fifties.

Dara Shikoh was said to be a fine painter, and many of his works, when criticized, were considered to be almost of a professional standard. Some of his works were collected and gifted to Nadira Banu, and it was a token of her affection for him that she cherished it until her death, when it went on display at a museum.

Shah Shuja (Mughal)

Shah Shuja (June 23, 1616 – 1660) was the second son of the Mughal emperor Shah Jahan and empress Mumtaz Mahal.

Emperor Shah Jahan appointed Shah Shuja as the *Subahdar* or governor of Bengal in 1639. In 1642, Shuja was also given the charge of the province of Orissa. He ruled the provinces for more than twenty years, from 1639 to 1660. During the period there were two short breaks: first in 1647-1648, when he was with the emperor on his campaigns against rebels in the Afghan passes; and the second in 1652, when he was at Kabul for about four months from April to July. During the later part of his Subahdari, from 1658 he twice proceeded towards the capital in his bid to contest for the throne.

Shah Shuja built the Bara Katra between 1644 and 1646 in Dhaka to serve as his official residence.

When Shah Jahan fell ill, a struggle for the throne started between his four sons-Dara Shikoh, Shah Shuja, Aurangzeb and Murad Baksh. Shuja immediately crowned himself the emperor and took imperial titles. He marched with a large army, backed by a good number of war-boats in the river Ganges. However, he was beaten by Dara's army in a hotly contested Battle of Bahadurpur (in modern Uttar Pradesh, India). Shuja turned back to Rajmahal to make further preparations. In the meantime, Aurangzeb defeated Dara twice (at Dharmat and Samugarh), caught him, executed him on a charge of heresy and ascended the throne. Shuja marched again to the capital, this time against Aurangzeb. A battle took place on 5 January 1658 at Khwaja (Fatehpur district, Uttar Pradesh, India) where Shuja was defeated.

After his defeat, Shuja retreated towards Bengal. He was pursued by the imperial army under Mir Jumla. Shuja put up a good fight against them. However, he was finally defeated in the last battle in April 1660. After each defeat he had to face desertions in his own army, but he did not lose heart. He, rather, reorganised the army with renewed vigor. But when he was going to be surrounded at Tandah, and when he found that reorganisation of the army was no longer possible, he decided to leave Bengal (and India) for good and take shelter in Arakan. He left Tanda with his family and retinue in the afternoon of 6 April 1660 and reached Dhaka on 12 April. He left Dhaka on 6 May and boarded the Arakanese ships on 12 May at Bhulua (near present-day Noakhali, Bangladesh).

Shuja made contacts with Arakan before his departure from Bengal. His plan was to go to Mecca and then to Persia or Turkey. But as the sea was rough in May and the rainy season, he asked for asylum in Arakan for a few months and help in procuring ships. On his arrival at Mrohaung (Mrauk-U), the capital of Arakan, the king warmly received him through his ministers. A house was allowed for Shuja's stay in the outskirts of the city. But as time passed, the king's attitude to his guest changed; either for getting hold of rich treasures Shuja carried with him, or to get one of the pretty and cultured daughters of Shuja as his spouse, the king picked up a quarrel with Shuja. Shuja, his family and his retinue were tortured to death. A few of his retinue, fleeing to the countryside, could escape the gruesome murder, but none of the Mughal princes or princesses survived.

6

Aurangzeb

Muhi ud-din Mohammad Aurangzeb Bahadur Alamgir I, more commonly known as Aurangzeb (November 4, 1618– March 3, 1707), also known by his chosen imperial title Alamgir I (Conqueror of the Universe), was the 6th Mughal Emperor whose reign lasted from 1658 until his death in 1707. Aurangzeb's reign as the Mughal monarch was marked by many wars of expansion.

Aurangzeb, having ruled most of the Indian subcontinent for nearly half a century, was the second longest reigning Mughal emperor after Akbar. In this period he successfully brought a larger area, notably in southern India, under Mughal rule than ever before. A devout Muslim, Aurangzeb tried to encourage all his people to follow the doctrines of Islam. He destroyed many works of art because he feared that they might be worshipped as idols.

After his death, the Mughal Empire gradually shrunk. Aurangzeb's successors, the "Later Mughals", lacked his strong hand and the great fortunes amassed by his predecessors.

Rise to Throne

Early life: Aurangzeb was the third son of the fifth Mughal emperor Shah Jahan and Mumtaz Mahal (Arjumand Banu Begum). After a rebellion by his father, part of Aurangzeb's childhood was spent as a virtual hostage at his grandfather Jahangir's court. Mohammad Saleh Kamboh Salafi had been one of his childhood teachers.

After Jahangir's death in 1627, Aurangzeb returned to live with his parents. Shah Jahan followed the Mughal practice of assigning authority to his sons, and in 1634 put Aurangzeb in charge of the Deccan campaign. Following his success in 1636, Aurangzeb became Subahdar (governor) of the Deccan. At this time, he began building a new city near the former capital of Khirki which he named Aurangabad after himself. In 1637, he married Rabia Durrani. During this period the Deccan was relatively peaceful. In the Mughal court, however, Shah Jahan began to show greater and greater favouritism to his eldest son Dara Shikoh.

In 1644, Aurangzeb's sister Jahanara Begum was accidentally burned in Agra. This event precipitated a family crisis which had political consequences. Aurangzeb suffered his father's displeasure when he returned to Agra three weeks after the event, instead of immediately. Shah Jahan dismissed him as the governor of the Deccan. Aurangzeb later claimed (1654) that he had resigned in protest of his father favouring Dara.

In 1645, he was barred from the court for seven months. But later, Shah Jahan appointed him governor of Gujarat; he performed well and was rewarded. In 1647, Shah Jahan made him governor of Balkh and Badakhshan (in modern Afghanistan and Tajikistan), replacing Aurangzeb's ineffective brother Murad Baksh. These areas at the time were under attack from various forces and Aurangzeb's military skill proved successful.

He was appointed governor of Multan and Sindh, and began a protracted military struggle against the Safavid army in an effort to capture the city of Kandahar. He failed, and fell again into his father's disfavour.

In 1652, Aurangzeb was re-appointed governor of the Deccan. In an effort to extend the empire, Aurangzeb attacked the border kingdoms of Golconda (1657), and Bijapur (1658). Both times, Shah Jahan called off the attacks near the moment of Aurangzeb's triumph. In each case Dara Shikoh interceded and arranged a peaceful end to the attacks.

Battle of Dharmat-I

The Battle of Dharmat: Fought by the rebel Mughal princes, Aurangzeb and Murad, against the leading Rajput mansabdar in the Mughal Empire, Raja Jaswant Singh, on the 15th of April 1658. The battle was fought near the village of Dharmat outside the city of Ujjain—the capital of the Mughal province of Malwa (the western portion of modern India's Madhya Pradesh state).

Background: To understand why the battle was fought, we need to understand the power structure in medieval India. The leading powers of that age were the Mughal Emperor (*badhsah or padishah*), his sons (*shahzada*), and his officers...in that order. These officers included the prime minister (*Wazir*), the army chief (*Mir bakshi*), the artillery chief (*Mir atish*), the provincial governors (*subahdars*), and the military officers (*mansabdars*). Each of these officers had their own separate armies and each was assigned agricultural estates by the emperor to finance those armies—the principal force of these armies was cavalry formed by horses imported from Central Asia, Iran, and Arabia.

In this power structure the large Hindu population was represented in the lower ranks as infantry, gunners of the artillery, and camp followers. These Hindus were recruited from the villages in every Mughal province where their brethren tilled the soil and paid land revenue but could always rebel and engage in plunder whenever they saw the opportunity (the leading infantry group were the Purbias for a variety of reasons.

There were also Hindus (and Muslims) engaged in commerce and trade, who financed the military activities of their rulers in the form of loans. From this class were recruited the clerks, secretaries, and accountants that administered each Mughal province and each Hindu state.

At the very top of Hindu society were the Rajas (of Rajasthan), the minor Rajas in other provinces, and their armed followers. For the minor Rajas in the provinces the local governor (subahdar) was like a mini-emperor with whom they could either negotiate or fight.

Rajasthan or, more accurately, Rajputana was in an entirely different category. Its rulers had the resources to fight, and negotiate as equals, directly with the Mughal Emperor or his sons. From their local breeds of horses the Rajputs of Rajasthan recruited large cavalry armies and by negotiations or battles raised their position from military officers to provincial governors. The highest ranks of prime minister, army chief, and artillery chief were out of their reach in an Islamic state but their position was one of equality with the Mughal princes, and sometimes with the Emperor himself.

The Mughal princes began their careers by administering provinces and by leading independent military campaigns on behalf of their father. In this process they acquired the resources and capability to fight for the position of Emperor on their father's death—the Islamic state did not recognize hereditary succession of the eldest son.

The War of Succession: In 1658 the Mughal Emperor Shah Jahan was ill and on his deathbed. He was extremely fond of his eldest son Dara and considered him the fittest to rule after him—to secure Dara's position Shah Jahan proclaimed him as his heir and transferred administrative matters to him. Dara held the provinces of Allahabad, Multan, and Punjab to pay for his army...in addition he had access to the Mughal treasury and to his father's capable officers at the capital Agra.

His three brothers Shuja, Aurangzeb, and Murad had always been jealous of the fatherly affection showered on their sibling and refused to accept his role in the administration. Shuja held the province of Bengal, the richest province in that period, and was the first to declare himself the new Emperor and the first to lead his army towards Agra. Against him Shah Jahan sent an army commanded by Raja Jai Singh of the Jaipur state in Rajasthan. To blood him in battle Dara's son Sulaiman was sent in the Raja's care along with several high officers.

Shah Jahan's youngest son Murad had been assigned the province of Gujarat. Murad looted the port city of Surat to acquire more money and then declared himself Emperor.

Shah Jahan's third son Aurangzeb was administering the Deccan (modern Maharashtra and parts of Karnataka) and was quietly intriguing with his brothers and with the nobles at Agra. He was the most austere and Islamic of the four brothers...but more than that Aurangzeb was the most capable of them in military matters. To further complicate matters for Dara, Shaista Khan, a partisan of Aurangzeb held the province of Malwa, lying north of the Deccan and east of Gujarat.

Dara naturally feared Aurangzeb the most, but the latter was too clever to follow the lead of his headstrong siblings and did not declare himself Emperor. He instead proposed to visit Agra and meet his sick father—in those days a prince could not travel without the protection of his army so this proposal was merely a ruse for attacking Agra. Dara had to take steps to defeat Murad, and more importantly, to prevent Aurangzeb from marching north through Malwa.Unfortunately most *mansabdars* refused the dangerous task of opposing the military genius and resources of Aurangzeb. From the geographical reality they knew that Murad was likely to join forces with his older brother and follow his lead. Opposing their combined might was only possible for a military commander who had comparable resources.

Maharaja Jaswant Singh of the Jodhpur state in Rajasthan had the resources in money and cavalry to oppose one of the princes. Seeing the fear of the other nobles he volunteered to not only defeat Aurangzeb but boasted of bringing him back to Agra as a prisoner! He was assigned the province of Malwa to boost his resources.

Dara did not do what he should have done as an Emperor-to-be....he did not place himself in the command. For opposing Murad another army was assembled and led by a Mughal officer Qasim Khan. For his payment Qasim Khan was assigned the province of Gujarat—and since the road to Gujarat passes through Malwa, Qasim was ordered to follow the lead of Jaswant Singh until the situation in Gujarat was clear.

The Rajput chief was first in the field. Murad, marching from Gujarat, was intimidated by Jaswant Singh's army and swerved south to join Aurangzeb. Their combined forces entered Malwa and began seizing the outlying forts and towns. Jaswant Singh made a clumsy attempt at diplomacy and intrigue by stating that he had no power to fight Aurangzeb and that if the princes pardoned him and returned to their provinces, Jaswant would take their case to the Emperor.

Aurangzeb was too clever to fall for that and replied that if he really wanted their pardon Jaswant should come *alone* and submit. Such submissions were only made by those who had been crushed into defeat and taken prisoner—so the Rajput chief prepared for battle. Military Resources: the core of Jaswant Singh's army was formed by 7000 Rajput cavaliers of his own kingdom, most of them belonging to the Rathor clan. 2000 of these stood around Jaswant in the center of the army while several thousand were posted in the vanguard that would take the attack to the enemy. The rest were placed in the advanced reserve between the center and the vanguard—in all three sections were hundreds of Rajputs from other clans of Rajasthan. After reaching Malwa, Jaswant had also recruited many local Rajput clans into his army,

Chandrawats, Bundelas, and Jhalas—these were also distributed evenly among the three sections while some were left to protect the camp. There were even *Maratha* chiefs among these recruits; two named Maluji and Parsuji were assigned to guard the camp.

The right wing of the army was under an imperial Rajput officer from Agra named Raja Rai Singh Sesodia who stood independent with his own clansmen. Similarly the left wing was led by an imperial Muslim officer named Iftikhar Khan. Both these wings had between 3000-5000 men and the vanguard was thus the strongest element of Jaswant's army. Qasim Khan and his 5000 men had set off one week behind the Rajputs and, now that Murad had joined Aurangzeb, Qasim's force was under Jaswant Singh's orders. Qasim was placed in the vanguard, raising its strength to nearly 10,000 men.

The vanguard was also the strongest portion of Aurangzeb's army comprising 8000 cavaliers under his son, Mohammad Sultan. A few thousand men were in the advanced reserve while in the center around Aurangzeb was the rest of his cavalry—this force was boosted by the cavalry under his officers to almost 5000 men. The left wing was under Aurangzeb's younger son Mohammad Azam while the right wing was composed of the entire army of Aurangzeb's brother Murad coming down from Gujarat.

In Aurangzeb's army were many Maratha chiefs recruited from his province in the Deccan. Some Rajput chiefs (Rao Karan of Bikaner and Subhkaran Bundela of Datia) assigned to him previously by Shah Jahan naturally followed their commander to war. One Rajput chief, Raja Indradyumna of Dhamdhera, was released from confinement in a Malwa fort and out of personal gratitude joined Aurangzeb's army.

In sheer numbers Aurangzeb's force far outnumbered Jaswant's army, but numbers by themselves are not important—*where* and *how* those numbers are used to apply force decides the outcome of a battle.

Aurangzeb's real superiority lay in artillery. His guns were manned by teams of Europeans; Dutch, Portuguese, French, and Italian, all of who had been recruited during the campaigns and battles in the south. While the fighting races of India (high-born cavaliers) despised artillery and placed their reliance on horses and swords, they appreciated artillery's utility in destroying the enemy forts and in stopping the charge of the enemy cavalry. Handling gunpowder and dragging the guns through the mud and the dust was anathema to them, hence they left the task of manning those guns to low-caste Muslims and Hindus.

This meant that there was little innovation in the use of artillery. Later in the 18th and 19th centuries this Indian artillery was found to be superior to European guns in *caliber and design* but the European gunners reduced that superiority by their *accuracy and better rate of firing*. This difference was seen also in the Battle of Dharmat.

The Battle: knowing the enemy's superiority in numbers and artillery Jaswant Singh had placed his army in a strong defensive position. On three sides they had dug ditches joined to a swamp, which made the ground muddy and soft, thus planning to bog down the advancing enemy cavalry. After that the Rajputs on their light cavalry would advance and cut down the stranded enemy.

On the morning of 15 April, the battle began with the general firing of the artillery, rockets, and muskets from both sides. Aurangzeb advanced slowly and the effect of his European gunners was soon felt—their shots, instead of bouncing along the ground or going wayward, were being fired from elevated positions and at such calculated angles as to land bang in the middle of the cavalry in the vanguard. Under cover of this barrage the musketeers and archers also came within range and began shooting down the trapped horsemen. Aurangzeb's band burst forth with the triumphant notes of the trumpets and the beating of kettledrums in anticipation of an easy victory—however they had not reckoned with Rajput valour.

The Rajput chiefs in the vanguard, Ratan Singh Rathor, Mukund Singh Hada, Dayal Singh Jhala, Arjun Singh Hada, and Sujan Singh Sesodia, loudly exhorted their clansmen to send the enemy to hell. Shouting cries of *Ram! Ram!* the Rajput cavalry burst out of their lines and charged headlong towards the enemy. Disregarding the first few salvos from Aurangzeb's army they cut down his gunners and his artillery chief, Murshid Quli Khan, and surged towards the enemy vanguard.

Another chief named Zulfiqar Khan was wounded and knocked senseless as the vanguard crumpled on itself. The alarmed Aurangzeb sent up the advanced reserve in support and, as the close combat raged, himself pushed forward with the center. His officers Saf Shikan Khan and Shaikh Mir brought their forces around the flanks and closed the path behind the charging Rajputs.

On Jaswant's side, men of the advanced reserve and the center had also gone up in support but the muddy ground slowed their advance...Qasim Khan's force in the vanguard had neither gone with the first charge nor had they advanced in support. Instead, when they beheld Aurangzeb's force moving forward, Qasim's men fled to save their own lives.

Aurangzeb's gunners recovered their artillery after losing it to the charging Rajputs and again commenced firing at the enemy. His right wing under Murad advanced to fight and kill Iftikhar Khan on Jaswant's left. Seeing that the awakened hopes of a victory, kindled by the charging Rajputs in the vanguard, were now snuffed out and the Muslims of the vanguard were running away, Rai Singh Sesodia left the field with his clansmen in the right wing. The locally raised Chandrawats and Bundelas also departed for their homes.

Jaswant Singh kept his place in the center with 2000 Rajputs of his own kingdom. All around them the enemy advanced and artillery shots landed in their midst but the Raja of Jodhpur would not leave the field. He had been out-manoeuvred in the campaign and out-generalled in the battle but he was not going to be *out-fought* by the enemy. Jaswant had resolved to die a hero's death while fighting to the last, which was the ideal for a Rajput defending his home from invaders.

This however was not such a battle—in an internecine quarrel of Mughal princes why should the head of the Rathor clan, and the future hope of Jodhpur in those uncertain times, sacrifice his life? So thinking, Jaswant's generals Askaran and Maheshdas Gaur, and his minister Govardhan, caught the bridle of his horse and forced him away from the field. They retired to their home of Jodhpur while the survivors of Iftikhar Khan's force and the untouched army of Qasim Khan were already on the road to Agra—some of them however stayed behind to join the service of Aurangzeb.

Criticism: Dharmat was the first battle in North India where European gunners were prominent in the artillery—these gunners later gave good service to Aurangzeb's sons who fought a similar war of succession half a century later (Still later in the 18th and 19th centuries European *infantry commanders* would come to lead the raw foot soldiers in the Indian armies.)

Despite the superior use of artillery the charge of the Rajput cavalry in the vanguard nearly turned the outcome of the battle. This proves how smaller numbers employed at the right place and at the critical moment can defeat a larger enemy force—the few thousand Rajputs silenced Aurangzeb's artillery and shattered his vanguard.

If the other units under Jaswant had moved in behind them to capture the guns and occupy the ground, Aurangzeb's men would have fled to save their own lives. However because of the muddy ground the heavy cavalry of the Muslim soldiers under Jaswant could not advance quickly enough. Only the Rajputs of the advanced reserve, on their light cavalry, could gallop across to join their brethren of the vanguard. But they were not enough to prevent the enemy from recovering his guns and closing around the shattered ranks of the vanguard.

A general advance of the center and the wings could not be made because their artillery would have become bogged down in that same ground. So when the victorious Rajputs of the vanguard were ultimately surrounded by Aurangzeb's advanced reserve and center, defection became general in these units.

Iftikhar Khan on the left wing was attacked by Murad and died fighting. His wing dispersed after his death and some of his officers went over to Aurangzeb after the battle. Similarly Qasim Khan's army in the vanguard was suspected of either sympathy to Aurangzeb or indifference to Jaswant Singh's army. However after the battle they did not join Aurangzeb and retreated to Agra, confirming that the second reason is more accurate.

The Rajputs of the vanguard sacrificed their lives, not for the sake of the Mughal throne, but for their own King, Jaswant. His victory would have raised the prestige of Jodhpur—the wealth looted from the enemy camp and the rewards showered by Shah Jahan and Dara would have been shared by every Rajput noble and each Rajput soldier in Jodhpur.

The Rajputs under Rai Singh Sesodia and the locally raised Chandrawats and Bundelas did not share this enthusiasm since they were junior commanders and their rewards would've been fewer. They were not interested in dying for the sake of the Mughals or for the sake of Jaswant Singh. Such feelings were common also among the Purbia and Jat infantry, the low-caste gunners, and the Maratha auxiliaries. In conclusion, Jaswant Singh's plan of holding off the enemy from a defensive position and then launching his cavalry at the advancing enemy bogged down in the mud, was negated by Aurangzeb's superior artillery. The Mughal prince did not make an attack even though he had larger numbers with him—instead he made a slow general advance carrying the artillery forward and letting his guns and muskets maul the enemy.

This useless slaughter was stopped by the ferocious charge of the Rajputs, which also gave the imperial army a glimmer of victory. Jaswant's defensive position, surrounded by ditches and muddy ground, which was meant to deter the advance of the enemy heavy cavalry, actually stopped the movement of his *own* men and snuffed out all chances of his victory.

To the end Jaswant maintained his position in the field along with his own clansmen and only retired when forced by his officers. That this decision was correct was proved by later events. There were times when Aurangzeb as emperor nearly launched an attack on Jodhpur, on various pretexts, but was held off by the power of Jaswant and his clansmen. It was only on the death of Jaswant, and the absence of his army in Afghanistan, that Aurangzeb could take a belated revenge on the Rajput ruler by occupying Jodhpur.

According to Jadunath Sarkar, Maharaja Jaswant Singh was a high-spirited leader of Hindus, and on the strength of his army and large state, was the hope of Hindus against the bigoted section of the Mughals who had grown powerful with the accession of Aurangzeb. The Rajput ruler is believed to have restored many Hindu temples by demolishing the mosques that had been built on their ruins. In fact, as Aurangzeb wrote to this father:

> My first battle was with wicked infidels, who had destroyed mosques, and erected on their sites temples to their idols.

Battle of Samugarh

Fought more than a month after the Battle of Dharmat on the 29th of May 1658. The rebel princes Aurangzeb and Murad outmanoeuvred the Mughal heir-apparent Dara Shikoh to reach the village of Samugarh on the outskirts of Agra.

Military Resources

Shah Jahan and Dara had received news of Jai Singh's victory over Shuja near the city of Benares in February. Dara's son Sulaiman was leading that army further east to hunt down his rebellious uncle but there was bad news from the south. Jaswant Singh had been defeated at Dharmat and his army had dissolved—this news reached Dara ten days after the battle had been fought.

Collecting a fresh army, the Mughal heir marched south to block the road to Agra. At Dholpur he built mud embankments, planting there his heavy artillery and posting his musketeers in the trenches. The road from Ujjain, after passing through Gwalior, crossed the Chambal at Dholpur but Dara Shikoh took the added precaution of sending patrols along the river to watch any other place of crossing.

In the meantime Aurangzeb and Murad were at Gwalior—the latter prince was now completely under the spell of his older brother. The losses they had suffered at the hands of the Rajputs in Dharmat were repaired by the adhesion of more imperial contingents joining them at every town and fort. Moreover the local powers of Malwa province also came to salute the rising sun and sought some gain by joining the winning side.

Among these were Champat Rao Bundela and the Jat zamindar of Gohad (a village near Gwalior). One of them told Aurgangzeb of a little-used ford further east that was unknown to most travellers. Since the way passed through thick jungles and rocky pathways Aurangzeb's army suffered losses but successfully crossed the Chambal on the 23rd of May. Now the rebel army was marching north to Agra, in the rear of Dara Shikoh's force. (*Gohad later became one of the three leading Jat states along with Bharatpur and Dholpur. On the other hand, Champat Rao Bundela was killed by order of Aurangzeb only three years later and his famous son Chhatrasal led a campaign to free Bundelkhand from Aurangzeb's oppression.)*

Dara had to abandon all his elabourate defence works and rush back to bar the enemy's path to Agra. In the process he lost some of his heavy artillery. Dara entrenched at Samugarh and waited for the enemy.

Aurangzeb reached the place after a non-stop march; Dara immediately marched out to give battle (*a good move*). But some distance from his camp he halted and decided to wait and watch (*a bad move...the general who hesitates is lost*). Aurangzeb profited from this by resting his men and horses throughout the heat of the day while Dara foolishly kept his soldiers armed and his artillery deployed without advancing an inch, and then retired from the field at sunset! His younger sibling had gained a moral victory without firing a shot. It became clear to all that Dara feared Aurangzeb's military capacity.

The Battle of Samugarh

The next morning (29th May) the two armies deployed for the battle in the usual formations and began the contest with the futile discharge of artillery at long range. Dara had no real experience of pitched battles and had drawn up his artillery in a single line, while Aurangzeb followed the normal practice of assigning guns to each division separately. In his ignorance Dara overestimated the effect of his cannonade and ordered his band (pipes, kettledrums, and brass drums) to play—the usual method of ordering a general advance on the enemy.

From Aurangzeb's side Prince Murad, commanding the left wing, rashly advanced towards the opposing right wing of Dara's army. This wing was under an imperial officer named Khalilullah Khan and his Uzbek clansmen who only made a show of fighting—Aurangzeb had already corrupted them to support his cause. The rest of Aurangzeb's army rigidly kept its place and the various divisions directed their artillery fire at the advancing enemy.

From Dara's left wing Rustam Khan and his charging Sayyid cavalry were stopped by the artillery shots of Aurangzeb's right wing and veered towards the vanguard under Mohammad Sultan. Trapped between the vanguard, the advanced reserve that came up in support, and the charging right wing, Rustam Khan and his men died fighting in desperation.

However a far greater crisis had developed for Aurangzeb on his left. Murad's reckless advance blocked the line of sight of the artillery in the vanguard and gave a golden opportunity to Dara's vanguard—commanded by Rao Chhatrasal Hada of the Rajput Kingdom of Bundi. Apart from the Hadas, there were Gaurs, Rathors, and Sesodias in the thousands wielding swords and lances and mounted on spirited horses.

These Rajputs saw their chance and charged forward, throwing themselves on Murad's contingent—the enemy artillery could not harm them without also killing Murad's men. The Mughal prince was severely wounded and lost his chief officers; his army crumpled when some Afghan retainers of Dara came up in support of the Rajput charge.

The victorious Rajputs turned their horses against Aurangzeb himself in the center. By this time their momentum had been spent and a severe hand-to-hand fight raged. Rao Chhatrasal's wounded elephant turned away but the battle-hardened Rajput jumped down and mounted a horse. One by one the Rajputs fell but no support came from their commander. The inexperienced Dara had made his last and most fatal mistake. Excited by the charge of Rustam Khan and his Sayyids, Dara had advanced his center in support. This movement blocked his own artillery from harming the enemy—worse the gunners, foot-soldiers and camp followers promptly turned aside to loot the camp, which was their practice when no one was sternly watching over them.

While Dara's guns fell silent the enemy artillery continued firing. As Rustam Khan's force crumbled Dara lost his chance to take the attack to Aurangzeb in the center. Just then he learnt that the Rajputs of his vanguard had defeated Murad and were then breaking through to attack Aurangzeb from the other side. The excited Dara once again goaded his elephant to swerve right and his men rode a long way across their entire front to support the Rajputs but it was too late. The vanguard had elicited a whiff of victory and ended its struggle with an act of desperate valour—Raja Rup Singh Rathor jumped off his horse and with his double-handed sword cut a way to Aurangzeb's elephant.

With the same heavy sword the Rajput chief slashed the legs of the elephant and cut the ropes holding Aurangzeb's howdah. Aurangzeb cried out to his men to spare the life of such a hero but they had already surrounded and cut down the last hope of Dara's side. The enemy's right wing was behind them and the vanguard was advancing forward, while artillery fire carried off many men and beasts. Dara left his elephant for a horse to avoid being hit by a gun—seeing this the Uzbek right wing, which had stayed aloof from the battle took the pretext to flee, and following their example the rest of the army broke up.

Dara's center, which had first moved forward, then swerved right a long way and now was facing artillery fire, played no part in the battle except to exhaust itself in the heat. Aurangzeb's band began playing the tune of victory—Dara's men in the center either fled or surrendered to the enemy. The luckless prince, inexperienced in campaigning and ignorant of warfare to the very end, fled to his mansion in Agra but at least kept some honor by sending the following message to his dear father Shah Jahan:

> *"I don't have the face to appear before your Majesty in my present plight...give up your wish to see my ashamed face...I only beg your Majesty to pronounce the fatiha on this confused and half-dead man in the long journey that he has before him."*

The *fatiha* is read for those who have passed away.

Conclusion

Dara's ignorance of warfare was the result of the doting love showered on him by his father, Shah Jahan.

Usually the best and quietest provinces were assigned to Dara and he stayed constantly at his father's side even after he had become a mature adult. Dara even lacked the basic fighting experience that could be gained by subduing the usual rebellions of the peasantry because his estates were orderly and well administered.

Dara's lack of real military experience was compensated by his strategic vision, his secular ethos, and his polite behavior with the nobles.

He had built around his person a group of loyal and dependable subordinates of different races and creeds. Unfortunately he divided and weakened this force by sending separate armies against each of his brothers. And even his closest followers abandoned him when he refused to face Aurangzeb later in Punjab.

Aurangzeb on the other hand tackled one brother at a time. He first flattered Murad and brought his drunkard brother's force under his own control; next he fought and defeated Dara and gave him no rest by chasing him from one end of the empire to the other; once Dara was on the run Aurangzeb concentrated his forces against Shuja and defeated him.

All through the war of succession, Murad acted as a mere divisional commander to Aurangzeb. At Samugarh his army had suffered heavy losses at the hands of the Rajputs and Aurangzeb easily overpowered him after they had gained Agra.

The Battle of Khwaja

Another event associated with the history of the eastern regions is the battle between the usurping Mughal Emperor Aurangzeb and his elder brother Shuja, who was viceroy of Bengal. It showcased the tactical use of elephants in war in such a late period—the battle was fought on January 5, 1659.

Aurangzeb had defeated his eldest brother Dara, and his allies, at the Battle of Dharmat and the Battle of Samugarh. He had forced his father Shah Jahan to surrender the capital city of Agra to him and had then put him in confinement—at Delhi Aurangzeb even sat on the throne as Emperor though his father was then still alive. His younger brother and former ally Murad was tricked into imprisonment and executed a few years later. With such a record of filial affection the letter Aurangzeb wrote to Shuja was dripping with hypocrisy, *"Like a true brother I shall not refuse you anything you desire, be it land or money."*

Military Resources

Shuja took his brother's words at their true worth and began preparations to fight him. Although earlier even *he* had crowned himself as an independent king and had also tried to seize Delhi from Dara, now he told his officers, *"I shall...secure the person of Shah Jahan and restore the old government. And then I shall stay at court as my father's obedient servant."* He was hopeful of securing the services of the men still loyal to his father on the way to Agra—at Rohtas, Chunar, and Allahabad many soldiers of Dara joined his army. At Varanasi Shuja extorted 300,000 Rupees from the merchants of that rich city—he now had a respectable force of 25,000 cavalry, 114 cannons of all sizes with the infantry to protect them, and the famous naval flotilla of Bengal that sailed up river to Benares.

Aurangzeb had heard of Shuja's movement from his spies and he rushed down from Punjab joined by subordinate Rajas and imperial officers along the way—Mir Jumla force-marched his army all the way from the Deccan to come to his master's aid. The usurping Emperor had a huge army of 90,000 cavalry, the bulk of the imperial artillery, and a sum of 10 million Rupees drawn from the Agra treasury. The two armies faced off on level ground near the village of Khwaja in the Fatehpur district. The night before the battle all was quiet in the two camps—but strangely the right wing of Aurangzeb's army was fully armed and mounted. The commander of this wing was Maharaja Jaswant Singh of Jodhpur who had earlier fought against Aurangzeb in the Battle of Dharmat, but had then joined his side after Dara abandoned his father and escaped to the Punjab. Aurangzeb too was keen to have this large Hindu Kingdom on his side while his position on the throne was still unstable. But Jaswant was not happy with Aurangzeb's usurpation of the throne nor did he see a happy future for his Rajputs in the bigoted prince's service.

At Dharmat Jaswant had told his soldiers that he did not engage in treachery or fight with subterfuge—after suffering a bloody defeat in that battle he seemed to have changed his mind. The Rajput king sent a message to Shuja that he would attack Aurangzeb's camp in the rear and lure him away from the front, leaving behind a disorganized army that Shuja could easily defeat. Just after midnight, when Aurangzeb was engaged in prayers, over 10,000 Rajput cavalry turned around from its position and charged the Mughal camp in the rear. They slaughtered the guards and pulled down the tents, carrying away horses, camels, baggage, and large amounts of money. The tumult in the camp spread to the army, groups of soldiers joined in the plunder or deserted to Shuja, and the entire frontline was in a shambles.

As the plunder-laden Jaswant Singh took the road to Agra, Shuja did not stir from his own camp—no one from his side even ventured to take advantage of the chaos in Aurangzeb's army. The Mughal prince had received Jaswant's message and heard the rumble of his charging cavalry at the promised hour, but Aurangzeb's reputation for deceit and treachery led him to believe that it was his *own brother's* scheme to draw Shuja out within range of his artillery! So Shuja did not budge from the safety of his tent——Aurangzeb took advantage of his brother's indecision to restore confidence in his men, saying to them, *"If the infidel (Jaswant) had played traitor in the midst of battle, all would have been lost. His flight is good for us."*

But when day broke the conditions were not so positive—Jaswant had effectively wiped out *half* the Mughal army as only 50,000 cavalry could be assembled around Aurangzeb. It was still a two to one superiority but now at least the 25,000 of Shuja had some chance of winning the battle. To neutralize the superior numbers of the enemy Shuja did not match his brother division for division, each spread out some distance from the other, but drew his entire army into a single line. His aim was to stake it all on one general attack across the entire front.

The Battle

As pointed out earlier the use of elephants in war had begun thousands of years ago in these very eastern regions. But over the centuries, and particularly with the Turk invasions, their role in battle had undergone several changes. The Turks relied primarily on cavalry and archery to defeat their opponents—hence they used elephants in smaller numbers than the older Hindu Kingdoms. These mountainous beasts were placed in the front and sent to initiate the attack—the gaps created by their charge would enable the main Turk cavalry to ride through and cut up the rest of the enemy force. Alternatively they would be used to deter an enemy advance while the cavalry engaged in maneuvers hidden behind them.

Under the Mughals though this role was taken up by the artillery—elephants were now used as mounts by royalty and by army commanders, to get a bird's eye view of the battle-field, and to be visible to their soldiers at all times. There were very few war-elephants and in fact the total number of elephants used even as mounts had been less than a dozen in all the campaigns of the Mughals.

At Khwaja Shuja sprung a nasty surprise on Aurangzeb by revealing three elephants trained for war, each driven by an experienced *mahout* and each carrying a huge iron chain in its trunk. These three were placed on the right of his army and behind the artillery, which was dueling with the opposing artillery at long range. When finally the two armies drew closer Shuja ordered a charge along his entire front—the left portion of his army under his son Buland Akhtar shook the opposing right wing of Aurangzeb. A Mughal officer named Islam Khan had taken Jaswant's place in that wing—while he was rallying his men to stand fast against the enemy, his own elephant was hit by a rocket. Since this was not a war-elephant, it took fright and fled away.

But the greatest damage to Aurangzeb was done by Shuja's war-elephants. Followed closely by the cavalry the three elephants threw aside the enemy soldiers and horses as they swung the heavy iron chains in their trunks. The entire left wing of the usurping Emperor broke down and fled before their charge—their shots, arrows, and lances had only succeeded in further goading the infuriated war-elephants. Two of the elephants swerved away to the right but one attacked Aurangzeb in the center—one of his matchlockmen shot down the enemy *mahout.* His officers on their own elephants surrounded the rampaging beast while one of their *mahouts* jumped on its back and finally brought it under control.

By this time Aurangzeb's reserves had come up to his rescue and succeeded in repelling the enemy cavalry that followed in the wake of the charging elephants. He now advanced to shore up his damaged right wing and here again the greater numbers finally broke the enemy's steady advance and pushed them back. All this while his artillery under European gunners had kept its place in the field through all the charges and counter-charges—they concentrated their fire on Shuja's men in the center. On his officers pleading Shuja stepped down from his elephant to escape being hit by the accurate firing of the Europeans—but this very move alarmed the remainder of the army, which saw the empty *howdah* and took him to be dead, and promptly ran away from the lost field.

With the rest of his army Shuja fled behind them until he reached the safety of his flotilla in Benares. Even though he managed to escape, there was no rest for the Mughal prince since his dear brother deputed Mir Jumla to hunt him down through the waterways of Bengal——a chase that ended finally with his death in faraway Arakan.

Aurangzeb's Reign

Enforcement of Islamic law: Francois Bernier (1625–1688), a French physician and traveler, became for 12 years the personal physician of Aurangzeb. He described his experiences in *Travels in the Mughal Empire.*

Soon after his ascension, Aurangzeb purportedly abandoned the "liberal" religious viewpoints of his predecessors. Though Akbar, Jahangir and Shah Jahan's approach to faith was more syncretic than the empire's founder, Aurangzeb's position is not so obvious. While his conservative interpretation of Islam and belief in the Sharia (Islamic law) is well documented, how this effected the empire remains unclear. Despite claims of sweeping edicts and policies, contradictory accounts exist. Specifically, his compilation of the Fatawa-e-Alamgiri, a digest of Muslim law, was either intended for personal use, never enforced, or only poorly done. While some assert the lack of broad adoption was due to an inherent flaw, others insist they were only intended for his observance. While it's possible the war of succession and a continued incursions combined with Shah Jahan's spending made cultural expenditures impossible, Aurangzeb's orthodoxy is also used to explain his infamous "burial" of music. The scene describing the "death of music" (and all other forms of performance) is paradoxically dramatic.

Niccolao Manucci's Storia do Mogor and Khafi Khan's Muntakhab al-Lubab are the only documents which describe the aforementioned event. In Storia do Mogor, Manucci describes the ramifications of Aurangzeb's 1668 decree. Here, Aurangzeb's instructions for the muhtasib seem particularly damning:

In Hindustan both Moguls and Hindus are very fond of listening to songs and instrumental music. He therefore ordered the same official to stop music. If in any house or elsewhere he heard the sound of singing and instruments, he should forthwith hasten there and arrest as many as he could, breaking the instruments. Thus was caused a great destruction of musical instruments. Finding themselves in this difficulty, their large earnings likely to cease, without there being any other mode of seeking a livelihood, the musicians took counsel together and tried to appease the king in the following way: About one thousand of them assembled on a Friday when Aurangzeb was going to the mosque. They came out with over twenty highly-ornamental biers, as is the custom of the country, crying aloud with great grief and many signs of feeling, as if they were escorting to the grave some distinguished defunct. From afar Aurangzeb saw this multitude and heard their great weeping and lamentation, and, wondering, sent to know the cause of so much sorrow. The musicians redoubled their outcry and their tears, fancying the king would take compassion upon them. Lamenting, they replied with sobs that the king's orders had killed Music, therefore they were bearing her to the grave. Report was made to the king, who quite calmly remarked that they should pray for the soul of Music, and see that she was thoroughly well buried. In spite of this, the nobles did not cease to listen to songs in secret. This strictness was enforced in the principal cities.

This implies he not only placed a prohibition on music, but actively sought and crushed any resistance. Without music, and implicitly dance, many Hindu-inspired practices would have been impossible. Lavish celebrations of the Emperor's birthday, commonplace since the time of Akbar, would certainly be forbidden under such conditions. Oddly, artistic work not only steadied during Aurangzeb's reign, it increased. Amidst these and other contradictions, the validity and bias of Manucci and Khafi Khan's work is being questioned.

Another particularly heinous claim against Aurangzeb, was his policy of temple destruction. Though figures vary wildly from 80 to 60,000, it clearly took place to some extent. However, Aurangzeb's Firmans on behalf of the Balaji or Vishnu Temple and his land grant for famous Hindu religious sites in Kasi, Varanasi insist these events weren't universal. Noted Historian Richard Eaton believes the overall understanding of temples to be flawed. As early as the sixth century, temples became vital political landmarks as well as religious ones. In fact, not only was temple desecration widely practiced and accepted, it was a necessary part of political struggle.

Alexander Hamilton, a British historian, toured India towards the end of Aurangzeb's fifty year reign and observed that every one was free to serve and worship God in his own way. Francois Bernier, travelled and chronicled Mughal India during the war of succession, notes that both Shah Jahan and Aurangzeb's distaste for Christians. This led to the demolition of Christian settlements near the British/European Factories and enslavement of Christian converts by Shah Jahan. Furthermore, Aurangzeb stopped all aid to Christian Missionaries (Frankish Padres) initiated by Akbar and Jahangir. Even Aurangzeb's dislike of non-Muslims has become the subject of scrutiny. Historian Shri Sharma states that while Emperor Akbar had fourteen Hindu Mansabdars (high officials) in his court, Aurangzeb actually had 148 Hindu high officials in his court." But this fact is somewhat less known, and all the more hidden and purposefully concealed in books ranging from general magazines to national curricula"

Aurangzeb's Views on the Jizya

From Aurangzeb's Fatwa: [Jizyah] refers to what is taken from the Dhimmis, according to [what is stated in] al-Nihayah. It is obligatory upon the free, adult members of [those] who are generally fought, who are fully in possession of their mental faculties, and gainfully employed, even if [their] profession is not noble, as is [stated in] al-Sarajiyyah. There are two types of [Jizyah]. [The first is] the Jizyah that is imposed by treaty or consent, such that it is established in accordance with mutual agreement, according to [what is stated in] al-Kafi. [The amount] does not go above or below [the stipulated] amount, as is stated in al-Nahr al-Faiq. [The second type] is the Jizyah that the leader imposes when he conquers the unbelievers (kuffar), and [whose amount] he imposes upon the populace in accordance with the amount of property [they own], as in al-Kafi. This is an amount that is pre-established, regardless of whether they agree or disagree, consent to it or not.

The wealthy [are obligated to pay] each year forty-eight dirhams [of a specified weight], payable per month at the rate of 4 dirhams. The next, middle group (wast al-hal) [must pay] Twenty-four dirhams, payable per month at the rate of 2 dirhams. The employed poor are obligated to pay twelve dirhams, in each month paying only one dirham, as stipulated in Fath al-Qadir, al-Hidayah, and al-Kafi. [The scholars] address the meaning of "gainfully employed", and the correct meaning is that it refers to one who has the capacity to work, even if his profession is not noble. The scholars also address the meaning of wealthy, poor, and the middle group. Al-Shaykh al-Imam Abu Jafar, may Allah the most high have mercy on him, considered the custom of each region decisive as to whom the people considered in their land to be poor, of the middle group, or rich. This is as such, and it is the most correct view, as stated in al-Muhit. Al-Karakhi says that the poor person is one who owns two hundred dirhams or less, while the middle group owns more than two hundred and up to ten thousand dirhams, and the wealthy [are those] who own more than ten thousand dirhams...The support for this, according to al-Karakhi is provided by the fatawa of Qadi Khan (d. 592/1196). It is necessary that in the case of the employed person, he must have good health for most of the year, as is stated in al-Hidayah. It is mentioned in al-Idah that if a dhimmi is ill for the entire year such that he cannot work and he is well off, he is not obligated to pay the Jizyah, and likewise if he is sick for half of the year or more. If he quits his work while having the capacity [to work] he [is still liable] as one gainfully employed, as is [stated in] al-Nihayah. No Jizyah is imposed upon their women, children, ill persons or the blind, or likewise on the paraplegic, the very old, or on the unemployed poor, as is stated in al-Hidayah.

Expansion of the Empire

Emperor Aurangzeb seated on a golden throne holding a hawk in the Durbar. Such scenes would be rare in the latter part of his reign as he was permanently camped in the Deccan, fighting wars.

From the start of his reign up until his death, Aurangzeb engaged in almost constant warfare. He built up a massive army, and began a program of military expansion along all the boundaries of his empire. Aurangzeb pushed north-west into the Punjab and what is now Afghanistan; he also drove south, conquering Bijapur and Golconda, his old enemies. He attempted to recover those portions of the Deccan territories where the Maratha king Shivaji was sparking rebellions.

This combination of military expansion and religious intolerance had deeper consequences. Though he succeeded in expanding Mughal control, it was at an enormous cost in lives and treasure. And, as the empire expanded in size, Aurangzeb's chain of command grew weaker. The Sikhs of the Punjab grew both in strength and numbers, and launched rebellions. The Marathas waged a war with Aurangzeb which lasted for 27 years. Even Aurangzeb's own armies grew restive — particularly the fierce Rajputs, who were his main source of strength. Aurangzeb gave a wide berth to the Rajputs, who were mostly Hindu. While they fought for Aurangzeb during his life, on his death they immediately revolted against his successors.

With much of his attention on military matters, Aurangzeb's political power waned, and his provincial governors and generals grew in authority.

Battle of Saraighat

The Battle of Saraighat was fought in 1671 between the Mughal empire (led by the Kachwaha king, Raja Ramsingh I), and the Ahom Kingdom (led by Lachit Borphukan) on the Brahmaputra river at Saraighat, now in Guwahati. Although much weaker, the Ahom army defeated the Mughal army by brilliant uses of the terrain, clever diplomatic negotiations to buy time, guerrilla tactics, psychological warfare, military intelligence and by exploiting the sole weakness of the Mughal forces—its navy.

The Battle of Saraighat was the last battle in the last major attempt by the Mughals to extend their empire in to Assam. Though the Mughals managed to regain Guwahati briefly after a later Borphukan deserted it, the Ahoms wrested control in 1682 and maintained it till the end of their rule.

Background

Mughal interest in the Brahmaputra valley began in 1602 when the Nawab of Dhaka attacked Parikshit Narayan of Koch Hajo at Dhubri, the western most corner of Assam. The first Mughal-Ahom conflict took place in 1615 when the Mughals attacked the Ahoms, then under Pratap Singha, for protecting Bali Narayan, the brother of Parikshit. This resulted in a period of Mughal-Ahom war with fluctuating fortunes that ended with the Treaty of Asurar Ali in 1639. The Treaty fixed Barnadi river in the north bank and Asurar Ali in the south bank of the Brahmaputra as the boundary between the Ahoms and the Mughals. This, and the defeat of the Koch king at Pandu in 1641, resulted in a period of Mughal administration in Kamrup (Guwahati and Hajo.)

Taking advantage of the Mughal succession wars after the fall of the Mughal emperor Shah Jahan in 1658, Pran Narayan of Koch Bihar tried to occupy Koch Hajo, but the Ahoms under Jayadhwaj Singha took Guwahati and pushed him back beyond Dhubri. That the Ahoms reached Dhubri by defeating the Koch king and not the Mughals would form a central tenet in later Ahom diplomacy. Soon after, Aurangzeb occupied the Delhi throne. Mir Jumla, pursuing Shah Shuja in Bengal, was appointed the Subahdar of Bengal in 1660 and asked to retake Assam. Mir Jumla marched in 1661 and defeated the Ahoms at successive encounters to finally take the Ahom capital Garhgaon. But the *daga juddha* (guerrilla warfare) of Atan Burhagohain and the rains succeeded in cutting off Mughal communication lines making it impossible for Mir Jumla to consolidate Mughal rule. Unaware of Mir Jumlas difficulties and unnerved by Baduli Phukan's defection, Jayadhwaj Singha sued for peace (Sarkar 1992:187), an opportunity Mir Jumla seized on. The Treaty of Ghilajharighat (1663) brought an end to Mughal occupation of Garhgaon, but the conditions of this treaty were so severe that the Ahoms were soon resolved to reverse them.

Ahom Preparations for War

After the humiliating defeat inflicted by Mir Jumla the Ahom king Jayadhwaj Singha died in despair. On his deathbed, he exhorted his cousin and successor Chakradhwaj Singha to "remove the spear of humiliation from the bosom of the nation." There followed a complete overhaul of the Ahom kingdom. People who had dispersed due to Mir Jumla's invasion were rehabilitated in the appropriate *khels*, food and military productions were increased, new forts were constructed and garrisoned and an experditionary army was organized under a new commander—Lachit Borphukan (Sarkar 1992:199). Alliances were renewed with the Jaintia and the Kachari kingdoms. During this period Mughal imperial demands were tactfully and diplomatically rebuffed, but when the new *faujdar* of Guwahati, Firuz Khan, forced the matter in March 1667, the Ahoms were compelled to move (Sarkar 1992:204). In August 1667 the Ahom army, under Lachit Borphukan and accompanied by Atan Burhagohain, sailed downstream to retake Guwahati.

Ahoms Retake Guwahati

Lachit made Kaliabor, the old seat of the Borphukan, his base camp and advanced toward Guwahati along both banks of the Brahmaputra. On the north bank the Deka Phukan retook Bahbari in early September 1667. On the south bank, the *Nausalia* Phukan and others, moving on land and water, captured Kajali, Sonapur, Panikhaiti, and Titamara forts between the Kapili river and Guwahati. The Ahoms then reached Guwahati which was defended by five *choukies* on each bank of the Brahmaputra (north—Kanai-borosi-bowa, Hillar, Hindurighopa, Patduar and Korai; south—Latasil, Joiduar, Dharamduar, Duarguria and Pandu). With some loss, the Ahoms captured Shah Buruz and Rangamahal forts, a little north of the city. An extended battle was fought for the Itakhuli fort (at the site of the current Deputy Commissioner's bungalow). The Ahoms besieged Joiduar, occupied Pandu, and in spite of a Mughal reinforcement, approached Itakhuli. The grand attack was launched on the night of November 4, 1667, when the Ahoms scaled the walls by ladders and after two months of seize, Itakhuli fell in mid-November 1667. Most of the defenders were massacred, many surrendered but a few managed to escape. War provisions, treasures and war material fell into Ahom hands (Sarkar 1992:206-207).

The Mughals received some reinforcement at this point and retaliated against the Ahoms. The Ahoms fought back with their naval forces and removed them from their bases in Umananda and Barhat. The Mughals, pursued by the Ahoms, managed to fortify the Manahmukh (the confluence of Manas river) and fend off the attackers for some time but Firuz Khan finally surrendered and was taken prisoner. This brought an end to the recapture of Guwahati and the Ahoms were able to control their old Manas border once again. But this did not last long and they had to beat a strategic retreat due to the advancing Mughal army of Raja Ram Singh.

Mughal Imperial Invasion

Mughal emperor Aurangzeb was informed of the losses on December 19, 1667 and he commissioned Raja Ram Singh of Amber, son of the famous Mirza Raja Jai Singh, to take back Guwahati. Ram Singh left Delhi on December 27, 1667, and finally reached Rangamati in February in 1669. He was accompanied, as was the Mughal custom of sending two generals, by Rashid Khan, ex-faujdar of Guwahati, and from Patna by the Sikh Guru Tegh Bahadur. The Ahoms, anticipating a Mughal strike, is said to have followed his movements from Delhi itself. Along the way Aurangzeb augmented Ram Singh's forces of 4,000 troopers (from his *char-hazaari mansab*), 1,500 *ahadis* and 500 *barqandezes* by an additional 30,000 infantrymen, 21 Rajput chiefs (Thakurs) with their contingents, 18,000 cavalry, 2,000 archers and shieldmen and 40 ships (Sarkar 1992:211) When Lachit surveyed the massive Mughal force later, he was moved to tears and he uttered: "It is a tragedy that my country is facing this dire catastrophe during my Phukanship. How will my king be saved? How will my people be saved? And how will my posterity be saved?" (Sarkar 1992:229)

Armies from Koch Bihar joined the Mughal forces since they were vassals.

Ahom Strategic Planning and Mughal Attacks

Aware of Mughal military might and the weakness of the Ahom soldiers, especially against cavalry and mounted forces in open fields, Lachit Borphukan and others decided to choose the terrain of the battlefield with care. The choice fell on Guwahati, which was hilly, on the way to the heart of the Ahom kingdom and without open fields where the Mughal forces would not have sufficient mobility.

The only way east was via the Brahmaputra river passing through it. The Brahmaputra at Saraighat, at its narrowest 1km width, was ideal for a naval defence. To check Mughal advance, Lachit prepared a complex system of mud embankments in Guwahati When the Mughals found Guwahati impregnable by land, they would be forced to use their navy, which was their weakest asset. Lachit set up his headquarters at Andharubali, the sandbanks between the Kamakhya and Sukreshwar hills. The deliberations of the war council were recorded and made into a manual (Sarkar 1992:213).

When the Mughal march reached the Manas river in March-April 1669 and defeated some Ahom forces, Lachit decided on a strategic retreat to Guwahati. Three Rajkhowas were asked to meet the Mughal forces and retreat to Guwahati, keeping the Mughal forces in sight but beyond the reach of their weapons. When the Mughals reached closer, he started a sham negotiation with Ram Singh, who had set up camp at Agiathuti, calling him a "Bhai Raja" (brother prince). And when he was ready for the Mughal attacks, he sent words to Ram Singh via Firuz Khan that "Guwahati and Kamrup do not belong to the Mughals" since they were taken from the Koch and that the Assamese were prepared to fight to the last (Sarkar 1992:214).

A period of battles between the Ahom and Mughal forces in the region of Guwahati followed, with varied results with forts changing hands many times. In these battles, the Mughal forces were arraigned in four divisions (Sarkar 1992:215):

1. The north bank, commanded by Ram Singh himself.
2. The south bank, under Ali Akbar Khan, Mir Sayyid Khan, Raja Indramani, Raja Jaynarayan and Marul Khan
3. The Sindurighopa entrance, under Jahir Beg, Kayam Khan, Ghanashyam Bakshi, and three Baruah's from Koch Bihar—Kavisekhar, Sarveshwar and Manmatha.
4. The river, guarded by the naval commanders Mansur Khan, Latif Khan, Iswarpati, *firinghees* (Europeans) and one Kapidan Raja.

In these attacks the Ahom allies—the Garos, the Jaintia, the Nagas, the Rani of Darrang, the Raja of Rani, and even the monsoons of 1669—joined battle. The Ahom defence was arraigned as (Gogoi 1968:39-43):

1. The north bank, under the command of Atan Burhagohain.
2. The south bank, under the command of Lachit Borphukan.

Both commanders had a number of *pali* commanders each defending a specific strategic area, with each *pali* reorganized in response to the challenge posed by Ram Singh's forces.

Aurangzeb received information of the lack of progress in August 1669 and made arrangements with the Subahdar of Bengal, Shaistha Khan, to provide reinforcements to Ram Singh. This period is also known for Atan Burhagohain's *dagga judha* (guerilla warfare). Ram Singh protested that these harassing campaigns lowered the "dignity of warfare", and withdrew from fighting (October 1664- March 1970), to no particular military advantage (Sarkar 1992:218-219).

Major Ahom Reversal at Alaboi

One of these battles stood out for a major Ahom reversal. Exasperated with the delaying tactics of the Borphukan, Ram Singh asked for a duel with the Ahom king. He promised to withdraw from Assam with his army if he was defeated. Lachit updated Chakradhwaj Singha about this proposal, who rejected the offer on the ground that it was beneath his dignity to duel a mere servant "who has no umbrella over his head." Annoyed with Ram Singh's proposal he ordered Lachit to confront the Mughals militarily. In a battle that was set up as a challenge, a force of 10,000 Mughals under Mir Nawab was to confront a force of 20,000 Ahom cavalry. Ram Singh's "approach was psychological, marked by pride, chivalry and revenge". The Ahom approach, to cover their basic weaknesses, was based on "diplomacy, deception and mispresentation". So instead of 20,000, they sent in 40,000 and using an anti-koch tactic that had worked against Chilarai, they dressed their vanguard archers and musketeers as Brahmans to make the Rajput warriors desist from killing them. Ram Singh, on the other hand, set a woman, Madanavati, dressed as a man, to command the vanguard to deny the Ahoms any glory in case of a victory. The battle took place in the fields adjoining the Alaboi hills about August 5, 1669.

In the first phase, Madanavati dispersed the first four lines of the Ahom vanguard with ease, but the Borphukan had trenches dug to conceal his other lines.

In the second phase, a diversion to cross the Brahmaputra was thwarted, and Madanavati was shot. The battle turned and in the third phase, Mir Nawab's forces were routed. Enraged at the deception, Ram Singh let loose his veteran horsemen and in the carnage that followed, 10,000 Ahom soldiers were massacred.

Aurangzeb was pleased with these Mughal successes and increased Ram Singh's mansab from 4000 to 5000. Ram Singh was also instructed to invest Guwahati soon, and if it was not possible, to devastate the land and plunder the people.

Final Diplomatic Aneuvers

After the Mughal advances in late 1669, Ram Singh began diplomatic efforts. The proposal was for the Assamese to evacuate Guwahati and a return to the 1639 status quo (Treaty of Asurar Ali) in return for a Mughal payment of 300,000 rupees.

The Ahoms did not respond favourably. Ram Singh next attempted to bribe and create divisions among the Ahom field commanders (Phukans). In the mean time, the Ahom king Chakradhwaj Singha died and was succeeded by his brother Udayaditya Singha.

The long war had resulted in popular discontent in the Ahom kingdom. Ram Singh again put forward his proposal on the 1639 status quo settlement and this time the Ahoms appeared receptive. The Ahom king, though displeased, left the decision to his commanders in Guwahati. In the meeting which included Lachit Borphukan, the only dissenter to the proposal was Atan Burhagohain, who displayed his statesmanship.

Atan Burhagohain argued that there was no guarantee that the Emperor at Delhi will abide by Ram Singh's assurance. Also, a settlement then would mean that the drain on the country's resources would have been in vain. Further, what was the guarantee that once the Mughals take Guwahati, they would not reach for Garhgaon or even Namrup (Sarkar 1990:224)?

Atan Burhagohain was able to persuade the other commanders and the Ahoms rejected this proposal. The diplomatic efforts of Ram Singh failed once again.

Final Battle at Saraighat

The Battle of Saraighat, March 1671

Meanwhile, Mughal reinforcements in the shape of war-vessels and imperial officers (*Omraos*) reached Ram Singh, along with the admiral, Munnawar Khan, and the message that Ram Singh was sent to fight the Assamese, not make friends with them (Sarkar 1992:225). Ram Singh now made preparations for his final and direct assault on Guwahati and began moving along the northbank. Near Sualkuchi he was joined by ships with artillery and archers under five sardars. The Mughals had large boats, some carrying as many as sixteen cannons. The Mughal ambassador, Paditrai, had reported a breach in the embankment at Andharubali a few days earlier, and Ram Singh wanted to exploit this opening.

The Ahom soldiers were demoralised after their losses at Allaboi. Their commander-in-chief, Lachit Borphukan and their admiral were both seriously ill, and the Nara Raja, the son of the Miri Sandikoi, was in command. An encounter both on land and water ensued near Ashwakranta. The Ahom land forces, under Laluk Borgohain Phukan, worsted the Mughals, but the Mughal boats compelled the Ahom boats to retreat to Barhila, north of Saraighat. The land forces, fearing an encirclement, too retreated (Sarkar 1992:226). The battle reached a crucial phase, when the Mughals were beginning to get close to Andharubali. The Borphukan, as well as the Nara Raja sent messages to inspire the soldiers. It looked as if there was a break in command and some boats began falling back to Kajali and Samdhara. Lachit Barphukan was observing this from his sickbed in the gatehouse of the Itakhuli fort.

At this crucial moment in the battle, when the Mughals were about to land at Andharubali, the Borphukan sent orders via *katakis* to all the land and naval forces to attack. He also ordered seven war-boats for himself and had Nadai of Kharangi carry him to a boat. He shouted "The King has put all the people in my hands to fight the Bongal. Shall I go back to my wife and children?" and pushed a few men into the water. With the other six war-boats the Borphukan headed toward the naval battle (Sarkar 1992:226).

The entry of the Borphukan transformed the Ahom soldiers. His small flotilla soon swelled with Ahom warships from all sides that smashed into the Mughal warships at Amrajuli on the north bank, opposite Kamakhya hills. The triangle in the river, between Itakhuli, Kamakhya and Aswakranta was filled with men and boat. The Ahoms spanned the river over an improviso bridge of boats and resorted to a combined front and rear attack. The Mughal admiral, smoking a hookah was killed by a gunshot from the back, throwing the Mughals out of gear. They suffered the loss of three top-ranking amirs, and another 4000 dead. The day of this decisive battle is not known for certain, only that it happened in the middle of March 1671.

Epilogue

The Mughals were pursued to the Manas river, the Ahom kingdom's western boundary. The Borphukan instructed his men not to attack the retreating army, reminding them of Alaboi (Gogoi 1968:476). Anticipating a counter attack, he set messengers at regular intervals, while Atan Burhagohain and other commanders stood ready for one. The Mughals in Darrang were also worsted, and Ram Singh left Kamrup on April 7, 1671 for Rangamati (Gogoi 1968:476). Ram Singh waited in vain for another opportunity, and finally had an audience with Aurangzeb on June 25, 1676.

Lachit Borphukan died at Kaliabor about a year later in April 1672, but not from the illness at Saraighat (Gogoi 1968:479). And this was not the final battle between the Ahoms and the Mughals, nor did Guwahati remain with the Ahoms. Lachit Borphukan's own brother and successor Borphukan, Laluk Sola, deserted Guwahati for the Mughals in 1679. It remained with the Mughals till 1682, when the Ahoms under Gadadhar Singha recovered it and ended Mughal control in Kamrup for ever, though the Mughal administration of 80 years cast a long shadow.

Rebellions

Many subjects rebelled against Aurangzeb's policies, among them his own son, Prince Akbar.

- In 1667, the Yusufzai Pashtuns revolted near Peshawar and were crushed.
- In 1669, the Jats around Mathura revolted and led to the formation of Bharatpur state after his death.

1669 Jat Uprising

Paradoxical though it might appear and strange though it

might seem, the Jat uprising of 1669 in India under the leader Gokula occurred at a time when the Mughal government was by no means weak or imbecile. In fact this period of Aurangzeb's reign witnessed the climax of the Mughal Empire., during the early medieval period frequent breakdown of law and order often induced the Jats to adopt a refractory course. But, with the establishment of the Mughal rule, law and order was effectively established and we do not come across any major Jat revolt during the century and a half proceeding the reign of Aurangzeb. Though in 1638 Murshid Quli Khan, the Mughal faujdar of Mathura was killed during an operation against Jats. During the reign of Aurangzeb, the faujdar of Mathura in 1669 was none other than Abdun Nabi who incurred the wrath of people.

Causes of the Revolt

The underlying causes of the Jat revolt of 1669 have not been properly analyzed so far. Historians have generally ascribed the said rebellion to Aurangzeb's religious discrimination and the oppression of local officers.,. These, however seem to have been the contributory causes but neither the sole nor the dominant factors which precipitated the revolt. The real cause of the Jat rebellion of 1669 lay deeper than have been assigned to it so far.

One of the main causes may be sought in the changed nature and scope of the Mughal government under Aurangzeb which was detrimental to the democratic and tribal way of life of the Jat fraternity. Akbar assiduously tried to build a comprehensive state based on religious and social freedom, respect for village autonomy and willing acquiescence of the people at large. The Nature of the Mugal despotism generally retained its previous character under Jahangir. In Spite of Shahjahan's intolerant attitude in the beginning, the government in his times also displayed a "sense of Justice "and kept the interests of the people in its view.

But, with the accession of Aurangzeb, the comprehensive nature of the state gradually yielded to a narrow and over centralized despotic regime., A despotic system rests upon the personality of the ruler, which motivates the entire administrative machinery.

The over-centralized set-up accompanied by the narrow outlook of the ruler, was naturally antagonistic to the tribal and democratic outlook of the Jats. An instinctive attachment to democratic ways and a "sturdy independence "have throughout been their chief characteristics. They have a pronounced aversion to external interference and have been accustomed to self governance of their internal affairs.

Giving due regard to their tradition customs and laws, Akbar issued two firmans, dated 8th Ramaza, 987 A.H. and 11th Ramzan, 989 A.H. granting internal freedom to the clan councils of the Jats of the upper Doab region in religious matters and "to carry out their functions according to their ancient customs and laws" Akbar's sagacious policy seems to have been followed until the time of Shah Jahan. Jahangir sometimes showed the top Jat leaders the unique favour of calling them to his audience and giving Khilats. But Aurangzeb reversed this policy. He "restricted the activities" of their customary institutions. This along with his religious fanaticism, created concern among the Jats. They discussed this issue in a meeting at Chhaprauli in 1661 (1718 V.S) and decided to protest against the new laws and pleaded for the reversion of the policy of the Delhi court.,

The courageous Jats who had reminiscences of their republican past and who still retained that spirit could hardly afford to remain quiet before in immensely centralized system based on a narrow outlook which threatened to devour their traditional tribal and democratic ways.

Probably, not less significant was the role of the economic factors in leading the Jat peasantry to rebellion. Emperor assigned a certain piece of land to the officials in lieu of their pay and also to enable them to defray the expenses over their troops on condition of their paying a sum to the Emperor out of the surplus revenue. Such grants were called Jagirs Since they were mainly grants of revenue out of which the holders (Who were usually Mansabdars) maintained their quota of troops for the Empire, the tendency was to fix revenue at the highest possible rate almost equal to the surplus produce. Even this high rate went on increasing with the passage of time under the circumstances the peasants were financially hit very hard. They were usually left with the barest minimum needed for supporting their lives.,

What added further to the hardships of the cultivators was the frequent transfer of the jagirs to different assignees. The jagirdars held their jagirs at the pleasure of the Emperor. Bhimsen remarks "There is no hope of a jagir being left with the same officer next year.", This constant insecurity of the tenure of office proved unfortunate in two ways. Firstly it offered little incentive to the holders to exert for alleviating the distress of their tenantry. Instead it led them to employ all possible tactics to extort money from the Peasantry. Secondly, quite often at the time of the transfer the hard hit peasants of the same Jagir were pressurized to pay the same sum twice, first to the collectors of the outgoing jagirdar and then to those of the incoming one. Thus this system ended in a mad looting of the peasants by the rival collectors.,

If the peasants refused to pay the revenue, very severe punishment was meted out to them. At times they were left with no other option than to sell their women, children and cattle, or to run away form their home to avoid extermination through-ill-treatment.,,

In its actual operation Mughal assignment system became extremely "ruinous to the peasants and ultimately harmful to the interests of the Empire" The exploitation by the collectors increased as time went on. At last a stage was reached when " excessive acts of oppression" by the officers could lead some of the peasants to shifting their hand from plough to the sword, as happened in the case of the Jats following the atrocities of Abdun Nabi. We know it on the testimony of Shah Waliullah that "the cultivators of the villages between Delhi and Akbarabad were of the Jat caste.

Against this background, it was quite natural for the Jats to ventilate their resentment over the prevailing assignment system as agriculture occupied the uppermost place in the there life.

It is obvious that an oppressive system goes hard with the agriculturists. Its sharp reaction among the Jats, culminating into a rebellion, appears to have been because of their adventurous disposition and martial character.

The Jats had been a race of warrior agriculturists.

Highly disapproved of the enhanced revenue, the levying of the "harmful taxes" and "looting by government tax collectors "they were prone to opposing such thing and other oppressions even by force, if the occasion demanded this may explain better why in face of similar provocations other weak agricultural communities remained more or less inactive while the Jat peasants unsheathed their swords.

Apart form it, the Jats more than any other people, are reputed to be deeply attached to personal freedom and to resenting external control. Aurangzeb pursued a fourfold course with regard to his religious policy, namely, promotion of Islamic practices, regulations against the Hindus, conversion to Islam and destruction of temples.

His supreme object was to make both Muslim and non-Muslim conform to the orthodox holy law. Hence he issued regulations aiming at suppressing the un-Islamic ceremonies and encouraging Muslim ways among the people at large.

In 1665 restrictions were imposed on the public celebration of the Hindu festivals of Holi and Diwali., In 1668, the Hindu fairs were prohibited in the Empire. In 1665 discriminative duties were imposed upon the Hindus. They were ordered to pay 5% while the Muslim merely 2.5% duty on their goods. In 1667, the Muslims were totally freed form this burden.,

These steps apart from being a source of revenue were intended to pressurise the Hindu into accepting Islam. In addition, Aurangzeb adopted seductive methods to attract the non Muslims to Islam, he offered posts money grants, public honour and even amnesty as rewards for embracing Islam.

Above all Aurangzeb embarked upon the policy of temple demolition; here he displayed his characteristic subtlety of approach. Early in 1659 he declared that his Canon Law prohibited the construction of new temples but did no ordain the demolition of the old ones. Gradually he opened out.

The temples of Somnath were razed to the ground early in his reign. In 1665, he ordered to redemolish the repaired temples of Gujarat which had once been destroyed by him during his viceroyalty of the province. He next ordered the pulling down of all the newly constructed temples in Orissa. In 1669, he fully unmasked himself. In that year he issued a general order for the destruction of the Hindu Schools and temples and the suppression of their teaching and religious practices throughout the Empire several temples pulled down in the wake of this order included those of Malarna and Vishwanath. Thus, within a short span of 11 years, Aurangzeb reversed the liberal and tolerant approach of Akbar, While Akbar's liberalism had secured him the willing co-operation of his people Aurangzeb's bigotry created mounting discontent among the suffering non Muslims.,

Mathura, the birth centre of the Jat rising, suffered heavily in Aurangzeb's reign. This venerated place of Hindu worship was naturally an object of annoyance to Aurangzeb. He appointed Abdun Nabi, "a religious man", as faujdar of the place to "suppress the Hindus". This officer amassed through questionable means, cash worth 93000 mohars and thirteen lakhs of Rupees and valuables worth four and a half Lakhs., Abdun Nabi demolished a temple in the city and upon its ruins erected a Jama Masjid in 1661-1662. Next, in pursuance of Aurangzeb's order, he removed the stone railing of the famous temple of Keshava Rai in 1666.

All these acts must have provoked the Jats further. We know that during the Sultanate danger to or suppression of their religion generated disaffection among them. There is no reason to believe that a more systematic religious persecutions by zealot Aurangazeb did not offend the religious feelings of the Jats. Generally speaking the Jats have never been orthodox in their religious belief.,, They do not bother about the philosophical or the ethical nuances of religion, but the outward ritualistic aspects do commonly touch them. Hence, measures like the closing of fairs and festivals and desecration of religious places could not but have caused concern among them. The religious bigotry of Aurangzeb and the consequent suffering of the non Muslims however had not assumed full proportion by 1668 – 1669. Jiziya, orders for the exclusion of the Hindus from public officers and even the destruction of the temple of Keshava Rai at Mathura followed later. And yet the Jats under Gokula unfurled the banner of revolt.

The 'floating literature' or the" Sakhas "as they are called among the Jats and other local people refers to the visit of Samarth Guru Ram Das, who exhorted the Jats for insurrection. He urged them to meet excess with excess. He also impressed upon them that tyranny is a sin but to tolerate tyranny is greater sin. Having been urged and inspired by the Guru, Gokula took a vow to save the Hindus from destruction and rose in rebellion.

The Jats being restive, fuel was ready. Only fire was needed and it was according to the "Sakhas" provided by Ram Das. K.R.Qanuago observes that in the revolt of 1669 "one flare of the might conflagration kindled throughout India by the missionary zeal of the Emperor" and revived the Hindu Nationalism. Thus religious factors played and appreciable part in the Jat Insurrection.

The economic causes although important, may not be over-emphasized. The vices in the operation of the assignment system did not multiply overnight in the reign of Aurangzeb. Their increasing tendency was discernible even before him. But when the tightening grip of Aurangeb threatened the age old democratic and tribal traditions of the Jats, the economic factors made their weight felt heavily.

From the foregoing discussion it may be concluded that the Jat rebellion of 1669 was essentially the result of the political provocation aggravated by the economic discontent and set ablaze by the religious persecution.

The Outbreak of the Rebellion

The year 1669 witnessed, the bursting forth of the pent up fury of the Jats into a very powerful revolt under the inspiring leadership of Gokula, the zamindar of Tilpat. A remarkable feature of this rebellion was its composite character. Though the Jats counted for its majority and provided leadership to it, it consisted of other local people as well such as, Mev, Meena, Ahir, Gujar, Naruka, Panwar and others. The rebels gathered at the village of Sahora (about 6 miles from Mathura). Abdun Nabi, the faujdar of Mathura, attacked them. At first he appeared to be gaining ground, but in the middle of the fighting he was killed on 12 may, 1669.

Overjoyed at this success, Gokula ravaged the paragana and town of Sadabad (24 miles from Mathura) in the Daob. The turbulance spread to Agra District also whereto Radandaz Khan was sent (13 May 1669 – 22nd Zil-Hijja, 1079 A.H.) with a force to put down the rebels. Aurangazeb appointed Saf Shikan Khan as the new faujdar of Mathura. As arms failed to prevail, diplomacy was resorted to. The Mughal government offered to forgive Gokula provided he surrendered his spoils. But Gukula spurned the offer. On the other side, as the situation was assuming serious proportions, the Emperor had to proceed (28 November-14th Rajab, 1080 A.H.) in person to the Disturbed area. On his way on 4 December 1669 (20th Rajab, 1080 A.H.) Aurangazeb learnt of the circumstance of rebellion in the villages of Rewara, Chandarakanta and Sarkhud (Sarkharu ?). He dispatched Hasan Ali khan to attack these places. Till noon the insurgent fought with bows and muskets. Getting desperate thereafter, many of them having performed the jauhar of their women fell upon the Khan, A fierce fight raged till the evening in which many imperialists and 300 rebels were killed. Hasan Ali Khan returned to the Emperor, taking 250 male and female prisoners. Aurangazeb was pleased with his performance. He made him the faujdar of Mathura in place of Saf Shikan Khan who had obviously failed in suppressing the rebels.

Under Hasan Ali Khan, were placed 2,000 barq and aztroops 1000 archers 1000 musketeers 1,000 rocketmen, and 25 pieces of cannons. Amanulla, the faujdar of the environs of Agra, was also ordered to help Hasan Ali. The latter immediately got engaged in quelling the rebellion. In January 1670, Gokula with 20,000 Jat and other followers, rushed forward to face the imperialists at a place 20 miles from Tilpat. Both the sides suffered many casualties in the battle in which the Jats, despite showing utmost bravery, could not cope with the trained Mughals and their artillery. They retreated to Tilpat. Hasan Ali followed them and besieged the fortalice. Fighting continued for three days in which muskets and bows were used by the contestants. On the fourth day, the royalists charged the besieged from all sides and having made a breach in the walls entered Tilpat. Then ensued a sanguinary conflict. The Jats displayed their reckless courage and undaunted valour. The experienced Mughals gained the day but not before losing 4,000 men. Of the vanquished 5000 lay dead, while 7000 were arrested. Gokula, with his two associates including " Sonki" (Udai Singh Singhi), was captured alive through the efforts of Shaikh Razi-ud-Din, the peshkar of Hassan Ali. They and other prisoners were presented to the Emperor. Being furious, he ordered Gokula and Singh to be cut limb on the Chabutara of the Kotwali (Agra). Other captives either met fate of their leader or were put in chains.

Aftermath of the Rebellion

Never before in the history of the Mughal Empire had the standard of such a formidable rebellion been raised by the Jats as was done by those of Mathura under Gokula in 1669. Although the rebellion failed, it had considerable though indirect, repercussions upon the future course of the Jat History and in the long run upon the Mughal Empire itself. The crushing defeat of the Jats in 1669 was not without a lesson. It exposed to them certain strategic flaws in their ways of fighting. They had seen their 20,000 gallant brethren being easily routed by the Mughal forces in a face to face combat. It must have been laid bare to them that, in the absence of proper military training and sufficient equipment their reckless courage and obstinate valour alone would not prove effective against the mighty Mughal army. Besides, the fall of Tilpat within the short duration of three days must have pointed out to them the hopeless vulnerability of their defence and its corresponding implications. The military tactics of Raja Ram and Churaman II clearly indicate that the Jats had benefited from the failure of 1669.

They gradually turned to making a change in their existing military methods. The subsequent Jat leaders grew alive to the efficacy of discipline and proper equipment in warfare. There developed an increasing tendency to build their forts in the fastness of dense Jungles capable of withholding the onslaught of powerful armies. Likewise they avoided the rashness of Gokula in inviting pitched battles with the mighty Mughals.

Gukula's rebellion also gave to the posterity an inspiration of political nature, namely, the usefulness of working under a united leadership.

We know that the Jats had the reputation of being impatient of any external control. Although success did not crown them in 1669, it was perhaps, heartening for them to perceive that their joint efforts could gather so powerful a momentum as to disturb even the Mughal Emperor, compelling him to rush to the disturbed region. On the other hand, it was disheartening to them that the effectiveness of their resistance withered away once their chief leader Gokula was no more. This seems to have emphasized to the Jats the advantage to working united under a common leader. Although progress in this direction was necessarily slow in due course it proved to be of considerable political importance to them. Once their combined efforts proved fruitful under later leaders and bright future prospects appeared ahead. Their circumstantial union assumed a little fixed character. Consideration of common benefit might also have been instrumental in leading the tribal and democratic Jats to prefer, accept and finally adopt the institution of kingship. To such circumstances may be traced the genesis of the Jat state of Bharatpur and the eventual emergence of the principalities of Patiala, Nabha and Jhind which were republican until recently.

In the light of the above considerations it seems that from the viewpoint of the long term interests of the Jats, Gokula's abortive exertions were no less significant than the more fruitful struggles of Raja Ram and Churaman II. The brighter careers of these two have dimmed the image of Gokula whose full importance has not been duly appreciated so for. The circumstances in which they worked were not altogether similar. Gokula had to face more formidable odds than the two later fortunate Jat leaders. It is doubtful whether, even with their better organizing capacity their success could have been assured in Gokua's circumstances. It is difficult to resist the conclusion that though Gokula failed, his failure paved the way for the subsequent success of Raja Ram and Churaman II.

Prior to the Jat uprising, other revolt had taken place in a different part of the Empire. But they were not so powerful and the place of their occurrence were comparatively too distant from the capital. The rebellion under Gokula was, however quite different. From the point of view of time, dimension and place it was the first fierce repudiation of the authority of Aurangzeb under his very seat. Though such evidence is not forthcoming, the possibility cannot be ruled out that his audaciousness provided a stimulus to the later rebels such as the Satnamis.

Aurangazeb pursued a course which seems to have estranged the Jats further. He wrecked terrible vengeance upon them. Apart from the treatment meted out to 7,000 captives, the family of their leader, Gokula was forcibly tried to convert to Islam. Even after the fall of Gokula the Mughal forces kept on imprisoning and plundering the Jats. Not content with it, as it were, Aurangzeb broke loose his fury upon the temple of Keshava Rai.

It was levelled to the ground (during the month of Ramzan, 1080 A.H. 13 January to 11 February 1670) and mosque was built upon its site. Its idols were desecrated and later buried under the footsteps of the Begum Sahiba mosque at Agra. The name of Mathura was changed to 'Islamabad' and that of Brindaban to 'Mominabad.' The temples and idols of the rest of the holy places in the Brij were gradually destroyed. This added insult to injury. The affront inflicted upon the families of their leader and kinsmen must have outraged the feelings of the entire tribe in whose social consciousness and tribal sentiments have always been uppermost.

Jat people are normally moderate light-hearted and not unmanageable unless of course when excited. It can hardly be called an act of political wisdom on his part to have tried to put down the warlike and stubborn Jats in ruthless manner.

So long as the Emperor had a firm grip over the north the Jats remained subdued but as soon as it loosened, their pent up fury was let loose and they resumed their lawless course with added vigour. Thus the policy of Aurangzeb towards them defeated its very object and in the long run proved harmful for the Empire. It has been rightly remarked that a little indiscretion and persistence in a wrong policy " converted " peaceful husbandmen (Jats) into flaming warriors as it did friends (Rajputs) into foes.

- In 1670, Chhatrapati Shivaji had opened the war against the Mughals. He opposed Aurangzeb with full strength and had initially stopped him from entering the Deccan, but by 1689 Auranzeb's armies had conquered the ruler of Maratha Empire Sambhaji. But even after Sambhaji's death, Aurangzeb could never conquer the Maratha Kingdom completely ever in his 27 years of war in Deccan..
- In 1672, the Satnami, a sect concentrated in an area near Delhi, under the leadership of Bhirbhan and some Satnami, took over the administration of Narnaul, but they were eventually crushed upon Auranzeb's personal intervention with very few escaping alive.

Satnami's

Apparently these Satnamis leader was Jeewandas Chandel, perhaps from Barabanki and wrote his own text which is similar to our ideology. He was brought to Sikhi by Bala Lal/Dayal Ji. And had meeting with Shri Guru Tegh Bahadur Ji and became close to Sri Guru Tegh Bahadur Ji. Later they rebelled against Aurangzeb (at Mahindergarh, district of south Haryana) and after initial success they were forced to run. Some say they were large in numbers, 20,000. It is said that Satnamis were so much a fear in Muslims that Aurangzeb, wrote ayets or verses of Holy Kuran on banners to put psycholgical motivations to his forces.

After their mass-persecution and defeating started, they took refuge in areas of present day Chhatisgarh state. There they lived the life of tribals. And faith became some rituals. Some of them became Christian, following Christian missionary preaching, including former CM of Chhatisgarh Ajit Jogi.

Very few people know that numbering more over one crore and spread in the areas of Jharkhand, Bengal and Chhatisgarh, Satnamis are those Sikhs who had taken on Emperor Aurangzeb at the behest of Guru Teg Bahadur against his decision to charge jeziya and destruction of temples and teaching centres of Hindus & Sikhs. Rebelling against Auranzeb, for a considerable time, they had in their possession the whole areas of Southern Haryana and North Rajasthan. These Sikhs associated themselves with Sikhism during the visit of Guru Nanak. They recited Satman and have kept themselves associated with Satnam till date.

In 1667, Aurangzeb declared that all Hindus would pay five per cent Jeziya tax. On April 9, 1969 he passed orders that all Hindu temples, and educational institutions be destroyed and their religious activities be banned. This decision was implemented ruthlessly. On hearing these orders, Guru Teg Bahadur started from Assam towards Punjab in December 1671 and reached Delhi in January 1672. In Delhi he gave the call "bhai kau ko det nahi, na bhai manat aan" (Neither I cause fear to anyone nor I accept fear). It were these Satnamis who implemented this call of the Guru.

When Guruji was in Delhi, the leader of Satnamis came to pay obeisance along with his associates and described the details of atrocities leased on Hindus. Guruji understood that the time had come to face the tyranny and that by sitting in fear, Mughals would only be more enthused. This was the main reason he called upon every Sikh to be fearless. It included Jagjivan Das also.

On receiving the call, Satnamis congregated and decided that they being followers of Guru Nanak would not pay anything to anyone else except the Guru. When government officials came to their houses to collect taxes they declined. The soldiers tried to force; but were beaten back. The ruler of the area attacked them, they retaliated. The Mughal forces fled from the area of Narnaul Rumour spread in the area that the Satnamis were blessed hence they cannot be defeated by anyone.

On the other hand, fear spread in the royal circles. The fact that Satnamis could not be defeated would result in rebellion in other parts as well. Situation would go out of control. Aurangzeb lost his sleep over this. He was already worried due to the rebellions in Afghanistan and Peshawar. Afghanistan had already been seceded for long to a rebellion. Rebellion at Narnaul being so near the capital could cause serious repercussions possibly resulting in loss of power also.

The Satnamis were not sitting complacent either. They had fortified themselves under the leadership of Jagjiwan Dass Chandel and were prepared for any eventuality. The entire information was constantly relayed to Aurangzed. He had the task in hand to break the fortification of Satnamis and to break the myth of their being invincible. Understanding the need of the hour, Aurangzeb decided to tackle this rebellion on a large scale. He prepared a contingent of forces under his general Salar Sayyad Ahmed Khan. He wrote with his own hands the ayats of quran on the thwart any magic. Addressing the forces he said," The ayats on your flags will keep you safe and nobody will be able to defeat you because you are going to annihilate the Kaafirs. Armed with guns and weaponry these forces reached Narnaul and encircled the few Satnamis. How could these unarmed-Satnamis take on the heavily armed enemy for long? None of the Satnamis surrendered. They reached Madhya Pardesh gradually, closely following by the Mughal forces. Along with their families they scattered themselves in the forest of what is now Chhatisgarh. Aurangzeb, army was recalled as they were required else where.

Since then these Satnamis remained in these forests. Worse happened when they were oppressed a lot by the rich and strong sections of local rich population. Satnamis lived in their huts reciting satnam and remained aloof from the rituals of Pandits. Later Ghasi Ram united them, thwarting the oppression of Pandits and spreading education among them. When the Britishers came they converted some of them to Christianity. Former Chief Minister Ajit Jogi's family is one of those Satnamis, who become Christians.

Few years back, the house of a Satnami near Dhamtari caught fire. Everything in his house was destroyed except a wooden box which contained a Granth. The news spread far and wide. The Script of the Granth could not be underdtood by the educated local. Few Punjabis also lived in the area. Once of them visited the site and found that this was and ancient beer of Sri Guru Granth Sahib. The housekeeper informed that his ancestors used to read and worship the Granth.

Where people of Dhamatri came to know of this, they expressed a wish to construct a Gudwara there. The housekeeper gifted the land for the Gurdwara and realising there his ancestors were Sikhs, Partook amrit himself. From then on, many of the Satnam Foundation of Raipur assisted by Scottish Sikh Council, alongwith other associations, which continues even now. Few organizations are contributing their mite for the welfare of these three tribes. Besides organization approved by the Panth, these include local organization, as Gurmat Parchar Sanstha Nagpur, Satnam Foundation Raipur, Guru Angad Dev Educational and Welfare Society Ludhiana, Trust for the Welfare of Vanjara and Other Weaker Sections of Society Chandigarh etc. But the monetary part is taken care mainly by foreign organization, prominent amongst them being the Scottish Sikh Council, British Sikh Council etc. These efforts keep them attached with the Gurughar. For this the whole Sikh community needs to made efforts unitedly at global level.

British Historian Accounts on Satnamis

Satnami. The word satnami is derived from satnam, lit the True Name, a term used in some religious traditions including Sikhism to denote the Supreme Being. Literally, a Satnami is one who believes in and worships only the True Being and as such every SIKH is a Satnami. However, the term has been adopted by at least three religious bodies as a title of their respective sects. The Sadhs, a unitarian sect of northern India founded in 1543 by Birbhan and which is also said to be an offshoot of the Raidasis, employ this term among themselves. Probably, it was this sect of the Sadhs which was responsible for the Satnami revolt against Aurangzib in 1672. The next sect calling itself Satnami was founded by Jagjivan Das (b. 1(582) of Sardaha in the Barabanki district in Bihar. He began his religious career as a Kabirpanthi and, according to some authorities, these Satnamis are merely a branch of that faith. These Satnamis profess to adore the True Name alone whom they consider the cause and creator of everything in this world. He is said to be formless, without a beginning and without an end. Although they profess to worship but one God, yet they also pay reverence to his manifestation revealed in incarnations, particularly those of Rama and Krishna.

Their moral code enjoins upon them indifference to the world ; devotion to the GURU ; clemency and gentleness ; rigid adherence to truth ; honest discharge of all social and religious obligations; and the hope of final absorption into the Supreme. Fasts are kept, at least to a partial extent, on Tuesday (the day of Hanuman) and on Sunday (the day of Sun). Their distinctive mark is a black and white twisted thread, usually of silk, worn on the right wrist. On the forehead is worn a tilak, consisting of one perpendicular streak. They bury their dead. Consumption of flesh and alcohol are taboo. They were nicknamed by the people as Mundiyas (Shavelings) because of their habit of shaving the body clean of all hair. Guru Naanak was also a Mundia \ Mundak \ Satnami. He proceed Satnam Culture and mission with the sikh name as per demand and time every sikh is first a Satnami. Soon afterwards the Afridi Pashtuns in the north-west also revolted, and Aurangzeb was forced to lead his army personally to Hasan Abdal to subdue them. When Maharaja Jaswant Singh of Jodhpur died in 1679, a conflict ensued over who would be the next Raja. Aurangzeb's choice of a nephew of the former Maharaja was not accepted by other members of Jaswant Singh's family and they rebelled, but in vain. Aurangzeb seized control of Jodhpur. He also moved on Udaipur, which was the only other state of Rajputana to support the rebellion. There was never a clear resolution to this conflict, although it is noted that the other Rajputs, including the celebrated Kachhwaha Rajput clan of Raja Jai Singh, the Bhattis, and the Rathores, remained loyal. On the other hand, Aurangzeb's own third son, Prince Akbar, along with a few Muslim Mansabdar supporters, joined the rebels in the hope of dethroning his father and becoming emperor. The rebels were defeated and Akbar fled south to the shelter of the Maratha Chhatrapati Sambhaji, Chhatrapati Shivaji's successor. The Ahoms (the people of Shan community of Thailand) were the kings who had established their kingdom in the basin of river Bramhaputra and made it impossible for the Mughals to conquer that area.

The Deccan Wars and the Rise of the Marathas

In the time of Shah Jahan, the Deccan had been controlled by three Muslim kingdoms: Ahmednagar (Nizamshahi), Bijapur (Adilshahi) and Golconda (Kutubshahi). Following a series of battles, Ahmendnagar was effectively divided, with large portions of the kingdom ceded to the Mughals and the balance to Bijapur. One of Ahmednagar's generals, a Hindu Maratha named Shahaji, joined the Bijapur court. Shahaji sent his wife Jijabai and young son Shivaji in Pune to look after his Jagir.

In 1657, while Aurangzeb attacked Golconda and Bijapur, Shivaji, using guerrilla tactics, took control of three Adilshahi forts formerly controlled by his father. With these victories, Shivaji assumed de facto leadership of many independent Maratha clans. The Marathas harried the flanks of the warring Adilshahi and Mughals, gaining weapons, forts, and territories. Shivaji's small and ill-equipped army survived an all out Adilshahi attack, and Shivaji personally killed the Adilshahi general, Afzal Khan. With this event, the Marathas transformed into a powerful military force, capturing more and more Adilshahi and Mughal territories.

Just before Shivaji Raje's his coronation in 1659, Aurangzeb sent his trusted general and maternal uncle Shaista Khan to the Deccan to recover his lost forts. Shaista Khan drove into Maratha territory and took up residence in Pune.

In a daring raid, Shivaji attacked the governor's residence in Pune, killed Shaista Khan's son, even hacking off Shaista Khan's thumb as he fled. This is the first known commando operation in the history, Shivaji and his band of mavla's dressed up as commoners and joined a wedding party and were successful in sneaking into Lal Mahal, where the governor was residing and drove him out from there by attacking him in his sleep.

Aurangzeb ignored the rise of the Marathas for the next few years. Shivaji continued to capture forts belonging to both Mughals and Bijapur. At last Aurangzeb sent his powerful general Raja Jai Singh of Amber, a Hindu Rajput, to attack the Marathas. Jai Singh's blistering attacks were so successful that he defeated Shivaji and had him arrested Shivaji agreed becoming a Mughal vassal. Jai Singh also promised the Maratha hero his safety, placing him under the care of his own son, the future Raja Ram Singh I. However, circumstances at the Mughal court were beyond the control of the Raja, and when Shivaji and his son Sambhaji went to Agra to meet Aurangzeb, they were placed under house arrest, from which they managed to effect a daring escape.

Shivaji returned to the Deccan, successfully drove out the Mughal armies, and was crowned Chhatrapati or Emperor of the Maratha Empire in 1674. While Aurangzeb continued to send troops against him, Shivaji expanded Maratha control throughout the Deccan until his death in 1680. Shivaji was succeeded by his son Sambhaji. Militarily and politically, Mughal efforts to control the Deccan continued to fail. Aurangzeb's son Akbar left the Mughal court and joined with Sambhaji, inspiring some Mughal forces to join the Marathas. Aurangzeb in response moved his court to

Aurangabad and took over command of the Deccan campaign. More battles ensued, and Akbar fled to Persia.

In 1689 Aurangzeb captured and had killed Sambhaji. Sambhaji's successor chhatrapati Rajaram and his, Maratha Sardars (commanders) fought individual battles against the Mughals, and territory changed hands again and again during years of endless warfare. As there was no central authority among the Marathas, Aurangzeb was forced to contest every inch of territory, at great cost in lives and treasure. Even as Aurangzeb drove west, deep into Maratha territory — notably conquering Satara — the Marathas expanded their attacks further into Mughal lands, including Mughal-held Malwa, Hyderabad, Jinji in Tamil Nadu. Aurangzeb waged continuous war in the Deccan for more than two decades with no resolution. Aurangzeb lost about a fifth of his army fighting rebellions. led by the Marathas in Deccan India He came down thousands of mile way to Deccan to conquer Marathas but finally was unable to crush Maratha kingdom. He never went back and died a natural death while fighting the Marathas.

The Pashtun Rebellion

The Pashtun tribesmen of the Empire were considered the bedrock of the Mughal Empire Army. They were crucial defenders of the Empire from the threat of invasion from the North-West as well as the main fighting force against the Sikh and Maratha forces. The Pashtun revolt in 1672 under the leadership of the warrior poet Khushal Khan Khattak was triggered when soldiers under the orders of the Mughal Governor Amir Khan allegedly attempted to molest women of the Safi tribe in modern day Kunar. The Safi tribes attacked the soldiers. This attack provoked a reprisal, which triggered a general revolt of most of the tribes. Attempting to reassert his authority, Amir Khan led a large Mughal Army to the Khyber pass. There the army was surrounded by tribesmen and routed, with only four men, including the Governor, managing to escape.

After that the revolt spread, with the Mughals suffering a near total collapse of their authority along the Pashtun belt. The closure of the important Attock-Kabul trade route along the Grand Trunk road was particularly critical. By 1674, the situation had deteriorated to a point where Aurangzeb himself camped at Attock to personally take charge. Switching to diplomacy and bribery along with force of arms, the Mughals eventually split the rebellion and while they never managed to wield effective authority outside the main trade route, the revolt was partially suppressed. However the long term anarchy on the Empire's North-Western frontier that prevailed as a consequence ensured that the Persian Nadir Shah's forces half a century later faced little resistance on the road to Delhi, being one of the causes for Mughal decline and eventual European dominance.

Khushal Khan Khattak

Khushal Khan Khattak (1613-1689) was a Pashtun warrior, poet and tribal chief of the Khattak tribe. He wrote in Pashto during the reign of the Mughal emperors in the seventeenth century, and admonished Afghans to forsake their divisive tendencies and unite. He was a renowned fighter who became known as the "Afghan Warrior Poet". He lived in the foothills of the Hindu Kush mountains in what is now the North-West Frontier Province of western Pakistan.

Biography

Khushal Khan was the son of Shahbaz Khan and was born in Akora (now in Nowshera District, Pakistan). His grandfather, Malik Akoray, was the first Khattak to enjoy widespread fame during the reign of the Mughal King Jalal-ud-din Akbar. Akoray moved from Teri (a village in Karak District) to Sarai Akora, the town which Akoray founded and built. Akoray cooperated with the Mughals to safeguard the trunk route and was generously rewarded for his assistance. The Akor Khels, a clan named after Akoray, still hold a prominent position in the Khattak tribe. The Khattak tribe of Khushhal Khan now (2007) lives in areas of Karak, Kohat, Nowshera, Peshawar, Mardan and in other parts of the North-West Frontier Province.

Khushhal Khan's life can be divided into two important parts— during his adult life he was mostly engaged in the service of the Mughal King, and during his old age he was preoccupied with the idea of the unification of the Pashtuns.

His first involvement in war occurred when he was just 13 years old. Shah Jehan appointed him as the tribal chief and Mansabdar at the age of 28 after the death of his father. By appointment of the Mughul emperor, Shah Jehan, Khushhal succeeded his father in 1641, but in 1658, Aurangzeb, Shah Jehan's successor, locked him away as a prisoner in the Gwalior fortress.

Rebellion

After Khushhal was permitted to return to Pashtun dominated areas (now constituting the NWFP), he incited the Afghans to rebel against the Mughal Emperor Aurenzeb.

Along with the Rajputs, the Pashtun tribesmen of the Empire were considered the bedrock of the Mughal Army. They were crucial defenders of the Mughal Empire from the threat of invasion from the West. The Pashtun revolt in 1672 was triggered when soldiers under the orders of the Mughal Governor Amir Khan attempted to molest women of the Safi tribe in what is now Kunar. The Safi tribes attacked the soldiers. This attack provoked a reprisal, which triggered a general revolt of most of the tribes. Attempting to reassert his authority, Amir Khan led a large Mughal Army to the Khyber pass. There the army was surrounded by tribesmen and routed, with only four men, including the Governor, managing to escape.

After that the revolt spread, with the Mughals suffering a near total collapse of their authority along the Pashtun belt. The closure of the important Attock-to-Kabul trade route along the Grand Trunk road was particularly critical. By 1674 the situation had deteriorated to a point where Aurangzeb himself camped at Attock to personally take charge. Switching to diplomacy and bribery along with force of arms, the Mughals eventually split the rebellion and while they never managed to wield effective authority outside the main trade route, the revolt was partially suppressed. However the long term anarchy on the Mughal frontier that prevailed as a consequence ensured that Nadir Shah's forces half a century later faced little resistance on the road to Delhi.

Forced to flee after the Mughals reasserted control, he died after many years of attempting to unite the various Pakhtun tribes together.

His grave carries the inscription: da afghan pa nang me watarla tura, nanagyalai da zamana khushal khattak yam "I have taken up the sword to defend the pride of the Afghan, I am Khushal Khattak, the honorable man of the age." Khushhal Khan Khattak died on February 25, 1689, in Dambara.

The Mazar of Khushal Khan Khattak is situated near the Railway Station of Akora Khattak in Nowshera district. N.W.F.P, Pakistan.

Published Works

His poetry consists of more than 45,000 poems. According to some historians the number of books written by him is more than 200. His more famous books are *Baz Nama, Fazal Nama, Distar Nama* and *Farrah Nama*. H. G. Raverty was the first translator of Khattak into English; *Selections from the Poetry of Afghans* (1862, Kolkata) has ninety eight poetic pieces. This was followed by Biddulph's translation *Selections from the Poetry of Khushhal Khan Khattak* in 1890 published in London. Evelyn Howell and Olaf Caroe jointly translated and published *The Poems of Khushhal Khan Khattak* in 1963, from the University of Peshawar. Another translation was that by Dr N. Mackenzie *Poems from the Diwan of Khushhal Khan Khattak* published from London in 1965.

Dost Mohammad Khan Kamil was the first Pakhtoon scholar to initiate research on Khattak along scientific lines. He wrote two important and comprehensive books, one in English called *On a Foreign Approach to Khushhal* and the other in Urdu titled *Khushhal Khan Khattak* published in 1952. *Diwan-i-Khushhal Khan Khattak* was published under the directive of H.W. Bellew in 1869 (Jail Press, Peshawar), the manuscript of which was provided by Sultan Bakhash Darogha, an employee of the British government. More recently his poetry has been translated again.

In October 2002, a book on Khushal Khan Khattak "*Khushal Khan, The Afghan Warrior Poet and Philosopher*" has been published. Sponsored by Pashtoon Cultural Society (Regd) and Pashto Adabi Society (Regd) Islamabad/Rawalpindi, written by a well known writer and scholar, Ghani Khan Khattak who is reputed for having established the literary and cultural societies and for promoting Pushto literary and cultural activities in the federal capital, Islamabad (Pakistan). The significance of the above named book lies in that this is the first book in English on Khushal. Most of the written material available on Khushal Khan Khattak is either in Pashto or in Urdu. Although orientalists have always given importance to Khushal in their findings but they have not ever presented a detailed picture of the exceptional man known as Khushal Khan.

Death

Khushal khan Khattak died in 1689, in his will which he described in one of his beautiful verses, he wished for his final resting place to be "as far from the soil disgraced by the Mogals" as his heirs could find. He is buried near Akora Khattak in N.W.F-P.. A tomb site with a rest house and a library in his name have also been erected at the site.

Legacy

Aurangzeb's influence continues through the centuries. He was the first ruler to attempt to impose Sharia law on a non-Muslim country. His critics decry this as intolerance, while his mostly Muslim supporters applaud him, some calling him a just ruler. Today, in Afghanistan and South Asia, Aurangzeb is considered the most powerful king ever to have ruled the subcontinent, an example of Islamic might. He engaged in nearly perpetual war, justifying the ensuing death and destruction on moral and religious grounds. He arguably eventually succeeded in the imposition of Islamic Sharia in his realm, but alienated many constituencies, not only non-Muslims, but also Shiite Muslims. This led to increasing Power of the Marathas, and militant tactics of the Sikhs, the Pashtuns, and the Rajputs, who along with other territories broke from the empire after his death; it also led to disputes among Indian Muslims.

Unlike his predecessors, Aurangzeb considered the royal treasury as a trust of the citizens of his empire and did not use it for personal expenses or extravagant building projects (except, perhaps, for one project: he built the Badshahi Masjid mosque (Imperial or Alamgiri Mosque) in Lahore, which was once the largest outside of Mecca). He also added a small marble mosque known as the *Moti Masjid* (Pearl Mosque) to the Red Fort complex in Delhi. His constant warfare especially with Marathas, however, drove his empire to the brink of bankruptcy just as much as the wasteful personal spending and opulence of his predecessors.

The conquest of the Deccan, to which [Aurangzeb] devoted the last 26 years of his life, was in many ways a Pyrrhic victory, costing an estimated hundred thousand lives a year during its last decade of futile chess game warfare...The expense in gold and rupees can hardly be accurately estimated. [Aurangzeb]'s moving capital alone-a city of tents 30 miles in circumference, some 250 bazaars, with a $^{1}D_{2}$ million camp followers, 50,000 camels and 30,000 elephants, all of whom had to be fed, stripped peninsular India of any and all of its surplus grain and wealth... Not only famine but bubonic plague arose...Even [Aurangzeb] had ceased to understand the purpose of it all by the time he..was nearing 90... "I came alone and I go as a stranger. I do not know who I am, nor what I have been doing," the dying old man confessed to his son in February 1707. "I have sinned terribly, and I do not know what punishment awaits me."

He alienated many of his children and wives, driving some into exile and imprisoning others. He died in Ahmednagar on Friday, February 20, 1707 at the age of 88, having outlived many of his children. His modest open-air grave in Khuldabad expresses his deep devotion to his Islamic beliefs.

Aurangzeb's legacy to India was factionalism, sectarianism, decentralization, and vulnerability to European encroachment.

After Aurangzeb's death, his son Bahadur Shah I took the throne. The Mughal Empire, due both to Aurangzeb's over-extension and to Bahadur Shah's weak military and leadership qualities, entered a period of long decline. Immediately after Bahadur Shah occupied the throne, the Maratha Empire — which Aurangzeb had held at bay, inflicting high human and monetary costs — consolidated and launched effective invasions of Mughal territory, seizing power from the weak emperor. Within 100 years of Aurangzeb's death, the Mughal Emperor had little power beyond Delhi.

Will Of Aurangzeb

After receiving and reading the Zafarnama sent by the tenth Sikh Guru, Guru Gobind Singh, Aurangzeb saw that had a bleak future. The will was recorded by Maulvi Hamid-ud Din in chapter 8 of his hand written book in Persian about the life of Aurangzeb:

1. There is no doubt that I have been the emperor of India and I have ruled over this country. But I am sorry to say that I have not been able to do a good deed in my lifetime. My inner soul is cursing me as a sinner. But now it is of no avail. It is my wish that my last rites be performed by my dear son Azam, nobody else should touch my body.
2. My servant, Aya Beg, has my purse in which I have carefully kept my earnings of 4 Rs. and 2 annas. In my spare time

I have been writing the Koran and stitching caps. It was by selling the caps that I made an honest earning of 4 Rs. and 2 annas. My coffin should be purchased with this amount. No other money should be spent for covering the body of a sinner. This is my dying wish. By selling the copies of the Koran I collected 305 Rs. That money is also with Aya Beg. It is my will that poor Muslims should be fed with sweet rice purchased by this money.

3. All my articles-clothes, ink stand, pens and books should be given to my son Azam Shah I. The labour charges for digging my grave will be paid by Prince Azam Shah I.
4. My grave should be dug in a dense forest. When I am buried my face should remain uncovered. Do not bury my face in earth. I want to present myself to Allah with a naked face. I am told whoever goes to the supreme court with a naked face will have his sins forgiven.
5. My coffin should be made of thick Khaddar. Do not place a costly shawl on the corpse. The route of my funeral should not be showered with flowers. No one should be permitted to place any flowers on my body. No music should be played or sung, I hate music.
6. No tomb should be built for me. Only a chabootra or platform may be erected
7. No mausoleum should be raised in my memory. No stone with my name should be placed at my grave. There should be no trees planted near the grave. A sinner like me does not deserve the protection of a shady tree.
8. My son, Azam Shah I has the authority to rule from the throne of Delhi. Kam Bakhsh should be entrusted with the governance of Bijapur and Golconda States.
9. Allah should not make anyone an emperor, the most unfortunate person is he who is an emperor. My sins should not be mentioned in any social gathering. No story of my life should be told to anyone.

Translated from an historical article published by S.Ajmer Singh MA in the Fateh weekly Nov. 7th, 1976. According to wishes of the emperor, his grave made of 'kuccha' bricks can still be seen in Aurangabad.

7

Later Mughals

Bahadur Shah I

His original name was Qutb ud-Din Mohammad Muazzam later titled as Shah Alam by his father. He took the throne name Bahadur Shah in 1707. He was a Mughal emperor who ruled India from 1707 to 1712. Bahadur Shah, who is commonly neglected because his reign lasted just five years, completes the gallery of the great Mughals. He was an old man of 63 when he came to power but his achievements in those five years would have done credit to most men in their prime. He made settlements with the implacable Marathas, tranquilized the Rajputs, added Assam to the Mughal Empire and became friendly with the Sikhs in the Punjab. He was travelling throughout his reign and only came to rest in Lahore in the last few months of his life.

Early Life

Muazzam, the second son of the emperor Aurangzeb through Nawab Bai Begum Saheba, the daughter of Raja of Rajauri (Jarral Rajput), was born in Burhanpur in 1643. In his father's lifetime, Muazzam was deputed governor of the northwest territories by Aurangzeb. His province included those parts of the Punjab where the Sikh faith was blossoming. As governor, Muazzam relaxed the enforcement of Aurangzeb's severe edicts, and an uneasy calm prevailed in the province for a brief time. In fact, he maintained a friendly relationship with the last Sikh spiritual leader, Guru Gobind Singh. When Muazzam was challenging his brothers for the Mughal throne, Guru Gobind Singh Ji provided military assistance and spiritual guidance to the liberal prince.

Reign

After Aurangzeb's death, Muazzam Bahadur Shah took the throne. A war of succession began immediately after Aurangzeb died. One younger brother, Prince Azam Shah, proclaimed himself emperor and marched towards Delhi, where he unsuccessfully fought Bahadur Shah and died after a nominal reign of three months. Another brother, Mohammad Kam Baksh, was killed in 1709.

Aurangzeb had imposed Sharia law within his kingdom with harsh enforcement of strict edicts. This led to increased militancy by many constituencies including the Marathas, the Sikhs and the Rajputs. Thus, rebellion was rife at the time of Aurangzeb's death and Bahadur Shah inherited a very unstable polity. A more moderate man than his father, Bahadur Shah sought to improve relations with the militant constituencies of the rapidly crumbling kingdom. Bahadur Shah was successful in retreating Sikh General Banda Singh Bahadur to hills and was also able to gain control over Assam purely because of the assistance he got from his son, Azim-ush-Shan. Bahadur Shah never abolished Jizyah, but the effort to collect the tax became ineffectual. Support to music was apparently renewed during his brief rule of five years. There was no destruction of temples in his reign. During Bahadur Shah's brief reign of five years, although the empire remained united, factionalism in the nobility reached a new height. However, he could do little to mitigate the damage already done by his father.

After his short reign of less than five years, the Mughal Empire entered a long decline, attributable both to his old age and to his father's geographical overextension. Reports are that he was courageous and intelligent, but that his father's repression had harmed his abilities. All accounts agree in representing Bahadur Shah as a man of mild and equable temper, learned, dignified, disciplined, magnanimous and generous to fault. Although not a great sovereign like his predecessors, Bahadur Shah may be called, at least in comparison with his successors, a fairly successful one. According to many historians Bahadur Shah was the last major Mughal emperor as the rulers who succeeded him were either proxies or puppets of some influential regional chieftains and their influence was hardly felt outside the imperial capital city of Delhi. Bahadur Shah hardly shared Aurangzeb's orthodox views. Unlike his father, Aurangzeb, he was a liberal sufi in outlook. In fact, it is true that after his sudden death the disintegration of the Mughal Empire became very much evident.

Bahadur Shah died on February 27, 1712 in Lahore while making alterations to the Shalimar Gardens. He was succeeded by his son Jahandar Shah. His grave lies, next to the dargah of 13th century, Sufi saint, Qutbuddin Bakhtiar Kaki at Mehrauli, in a marble enclosure, along with that of Shah Alam II, and Akbar II.

Azim-ush-Shan

Sultan Azhar ud-din Mohammad Azim Mirza, Azim us-Shan Bahadur (December 15, 1664- March 18, 1712) was the third son of Mughal emperor Bahadur Shah I, by his second wife, Maharajkumari Amrita Bai Sahiba.

In 1712, at the time of his father's death, Azim-ush-shan was serving as governor of Bengal, Bihar, and Orissa. He immediately proclaimed himself emperor. However, he was killed (drowned in the Ravi River) shortly afterwards in the succession struggles that ensued.

Azim-ush-shan was married four times. His first marriage was in 1668, to Rajkumari Bai Jas Kanwar Sahiba, the daughter of the Rajput Raja of Kama. In 1692, he married his second wife, Nawab Aisha Begum Sahiba, a daughter of a Mughal courtier. He married in third wife, Nawab Giti Ara Begum Sahiba, daughter of Prince Mohammad Azam Shah in 1709. Finally, in 1715, he married his fourth wife, Sahiba Nizwan, a sister of Nawab Khwaja Inayatullah Shaista Khan III, the erstwhile governor of Kashmir. He had six sons and a daughter, including Farrukhsiyar (son of Sahiba Nizwan), who reigned as Mughal emperor between 1713 and 1719 AD.

Jahandar Shah

Jahandar Shah was born on May 10, 1661, a son of the emperor Bahadur Shah I. Upon the death of their father on 27 February 1712, he and his brother Azim-ush-Shan both declared themselves emperor and conducted a struggle for the succession. Azim-ush-shan was killed on 17 March 1712 and Jahandar Shah was able to rule for a further eleven months. His court was depraved. He was a mere puppet in the hands of his favourite wife, Lal Kunwar, who, before her elevation to the position of Queen Consort was a mere dancing girl. Her children were promoted to the highest offices of the Empire. He was defeated in the battle at Agra on 10 January 1713 by Farrukhsiyar, his nephew the second son of Azim-ush-shan, with the support of the Sayyid Brothers. He fled to Delhi, from where he was captured and handed over to the new Emperor, who confined him along with Lal Kunwar. He lived in confinement for a month, until 11 February 1713, when professional stranglers were sent to murder him. When the stranglers were admitted into the prison, Lal Kunwar shrieked," clasped hold of her lover and refused to let go." Violently forcing the two apart, they laid hands on Jahandar Shah and finished him off. His head was severed and presented to Farruksiyar, while his body was taken to Humayun's Tomb and interred there. Lal Kunwar was sent to "suragpura" (Hamlet of Happy Wives), where the widows of previous emperors lived in retirement. Before coming to the throne, Jahandar Shah had sailed around the Indian ocean, and had been a very prosperous trader. He was the father of three sons, including, Aziz-ud-Din, or Alamgir II, who reigned as Mughal emperor between 1754 and 1759.

Farrukhsiyar

Abul Muzaffar Muin ud-din Mohammad Shah Farrukh-siyar Alim Akbar Sani Wala Shan Padshah-i-bahr-u-bar [Shahid-i-Mazlum] (or Farrukhsiyar, August 20, 1685-April 19, 1719) was the Mughal emperor between 1713 and 1719. Noted as a handsome but weak ruler, easily swayed by his advisers, Farukhsiyar lacked the ability and character to rule independently. His reign witnessed the primacy of the Syed Brothers who became the effective powers of the land, behind the facade of Mughal rule.

Biography

Farrukhn Siyar was born at Aurangabad in the Deccan on September 11, 1683. He was the second son of Azim ush Shan, a son of former emperor Bahadur Shah I. His mother was Sahiba Niswan, a sister of Nawab Shaista Khan, the erstwhile Mughal Subadar of Kashmir. He married his first wife, Nawab Fakhr-un-Nisa Begum Sahiba, daughter of Nawab Sahadat Khan Bahadur [Mir Mohammad Taqi Husaini], a Kashmiri nobleman from the Marashi clan, sometime prior to December, 1715. In September 1715, Farrukhsiyar married Indira Kanwar, daughter of Maharaja Ajit Singh of Jodhpur. He was also married to at least one other lady.

Reign

Jahandar Shah was defeated at Samugarh near Agra on 10 January 1713. Following this, the Syed Brothers, helped Farukhsiyar to secure his throne. He took the throne On January 11, 1713, at the age of 30. His reign marked the ascendancy of the Syed Brothers who monopolized state power and reduced the Emperor to an effective figurehead. The town of Farrukhnagar in Gurgaon district, 32 km south of Delhi, was rechristened after his name, during his reign, here he built a Sheesh Mahal and also a mosque.

Trade Concessions

It was during Farrukhsiyar's reign, in 1717, that the British East India Company purchased duty-free trading rights in all of Bengal for a mere three thousand rupees a year. It is said that the Company's surgeon, William Hamilton, cured Farrukhsiyar from some ailment and the emperor was moved to grant trading rights to the Company.

Another story tells of a bribe to a eunuch of the seraglio and a rumoured British Naval attack on the Moghul navy at Surat. This order, which the Company hailed as the golden firman, was not of much practical use. Even though the Company claimed duty exemptions based on this firman, the Mughal governors of Bengal, from Murshid Quli Khan onwards, ignored this order of their suzerain and continued to collect customs duty from the East India Company.

Death

However Farrukhsiyar in the very short term met a humiliating and bloody end, his constant plotting eventually led the Syed Brothers to officially depose him as the Emperor. Farrukhsiyar was imprisoned and starved; later, on February 28, 1719, he was blinded with needles at the orders of the Saiyad brothers. Farrukhsiyar was strangled to death on the night of April 27/28, 1719. After accomplishing his assassination, the Syed Brothers placed his first-cousin, Rafi Ul-Darjat on the throne. Rafi-ud-durjat's father and Farukhsiyar's father had been

Syed Brothers

The Syed brothers refers to Syed Hassan Ali Khan Barha (afterwards Abdullah Khan) and Syed Hussain Ali Khan Barha.

Syeds of Barha

The Syeds of Barha are descendents of Abul Farah, of Wasit in Iraq; Several hundred years ago, at a date which cannot be fixed exactly, Abul Farah and his twelve sons came from Wasit to Mughal Empire, settling at first in four villages near Patiala, in the sarkar of Sirhind and subah of Delhi. From these villages the four branches, into which they are divided, derive their names. Then crossing the Jamuna, they formed a settlement on the eastern side of the upper Doaba, half way between Mirat and Saharanpur, in a sandy, unproductive piece of country, possibly at that time very sparsely inhabited. The etymology of the name Barha is disputed; perhaps it is from the word bara (twelve), with some allusion to the number of their villages.

From the time of Akbar the Great, the men of this brave, proud and lavish clan were famous as military leaders, and by their bravery had acquired a traditional right to lead the vanguard of the Mughal troops.

Early Appointments of the Syed Brothers in the Mughal Empire

The two Syed brothers, who now come into such prominence, were not the mere upstarts, men of yesterday. Besides the prestige of Syed lineage, of descent from the famous Barha branch of that race, and the personal renown acquired by their own valor, they were the sons of a man who had held in Emperor Alamgir's reign first the *subahdari* or Governorship of Bijapur in the Deccan and then that of Ajmer, appointments given in that reign either to Princes of the blood or to the very foremost men in the State. Their father, Syed Abdullah Khan titled *Syed Miyan*, had risen in the service of Ruhullah Khan, Emperor Alamgir's *Mir Bakhshi*, and finally, on receiving an imperial *mansab* (rank), attached himself to the eldest Prince Mohammad Muazzam Shah Alam (later Emperor Bahadur Shah).

Syed Hassan Ali Khan (afterwards Abdullah Khan) and Syed Hussain Ali Khan, two of the numerous sons of Syed Miyan were men of about 46 and 44 years of age respectively in 1712. About 1697 or 1698 the elder brother was faujdar of Sultanpur, Nazarbar in Baglana, subah Khandesh, after that, of Siuni-Hoshangabad also in Khandesh, then again of Nazarbar coupled with Thalner in sarkar Asir of the same subah. Subsequently he obtained charge of Aurangabad. The younger brother, Hussain Ali Khan, who is admitted by every one to have been a man of much greater energy and resolution than his elder brother, had in Emperor Alamgir's reign held charge first of Ranthambore, in subah Ajmer, and then of Hindaun-Bayana, in subah Agra.

After Prince Muizz ud-Din Jahandar Shah, the eldest of Emperor Bahadur Shah's sons, had been appointed in 1106 H. (1694-5) to the charge of the Multan province, Hassan Ali Khan and his brother followed him there. In an expedition against a refractory Baloch zamindar, the Syeds were of opinion that the honours of the day were theirs. Prince Muizz ud-Din Jahandar Shah thought otherwise, and assigned them to his then favourite administrator Isa Khan Mian. The Syeds quitted the service in dudgeon and repaired to Lahore, where they lived in comparative poverty, waiting for employment from Munim Khan, the nazim of that place. When Emperor Alamgir died and Prince Mohammad Muazzam Shah Alam, reached Lahore on his march to Agra to contest the throne, the Syeds presented themselves, and their services were gladly accepted. In the battle of Jajau or Jajowan on the 18th Rabi I, 1119 H. (June 18, 1707), they served in the vanguard and fought valiantly on foot, as was the Syed habit on an emergency. A third brother, Syed Nur ud-Din Ali Khan, was left dead on the field, and Hussain Ali Khan was severely wounded. Though their rank was raised and the elder brother received his father's title of *Abdullah Khan*, they were not treated with such favour as their exceptional services seemed to deserve, either by the new Emperor or his vizier.

The two Syeds managed to quarrel with Khanazad Khan, the vizier Munim Khan's second son, and though the breach was healed by a visit to them from the vizier in person, there is little doubt that this difference helped to keep them out of employment. Hussain Ali Khan is also said to have offended Prince Muizz ud-Din Jahandar Shah. The morning after the battle of Jajau, the Prince visited their quarters to condole with them on the death of their brother, Syed Nur ud-Din Ali Khan, and in so doing launched out into praises of their valor.

Hussain Ali Khan met these overtures in an aggressive manner, saying that what they had done was nothing, many had done as much, their valor would be known when their lord was deserted and alone, and the strength of their right arm had seated him on the throne. Prince Muizz ud-Din Jahandar Shah was vexed by this speech, and refrained from making any recommendation to his father in their favour. Nay, he did his best to prevent their obtaining lucrative employment, and we read of their being obliged to rely upon the Emperor's bounty for their travelling expenses, which were necessarily great, as they were kept in attendance on the Court while it was constantly on the march.

In Shaban 1120 H. (Oct. 1708) Abdullah Khan had been named to the subah of Ajmer, then in a disturbed state owing to the Rajput rising, a condition of things with which Syed Shujaat Khan seemed hardly capable of dealing. Syed Abdullah Khan had barely more than reached Delhi, in order to raise new troops and make other preparations, when the Emperor, Bahadur Shah, changed his mind and Shujaat Khan was received again into favour and maintained in his Government. At length, by the favour of Prince Azim-ush-shan, Abdullah Khan on the 21st Dhu al-Qida 1122 H. (10th Jan. 1711) became that Prince's deputy in the province of Allahabad. About two years earlier (11th Muharram 1120 H., 1 April 1708), the same patron had nominated the younger brother Hussain Ali Khan, to represent him in another of his Governments, that of Bihar, of which the capital was at Azimabad Patna.

Succession Crises of 1712

When Prince Farrukhsiyar first arrived at Azimabad, Hussain Ali Khan was away on an expedition, apparently the recapture of Rohtas fort of Bihar, which about this time had been seized by one Mohammad Raza *Rayat Khan*. The Syed had felt annoyed on hearing that Farrukhsiyar had issued coin and caused the khutba to be read in his father, Prince Azim-ush-shan's, name, without waiting to learn the result of the impending struggle at Lahore. Thus on his return to his headquarters his first impulse was to decline altogether that Prince's overtures. In truth, no attempt could well look more hopeless than that upon which Prince Farrukhsiyar wished to enter. The Prince's mother now hazarded a private visit to the Syeds mother, taking with her little grand-daughter. Her arguments rested on the fact that the Syeds position was due to the kindness of the Prince's father. That father, two brothers, and two uncles had been killed, and the Prince's own means were insufficient for any enterprise. Let Hussain Ali Khan then choose his own course, either let him aid Prince Farrukhsiyar to recover his rights and revenge his father's death, or else let him place the Prince in chains and send him a prisoner to Emperor Jahandar Shah. Here the Prince's mother and daughter bared their heads and wept aloud. Overcome by their tears, the Syeda called her son within the harem. The little girl fell bareheaded at his feet and implored his aid. His mother told him that "whatever was the result he would be a gainer: if defeated, his name would stand recorded as a hero till Judgment Day; if successful, the whole of Hindustan would be at their feet and above them none but the Emperor". Finally she exclaimed, "If you adhere to Emperor Jahandar Shah, you will have to answer before the Great Judge for disavowing your mother's claim upon you."

At these words Hussain Ali Khan took up the women's veils and replaced them on their heads swearing a binding oath that he would espouse the Prince's cause. The next night Prince Farrukhsiyar presented himself at the Khan's house, saying that he had come either to be seized and sent to Emperor Jahandar Shah or to enter into an agreement for the recovery of the throne. The Syed bound himself finally to fight on Prince Farrukhsiyar's behalf. He wrote at once to his elder brother, Abdullah Khan, at Allahabad, inviting him to join the same side, and Prince Farrukhsiyar addressed a farman to him making many promises, and authorizing him to expend the Bengal treasure, then at Allahabad, on the enlistment of troops. It is quite clear that at this time, or soon afterwards, the two chief places in the Empire, those of *Vizier* and of *Amir ul Umara* were formally promised to the two brothers as their reward in case of success. Abdullah Khan, on being superseded at Allahabad, gives in his adhesion to Prince Farrukhsiyar.

At first Abdullah Khan's intention was to submit to Emperor Jahandar Shah, the de facto Emperor, to whom he sent letters professing his loyalty and offering his services. Three months before the death of Emperor Bahadur Shah, he had gone out towards Jaunpur to restore order. In this he was not successful and the pay of his soldiers fell into arrears. The men raised a disturbance, and Abdullah Khan's only anxiety was to escape from them and take shelter within the fort of Allahabad. He promised publicly that as soon as he reached the city, all the collections then in the hands of his agents should be made over to the troops. On the return march, word came of Emperor Bahadur Shah's death. While

Abdullah Khan was still in expectation of a favourable reply to his letter to Emperor Jahandar Shah, he was surprised to learn that his Government had been taken from him, and that the deputy of the new governor was on his way to take possession. The province had been granted to a Gardezi Syed of Manikpur, subah Allahabad, one Raji Mohammad Khan, who had risen to notice in the recent righting at Lahore, and through the reputation thereby acquired, had been appointed *Mir Atish* or general of artillery. The new governor nominated as his deputy his relation, one Syed Abdul Ghaffar (a descendant of Syed Sadar Jahan, *Sadar-us-Sadur, Pihanwi*).

Syed Abdul Ghaffar obtained contingents from one or two zamindars and collected altogether 6,000 to 7,000 men. When he drew near to Karra Manikpur, Abul Hasan Khan, a Syed of Bijapur, who was Abdullah Khan's *Bakhshi*, advanced at the head of 3,000 men to bar his progress. At the Battle of Sarai Alam Chand on August 2, 1712 with Abul Hasan Khan's victory for Abdullah Khan it became clear now that the Syeds were allied against the Emperor for the new contender Prince Farrukhsiyar.

Prince Farrukhsiyar, meanwhile, had marched out with an army along with Syed Hussain Ali Khan Barha from Patna to Allahabad to join Syed Abdullah Khan as soon as possible. Emperor Jahandar Shah learning of the defeat of his General Syed Abdul Ghaffar sent his own son Prince Azzu-ud-Din along with Generals Lutfullah Khan and Khwaja Hussain *Khan Dauran* to face this army. The Second Battle of Khajwah was fought in Fatehpur District, Uttar Pradesh on November 28, 1712. Prince Farrukhsiyar decisively defeated Prince Azzu-ud-Din forcing Emperor Jahandar Shah and his Vizier the Great Zulfiqar Khan *Nusrat Jung* to take the field. At the Battle of Agra 1713 fought on January 10, 1713, Prince Farrukhsiyar won decisively and became the Emperor of the Mughal Empire succeeding his uncle Jahandar Shah.

Rise of the Syed Brothers

After his victory at the Battle of Agra 1713 Emperor Farrukhsiyar on the way from Agra to Delhi, and after arrival at Delhi, conferred many new appointments and new titles on his generals and noblemen. Syed Abdullah Khan was awarded titles *Nawab Qutb-ul-Mulk, Yamin-ud-daulah, Syed Abdullah Khan Bahadur Zafar Jung, Sipah-salar, Yar-i-wafadar* and became *Vizier* or Prime

Minister. Syed Hussain Ali Khan was appointed first *Bakhshi* with the titles of *Umdat-ul-Mulk, Amir-ul-Umara, Bahadur, Feroze Jung, Sipah Sardar*.

Rajputana Campaign 1714

The Rajput States had been in veiled revolt from the imperial authority for 50 years. Emperor Bahadur Shah had been unable, owing to more pressing affairs, to reduce the Raja's effectually. During the confusion which arose on that monarch's death, Ajit Singh, after forbidding slaughtering cows by Muslims for food and the call for prayer from the Alamgiri mosque, besides ejecting the imperial officers from Jodhpur and destroying their houses, had entered the imperial territory and taken possession of Ajmer. Early in Emperor Farrukhsiyar's reign it was determined that this encroachment must be put an end to; and as the Raja's replies to the imperial orders were not satisfactory, it was necessary to march against him.

Hussain Ali Khan left Delhi on January 6, 1714. After a brief campaign Raghunath, a *munshi* in the service of Maharaja Ajit Singh of Jodhpur came to negotiate peace. Hussain Ali Khan thus advanced to Mairtha, where he halted until the terms of peace had been arranged. The terms were that the Raja should give one of his daughters in marriage to the Emperor, in the mode which they styled Dola that the Raja's son, Abhay Singh, should accompany Hussain Ali Khan to Court, and that the Raja in person should attend when summoned. Zafar Khan *Roshan ud-Daulah* arrived at Court on the 5th Jamadi I, 1126 H. (18 May, 1714), with the news.

Clash of the Nobles

During Hussain Ali Khan's absence, Ubaidullah Khan better known as Mir Jumla III became more and more powerful. Emperor Farrukhsiyar had made over his seal to this favourite, and was often heard to say openly:

> *"The word and seal of Mir Jumla are the word and seal of Farrukhsiyar."*

On his side, Abdullah Khan was immersed in pleasure and found little or no leisure to devote to State affairs. Nor, being a soldier who had come into office without much preparation for civil affairs, was he very competent to deal with the details of administration, for which, moreover, he had no natural taste.

Everything was left to his man of business, Ratan Chand, a Hindu of the Baniya caste, and a native of a village near the Syeds home at Jansath. He had been recently created a Raja with the rank of 2,000 zat. The chief dispute centered upon the question of appointments to office, the fees paid by those receiving appointments being a recognized and most substantial source of emolument. Ratan Chand, in addition to these customary fees, exacted large sums, which were practically bribes or payments for the grant of the appointment.

By Mir Jumla's independent action in bringing forward candidates and affixing the seal to their warrants of appointment, without following the usual routine of passing them through the Vizier's office, the emoluments of both Abdullah Khan and of his head officer were considerably curtailed. It is a matter of little wonder, therefore, that Abdullah Khan felt aggrieved at the unusual powers placed in the hands of a rival such as Mir Jumla. This noble was much more accessible than the Vizier, and was not given to the extortionate practices of Ratan Chand. Naturally, men in search of employment or promotion sought his audience-hall rather than that of Abdullah Khan.

The Vizier suffered, in this way, both in influence and in income. Moreover, Mir Jumla allowed no opportunity to pass without depreciating the Syed brothers, and brought forward arguments of every sort to prove that they were unfitted for the offices that they held.

The Syed brothers could never be certain from day to day that some new plot was not being hatched for their destruction. The Rajputana campaign was the means of unmasking one of these schemes. Secret letters had been, dispatched to Maharaja Ajit Singh, urging him to strenuous resistance, and inviting him, if he could, to make away with Syed Hussain Ali Khan Barha. These letters came into Hussain Ali Khan's possession and through them he acquired proof of Emperor Farrukhsiyar's double-faced dealings. In the interval of Hussain Ali Khan's absence, Abdullah Khan had found the greatest difficulty in maintaining his position at Court. All the power was in the hands of Mir Jumla. Every day messages came from Emperor Farrukhsiyar, couched in various forms, but all urging him to resign the office of Vizier. Abdullah Khan now wrote letters to his brother enjoining him to return to Delhi with all possible speed. In response to these calls, Hussain Ali Khan, as we have seen, reached the capital again on the 5th Rajab 1126 H. (16 July, 1714).

For the next two or three months the breach between the Emperor and the minister, although far from closed, was not sensibly widened. The Syeds, as was natural, looked on Farrukhsiyar's accession to the throne as the work of their hands, and resented the grant of any share of power to other persons. On the other hand, the small group of Farrukhsiyar's intimates, men who had known him from his childhood and stood on the most familiar terms with him, were aggrieved at their exclusion from a share in the spoil. The two men selected to confront the Syeds were Khwaja Asim *Khan Dauran* and Mir Jumla III. They were both promoted to the rank of 7,000 horse: they were placed, the former at the head of 5,000 Wala-shahi, and the latter of 5,000 Mughal troopers. Many of their relations were pushed forward into high rank, and counting these men's troops, each of the two nobles had at his command over ten thousand men. Among the signs of this favouritism was the order passed on the 12th Shaban September 2, 1713, permitting Mir Jumla to entertain 6,000 horsemen, who were to be specially paid from the imperial treasury. These were raised by Amanat Khan, his adopted son, from Mughals born in India, and some seventy lakhs of Rupees for their pay were disbursed from the treasury, the rules as to descriptive rolls of the men and branding of the horses being set aside. No order was issued by Farrukhsiyar without the advice and approval of the above two men. In this exercise of authority Mir Jumla assumed the lead, till at length Abdullah Khan was only the nominal, while he was the real vizier. The two Syeds bowed for the time to the Emperor's will, and made no opposition to these usurpations.

Mir Jumla and Khan Dauran talked well, but evaded dealing with the kernel of the matter. Mir Jumla, having no real strength of character, knew that he was not fitted to enter the lists as a champion to fight the Syeds. He therefore made excuses and drew to one side. Khan Dauran was in reality a mere braggadocio, a big talker; and he was frightened that if he should ever be called on to take the lead, he may lose his life in the attempt to destroy the Syeds.

As for the Emperor, his own troops and those of his relations were unequal to an attack on the Syeds. The imperial and Wala-shahi troops comprised many low-caste men and mere artisans held commands. The Emperor had no proof of their fighting quality. So it was decided once more to resume friendly relations with the Syed brothers. Eventually Islam Khan would negotiate a settlement whereby Mir Jumla was forced out of office in Delhi and sent to Bihar.

As Hussain Ali Khan would not come to Court until Mir Jumla had left, the latter received his audience of dismissal on December 16, 1714. Four days afterwards, December 20, 1714, Hussain Ali Khan entered the palace with his men, observing the same precautions as in the case of Abdullah Khan. The Emperor and the *Mir Bakhshi* exchanged compliments, under which their real sentiments were easily perceived. Some months before this time Hussain Ali Khan had obtained in his own favour a grant of the Deccan provinces, in super session of *Nizam-ul-Mulk-ul-Mulk* Chin Kilich Khan (Mir Qamar ud-Din). He had then no intention of proceeding there in person, but meant to exercise the government through a deputy, Daud Khan Panni.

William Hamilton (Surgeon)

William Hamilton (died 4 December 1717) was a surgeon in the British East India Company. He was a part of the delegation that went from Calcutta, the base of the company, to meet Mughal emperor Farrukhsiyar in his court in Delhi in 1715.

Treatment of Farrukhsiyar

In Delhi, Hamilton first had to treat Taqarab Khan (the *khansama,* or lord steward). In August 1715, the surgeon was called to treat a swelling in the groin of the emperor Farrukhsiyar, which he treated successfully. In October of the same year, the emperor again suffered from violent pain and feared it would be a fistula. Hamilton's treatment was again successful. As a result, in December 1715 Farrukhsiyar finally arranged his marriage to the daughter of Raja Ajit Sinh of Jodhpur, which had been delayed by his recurrent illness.

Royal Gift to Hamilton

Hamilton was generously rewarded on the occasion of the wedding. He received "an elephant, a horse, five thousand rupees in money, two diamond rings, a jewelled aigrette, a set of gold buttons, and models of all his instruments in gold."

The Farman

More important than these personal rewards to Hamilton was what the British East India Company achieved. The Company's delegation was placed in high regard in the royal court of Farrukhsiyar. In April 1717, the emperor's *farman* (grant) was issued, meeting all the requests that the Company had made in its petitions. Permission was granted to purchase 38 villages surrounding the three already held by the company (*Sutanuti, Gobindapur* and *Kalikata,* the predecessor of modern Calcutta). The Company was also granted trading privileges in Bengal and further fortification of Calcutta. This grant was instrumental in the setting up of business and the colonisation of Bengal, later to be followed by the rest of India, by the East India Company.

Farrukhsiyar's wish to Retain Hamilton

After the grant, Farrukhsiyar expressed his wish to retain Hamilton in Delhi as his personal physician, but Hamilton was unwilling to stay. Hamilton promised to the emperor that after a visit to Europe he would return and join him as his personal physician.

Death

Hamilton died in Calcutta on [4 December] 1717. He was buried at the churchyard of St. John's Church, Calcutta. The inscription tells the story of his curing a "Malignant Distemper" of Farrukhsiyar.

Rafi ud-Darajat

Rafi-ul Darjat, youngest son of Rafi-us-shaan (brother of Azim ush Shan) was the 10th Mughal Emperor. He was born on 30 November 1699, and succeeded Furrukhsiyar on 28 February 1719, being proclaimed Badshah by the Syed Brothers.

Role of the Syed Brothers

As Rafi-ul Darajat owed his throne to the Syed Brothers they took full advantage of this. They wanted him to be a puppet ruler and so took steps to curtail his power, the previous emperor Furrukhsiyar was deposed by the Syed Brothers as he had tried to maintain his independence. On one occasion a warrant of appointment, having been signed by the Emperor, a second was brought to him the next day by the Wazir, giving the appointment to someone else. The emperor asked," Is this the same village or some other village by the same name?" On being told that it was the same, but this new man was more suitable for the post because he offered more money, the Emperor refused to sign it, saying it was foolish to act this way. He was also slighted by the Syed Brothers. Once, Husain Ali Khan sat in his presence without his permission (which was contrary to the royal etiquette). In response, the emperor requested him to take off his (the emperor's) stockings [moza]. Although inwardly boiling, Husain was forced to comply. His younger brother went a step forward, flirting with Inayat Banu, the emperor's wife, saying that he had fallen in love with her "long curling locks." So the former cut her "locks" off, and sent them to her lover.

Rival Claim to Throne

The reign of Rafi Ul-Darjat was one of turbulence. On 18 May 1719, less than three months after his own accession, Rafi Ul-Darjat's uncle, Nekusiyar assumed the throne at the Agra Fort as he thought he had more right to the throne than the "new born child".i.e. Rafi Ul-Darjat. (Nekusiyar was twenty years older than the former). The Syed Brothers were extremely determined, of course, to defend the emperor they had raised to the throne and punish the offender. In this they easily and swiftly succeeded, and only three months after Nekusiyar's enthronement, the fort surrendered and Nekusiyar was captured. He was respectfully received by the *Amir Ul-Umara,* and confined at Salimgarh where he died in 1723. Meanwhile, Rafi Ul-Darjat had died. His lungs had failed. When it became clear that he was dying, he requested that his elder brother be raised to the throne, so that he could die a happy man. Accordingly, on 4 June 1719, after a reign of 3 months and four days, he was dethroned and sent to the "haram". Two days later his brother, Rafi Ul-Daulah was enthroned. Thus delighted, Rafi Ul-Darjat died five days later. His remains were interred near the shrine of Khawaja Qutub ud-din in Delhi

Rafi ud-Daulah

Rafi-ud-Daulah also known as Shah Jahan II (born 1696) was Mughal emperor for a brief period in 1719. He succeeded his short-lived brother Rafi Ul-Darjat in that year, being proclaimed Badshah by the Syed Brothers. Like his brother, he also died in

1719 at Delhi, being deposed and killed at the behest of the Syed Brothers.

After his death he was succeeded by the unfortunate Nikusiyar who was a nominal sovereign (and whose reign is sometimes discounted).

Neku Siyar

Neku Siyar or Nikusiyar Mohammed was the 12th Mughal Emperor. He took the throne in 1719 at the age of 40 plus. He was son of rebel Mohammad Akbar, son of Aurangzeb and was brought up in a harem in Agra. The local Minister Birbal (not the Birbal of Akbar's fame) used him as puppet and proclaimed him emperor. But as the prince had spent his life inside harem and talked like a catamite, he was laughingly ignored and again put in jail by the Syed Brothers. He died around 1743 at age of 63.

Mohammad Ibrahim (Mughal Emperor)

Mohammed Ibrahim was the 13th Mughal emperor. The brother of Rafi Ul-Darjat and Rafi Ud-Daulat, he took the throne in 1720, after a war of succession to inherit the short-lived Furrukhsiyar throne against the Syed Brothers. He was the claimant of the Syed Brothers after Mohammad Shah joined *Nizam-ul-Mulk* Chin Kilich Khan Mir Qamar ud-Din Khan's camp. After the Syed Brothers' defeat, he was sent back to harem. He died in 1744.

Mohammad Shah

Mohammad Shah (1748 – 1702) also known as Roshan Akhtar was a Mughal emperor of India between 1719 and 1748. He was son of Khujista Akhtar Jahan Shah, the 4th son of Bahadur Shah I. Ascending the throne at the age of seventeen with the help of the Syed Brothers, he later got rid of them with the help of *Nizam-ul-Mulk ul Mulk* Chin Qilich Khan. He was nicknamed as *Rangeela* meaning merrymaker by many historians.

Reign

During his reign, the Mughal empire eventually broke up into a loosely-knit collection of several regional states, each with its own ruler, thus declining the authority of the emperor into a greater extent. In 1722, Mohammad Shah got rid of the Syed Brothers. The following year he lost Malwa to the Marathas. In

1725, the Marathas took Gujrat. In 1737, the Mughal emperor Mohammad Shah had to fight the Marathas once again. He asked the Nizam-ul-Mulk-ul-Mulk to help him. Both forces fought the Marathas at Bhopal but were defeated. Under the terms of a treaty, Mohammad Shah gave the Marathas 5 million rupees and also ceded Malwa to them.

Invasion of Nadir Shah

In February 1739, the Persian emperor, Nader Shah decided to conquer India. Due to poor tactics, Mohammad Shah's army was easily defeated, and Nader Shah triumphantly entered Delhi within the span of one month, where he had the Khutba read in his name. In the violence that followed, more than 30,000 civilians were killed by the Persian troops, forcing Mohammad Shah to beg for mercy and handing the keys to his treasury.

In response, Nader Shah agreed to withdraw, but Mohammad Shah paid the consequence-handing over the keys of his royal treasury and losing even the Peacock Throne, along with the Koh-i-Noor and Darya-ye Noor diamonds, to the Persian emperor.

Aftermath

After Nadir Shah's invasion, the Mughal Empire disintegrated rapidly. Nawab Ali Wardi Khan of Bengal proclaimed independence in 1740. In 1748, to the people's relief, the Mughal prince Ahmad Shah Bahadur defeated Ahmad Shah Abdali.

Mohammad Shah died in 1748 at the age of 46.

Qamar-ud-din Khan, Asaf Jah I

Qamar ad-Din Chin Qilij Khan (Qamar Uddin Siddiqi) Asaf Jah I (20 August 1671-1 June 1748), later known as "Nizam-ul-Mulk-ul-Mulk" was the founder of the Asaf Jahi dynasty which ruled the Hyderabad state from 1720 to 1948.

Birth

He was born to Ghazi ud-Din Khan Feroze Jung and his first wife Wazir un-nisa Begum at Agra, 20 August 1671 as Mir Qamar ud-din Khan. The name was given to him by the Mughal Emperor Aurangazeb. His Paternal grandfathers were both important Mughal Generals and courtiers namely; Kilich Khan II (Paternal) and *Jumlat-ul-Mulk* Allami Saadullah Khan (Maternal), the Prime Minister of Emperor Shah Jahan.

Early Life

At the age of six, Mir Qumaruddin Siddiqi accompanied his father to the Mughal court in 1677. Aurangzeb awarded him a Mansab. Mir Qumaruddin Siddiqi displayed considerable skill as a warrior and before he reached his teens began acompanying his father into battle. In 1688 aged 17 he joined his father in the successful assault on the fort of Adoni and was promoted to the rank of 2000 zat and 500 horse and presented with the finest Arab steed with gold trappings and a pastille perfumed with ambergris from the mughal court.

At the age of nineteen, the Emperor bestowed on him the title "Chin Fateh Khan". He was also gifted a female elephant and now aged 20 he was bestowed with the title of "Chin Qilich Khan" (boy swordsman) for surviving an attack that blew off three of his horse's legs during the siege of Wakinhera Fort. For fighting on and capturing the fort he was raised to rank of 5000 horse and awarded 15 million dams, a jewelled sabre and a third elephant. At 26, he was appointed Commander in Chief and Viceroy, first at Bijapur, then Malwa and later of the Deccan.

He inherited his grandfather's piety and his fathers military prowess. Henry George Briggs (a historian) wrote "If Musalman were accustomed to perpetuate the memory of their heroes by posthumous ovations, india might have seen a hundred statues of her greatest mohammedan hero of the eighteenth century".

Second Only to The Emperor

After Aurangzeb's death he was appointed Governor of Oudh, but after Bahadur Shahs death he opted for a private life in Delhi. His sabbatical was cut short when in 1712 the sixth of Aurangzeb's successors, Farrukhsiyar convinced him to take up the post of Viceroy of the Deccan with the title of Nizam-ul-Mulk (Regulator of the Realm) Fateh Jung.

Diwan

Nizam-ul-Mulk began building up his own power-base independently of the Mughals in Delhi, while continuing to give obeisance to the throne and even remitting money to the centre. He was then called upon by Farrukhsiyar to help fight off the Saiyid brothers. Farrukhsiyar was found and killed but Nizam-ul-Mulk was rewarded for defeating the Saiyids with the post of

Diwan (Prime minister) in the court of Mohammad Shah, Farrukhsiyar's 18 year old successor.

But all did not work as well as planned. Nizam-ul-Mulk attempts to reform the corrupt Mughal administration with its cliques of concubines and eunuchs created many enemies. According to his biographer, Yusuf Husain, he grew to hate the "harlots and jesters" who were the Emperor's constant companions and greeted all great nobles of the realm with lewd gestures and offensive epithets. Nizam-ul-Mulk desire to restore the etiquette of the Court and the discipline of the State to the standard of Shah Jahan's time earned him few friends. By envious malicious insinuations (the courtiers) poisoned the mind of the Emperor against his devoted servant.

Viceroy of the Deccan

In 1724 Nizam-ul-Mulk resigned his post in disgust and set off for the Deccan to resume the Vice-royalty, only to find Mubariz Khan, who had been appointed governor by Emperor Farrukhsiyar nine years earlier, refusing to vacate the post. Mubariz khan had successfully restored law and order in the Deccan but he was also paying lip service to the Mughal throne making only token payments and dividing plum administrative posts among his sons, his uncle and his favourite slave eunuchs. Unimpressed by the upstart occupying what he considered to be his rightfull place, Nizam-ul-Mulk gathered his forces at Shakarkhelda in Berar for a showdown with Mubariz Khan's army. The encounter was short but decisive. Wrapped in his bloodsoaked shawl, Mubariz Khan drove his war elephant into battle until he died from his wounds. His severed head was then sent to Delhi as proof of Nizam-ul-Mulk determination to annihilate anyone who stood in his way.

Now there came from the Emperor an elephant, jewels and the title of Asaf Jah, with directions to settle the country, repress the turbulent, punish the rebels and cherish the people. Asaf Jah or the equal to Asaf, the Grand Vazir in the court of the biblical ruler King Solomon, was the highest title that could be awarded to a subject of the Mughal Empire. There were no lavish ceremonies to mark the establishment of the Asaf Jahi dynasty in 1724. The inauguration of the first Nizam-ul-Mulk took place behind closed doors in a private ceremony attended by the new ruler's closest advisors. Nizam-ul-Mulk never formally declared his independence and insisted that his rule was entirely based on the trust reposed in him by the Mughal Emperor.

The Nizams has no throne, no crown and no symbol of sovereignty. Coins were still minted with the Emperor's name until 1858. It was in the name of the Mughal ruler and not the Nizam that prayers were read out in the Friday Sermon. Qamaruddin Khan was essentially the servant of the Mughal Emperor.

As the Viceroy of the Deccan, the Nizam was the head of the executive and judicial departments and the source of all civil and military authority of the Mughal empire in the Deccan. All officials were appointed by him directly or in his name. Assisted by a Diwan the Nizam drafted his own laws, raised his own armies, flew his own flag and formed his own government.

Acknowledging Mohammad Shah's farman, Nizam-ul-Mulk had good reason to be grateful. Alongside his own personal wealth came the spoils of war and status, he was also entitled to the lions share of gold unearthed in his dominions, the finest diamonds and gems from Golconda mines and the income from his vast personal estates.

He then divided his newly acquired kingdom into three parts. One third became his own private estate known as the Sarf-i-Khas, one third was allotted for the expenses of the government and was known as the Diwans territory, and the remainder was distributed to muslim nobles (Jagirdar, Zamindars, Deshmukh), who in return paid nazars (gifts) to the Nizam for the privilege of collecting revenue from the villages under their suzerainty. The most important of these were the Paigah estates. The Paigah's doubled up as generals, making it easy to raise an army should the Nizams Dominions come under attack. They were the equivalent to the Barmakids for the Abbasid Caliphate. Only second to the Nizams family, they were very important in the running of the government and even today their legacy lingers on with ruined palaces and tombs doted around the once very feudal city of Hyderabad. On the sanads (scrolls) granting them their lands, inscribed in Persian were the words "as long as the Sun and the Moon are in rotation". The owners of the estates were mostly absentee landlords who cared little for the condition of the lands under their control. Jagirs were usually split into numerous pieces in order to prevent the most powerful of the nobles from entertaining any thought of carving out an empire for themselves. The system, which continued relatively unchanged until 1950, ensured a steady source of income for the state treasury and the Nizam himself.

Clash with the Marathas

In 1725, the Marathas clashed with the Nizam, who refused to pay Chauth and Sardeshmukhi to the Marathas. The war began in August 1727 and ended in March 1728. The Nizam was given a crushing defeat at Palkhed near Daulatabad. By the treaty of Munji Shivagaon, the Nizam-ul-Mulk was forced to abide by the following terms:

- Chhatrapati Shahu was recognised as the only Maratha ruler.
- Marathas were given the right to collect Chauth and Sardeshmukhi of Deccan.
- Those revenue collectors driven out would be reappointed.
- The balance revenue was to be paid to Chhatrapati Shahu.

Nadir Shah

In 1738, from beyond the Hindu kush, Nadir Shah started advancing towards Delhi through Afghanistan and the Punjab.

Nizam-ul-Mulk sent his troops to Karnal, where Mughal Emperor Muhammed Shah's forces had gathered to turn back the Persian army. But the combined forces were cannon fodder for the Persian cavalry and its superior weaponry and tactics. Nadir Shah defeated the combined armies of Muhammed Shah and the Nizam.

Nadir Shah entered Delhi and ordered it to be ransacked. Unable to prevent his capital being destroyed, Muhammed Shah again summoned Nizam-ul-Mulk for help. Accordingly, Nizam-ul-Mulk negotiated with Nadir Shah to stop the ransacking.

Later Life

The Nizam was not so well suited to ruling his own territory. The Feudal Lords had the power of life and death and exercised a kind of "imperium-in-imperio". His territory was almost depopulated in some areas and chaos reigned almost everywhere.

In March 1742, the British who were based in Fort St. George in Madras sent a modest hamper to Nizam-ul-Mulk in recognition of his leadership of the most important of the Mughal successor states. Its contents included a gold throne, gold and silver threaded silk from Europe, two pairs of large painted looking glasses, and equipage for coffee cups, 163.75 yards of green and 73.5 yards of crimson velvet, brocades, Persian carpets, a gold ceremonial cloth, two Arab horses, half a dozen ornate rose-water bottles and 39.75 chests of rose water-enough to keep the Nizamul and his entire darbar fragrant for the rest of his reign. In return, the Nizam sent one horse, a piece of jewellery and a note warning the British that they had no right to mint their own currency, to which they complied.

It was after Nizam-ul-Mulks death that his son and grandson sought help from the British and French in order to win the throne. Just days before he died in 1748, Asaf Jah dictated his last will and testament. The 17 clause document was a blueprint for governance and personal conduct that ranged from advice on how to keep the troops happy and well fed to an apology for neglecting his wife. He then reminded his successors to remain subservient to the Mughal Emperor who had granted them their office and rank. He warned against declaring war unnecessarily, but if forced to do so to seek the help of elders and saints and follow the sayings and practices of the Prophet. Finally, he insisted to his sons that "you must not lend your ears to tittle-tattle of the backbiters and slanderers, nor suffer the riff-raff to approach your presence.

Legacy

Nizam-ul-Mulk-ul-Mulk is remembered as laying the foundation for what would become the one of the most important Muslim states outside the Middle East by the first half of the twentieth century. Hyderabad state survived right through the period of British rule up to the time of Indian independence 1947, and was indeed the largest-the state covered an extensive 95,337 sq. miles, An area larger than Mysore or Gwalior and the size of Nepal and Kashmir put together (although it was the size of France when the first Nizam held reign)- and one of the most prosperous, among the princely states of the British Raj.

Death

Nizam-ul-Mulk died aged 76. He had four sons and a daughter, Mir Ahmed Ali Khan Nasir Jung, Mir Ghazi uddin Khan Bahadur Firuz jung, Nawab Syed Mohammed Khan Salabath Jung, Nawab Mir Nizam Ali Khan Bahadur Nizam Ul Mulk Azaf Jah II, Sahibzadi Khair unisa Begum.

He died at Burhanpur, 1 June 1748 and was buried at *mazaar* of Shaikh Burhan ud-din Gharib Chisti, Khuldabad, near Aurangabad.

Titles

- 1685 : Khan
- 1691 : Khan Bahadur
- 1697 : Chin Qilich Khan (by Emperor Aurangazeb)
- 9 December 1707 : Khan-i-Dauran Bahadur
- 1712 : Ghazi ud-din Khan Bahadur and Firuz Jang
- 12 January 1713 : Khan-i-Khanan, Nizam-ul-Mulk and Fateh Jang (by Emperor Farukh Siar)
- 12 July 1737 : Asaf Jah (by Emperor Mohammad Shah)
- 26 February 1739 : Amir ul-Umara and Bakshi ul-Mamaluk (Paymaster-General).

Positions

- 1701-1705 : Faujdar of the Carnatic and Talikota
- 1705-1706 : Faujdar of the Bijapur, Azamnagar and Belgaum
- 1706-1707 : Faujdar of Raichur, Talikota, Sakkhar and Badkal
- 1707 : Faujdar of Firoznagar and Balkona
- 9 December 1707-6 February 1711 : Subedar of Oudh and Faujdar of Gorakhpur
- 12 January 1713-April 1715 : Subedar of the Deccan and Faujdar of the Carnatic
- April 1717-7 January 1719 : Faujdar of Moradabad
- 7 February-15 March 1719: Subedar of Patna
- 15 March 1719-1724 : Subedar of Malwa
- 1722-1724 : Subedar of Gujarat.

Ahmad Shah Bahadur

Ahmed Shah Bahadur (1725–1775) was born to Mohammed Shah. He succeeded his father to the throne as the 15th Mughal Emperor in 1748 at the age of 23. His mother was Udhambai, (also known as Kudsiya Begum). When Ahmed Shah came to power the rule of the Mughal Empire was collapsing. During the reign of his father the city of Delhi (the Mughal capital) had been plundered and much of northern India had been ransacked by the invading army of Nadir Shah). Ahmed Shah inherited a much weakened Mughal state and after ruling unsuccessfully for 6 years, he was deposed by the Vizier Ghazi ud-Din Khan Feroze Jung III in 1754 and later blinded along with his mother. He spent the remaining years of his life in prison and died of natural causes in January 1775. His son Bidar Bakhsh II temporarily rose to power in 1788 as puppet of Ghulam Qadir.

Alamgir II

Aziz-ud-din Alamgir II (1759-1699) was the Mughal Emperor of India from June 3, 1754 to December 11, 1759. He was the son of Jahandar Shah.

Aziz-ud-Din, the second son of Jahandar Shah, was raised to the throne by Ghazi-ud-Din after he deposed Ahmad Shah Bahadur in 1754. On ascending the throne, he took the title of Alamgir and tried to follow the approach of Aurangzeb Alamgir. At the time of his accession to throne he was an old man of 55 years. He had no experience of administration and warfare as he had spent most of his life in jail. He was a weak ruler, with all powers vested in the hand of his Wazir, Ghazi-ud-Din Imad-ul-Mulk. In 1756, Ahmad Shah Abdali invaded India once again and captured Delhi and plundered Mathura. Marathas became more powerful because of their collabouration with Ghazi-ud-Din, and dominated the whole of northern India. This was the peak of Maratha expansion, which caused great trouble for the Mughal Empire, already weak with no strong ruler. The relations between Alamgir and his Wazir, Ghazi-ud-Din, by this time had gotten worse. Alamgir was murdered by Nawab Mir Nawab Mir Ghaziudin Khan Bahadur (grandson of Asaf Jah I), and the son of Alamgir, Ali Gauhar succeeded him.

Shah Jahan III

Shah Jahan III also known as Muhi-ul-millat was Mughal Emperor briefly. He was son of Muhi-us-sunnat, the eldest son of Mohammad Kam Baksh who was the youngest son of Aurangzeb. He was placed on the Mughal throne in 1759 but subsequently deposed by Wazir Ghazi-ud-Din 1760.

In 1759, Delhi was briefly captured by the Marathas.

Ghazi ud-Din Khan Feroze Jung III

Ghazi ud-Din Khan Feroze Jung III was the son of Ghazi ud-Din Khan Feroze Jung II (the son of Nizam ul Mulk Asaf Jah). His original name was Shahabuddin Mohammad Khan but after the death of his father in 1752, he was, by the recommendation of Nawab Safdar Jung appointed *Mir Bakhshi* (Pay Master General), and received the titles of *Amir ul-Umara* (Noble of Nobles) and *Imad ul-Mulk* by the Mughal Emperor Ahmad Shah Bahadur of Delhi.

He blinded and imprisoned Emperor Ahmad Shah Bahadur in 1754 and assassinated Emperor Alamgir II in 1759. He was later the *Wazir ul-Mamalik-i-Hindustan* of the Mughal Emperor Shah Jahan III. His wife was the celebrated Ganna or Gunna Begam who died in the year 1775.

The year of Khan's death is unknown but according to the biography of the poet called Gulzar Ibrahim he was living in 1780 in straitened circumstances. His poetical name was *Nizam*. According to the work called *Masir ul Umra* he went to the Deccan in 1773 and received a *jagir* in Malwa subsequently he proceeded to Surat where he passed a few years with the English and then went on a pilgrimage (Hajj) to Makkah. He composed Persian and Rekhta poetry and left Arabic and Turkish Ghazals and a thick Persian Diwan and a Masnawi in which the miracles of Maulana Fakhr uddin are related. Some say he died at Kalpi on 31 August 1800 and was buried in the Shrine of Fariduddin Ganjshakar, Pakpattan.

Shah Alam II

Shah Alam II (1728–1806), also known as Ali Gauhar, was a Mughal emperor of India. He inherited the throne from his father, Alamgir II as Shah Alam II (1761–1805).

Escape from Delhi

Prince Ali Gauhar, afterwards Emperor Shah Alam II, had been the heir apparent of his father, Emperor Azizuddin Alamgir II. Alamgir's unscrupulous minister (Wazir), Ghaziuddin, had completely dominated the emperor and kept Ali Gauhar under surveillance. After an escape from Delhi, Ali Gauhar appeared in the eastern provinces in 1759, hoping to strengthen his position by gaining control over Bengal, Bihar and Orissa.

Battle of Buxar

The political disorders in Bengal and the unpopularity of Mir Jafar raised high hopes in his mind. Mir Jafar was entirely dependent upon British support for maintaining himself on the throne. Shah Alam also asked for British help, but Robert Clive chose to continue with Mir Jafar. Shah Alam's forces were defeated at Buxar in 1764 and driven back by the British.

Further intrigues of the Wazir at Delhi compelled the prince to seek the protection of the British and ask for a sum of money for his subsistence, and offer, in return, to withdraw from the province. Clive sent about a thousand Pounds, and Shah Alam left Bengal and took up residence in Allahabad where he became a pensioner of the British state. Although a Muslim, Shah Alam developed a keen interest in Christianity, requesting Persian Psalters from the first Protestant missionary to North India, John Zacharias Kiernander at Calcutta.

Loss of Bengal

Thus, the Wazir deprived Shah Alam of the title of Subahdar of Bengal, Bihar and Orissa. However, upon the assassination of his father by Ghaziuddin in 1759, the prince proclaimed himself Emperor, assuming the title of Shah Alam II. The new Mughal emperor, the nominal suzerain of Mir Jafar and the theoretical overlord of the company, invaded Bihar. He was defeated by a British force, but entered into friendly relations with his conquerors. The British forces escorted him to Patna. Here the new Nawab Mir Qasim waited on him. Mir Qasim had his investiture as Subahdar of Bengal, Bihar and Orissa, and agreed to pay an annual revenue of 2.4 million Rupees. Shah Alam was under the shelter of the nawab of Awadh from 1761 until the Battle of Buxar, in 1764.

Diwani Rights

Soon after the Battle of Buxar, Shah Alam, a sovereign who had just been defeated by the British troops and was in fact a homeless fugitive, sought the protection of the British. By the Treaty of Allahabad (1765) Shah Alam granted the diwani (right to collect revenue) of Bengal (which included Bihar and Orissa) to the British East India Company in return for an annual tribute of 2.6 million rupees. The company further secured for him the districts of Kora and Allahabad.

Return to Delhi

Shah Alam took up residence at Allahabad and no doubt could have passed his life peacefully there. But he wished to go back to Delhi to restore the bygone glories of the great Mughals. An opportunity came when the Marathas, having occupied Delhi, invited him there to occupy the throne of his forefathers. The Marathas had acknowledged that they were servants of the emperor. Shah Alam left Allahabad in May 1771 and in December reached Delhi. He had consulted the British and they had advised him not to trust the Marathas. The emperor resided in the fort of Allahabad for six years as a virtual prisoner of the British. Warren Hastings who had been appointed Governor of Bengal in 1772 discontinued the tribute of 2.6 million Rupees and also made over the districts of Allahabad and Kora to the Nawab of Oudh. These measures amounted to a repudiation of the company's vassalage as Diwan and the annexation of Bengal. Shah Alam then left for Delhi with a small force trained on the European model, under the command of his able general, Mirza Najaf Khan. He arrived there in December 1772 and sought to restore some of the glories of the Mughal empire.

Reform of Mughal Army

One of his first acts was to strengthen and raise an army capable of enforcing the diktat of the Mughal state. Once the army was ready it invaded the Rohillas with Maratha help to exact revenue from them. The army then marched south of Delhi against the troublesome Jats, defeating them and capturing the lucrative revenue bearing district of Agra along with the fort. The revenue from Agra permitted the Mughal army to pay regular imperial salaries rather than living in arrears as had become the trend in the latter half of the 18th century. However times were troubled and the Mughal state was surrounded by enemies on every side.

Sikh Raids

Trouble with the Sikhs was endless; they raided as far as Delhi practically every year for plunder. They entered Delhi three times in 11 years from 1772 to 1783 — in 1772, 1778 and 1783 with underhand help from the then wazirs of Shah Alam II. There was ongoing warfare with the Sikhs who were marauding in eastern Punjab and plundering the Rohilla, Mewar (Rajput) and Jat lands.

During Shah Alam's reign the Sikhs fought not just with the Mughals, but with the Marathas, Rajputs, and Rohillas.

The Marathas took Delhi in 1772 before Shah Alam arrived. Mirza Najaf Khan had restored a sense of order to the Mughal finances and administration. In 1777 Mirza Najaf Khan decisively defeated Zabita Khan's forces and repelled the Sikhs.

In 1778, after a Sikh incursion into Delhi, Shah Alam ordered their chastisement. His corrupt Wazir, Abdul Ahid Khan — known to us by his title of Nawab Majad-ud-daulah — marched alongside the Crown Prince with 20,000 Mughal troops against the Sikh forces. On payment of several bribes he colluded with them which led to the defeat of the Mughal army at Muzzaffargarh. Much like Mir Jafar before him, the Wazir removed the bulk of the army and left the much reduced Mughal forces of 5,000 to 6,000 soldiers to fight the numerically larger Sikh force. The result was a fighting retreat back to Mughal lines.

Downfall

After this defeat, Nawab Majad-ud-daulah was taken into custody by the crown prince and Shah Alam II recalled Mirza Najaf Khan. This led to the Wazir's arrest. The traitor was imprisoned and a sum of Rs.2 million in stolen revenue recovered from him. It was Shah Alam's poor judgement and vacillation that led to his own downfall. Mirza Najaf Khan had given the Mughal state breathing space by having a powerful, well managed army in its own right. In 1779 the Mughal army decisively defeated Zabita Khan and his Sikh allies, who — losing 5,000 men and their leader — did not return in the lifetime of Mirza Najaf Khan. Unfortunately upon the general's death, Shah Alam's bad judgement prevailed. The dead man's nephew, Mirza Shaffi whose valour had been proven, was not appointed commander in chief. Shah Alam instead appointed worthless individuals whose loyalty and record were questionable at best. They were soon quarrelling over petty matters. Even the corrupt and treasonous ex-Wazir Nawab Majad-ud-daulah was restored to his former office. This man then proceeded to practice policies both corrupt and destructive towards the Mughal realm.

Nawab Majad-ud-daulah was followed by a known enemy of the Mughals, the Afghan Rohilla, Ghulam Qadir with his Sikh allies as Wazir. Petty, avaricious and insane the Afghan Rohilla took advantage of Mahadaji Scindia's temporary evacuation of Delhi to ravage the palaces in search of the Mughal treasure rumoured to be worth Rs. 250 million. Unable to locate even a fraction of that sum, he blinded Shah Alam in 1788. Scindia, at the head of Maratha and Jat troops, came to the Emperor's rescue and chased down the fleeing Ghulam Qadir whose body was tortured and mutilated as an example. Shah Alam, who for a short period had been a great king, was now a mere shadow of his former self. The power of his realm had been reduced to the red fort and his Mughal army — so formidable less than half a decade a back — no longer even in existence.

Arrival of British Troops

The French threat in Europe and its possible repercussions in India caused the British to strive to regain the custody of Shah Alam. The British feared that the French military officers might overthrow Maratha power and use the authority of the Mughal emperor to further French ambition in India. After the Battle of Delhi, on September 14, 1803 British troops entered Delhi and Shah Alam, a blind old man, seated under a tattered canopy, came under British protection. The Mughal emperor no longer had the military power to enforce his will, but he commanded respect as a dignified member of the House of Timur in the length and breadth of the country. The nawabs and subahdars still sought formal sanction of the emperor on their accession and valued the titles he bestowed upon them. They struck coins and read the Khutba (Friday sermons) in his name. The British, not yet strong enough to claim sovereignty on their own, kept Shah Alam as a puppet until his death in 1805.

His grave lies, next to the dargah of 13th century, Sufi saint, Qutbuddin Bakhtiar Kaki at Mehrauli, in a marble enclosure, along with that of Bahadur Shah I (also known as Shah Alam I), and Akbar II.

Akbar Shah II

Akbar Shah II (1760-1837), also known as Mirza Akbar, was the second-to-last of the Mughal emperors of India. He held the title from 1806 to 1837. He was the second son of Shah Alam II and the father of Bahadur Shah Zafar II. Akbar had little real power due to the increasing British control of India through the

East India Company. Shortly before his death he sent Ram Mohan Roy as an ambassador to Britain. During his regime, in 1835, the East India Company discontinued calling itself the lieutenant of the Mughal Emperor and issuing coins in his name. The Persian lines in the Company's coins to this effect were deleted.

His grave lies, next to the dargah of 13th century, Sufi saint, Qutbuddin Bakhtiar Kaki at Mehrauli, in a marble enclosure, along with that of Bahadur Shah I (also known as Shah Alam I) and Shah Alam II.

Reign

Emperor Akbar Shah II presided over an empire titularly large but in effect limited to the Red Fort in Delhi alone. His attitude with the British was honourable to him but it angered the British. They reduced even his titular authority to Delhi in 1835. The British no more called itself the lieutenant of Mughal Empire as they did so from 1803 to 1835. They replaced the Persian lines of the company with English lines on coins. The British allowed the Nawab of Oudh and the Nizam of Hyderabad to take the royal title. The Nizam did not do so but the Nawab of Oudh did so. For this he sent Ram Mohan Roy as ambassador to Britain for trial. But he died before any thing could proceed further on.

Bahadur Shah II

Abu Zafar Sirajuddin Mohammad Bahadur Shah Zafar, also known as Bahadur Shah or Bahadur Shah II (October 1775 – 7 November 1862) was the last of the Mughal emperors in India, as well as the last ruler of the Timurid Dynasty. He was the son of Akbar Shah II and Lalbai, who was a Hindu Rajput. He became the Mughal Emperor upon his father's death on 28 September 1837. *Zafar* (Urdu: 8A1), meaning "victory" was his *nom de plume* (*takhallus*) as an Urdu poet. Even in defeat it is traditionally believed that he said

> *"Ghazion mein bu rahegi jab talak iman ki; Takht-e-London tak chalegi tegh Hindustan ki"*
>
> *"As long as there remains the least trace of love of faith in the hearts of our heroes, so long, the sword of Hindustan shall be sharp, and one day shall flash even at the gates of London."*

Zafar's father Akbar Shah Saani II ruled over a rapidly disintegrating empire between 1806 to 1837. It was during his time that the East India Company dispensed with even the fig leaf of ruling in the name of the Mughal Monarch and removed his name from the Persian texts that appeared on the coins struck by the company in the areas under their control.

Bahadur Shah Zafar who succeeded him was not Akbar Shah Saani's choice as his successor, Akbar Shah was, in fact, under great pressure by one of his queens, Mumtaz Begum to declare her son Mirza Jahangir as the successor. Akbar Shah would have probably accepted this demand but Mirza Jahangir had fallen foul of the British and they would have none of this.

As Emperor

Bahadur Shah presided over a Mughal empire that barely extended beyond Delhi's Red Fort. The British were the dominant political and military power in 19th-century India. Outside British India, hundreds of kingdoms and principalities, from the large to the small, fragmented the land. The emperor in Delhi was paid some respect by the British and allowed a pension, the authority to collect some taxes, and to maintain a small military force in Delhi, but he posed no threat to any power in India. Bahadur Shah II himself did not take an interest in statecraft or possess any imperial ambitions.

Bahadur Shah Zafar was a noted Urdu poet. He wrote a large number of Urdu ghazals. While some part of his opus was lost or destroyed during the Indian Rebellion of 1857-1858, a large collection did survive, and was later compiled into the *Kulliyyat-i Zafar.* The court that he maintained, although somewhat decadent and arguably pretentious for someone who was effectively a pensioner of the British East India Company, was home to several Urdu writers of high standing, including Ghalib, Dagh, Mumin, and Zauq (Dhawq).

Religious Attitudes

Bahadur Shah Zafar was a devout Sufi. Zafar was himself regarded as a Sufi pir and used to accept *murids* or pupils. The loyalist newspaper *Delhi Urdu Akhbaar* once called him one of the leading saints of the age, approved of by the divine court. Prior to his accession, in his youth he made it a point to live and look like a poor scholar and dervish, in stark contrast to his three well dressed dandy brothers, Mirza Jahangir, Salim and Babur. In 1828, when Zafar was 53 and a decade before he succeeded the throne, Major Archer reported, *"Zafar is a man of spare figure and stature, plainly apparelled, almost approaching to meanness. His appearance is that of an indigent munshi or teacher of languages"*.

As a poet and dervish, Zafar imbibed the highest subtleties of mystical Sufi teachings. At the same time, he was deeply susceptible to the magical and superstitious side of Orthodox Sunni Islam. Like many of his followers, he believed that his position as both a Sufi pir and emperor gave him tangible spiritual powers. In an incident in which one of his followers was bitten by a snake, Zafar attempted to cure him by sending a "seal of Bezoar" (a stone antidote to poison) and some water on which he had breathed, and giving it to the man to drink.

A panorama in 12 folds showing the procession of the Emperor Bahadur Shah to celebrate the feast of the 'Id, 1843. The emperor also had a staunch belief in *taaviz* or charms, especially as a palliative for his constant complaint of piles, or to ward off evil spells. During one period of illness, he gathered a group of Sufi pirs and told them that several of his wives suspected that some party or the other had cast a spell over him. Therefore, he requested them to take some steps to remedy this so as to remove all apprehension on this account. They replied that they would write off some charms for him. They were to be mixed in water which when drunk would protect him from the evil eye. A coterie of pirs, miracle workers and Hindu astrologers were in constant attendance to the emperor. On their advice, he regularly sacrificed buffaloes and camels, buried eggs and arrested alleged black magicians, in addition to wearing a special ring that cured indigestion. On their advice, he also regularly donated cows to the poor, elephants to the sufi shrines and a horse to the *khadims* or clergy of Jama Masjid.

Zafar consciously saw his role as a protector of his Hindu subjects, and a moderator of extreme Muslim demands and the intense puritanism of many of the Orthodox Muslim sheikhs of the Ulema. In one of his verses, Zafar explicitly stated that both Hinduism and Islam shared the same essence. This syncretic philosophy was implemented by his court which came to cherish and embody a multicultural composite Hindu-Islamic Mughal culture. For instance, the Hindu elite used to frequently visit the *dargah* or tomb of the great Sufi pir, Nizamuddin Auliya. They could quote Hafiz and were very fond of Persian poetry. Their children, especially those belonging to the administrative Khatri and Kayasth castes studied under maulvis and attended the more liberal madrasas, bring food offerings for their teachers on Hindu festivals. On the other hand, the emperor's Muslim subjects emulated him in honouring the Hindu holy men, while many in court, including Zafar himself, followed the old Mughal custom that was originally borrowed from high class Hindus, of only drinking the water from the Ganga.

Zafar and his court used to celebrate Hindu festivals. During the spring festival of Holi, he would spray his courtiers, wives and concubines with different coloured paints, initiating the celebrations by bathing in the water of seven wells. The autumn Hindu festival of Dusshera was celebrated in the palace by the distribution of *nazrs* or presents to Zafar's Hindu officers and the colouring of the horses in the royal stud. In the evening, Zafar would then watch the *Ram Lila* processions annually celebrated in Delhi with the burning of giant effigies of Ravana and his brothers. He even went to the extent of demanding that the route of the procession be changed so that it would skirt the entire flank of the palace, allowing it to be enjoyed in all its glory. On Diwali, Zafar would weigh himself against seven kinds of grain, gold, coral, etc., and directed their distribution among the city's poor.

He was reputedly known to have profound sensitivities to the feelings of his Hindu subjects. One evening, when Zafar was riding out across the river for an airing, a Hindu waited on the king and disclosed his wish to become a Muslim. Hakim Ahsanullah Khan, Zafar's prime minister flatly denied this request and the emperor had him removed from his presence. During the *Phulwalon ki Sair* or Flower-sellers fair held annually at the ancient Jog Maya Temple and the Sufi dargah of Qutb Sahib, Qutbuddin Bakhtiar Kaki in Mehrauli, Zafar declared that he would not accompany the *pankah* into the shrine as he could not accompany it into the temple. On a separate occasion, a mob of 200 Muslims showed up at the royal palace demanding to be allowed to slaughter cows, which are holy to Hindus, in Id. To this, Zafar angrily replied that the religion of Muslims did not depend upon the sacrifice of cows.

The Delhi Ulema and Bahadur Shah Zafar staunchly disdained each other. Zafar perceived the Muslim sheikhs to be narrow minded. One evening's entertainment at the Palace consisted of Kadir Baksh impersonating a Maluvi in the presence of the king.

Zafar was reportedly so pleased that he ordered Mahbub Ali Khan, the chief eunuch to give him the usual present. On the other hand, many of the Delhi maulvis and their followers considered the king to be a *mushrik* or heretic. They were of the opinion that it was not right to pray in the mosques that were frequented by the emperor or were under royal patronage. Zafar was devoted to Ali (son-in-law of the Islamic prophet Muhammed) and the festival of Muharram was celebrated with great enthusiasm in the palace, with the king listening to the *marsiya* mourning poems. This led to persistent rumors that Zafar had actually converted to the Shiite sect of Islam, which were seen as heretical by the Sunni Muslim clergy. This led to Zafar receiving several outraged delegations from the Delhi ulema threatening to take the ultimate sanction of excluding his name from the Friday prayers, effectively excommunicating him and delegitimising his rule, if the rumour ever proved true.

Zafar Mahal

Closely woven into the history of the last remains of Mughal rule is the history of Zafar Mahal in Mehrauli, a locality of Delhi. Zafar Mahal was originally built by Akbar II, but it was his son, Bahadur Shah Zafar, who constructed the gateway and added to the palace in the mid-1800s. Mehrauli was then a popular venue for hunting parties, picnics and jaunts, and the dargah was an added attraction. The emperor visited often with his retinue-and stayed in royal style at Zafar Mahal. Another interesting feature of Zafar Mahal is that it literally spans centuries. A plastered dome near the gate is probably 15th century; other sections are relatively newer and show definite signs of Western influences. There is, for instance, a fireplace in one of the walls that stands near the Moti Masjid. And the staircase to the balcony is a wide one with low steps-very unlike the steep, narrow staircases of most Indian Islamic architecture.

The balcony, with its 'jharokha' windows, is where the emperor and his family could look out over the road. In Bahadurshah's time, the main Mehrauli-Gurgaon road passed in front of Zafar Mahal, and all passersby were expected to dismount as a sign of respect for the emperor. When the British refused to comply, Bahadurshah solved the problem creatively-he bought the surrounding land and diverted the road so that it would pass well away from Zafar Mahal! The Phool Walon Ki Sair gradually turned into a major three day celebration during the time when Bahadur Shah Zafar, son and successor to Akbar Shah Saani ruled from Delhi. Zafar used to move his court to a building adjacent to the Shrine of Khwaja Bakhtiyar Kaki and stayed at Mehrauli for a week during the celebrations. The building where he stayed during the period was originally built by his father and Zafar added an impressive gate and a Baaraadari to the structure and renamed it Zafar Mahal. The celebrations spread out in different parts of Mehrauli with the Jahaz Mahal, (a Lodhi period structure, that was once in the middle of the Hauz-e-Shamsi but is now at one end of the much depleted Hauz, becoming a center where Qawwali mehfils would be organised while the Jharna, built by Firoz Shah Tughlaq and later added to by Akbar Shah II became a place where the women of the court relaxed.

Events of 1857

As the Indian rebellion of 1857 spread, Sepoy regiments seized Delhi. Seeking a figure that could unite all Indians, Hindu and Muslim alike, most rebelling Indian kings and the Indian regiments accepted Zafar as the Emperor of India., under whom the smaller Indian kingdoms would unite until the British were defeated. Zafar was the least threatening and least ambitious of monarchs, and the legacy of the Mughal Empire was more acceptable a uniting force to most allied kings than the domination of any other Indian kingdom. When the victory of the British became certain, Zafar took refuge at Humayun's Tomb, in an area that was then at the outskirts of Delhi, and hid there. British forces led by Major William Hodson surrounded the tomb and compelled his surrender on 20 September 1857. The next day British officer William Hodson shot his sons Mirza Mughal, Mirza Khizr Sultan, and grandson Mirza Abu Bakr under his own authority at the Khooni Darwaza (the bloody gate) near Delhi Gate. On hearing the news Zafar reacted with shocked silence while his wife Zeenat Mahal was happy as she believed her son was now Zafar's heir.

Numerous male members of his family were killed by British forces, who imprisoned or exiled the surviving members of the Mughal dynasty. After a show trial, Zafar himself was exiled to Rangoon, Burma (now Yangon, Union of Myanmar) in 1858 along with his wife Zeenat Mahal and some of the remaining members of the family. His departure as Emperor marked the end of more than three centuries of Mughal rule in India. Bahadur Shah died in exile on 7 November 1862. He was buried near the Shwedagon Pagoda in Yangon, at the site that later became known as Bahadur Shah Zafar Dargah. His wife Zeenat Mahal died in 1886. In a marble enclosure adjoining the dargah of Sufi saint, Qutbuddin Bakhtiar Kaki at Mehrauli, an empty grave or *Sardgah* marks the site where he had willed to be buried along with some of his Mughal predecessors, Akbar Shah II, Bahadur Shah I (also known as Shah Alam I) and Shah Alam II. He, unfortunately, was not so lucky, though talks of bringing back his remains here have been raised from time to time.

Family

Bahadur Shah Zafar is known to have had four wives and numerous concubines. In order of marriage, his wives were:

- Begum Ashraf Mahal
- Begum Akhtar Mahal
- Begum Zeenat Mahal
- Begum Taj Mahal.

Zafar had 22 sons, including:

- Mirza Fath-ul-Mulk Bahadur (alias Mirza Fakhru)
- Mirza Mughal
- Mirza Khazr Sultan
- Jawan Bakht
- Mirza Quaish
- Mirza Shah Abbas.

He also had at least 32 daughters, including:

- Rabeya Begum
- Begum Fatima Sultan
- Kulsum Zamani Begum
- Raunaq Zamani Begum (possibly a granddaughter).

Most of his sons and grandsons were killed during or in the aftermath of the rebellion of 1857. Of those who survived, the following four lines of descent are known:

- Delhi line—son: Mirza Fath-ul-Mulk Bahadur (alias Mirza Fakhru); grandson: Mirza Farkhunda Jamal; great-grandchildren: Ahmad Shah, Hamid Shah and Begum Qamar Sultan; Children of Ahmad Shah: Nadir Mirza, Farrukh Mirza, Mirza Taimur, Akbar Shah and Mohammad Shah Taimur; Children of Mohammad Shah temuri: Mirza Babar Shah Temuri, Mirza Birjees Shah Temuri, Sabahat Temuri, Mirza Zafar Shah Temuri, Saira temuri and Mirza Azfar Shah Temuri.

- Howrah line—son: Jawan Bakht, grandson: Jamshid Bakht, great-grandson: Mirza Mohammad Bedar Bakht (married Sultana Begum, who currently runs a tea stall in Howrah).
- Varanasi Line — [Shah Alam Ameer of Delhi, Son: Mirza Jahaandar Shah Alais Mirza Khan Bakht (Married-Jahanbaad Begum)], [Ali Gohar Mirza Ali Bahadur had five sons], [Mirza Kazim Bakht married Birjis Ara Begum, Son: Mirza Yousuf Bakht married Hasina Sultan Begum, Grand Son: Mirza Zaheeruddin Alim Bakht married Khurshid Laqah Begum (had five sons-two daughters), Great Grand Son: Mirza Daud Bakht married fakhre ara kaniz mehndi begum (D/O. Late Mobarrak Bakht Mirza Illyas Hussain Bahadur G/son of late King of oudh-Wife: Sultan Bano Mehndi Begum (in Kolkata).
- Hyderabad line—son: Mirza Quaish, grandson: Mirza Abdullah, great-grandson: Mirza Pyare (married Habib Begum), great-great-granddaughter: Begum Laila Ummahani (married Yakub Habeebuddin Tucy).

Descendants of Mughal rulers other than Bahadur Shah Zafar also survive to this day. They include the line of Jalaluddin Mirza in Bengal, who served at the court of the Maharaja of Dighapatia, and the Toluqari family.

Decline of Mughal Empire

CULTURAL and artistic achievements did not come to an end with Aurangzeb's death in 1707, and for a century and more, the Mughals dominated the cultural life of North India. In political life, one visible sign of the enduring power of the empire was the eagerness of every usurper of territory to gain recognition from Delhi. Another was that until 1835, the East India Company, which had become the effective successor to Mughal power, still minted coins in the emperor's name. In general, however, the eighteenth century saw a progressive decline in Mughal political control.

The Struggle for Succession

After Aurangzeb's death, the usual war of succession followed, with his eldest surviving son, Muazzam, the subedar of Kabul, who was the first to reach Agra, being successful. He ascended the throne as Bahadur Shah. A mild and forbearing man, he tackled the problems confronting him with tolerable competence. Rebellious chieftains in Rajputana troubled him but were overcome without much difficulty. His longest campaign was against Banda, a leader of the Sikhs. Govind Singh, the last Sikh guru, after years of bitter fighting against Aurangzeb, had entered into friendly relations with Bahadur Shah, accepting the position of mansabdar in the Mughal army. His assassination in 1708 ended this period of amity. Govind Singh's successor as temporal leader of the Sikhs was Banda, who returned to the Punjab declaring he was Guru Govind Singh miraculously brought back to life. In response to his call for disciples, many zealous Sikhs assembled and marched in arms to Sonepat, some twenty-five miles north of Delhi. There the faujdar, who was utterly unprepared, was routed. This success emboldened Banda. Accompanied by forty thousand men he set out to establish his power in the north. The town of Sadhaura, near Ambala, was captured, and the Muslim inhabitants were cruelly treated. He then moved against Sirhind, whose governor, Wazir Khan, was held responsible for the execution of Govind Singh's children. Banda's army pillaged the city for four days, and the whole Muslim population was slaughtered.

The situation became so serious that Bahadur Shah himself moved against Banda, and on December 4, 1710, he forced the evacuation of Sadhaura. The Sikhs then moved to the strong fort of Lohgarh, where Banda had issued coins in his own name. Bahadur Shah captured Lohgarh, but Banda escaped. Sirhind was reoccupied in January, 1711, and Banda took shelter in the hills.

After a halt at Sirhind, Bahadur Shah moved to Lahore. His stay here was marked by the one major controversy of his reign. Soon after his accession to the throne, he had given orders that the title *wasi* should be used after the name of Hazrat Ali in the Friday prayers. This usage, indicating that Ali was the testamentary successor to the Prophet, and considered by the Sunnis to be a Shia innovation, was bitterly resented. During his stay in Lahore Bahadur Shah tried to persuade the local ulama to accept the change, but without success. He then ordered his chief of artillery to have the new form of prayer recited from the pulpit of the Badshahi Masjid on April 22, 1711. When he found that a vast crowd, ready for violent resistance, had gathered in the streets of Lahore, he gave way and in the end the old form in use in the days of Aurangzeb was recited. Seven leading ulama of Lahore were sent, however, to the state prison in the Gwalior fort. The episode indicates the limitations imposed on the emperor by the ulama, but the punishment given the leaders shows that resistance, even if successful, could be dangerous.

Bahadur Shah died on February 27, 1712. His favourite son, Azim-ush-Shan, expected to succeed him, but a powerful general, Zulfiqar Khan, the son of Aurangzeb's Wazir, Azad Khan, formed an alliance with Azim's three brothers against him. They agreed to partition the empire among them, with Zulfiqar Khan as their common minister. In the battle that followed Azim was drowned in the Ravi, and Zulfiqar threw aside the two youngest princes in favour of the worthless Jahandar Shah. Zulfiqar became the all-powerful minister, and the emperor, infatuated with his concubine Lal Kunwar and relieved by Zulfiqar from all responsibilities of the state, spent his time in frivolous amusements.

Disaster was not long in coming. Mohammad Farrukhsiyar, the second son of Azimush Shan, and deputy governor of Bengal, had not reconciled himself to Jahandar Shah's enthronement; and when he heard of his father's death, he proclaimed himself emperor at Patna in April, 1712. He interested the two powerful Sayyid brothers, Husain Ali and Hasan Ali, in his fortunes; and having collected an army, the allies moved towards the capital. They defeated Jahandar Shah at Samugarh on January 6, 1713. Jahandar Shah fled from the battlefield, hidden in the howda of Lal Kunwar. Entering Delhi surreptitiously at night, he sought help from Zulfiqar and Asad Khan. Realizing that Jahandar was of no more use, Zulfiqar and Asad Khan tried to gain favour with the new power by imprisoning him. Jahandar was murdered in prison, but Zulfiqar also was put to death two days later.

Farrukhsiyar's reign (1713–1719) saw a general deterioration in the power of the central government, but in one area its authority was strongly asserted. Bahadur Shah had not succeeded in overcoming the menace of the resurgent power of the Sikhs. Early in his reign, Farrukhsiyar appointed Abdus Samad Khan as governor of Lahore with instructions to destroy Banda, who had taken refuge in the hills and used them as a base for raids on the countryside. Abdus Samad finally penned him up in the fort of Gurdaspur. Banda's followers offered fanatical resistance, but all their attempts to escape failed, and the garrison was forced to surrender unconditionally on December 17, 1715, after an eight-month siege. Banda was taken to Delhi and put to death. Stern vengeance was wreaked on his followers, but the peace of the area was ensured for a generation or more.

Farrukhsiyar owed his throne to the Sayyid brothers, and he rewarded them with the highest offices in the realm. He soon found their power galling, but a number of ineffectual attempts to get rid of them only worsened his position. Husain Ali left Delhi in 1715, as viceroy of the Deccan, but before leaving he warned the emperor that if ever his brother was harassed at Delhi he would promptly return to the capital. Matters came to a head in 1718 when Hasan Ali, believing he was in danger, asked his brother to come to Delhi. A peculiarly sinister feature of Husain Ali's return was that he was accompanied by eleven thousand Maratha troops as well as by his own army. Maratha support had been bought for a heavy price—among other concessions, they were promised one-fourth of the revenue from the Deccan. The emperor was imprisoned and blinded in February, 1719; two months later he was strangled to death. Two of the puppets placed on the throne by the king-making Sayyids died within a year, but a third, Raushan Akhtar, a grandson of Bahadur Shah, who became emperor in 1719 as Mohammad Shah, reigned for thirty years. In its duration, his reign recalls that of his great predecessors, but possibly even they could not have prevented the decline that was now obvious in the imperial power.

The power of the Sayyids was broken early in the reign of the new emperor when two of the opposing factions at the court, the Irani nobles and the Turani, formed an alliance against them. Both brothers were killed in 1720, one by an assassin and the other in battle. For a short time the wizarat was held by Mohammad Amin Khan, one of the Turani nobles who had helped overthrow the Sayyids, but after his death in 1721, an important new figure appeared on the Delhi scene.

This was Chin Qilich Khan, another of the Turani nobles who had been an enemy of the Sayyids. He is best known in history by his title, Nizam-ul-Mulk. An able administrator and soldier who had been governor of the Deccan provinces, Nizam-ul-Mulk was made Wazir of the empire in 1722. His experience in the office illustrates the increasing weakness of the administration and the reason it could not meet the challenges of the time. His advice to the gay young sovereign to reform the court was not followed, and his attempts to bring about changes in the administration were met by obstruction and indifference. He was especially anxious to stop the farming of imperial revenues, a practice that was diverting much of the resources that should have come into the central treasury; to reimpose the jizya; and to eradicate bribery. This call to return to the austerity of the court of Aurangzeb had little chance of being heeded in Delhi in the eighteenth century, and Nizamul-Mulk left Delhi late in 1723 for Hyderabad. There he established the power which he was able to transmit to his descendants as the largest of the Indian states.

After Nizamul-Mulk's departure from Delhi the Marathas became an increasingly grave menace to the empire. By 1732 they had partially occupied Gujarat, had partitioned Bundelkhand, and had temporarily overrun Mewar in Rajputana. Mohammad Shah moved against them in 1733, but the imperial army never went beyond Faridabad, sixteen miles south of Delhi. The Marathas continued to advance; and although they suffered defeats, in 1737 under one of their greatest leaders, Baji Rao I (r. 1720–1740), they reached Delhi itself. They looted the suburbs but when they heard that the whole Mughal army was approaching the capital, they retired southwards. It was the Maratha danger that led to the recall of Nizamul-Mulk to Delhi in 1737. He was received by the Wazir outside the capital with great honor, and during the winter months was engaged in a series of negotiations and skirmishes with Baji Rao and his troops. In return for concessions in Central India, the Marathas withdrew from the north, but Nizamul-Mulk had scarcely returned to Delhi when a new danger, invasion from the northwest by Nadir Shah, was threatening the empire.

Disintegration of the Empire

Mohammad Shah died in 1748, a few weeks after this last victory. His long reign had seen a growing paralysis in imperial power, of which the most visible symptom was the establishment of hereditary viceroyalties in the major provinces of the empire. The pattern was one that had been seen before in India history: as the central power weakened, either as a cause or a result the outlying provinces assumed independent status. These states were the administrative units of the Mughal empire, but they were also the traditional "nuclear" regions of Indian history, defined by geography, language, and past traditions.

The provincial governors long continued to demonstrate the symbolic function of the Mughal emperor by their desire to gain his recognition for their rule, but from the time of Mohammad Shah they sought such recognition after, not before, their seizure of power. In the Punjab, largely because of the intervention of external forces from the northwest, independent kingdoms were not formed in the middle of the eighteenth century, but elsewhere the process of the disintegration of central authority was complete. In the Deccan, Oudh, Bengal, and to some extent Rohilkhand, large principalities over which the central government of Delhi had only nominal authority came into existence. By depriving the empire of financial resources, even though they continued to send an annual tribute to Delhi, and by reducing the possibility of united action, these kingdoms lessened the chances of the empire's survival when attacks came from without.

The most important of the new principalities was Hyderabad, made up of six subas of the Deccan, which at this time had a revenue of sixteen crores of rupees, compared with seventeen crores from the other twelve provinces of the Mughal empire. As already noted, the founder of the state was Nizam-ul-Mulk, who had been made viceroy of the Deccan by Farrukhsiyar in 1714, and Wazir of the empire by Mohammad Shah in 1722. On his return to the Deccan in 1724, he began to build up a strong state, although still offering assistance to the emperor. At his death in 1748, he passed on a well-administered state that continued to be a center of Muslim culture in the Deccan for two centuries.

In Bengal, power passed into the hands of two remarkable men, Murshid Quli Khan and Alivardi Khan. Under these able administrators Bengal was among the most peaceful and prosperous areas of India, and paid an annual tribute of ten million rupees to the Delhi court. In the Punjab, the Sikhs used Nadir Shah's invasion in 1739 as an opportunity to attack Mughal authority; but the able governor, Zakariya Khan, crushed them. After his death in 1745 the province passed out of effective Mughal control. Sind does not figure greatly in Mughal history, and authority had always tended to reside in the hands of local chiefs.

The most important of these belonged to the Kalhara family, descendants of the disciples of a sixteenth-century spiritual leader. Through the course of the next hundred years they built up great land holdings, and by the beginning of the eighteenth century were recognized as governors of a large area of Upper Sind. Mohammad Shah completed the process in 1736 by conferring on the chief of the Kalharas a title that acknowledged his control of the whole province of Sind.

Cultural Life

Against this picture of a disintegrating empire must be set the undoubted fact that Mohammad Shah's reign was a time of very considerable cultural activity. Urdu, which had gained admission in the literary and cultural circles of the metropolis only a few years before the beginning of Mohammad Shah's reign, was a fully developed literary language at its end. A new school of music grew up around the Mughal court, and the names of Sadarang and his brother occupy a high place in the evolution of khiyal, which was to supersede all other varieties of Hindustani music. Indian dancing, freed from the atmosphere of the temple, became an art ministering to human pleasure. A new style of painting, closely related to the rise of Urdu literature, brought fresh vigor to the tradition of pictorial art. Indian astronomy also reached a new level of excellence in this period, as indicated by the magnificent astronomical instruments at Delhi and Ujjain. The creator of these works, Maharaja Jai Singh of Jaipur, was Mohammad Shah's governor in Malwa from 1728 to 1734.

Most significant of all the cultural activities of Mohammad Shah's reign was the beginning of the work of Shah Waliullah (1703–1762), the greatest Islamic scholar India ever produced. That the political disintegration of Islamic power in the eighteenth century was not accompanied by a religious collapse was largely due to his work; and more than anyone else, he is responsible for the religious regeneration of Indian Islam.

Shah Waliullah received his training from his father, who as a theologian, Sufi, and philosopher combined in his own person these three main strands of Indian Islam. He was in his teens when he started teaching in his father's madrasah. He continued this for twelve years, after which he left for Arabia for higher studies and for performing the Hajj. He was in Arabia for nearly fourteen months, pursuing his studies under famous teachers at Mecca and

Medina. During his stay at Mecca, Shah Waliullah saw a vision in which the Holy Prophet informed him that he would be instrumental in the organization of a section of the Muslim community. Friends urged him to stay in Hijaz, and not to return to the unsettled conditions of India, but he was convinced that his mission was to work there. He returned to Delhi in 1732, and began what was to be his life's work. He had been a teacher before he went to Arabia, and while he resumed his occupation, he no longer followed the traditional methods of instruction. He trained pupils in different branches of Islamic knowledge, then entrusted them with the teaching of the students, while he devoted himself to writing. Before his death in 1762, he had completed practically a library of standard works in all branches of "Islamic sciences" of the type particularly suited to the Indian conditions.

Shah Waliullah's most important single work was his translation of the Quran into simple Persian, the literary language of Muslim India. Translations had been attempted earlier, but they either were incidental to a voluminous commentary, or did not gain wide acceptance. After some opposition Shah Waliullah's translation became popular, either because of the translator's eminence in religious circles, or because his translation was connected with a broad-based movement aimed at bringing the knowledge of the Quran within the reach of the average, literate Indian Muslim. Shah Waliullah's action, which involved not only scholarship, but also imagination and great moral courage, smoothed the way for others. Within sixty years his two sons prepared their Urdu translations—one completely literal and following the Arabic sentence-structure, and the other idiomatic and in accordance with Urdu usage. Not only did his sons follow his example, but in course of time, so did scores of others; and it is because of his initiative that, outside the Arabic-speaking countries, Muslims in India and Pakistan have taken the lead in the study and propagation of the Quran.

Not less important was his balanced understanding and fair-minded approach to different religious questions. In his day Indian Islam was rent by controversies and conflicts between the Shia and the Sunni, the Sufi and the Mullah, the Hanafi and the Wahhabi, the Mujaddidi and the Wahdat-al-Wajudi, and the Mu'tazali and the Ashaari. To Shah Waliullah, *adl* (justice, equity) was the prime virtue and the basis of civilized existence, and he studied the writings of all schools of thought, trying to understand the attitudes of each of them. He then wrote authoritative volumes expounding what was just and acceptable to different points of view. In this way, by working out a system of thought on which all but the extremists could agree, he helped to provide a spiritual basis for national cohesion and harmony.

Shah Waliullah's success was also due to his able and devoted successors. One of his grandsons was the great reformer Shah Ismail Shahid. Three of his sons were leading scholars and writers, including Shah Abdul Aziz, who dominated Delhi religious life for nearly fifty years. The brothers taught and trained a large body of men who carried the message of Shah Waliullah to all parts of India. Their students and successors organized jihad against persecution of Islam by the Sikhs in the northwest, brought about a revival of Islam in Bengal, and were held in equal veneration by Sir Sayyid Ahmed Khan, the leader of the Aligarh movement, and Maulana Mohammad Qasim, the founder of the Deoband seminary.

While Islam is not organized along national lines, owing to historic, racial, linguistic, and geographic factors, a variety of schools and viewpoints have gained prominence in different Muslim countries. In Iran, for example, the Shia form of Islam is the national religion, while in the desert of Najd, Wahhabi puritanism is dominant. Similarly, different countries have adopted, according to their peculiar developments, different schools of law—the Shafii, the Hanbali, the Maliki, and the Hanafi. If the beliefs, the legal traditions, and the religious tendencies of modern Muslim India and Pakistan were to be examined from this point of view, it would be seen that the foundation of the religious structure which is dominant there was laid by Shah Waliullah.

Shah Mohammad's Successors

Looking at Shah Mohammad's reign, the author of the late eighteenth-century history, *Siyar-ul-Mutakhkhirin*, declared: "In his reign the people passed their lives in ease, and the empire outwardly retained its dignity and prestige. The foundations of the Delhi monarchy were really rotten, but Mohammad Shah by his cleverness kept them standing. He may be called the last of the rulers of Babur's line, as after him the kingship had nothing but the name left to it." The records of the last fifty years of the century suggest no reason for challenging this melancholy verdict. After Mohammad Shah's death, Prince Ahmad Shah, the hero of the battle of Sirhind, ascended the throne, and although he was a well-meaning and active young man, he could effect no improvement in government affairs. His appointment of Safdar Jang as Wazir was especially unfortunate. An opportunist whose measures helped to destroy the Mughal empire, Safdar Jang seems to have been motivated by two aims. One was to humiliate any relatives of his predecessors in the wizarat; the other was to drive out all Afghans from positions of authority.

Safdar's policy brought him in conflict with the principal Turani families, but his initial difficulties came from the royal favourites headed by the chief eunuch, Javed Khan, and the emperor's mother. Safdar Jang had Javed Khan assassinated in August, 1752, but then the emperor started favouring Ghazi-ud-din, a grandson of Nizam-ul-Mulk, and a clever but completely unscrupulous youth of eighteen. Safdar Jang lost the support of the emperor, and in May, 1753, though still the Wazir of the realm, rebelled against his master. Ghazi-ud-din organized the opposition to Safdar Jang, and with his usual lack of scruples, whipped up Shia-Sunni and Afghan-Irani differences to gain supporters. Safdar was defeated and forgiven; but realizing that the best field for the satisfaction of his ambitions was away from the capital, withdrew to Oudh. Ghazi-ud-din was now all-powerful at the capital. This was dramatically attested when the emperor, who had soon become estranged from him, sought to have him removed from the court. With the help of the Maratha chiefs, Ghazi-ud-din made himself Wazir and in June, 1754, deposed the emperor.

The man placed on the throne in 1754 as Alamgir II was a son of Jahandar Shah. A man of good intentions, his adoption of Aurangzeb's title was an indication of his desire to follow in his great predecessor's footsteps, but the situation in the empire was beyond his control. The Marathas, who had grown more powerful because of their collaboration with Ghazi-ud-din, now dominated the whole of northern India. In 1758 they occupied Lahore and drove out Taimur Shah, the son and viceroy of the Afghan ruler, Ahmad Shah Abdali. This was the high-water mark of the Maratha expansion. "Their frontier extended on the north to the Indus and the Himalaya, and in the south nearly to the extremity of the peninsula; all the territory within those limits which was not their own, paid tribute." The whole of this great power was wielded by one hand, that of the Peshwa, who talked of placing Bishvas Rao on the Mughal throne.

Maratha dreams, however, received a shattering blow. The expulsion of Taimur Shah provoked the wrath of Ahmad Shah Abdali, who was joined in the war against the Marathas by the principal Muslim nobles of North India. The main battle was fought at Panipat on June 14, 1761. This was the most desperate of the three historic battles of Panipat (the first fought by Babur in 1526, and the second by Humayun in 1556), and its results were of great significance for Indian history. The Marathas were completely defeated, and while their chiefs retained power in Central India, the centralizing power of the Peshwa was destroyed. Panipat meant that whoever succeeded the Mughals on the throne of Delhi, it would not be the Marathas. Ahmad Shah Abdali's own design of building up an Afghan empire in India was frustrated by the impetuosity of his soldiers, who hated the heat of the plains and clamored for an immediate return to Kabul with their plunder. Since they had been away from their homes for a long time and were on the verge of mutiny, Ahmad Shah had to abandon his dreams and return to his own country.

Ghazi-ud-din had put Alamgir II to death in 1759, replacing him with a puppet, but after the battle of Panipat, Ahmad Shah nominated a son of Alamgir II as emperor, with the title of Shah Alam (1761–1803). In the struggles that followed, Ghazi-ud-din lost power and fled from the capital. The administration of the shrunken empire—by now reduced to little more than the area around Delhi—was in the hands of Najib-ud-daula. It was he who had organized the Muslim confederacy that defeated the Marathas at Panipat, and he remained loyal throughout his life to the Mughal emperor. This was all the more remarkable since Shah Alam was absent from Delhi almost continuously until 1772. Najib's main task was to maintain order in the Mughal domain around Delhi. After the battle of Panipat the Marathas were quiescent for some time, but the Jats and the Sikhs began to threaten the integrity of the remaining imperial territories. Najib defeated the Jats and killed their leader, Suraj Mal, but he was less successful with the Sikhs. They were kept from creating too much trouble, however, by an internal split between two groups.

Bibliography

Adikaram, E. W.: *Early History of Buddhism in Ceylon,* D. S. Puswella, Migoda, 1946.

Agrawala, V. S.: *Shiva Mahadeva: The Great God,* Veda Academy, Varanasi, 1966.

Ahmad, Imtiaz: *State and Foreign Policy: India's Role in South Asia,* Vikas, New Delhi, 1993.

Ahmad, Jamil-ud-din: *Some Recent Speeches and Writings of Mr. Jinnah,* Lahore, Ashraf, 1952.

Aiyar, R. Krishnaswami: *Outlines of Vedaanta,* Chetana, Bombay, 1978.

Archer, W. G.: *The Kama Sutra,* Unwin Hyman, London, 1990.

Ashton, S.R. : *British Policy Towards the Indian States, 1905-1939,* London, Curzon, 1982.

Aurobindo, Sri: *Vyasa and Valmiki,* Acharya Press, Pondicherry, 1956.

Avalon, Arthur and Ellen: *Hymns to the Goddess,* Ganesh and Co., Madras, 1964.

Aziz, Ashraf: *Light of the Universe: Essays on Hindustani Film Music,* Three Essays Collective, New Delhi, 2003.

Bagchi, P. C.: *Studies in Dharmashastra,* University of Calcutta Press, Calcutta, 1939.

Bahadur, K.P.: *The Wisdom of Vedaanta,* Sterling Publishers Private Limited, New Delhi, 1996.

Banerjea, J. N.: *Pauranic and Vedanta Religion,* University of Calcutta, Calcutta, 1996.

Bankimchandra, C.: *Essentials of Dharma,* Sanskrit Book Depot, Calcutta 1979.

Basu, Manoranjan: *Dharmashastra: A General Study,* Shrimati Mira Basu, Calcutta, 1976.

Beaumont, Roger : *Sword of the Raj: The British Army in India, 1747-1947*, Indianapolis, Bobbs-Merrill, 1977.

Benjamin, Joseph : *Scheduled Castes in Indian Politics and Society*, New Delhi, Ess Ess Publications, 1989.

Bhattacharyya, B.: *Nispannayogavali of Mahapandita Abhyakara Gupta*, Oriental Institute, Baroda, 1949.

Borchert, Bruno: *Mysticism: Its History and Challenge*, Samuel Wiser, York Beach, 1994.

Bose, D. N.: *Dharmashastra: Their Philosophy and Occult Secrets*, Kali Press, Calcutta, 1965.

Bowle, John: *The Imperial Achievement: The Rise and Transformation of the British Empire*, Little, Brown, 1974.

Brockington, J. L.: *Righteous Rama: The Evolution of an Epic*, Oxford, London, 1984.

Bromley, D.: *Krishna Consciousness in the West*, Bucknell University Press, Lewisburg, 1989.

Brooks, E.: *The Original Analects: Sayings of Confucius and His Successors*. Columbia University Press, New York, 1988.

Bruhn, Klaus: *The Jina-lmages of Deogarh*, MacMillan, Leiden, 1969.

Burke, Mary Louise: *Swami Vivekananda in America: New Discoveries*, Advaita Ashrama, Calcutta, 1966.

Chaudhary, M.: *Partition and the Curse of Rehabilitation*, Calcutta, Bengal Rehabilitation Organization, 1964.

Chaudhuri, Nirad: *Thy Hand, Great Anarch! India: 1921-1952*, London, Chatto & Windus, 1987.

Coomeraswamy, Ananda K.: *Buddha and the Gospel of Buddhism*, MacMillan, London, 1928.

Crawford, Cromwell S.: *Ram Mohan Roy: His Era and Ethics*, Acharya Press, New Delhi, 1984.

Dalton, Dennis : *Gandhi's Power : Nonviolence in Action*, New Delhi, OUP, 2001.

Danielou, Alain: *The Complete Kama Sutra*, Park Street Press, Rochester, 2000.

Dasgupta, Shahana: *Rani Lakshmibai: The Indian Heroine*, Rupa & Company, Calcutta, 2002.

Datta, V.N.: *Sati: Widow Burning in India*, Manohar, New Delhi, 1990.

David, M. D.: *John Wilson and his Institutions*, Mumbai, 1957.

De Bary: *Self and Society in Ming Thought*, Columbia University Press, New York, 1970.

De, Sushil Kumar: *Ancient Indian Erotics and Erotic Literature*, Firma K. L. Mukhopadhyay, Calcutta, 1959.

Deak, Istvan: *The Lawful Revolution: Louis Kossuth and the Hungarians 1848-1849*, Columbia University Press, 1979.

Dhar, Niranjan: *Vedanta and Bengal Renaissance*, Minerva Associates, Calcutta, 1977.

Dikshit, D.P. *Political History of the Chalukyas of Badami*. New Delhi: Abhinav, 1980.

Donat, K.: *Meditate the Tantric Yoga Way*, George Allen and Unwin, London, 1973.

Doniger, W.: *The Rig Veda: An Anthology*, Penguin, New York, 1981.

Duboi, Abbe: *Hindu Manners, Customs and Ceremonies*, Fifth Indian Impression, CUP, 1985.

Dwivedi, M.: *The Principal Upanishads*, Adyar Library, Madras, 1931.

Eaton, Richard M.: *Sufis of Bijapur, 1300-1700: Social Roles of Sufis in Medieval India*, Princeton University Press, Princeton, 1978.

Edwardes, Michael: *Battles of the Indian Mutiny*, London; B. T. Batsford Ltd., 1963.

Erickson, Erik H.: *Gandhi's Truth: On the Origins of Militant Nonviolence*, Norton, New York, 1970.

Farquhar, J.N.: *Modern Religious Movements in India*, Munshiram, New Delhi, 1967.

Fay, Peter Ward: *The Opium War, 1840-42*, University of North Carolina Press, 1975.

Fisher, Michael H.: *The Politics of British Annexation of India - 1757-1857*, Oxford, 1996.

Frauwallner, E..: *History of Indian Philosophy*, Motilal, Delhi, 1973.

Gambhirananda, S.: *Brahma Sutra Shamkar Bhasya*, Adavita Ashrama, Calcutta, 1977.

Gambhirananda, Swami: *Brahma Sutra Shamkar Bhasya*, Adavita Ashrama, Calcutta, 1977.

Gandhi, M. K.: *The Story of My Experiment With Trust*, Washington, Public Affairs Press, 1948.

Garbe, R.: *The Philosophy of Ancient India*, Chicago University Press, Chicago, 1899.

Goradia, Nayana: *Lord Curzon: The Last of the British Moghuls*, New Delhi, Oxford University Press, 1993.

Goudriaan, T.: *Ritual and Speculation in Early Tantrism*, State University of New York Press, New York, 1992.

Gough, A.E.: *The Philosophy of the Upanisads and Ancient Indian Metaphysics*, MacMillan, London, 1882.

Grant, G. P.: *Philosophy in the Mass Age*, Copp Clark, Toronto, 1959.

Grisenold, H.D.: *Insights into Modern Hinduism*, Oxford, New York, 1934.

Growse, F. S.: *The Ramayana of Tulasidasa*, Motilal Banarsidass, Delhi, 1995.

Gurumurthy, S. : *Hindu Heritage, Assimilative, Not Divisive*, Vigil, Madras 1993.

Haich, E.: *Sexual Energy and Yoga*, Aurora Press, New York, 1982.

Hasan, Murhirul: *Legacy of a Divided Nation: India's Muslims Since Independence*, New Delhi, Oxford, 1997.

Hasan, Mushirul: *India's Partition: Process, Strategy and Mobilization*, New Delhi, Oxford UP, 1993.

Heifetz, Hank: *The Origin of the Young God: Kalidasa's Kumara-sambhava*, University of California Press, Berkeley, 1985.

Heimann, Betty: *Facets of Indian Thought*, Geroge Allen & Unwin, London, 1964.

Heinsath, Charles: *Indian Nationalism and Hindu Social Reform*, Princeton University Press, Princeton, 1964.

Heschel, J.: *God in Search of Man: A Philosophy of Judaism*, Noonday Press, New York, 1997.

Hirschman, Edwin: *White Mutiny: The Ilbert Bill Crisis in India and the Genesis of the Indian National Congress*, New Delhi, Heritage, 1980.

Hixon, L.: *Mother of the Universe: Visions of the Goddess, Tantric Hymns of Enlightenment*, Quest Books, Wheaton, 1994.

Hopkins, J.: *Kalachakra Tantra Rite of Initiation*, Wisdom Publications, Boston, 1982.

Hopkirk, Peter: *The Great Game: The Struggle for Empire in Central Asia*, Kodansha, 1992.

Hume, R.E.: *The Thirteen Principle Upanishads,* Oxford University Press, London, 1971.

Hutchins, Francis: *Spontaneous Revolution: The Quit India Movement,* New Delhi, Manohar, 1971.

Irene, S.: *Vedic Heritage Teaching Program.* Arsha Vidya Gurukulam, Coimbatore, 1994.

Iyar, K.: *Vedanta: The Science of Reality,* Ganesh and Co., Mardas, 1930.

Iyengar, B.K.S.: *Light on the Yoga Sutras of Patanjali,* Aquarian Press, London 1993.

Jacob, K.: *Religion and Ethics in Advaita,* C.M.S. Press, Kottayam, 1982.

Jafar, Malik Muhammad: *Jinnah as a Parliamentarian,* Lahore, Afzar Publications, 1977.

Jain, Kailash Chand, *Lord Mahavira and His Times,* Saraswati Press, Delhi, 1974.

James, Lawrence: *The Rise and Fall of the British Empire,* St. Martin's, 1997.

James, Robert Rhodes: *The British Revolution, 1880-1939,* New York, Knopf, 1976.

Jean, M.: *Tantrik Yoga,* The Aquarian Press, Wellingborough, 1970.

John, B.: *Mantras: Sacred Words of Power,* George Allen and Unwin, London, 1977.

John, Elsner: *Pilgrimage: Past and Present in the World Religions,* Harvard University Press, Cambridge, 1995.

John, K.: *The Origin and Development of the State Cult of Confucius,* Paragon Book, New York, 1966.

Karmarkar, D.: *Sankara's Advaita,* Karnatak University, Dharwar, 1976.

Kaushik, Asha : *Globalization, Democracy and Culture : Situating Gandhian Alternatives,* Jaipur, Pointer, 2002.

Kaviraj, G.: *Aspects of Indian Thought,* University of Burdwan, Calcutta, 1966.

Kavlekar, K.K. : *Non-Brahmin Movement in Southern India, 1873-1949,* Kolhapur, Shivaji University, 19790

Keith, A.B. : *Rigveda Brahmanas,* Harvard University Press, Cambridge, 1920.

Keith, Arthur Berriedale: *The Religion and Philosophy of the Veda and Upanishads,* MacMillan, Delhi, 1925.

Kishwar, Madhu : *Religion at the Service of Nationalism, and Other Essays,* OUP, Delhi, 1998.

Klaus, K.: *A Survey of Hinduism,* State University of New York Press, Albany, 1989.

Knipe, M.: *Hinduism: Experiments in the Sacred,* Harper, San Francisco, 1991.

Knott, K.: *Hinduism, A Very Short Introduction,* Oxford University Press, New York, 1998.

Kosambi, D. D. : *The Culture and Civilisation of Ancient India in Historical Outline,* London, Routledge and Kegan Paul, 1956.

Kottackal, Jacob: *Religion and Ethics in Advaita,* C.M.S. Press, Kottayam, 1982.

Kuiper, F.B.J. : *Aryans in the Rigveda,* Rodopi, Amsterdam, 1991.

Kuppuswamy, Sastri S.: *Compromises in the History of Advaitic Thought,* Kalyani Press, Madras, 1940.

Louis, Fischer: *Essential Gandhi: An Anthology of His Writings,* Vintage, New York, 1983.

Low, D. A. and Brasted, Howard: *Freedom, Trauma, Continuities: Northern India and Independence,* New Delhi, Sage Publications, 1998.

Maheshwari, Shriram: *Rural Development in India: A Public Policy Approach,* New Delhi, Sage, 1995.

Makhan, L.: *The Ramayana of Valmiki,* Munshiram Manoharlal, New Delhi, 1978.

Mathew, Arnold: *Culture and Anarchy,* The University Press, Cambridge, 1935.

Mayer, A. : *Caste in an Indian Village: Change and Continuity 1954-1992,* Delhi, OUP, 1996.

Mazumder, Sukhendu : *Politico-Economic Ideas of Mahatma Gandhi: Their Relevance in the Present Day,* New Delhi, Concept Pub., 2004.

Mearns, David J.: *Shiva's Other Children: Religion and Social Identity amongst Overseas Indians,* Sage, Walnut Creek, 1995.

Mearns, J.: *Shiva's Other Children: Religion and Social Identity amongst Overseas Indians,* Sage, Walnut Creek, 1995.

Mehra, Parshotam: *A Dictionary of Modern Indian History, 1707-1947*, New Delhi, Oxford University Press, 1985.

Metcalf, Thomas R.: *The Aftermath of the Revolt: India, 1857-1870*, Princeton, Princeton University, 1964.

Mohan, K.: *The Mahabharata*, Munshiram Manoharlal, Delhi 1997.

Mookerjee, Ajit: *Kali The Feminine Force*, Thames and Hudson, London, 1988.

Mookerji, Satkari: *Modern Polity and Vedanta*, Sanskrit College, Calcutta, 1972.

Moon, Penderel: *The British Conquest and Dominion of India*, London, Duckworth, 1989.

Morris-Jones, W.H.: *The Government and Politics of India*, London, Hutchinson, 1971.

Nanda, B. R. : *Gandhi and His Critics*, Oxford University Press, Delhi, 1993.

Neale, Walter C.: *Economic Change in Rural India: Land Tenure and Reform in the United Provinces, 1800-1955*, New Haven, 1962.

Nevile, P.: *Lahore: A Sentimental Journey*, New Delhi, Penguin, 1993.

Oddie, G.A. : *Hindu and Christian in South-East India*, London, Curzon Press, 1991.

Pathak, Dr S.P.: *Jhansi during the British Rule*, Ramanand Vidya Bhawan, Delhi, 1987.

Preston, Diana: *The Boxer Rebellion*, Berkley Books, 2000.

Raimundo Panikkar: *The Vedic Experience: Mantramanjari*, Longman Todd, London, 1977.

Raja, C. Kunhan : *The Taittiriya Sarvanukramani of Yaska*, Madras, 1931.

Ramamurti, A.: *Advaitic Mysticism of Sankara*, Visvabharati, Santiniketan, 1974.

Ranajit Guha: *A Construction of Humanism in Colonial India*, CASA, Amsterdam, 1993.

Renou, Louis: *The Nature of Dharmashastra*, Walker and Co., New York, 1997.

Robson, Brian: *Sir Hugh Rose and the Central India Campaign*, Sutton Publishing Ltd for the Army Records Society, UK, 2000.

Satyapal Verma: *Role of Reason in Sankara Vedanta*, Parimal Publication, Delhi, 1992.

Savarkar, Vinayak Damodar : *The Indian War of Independence* 1857 Rajdhani Granthagar, Delhi, 1988.

Scheftelowitz, Isidor : *Die Kasmirische Rezension von Katyayanas Sarvanukramani,* Zeitschrift fur Indologie und Iranistik, 1922.

Shukla, D. N.: *Vastu-Shastra,* Motilal Banarsidass, Delhi, 1966.

Singh, Birendra Kumar: *Early Chalukyas of Vatapi, circa A.D. 500 to 757,* Delhi, Eastern Book Linkers, 1991.

Smith, Col. J. T. : *Silver and the India Exchanges,* Effingham Wilson, London, 1876.

Strauss, L.: *Political Philosophy,* The Bobbs Merrill Co., New York, 1975.

Swami Vishnu Tirtha: *Devatma Shakti,* Swami Shivom Tirth, Rishikesh, 1962.

Talageri, Shrikant : *Aryan Invasion Theory and Indian Nationalism,* Voice of India, Delhi, 1993.

Tejomayananda, Swami: *Hindu Culture: An Introduction,* Chinmaya Publications, Piercy, 1993.

Thapar, Romila : *Ashoka and the Decline of the Mauryas,* London, Oxford University Press, 1961.

Thompson, Edward: *The Making of the Indian Princes,* Oxford University Press, London, 1943.

Trautmann, Thomas R.: *Kautilya and the Arthasastra: A Statistical Study,* Leiden, Brill, 1971.

Trimingham, J.: *Sufi Orders in Islam,* Oxford University Press, New York, 1998.

Utpat, V.N.: *Riddles of Buddha and Ambedkar,* Itihas Patrika Prakashan, Thane 1988.

Vable, D.: *The Arya Samaj. Hindu without Hinduism.* Vikas Publ., Delhi, 1983.

Vedalankar, Pandit Nardev : *Basic Teachings of Hinduism,* Veda Niketan, Durban, 1978.

Visvantha, K.: *Essentials of Hinduism,* Narosa Pub. House, New Delhi, 1989.

Wendy Doniger: *Siva: The Erotic Ascetic,* Oxford University Press, Delhi, 1998.

Zaidi, A. Moin: *Evolution of Muslim political Thought in India,* New Delhi: S. Chand, 1975.

Index

A

Abdul Hasan Asaf Khan, 145, 151, 163.
Abul Fazl, 44, 48, 51, 64, 99, 102, 103, 104, 109, 119, 122, 123, 124, 125, 156.
Achievements, 21, 64, 70, 138, 167, 237, 274.
Adham Khan, 66, 67, 68, 69, 70, 96.
Agra Fort, 69, 70, 167, 168, 169, 174, 252.
Ahmad Shah Bahadur, 254, 260, 261, 262.
Ain-i-Akbari, 54, 102, 103, 119, 123, 124.
Akbar, 3, 10, 23, 33, 38, 39, 40, 41, 43, 47, 48, 49, 50, 51, 52, 53, 54, 55, 56, 57, 58, 60, 61, 62, 63, 64, 65, 66, 67, 68, 69, 70, 71, 73, 74, 75, 76, 77, 78, 81, 82, 83, 84, 86, 87, 88, 89, 93, 94, 95, 96, 97, 98, 99, 100, 101, 102, 103, 104, 105, 106, 107, 108, 109, 110, 112, 113, 115, 116, 117, 118, 119, 122, 123, 124, 125, 126, 128, 130, 131, 132, 133, 134, 135, 136, 137, 138, 139, 141, 142, 145, 146, 148, 149, 151, 153, 158, 160, 161, 162, 169, 176, 185, 202, 204, 210, 214, 215, 216, 218, 228, 229, 230, 231, 239, 240, 242, 253, 266, 267, 268, 271, 272, 273, 274.
Akbarnama, 47, 48, 53, 54, 95, 106, 119, 122, 123, 124, 154.
Amir Khusro, 129, 130.
Architecture, 31, 33, 40, 42, 56, 118, 159, 161, 164, 173, 177, 271.
Ataga Khan, 66, 69, 70, 139.
Aurangzeb, 74, 87, 91, 92, 95, 112, 113, 114, 138, 151, 161, 165, 167, 168, 169, 170, 171, 172, 174, 175, 176, 177, 182, 183, 184, 185, 186, 188, 189, 190, 191, 192, 193, 194, 195, 196, 197, 198, 199, 200, 201, 202, 203, 204, 206, 207, 209, 211, 212, 214, 215, 216, 218, 219, 220, 223, 224, 225, 226, 228, 229, 230, 232, 234, 235, 237, 238, 253, 255, 261, 274, 275, 276, 278, 283.

B

Babri Masjid, 32.
Babur, 1, 2, 3, 4, 5, 6, 7, 8, 9, 10, 11, 12, 13, 14, 15, 16, 17, 18, 19, 20, 22, 23, 24, 25, 26, 27, 28,

29, 30, 31, 32, 33, 34, 38, 43, 44, 45, 47, 48, 49, 50, 53, 55, 57, 65, 66, 87, 88, 91, 93, 140, 153, 161, 162, 268, 282, 284.
Bagh-e Babur, 31.
Bahadur Shah Zafar, 266, 267, 268, 270, 271, 272, 273, 274.
Baiju Bawra, 128, 130.
Bairam Khan, 42, 54, 56, 57, 58, 61, 64, 65, 66, 67, 68, 139.
Baji Rao, 278.
Basawan, 123.
Battle at Saraighat, 213.
Battle of Buxar, 263.
Battle of Dharmat, 186, 191, 194, 199, 200.
Battle of Ghaghra, 10, 18, 24.
Battle of Haldighati, 76, 77, 79, 84, 85, 134, 135.
Battle of Khanwa, 10, 19, 20, 21, 22, 24, 25.
Battle of Khwaja, 199.
Battle of Panipat, 8, 10, 11, 18, 24, 55, 56, 57, 58, 59, 64, 65, 87, 88, 284.
Battle of Samugarh, 194, 196, 199.
Battle of Saraighat, 206, 207, 213.
Bhama Shah, 80, 85.
Birbal, 105, 117, 130, 131, 132, 136, 253.
British India, 268.
British Rule, 259.

C

Chhatrapati Shivaji, 224.
Civilization, 133.
Company, 114, 241, 250, 251, 263, 267, 268, 274.
Constitution, 121.

D

Dara Shikoh, 167, 168, 169, 170, 171, 172, 175, 176, 177, 180, 181, 183, 186, 194, 195.
Dargah, 66, 70, 141, 170, 239, 266, 267, 269, 270, 271, 273.
Deccan Wars, 228.
Delhi Sultanate, 6, 25, 28, 43, 98, 105.
Din-i-Ilahi, 56, 102, 103, 116, 117, 131, 133, 139.
Disintegration, 239, 278, 279, 280.

E

East India Company, 241, 250, 251, 263, 267, 268, 274.
Economic, 154, 216, 219, 220.
Emergence, 167, 222.

F

Fatehpur Sikri, 10, 12, 94, 116, 117, 128, 136, 138, 141.
Firoz Shah, 272.
Foundation, 59, 94, 102, 134, 176, 179, 226, 227, 259, 282.
Francois Bernier, 165, 202, 204.
Freedom, 79, 81, 85, 215, 216, 217.

G

Gauhara Begum, 163.
Golden Temple, 176.
Governments, 244.
Gulbadan Begum, 34, 43, 46, 47, 48, 49, 50, 51, 52, 54.
Guru Arjan Dev, 178.
Guru Granth Sahib, 31, 226.
Guru Tegh Bahadur, 179, 209, 224.

H

Hamida Banu Begum, 52, 56, 66.
Hindu Philosophy, 124.
Humayun, 2, 3, 8, 9, 11, 16, 23, 26, 31, 33, 34, 35, 36, 37, 38, 39, 40, 41, 42, 43, 44, 45, 47, 48, 49, 50, 51, 52, 53, 54, 55, 56, 57, 58, 59, 61, 64, 65, 66, 70, 86, 88, 93, 124, 139, 140, 161, 240, 272, 284.

I

Ibadat Khana, 98, 101, 115, 116, 117.
Ibrahim Lodi, 6, 8, 11, 17, 26, 27, 57, 87.
Indian Mutiny, 87.
Indian Subcontinent, 1, 116, 133, 161, 175, 176, 185.
Islamic Architecture, 271.
Islamic Law, 99, 143, 202.

J

Jahanara Begum Sahib, 167, 168.
Jahangir, 3, 54, 64, 94, 95, 96, 109, 110, 111, 112, 119, 123, 125, 134, 138, 141, 142, 143, 144, 145, 146, 147, 148, 149, 150, 151, 152, 153, 154, 155, 156, 157, 158, 159, 160, 161, 162, 163, 164, 165, 166, 174, 177, 178, 179, 185, 202, 204, 215, 216, 268, 270, 271.
Jaimal and Patta, 67, 73, 74.
Jama Masjid, 9, 162, 167, 174, 219, 269.
Jat Uprising, 214.
Jizya, 113, 116, 154, 204, 278.

K

Kabir, 93, 129.
Kamran Mirza, 33, 38, 44, 69.
Khalifa, 13, 14, 101, 107.
Khalsa, 131.
Khushal Khan Khattak, 230, 231, 233.
Khushal Khan Khattak, 234.

L

Ladli Begum, 147, 148, 150.
Lahore Fort, 167, 174.
Later Mughals, 185, 237.

M

Mahabharata, 115.
Maham Anga, 66, 68, 69.
Maharana Udai Singh, 67, 72, 74, 76, 77.
Maratha Clans, 229.
Maratha Forces, 230.
Mariam-uz-Zamani, 94.
Mecca, 42, 44, 49, 51, 65, 107, 184, 234, 280, 281.
Mian Tansen, 126.
Military Achievements, 64.
Mirza Ghiyas Beg, 151.
Misl, 156.
Mohammad Ibrahim, 253.
Moti Masjid, 162, 174, 234, 271.
Mughal Art, 158, 167.
Mughal Culture, 269.
Mughal Decline, 231.
Mughal India, 159, 204.
Mughal Painting, 143.
Mughal Rule, 57, 85, 173, 185, 207, 215, 240, 271, 273.
Musical Instruments, 129, 203.

N

Nadir Shah, 254, 258, 261, 278.
Neku Siyar, 253.
Nur Jahan, 144, 145, 146, 147, 148, 149, 150, 151, 152, 162, 165, 166, 174..

O

Organization, 93, 99, 110, 227, 281.
Origins, 33, 152.
Orthodox Reaction, 108.

P

Pashtun Rebellion, 230.
Political Government, 93.
Politics, 54, 60, 153.
Pratap Singh, 73, 74, 76, 77, 81, 82, 86, 207.
Production, 85, 137.
Projects, 171, 234.
Promotion, 126, 218, 248.

R

Rafi ud-Darajat, 251.
Rafi ud-Daulah, 252.
Raja Man Singh, 32, 76, 77, 95, 105, 133, 136, 137, 138, 149.
Rajaram, 230.
Rama, 32, 139, 227.
Rana Pratap, 20, 83, 86, 133, 134, 135.
Rani Durgavati, 67, 70, 71.
Red Fort, 167, 174, 234, 267, 268.
Relation with Hindus, 106.
Religious Policy, 105, 112, 113, 218.
Research, 233.
Revenue Collection, 43.
Roshanara Bagh, 171, 173.
Roshanara Begum, 169, 170, 171, 172.

S

Shah Jahan, 3, 142, 144, 147, 148, 150, 151, 152, 153, 161, 162, 163, 164, 165, 166, 167, 168, 169, 170, 171, 172, 173, 174, 175, 176, 177, 181, 182, 183, 185, 186, 188, 190, 193, 195, 198, 199, 202, 203, 204, 207, 216, 228, 252, 254, 256, 261, 262.
Shaista Khan, 188, 229, 239, 240.
Shalimar Gardens, 167, 174.
Sher Afghan Quli Khan, 148.
Shivaji, 206, 224, 228, 229.
Sikh Community, 227.
Spiritual Development, 109.
Swami Haridas, 127, 128.
Syed Brothers, 240, 241, 242, 246, 251, 252, 253.

T

Technology, 7, 18, 23, 137.
Thomas Roe, 144, 155, 160.

U

Union Home Minister, 84.
Upanishads, 176, 177.

W

Warfare, 10, 12, 15, 34, 35, 49, 78, 80, 82, 135, 198, 206, 207, 211, 222, 230, 234, 261, 264.
Welfare, 227.
William Hamilton, 241, 250.
Wisdom, 100, 122, 126, 131, 223.
Worship, 96, 97, 98, 105, 115, 117, 157, 204, 218, 226, 227.

Z

Zamindars, 87, 139, 246, 257.

□□□